FICTIONS OF YOUTH

Pier Paolo Pasolini, Adolescence, Fascisms

Fictions of Youth examines Pier Paolo Pasolini's redefinition of intellectual commitment through his lifelong contribution to the discourse of youth. In this book Simona Bondavalli explores the many ways in which youth, real or imagined, shaped Pasolini's poetics and critical position; simultaneously, she shows how Pasolini's poetry, films, fiction, and non-fiction served as a source for representations of contemporary young people, in Italy especially, during a key period in the formation of national identity. This period begins with Pasolini's own intellectual coming of age during Fascism in the 1940s, and ends with the emergence of neo-capitalism in the 1970s, which he labelled a "new Fascism" because of its disastrous effects on young people. In the decades between these two Fascisms, youth symbolized innovation and rejuvenation, innocence and peril, idealism and rebellion. Pasolini's portrayals of young people in literature and visual media both reflected and shaped those ideas.

The book consists of six diachronically arranged chapters, each centred on a paradigm of youth, which is explored in several genres and analysed in the context of contemporary discourse. *Fictions of Youth* is the only work to date that systematically addresses Pasolini's focus on youth and establishes it as a fundamental category for understanding his eclectic body of work.

(Toronto Italian Studies)

SIMONA BONDAVALLI is an associate professor in the Department of Italian at Vassar College.

SIMONA BONDAVALLI

Fictions of Youth

Pier Paolo Pasolini, Adolescence, Fascisms

UNIVERSITY OF TORONTO PRESS
Toronto Buffalo London

© University of Toronto Press 2015
Toronto Buffalo London
www.utppublishing.com

ISBN 978-1-4426-4974-3 (cloth)
ISBN 978-1-4426-2707-9 (paper)

Toronto Italian Studies

Library and Archives Canada Cataloguing in Publication

Bondavalli, Simona, 1969–, author
Fictions of youth : Pier Paolo Pasolini, adolescence, fascisms / Simona Bondavalli.

(Toronto Italian studies)
Includes bibliographical references and index.
ISBN 978-1-4426-4974-3 (bound).–ISBN 978-1-4426-2707-9 (pbk.)

1. Pasolini, Pier Paolo, 1922–1975—Criticism and interpretation.
2. Youth in literature. 3. Adolescence in literature. 4. Fascism in literature. 5. Youth in motion pictures. 6. Fascism in motion pictures.
I. Title. II. Title: Pier Paolo Pasolini, adolescence, fascisms. III. Series: Toronto Italian studies

PQ4835.A48Z55 2015   858'.91409   C2015-900191-9

This book has been published with the assistance of the Salmon Fund and the Tatlock Endowment for Career Enhancement at Vassar College.

University of Toronto Press acknowledges the financial assistance to its publishing program of the Canada Council for the Arts and the Ontario Arts Council, an Ontario government agency.

 Canada Council   Conseil des Arts
for the Arts   du Canada

 ONTARIO ARTS COUNCIL
CONSEIL DES ARTS DE L'ONTARIO
an Ontario government agency
un organisme du gouvernement de l'Ontario

University of Toronto Press acknowledges the financial support of the Government of Canada through the Canada Book Fund for its publishing activities.

In loving memory of my parents.

Contents

Acknowledgments ix

Permissions xi

Introduction 3

1 *Giovinezza,* **or The Best of Youth** 17
  Largo ai Giovani!: Youth and Fascism in the 1940s 17
  Pasolini and Fascist University Youth: *Architrave* and
    Il setaccio 20
  Generational Identity, Personal Exclusion: *Eredi,* Exile,
    Nostalgia 26
  Poesie a Casarsa: The Very Best of Youth 36

2 Being Young: *Bildung,* **Development, and Growing
  Up** *Ragazzi* **49**
  Being Young: *Ragazzi di vita* as a Reversed *Bildungsroman* 50
  Alternative Lessons in the Streets of Rome 61
  Redeeming the *Ragazzi: Una vita violenta* 71
  Urban Development and Neorealism: The Tiburtino Quarter 74

**3 Looking Back in Longing: Lost Youth, Teddy Boys,
  and** *Il sogno di una cosa* **84**
  Giovani, Giovani, Giovani: Youth and Mass Media in 1960 85
  Where Is the Best of Youth?: Timeless and Contemporary
    Adolescence in *Il sogno di una cosa* 91
  The Boys with the Striped T-Shirts 102
  Second Best?: Portraits of Young Women in the 1940s 104
  Two Weddings and a Funeral: Rites of Passage 111

4 Revolutionary Youth: From the Page, to the Streets, to the Screen 115

The Generation of 1968 115
A New Poetry of Youth: New Linguistic Questions and the Cinema of Poetry 119
Coming of Age on Screen: *Comizi d'amore* 123
Moving beyond Pedagogy, One Step at a Time: *Uccellacci e uccellini* 130
Flower Power and Flower Shops: A Brief Encounter with Counterculture 135
The Written Language of Action: Poetry and Cinema 143

5 Fatherless Youth: Fathers, Children, Orphans 149

Ugly Verses for Spoiled Children: "The PCI to the Young!" 149
Wanting to Be Orphans, Refusing to Be a Father: *Il Caos* 158
Generational Conflicts: Rebellious Children and Fascist Fathers 162
The Cinematic Poetry of Youth: *Teorema* 169
Disobeying the Almighty Father: *La sequenza del fiore di carta* 180

6 *Giovani Infelici*: Consumer, Disobedient, Unhappy Youth 182

Consuming Disobedient Adolescence: *Porcile* 182
Beyond the *Sessantottini:* Neo-capitalism as the New Fascism 196
Sharing Responsibilities: Fathers and Children 204
Gennariello: A Concise Study Guide to Pasolini 207

Epilogue. Coming of Age as Sadists: *Salò* and the Repudiation of Youth 211

Notes 216

Bibliography 261

Index 270

Acknowledgments

Many people and institutions have contributed to the successful completion of *Fictions of Youth*. First of all, I wish to thank the editors at University of Toronto Press: the late Ron Schoeffel for believing in this book when it was still in the making, and Siobhan McMenemy for generously adopting the project and seeing it through to conclusion. Her precious editorial assistance and constant encouragement made *Fictions* a reality. I also wish to thank the Press' external readers, whose insightful suggestions facilitated revisions and significantly improved the book.

I would like to thank the Pasolini Estate and Garzanti Editore for permission to reproduce excerpts from Pasolini's work, particularly from *Tutte le Poesie*, *Trasumanar e organizzar*, *Le lettere*, *Ragazzi di vita*, and *Una vita violenta*. The University of Chicago Press generously allowed me to reproduce translations from its forthcoming volume *The Selected Poetry of Pier Paolo Pasolini: A Bilingual Edition*, edited and translated by Stephen Sartarelli. My sincerest thanks to Stephen Sartarelli, Randy Petilos, Ines ter Horst, and Perry Cartwright. In Italy, I am grateful to Roberto Chiesi and the staff of the Centro Studi - Archivio Pier Paolo Pasolini in Bologna for facilitating access to their valuable collection. Some of the material included here appeared elsewhere in earlier versions. A portion of chapter 3 was published in *Quaderni del '900* as "Enamored of Distance: Youth, History, and Nostalgia in Pier Paolo Pasolini's *Il sogno di una cosa*" (11: 2011). I thank Nicoletta Marini-Maio, who edited the issue, and the journal for granting permission to reprint. Parts of chapter 4 appeared as "Giving Flowers to Policemen: Pasolini, "Flower Children," and *Figli di Papà*" in the volume *Pier Paolo Pasolini: In Living Memory*, edited by Ben Lawton and Maura Bergonzoni (Washington, DC: New Academia

Publishing, 2009). I also wish to thank *Italica*, where portions of chapter 6 were first published as "Lost in the Pig House: Vision and Consumption in Pier Paolo Pasolini's *Porcile* (87:3 [2010]).

My research on Pasolini began with graduate study in Comparative Literature at the University of Washington. I thank Albert Sbragia, Gary Handwerk, and Massimo Scalabrini (now at Indiana University) for their guidance. In Seattle, my heartfelt thanks go to Deborah Woodard, who shared with me her love of poetry and translation. Although my interest in Pasolini long predates my arrival at Vassar College, *Fictions of Youth* is primarily a Vassar project. Research and publication were made possible by grants from the Salmon Fund and the Tatlock Endowment for Career Enhancement. I am thankful to the Vassar College Research Committee and the Dean of the Faculty for their support. Students who took various incarnations of my seminar on Youth in Twentieth-Century Italian Literature over the years helped me sharpen my focus and question many of my assumptions on youth nourished by literature. Hilary Mauro, my student research assistant for the last two years, deserves thanks for her meticulous bibliographical and editorial work.

My colleagues in the Italian Department have my deepest gratitude for their mentorship, support, and friendship. I am especially grateful to John Ahern, who read the manuscript with his sharp eye for detail and broad perspective on Italian culture, and offered invaluable advice. Fellow Pasolini enthusiasts Guzzi Blumenfeld and Lucia Lermond merit special thanks for their patience in reading subsequent versions of the manuscript and providing each time insightful criticism and helpful suggestions. It saddens me immensely that Lucia is not here to celebrate its completion with a glass of champagne. Roberta Antognini's keen philological observations and the lively discussions on Pasolini I had with Eugenio Giusti sent me back to the source more often than I can recall. I am fortunate to work with such a collegial and stimulating team.

I am grateful for the support I continue to receive from family and friends, many of whom have contributed material for this book in various forms.

Finally, my warmest thanks are for David Poole, critical reader and supportive companion, who makes everything possible and worthwhile.

Permissions

We acknowledge with thanks permission received from the following publishers for quotations that appear in this book.

Pasolini, Pier Paolo, *Ragazzi di vita*
© Garzanti Editore s.p.a, 1955, 1988, 1996
© 1999, 2000, 2005, Garzanti Libri spa, Milano
(The Ragazzi, translated by Emile Capouya, Manchester: Carcanet Press Ltd, 1986)

Una vita violenta
© Garzanti Editore s.p.a, 1959, 1988, 1996, 1998
© 1999, 2001, 2005, Garzanti Libri s.p.a, Milano
(A Violent Life, translated by William Weaver, Manchester: Carcanet Press Ltd, 1985)

Trasumanar e organizzar
© Garzanti Editore s.p.a, 1971, 1976
© 1999, 2002, Garzanti Libri s.p.a, Milano

Le Lettere: 1945-1954. Edited by Nico Naldini, Turin: Einaudi 1986
Tutte le poesie, 2 vols. Edited by Walter Siti, Milan: Arnoldo Mondadori, 2003

The Selected Poetry of Pier Paolo Pasolini: A Bilingual Edition. Edited and translated by Stephen Sartarelli. Chicago and London: The University of Chicago Press, 2014.

FICTIONS OF YOUTH

Pier Paolo Pasolini, Adolescence, Fascisms

Introduction

Adulto? Mai – mai, come l'esistenza
che non matura – resta sempre acerba ...

Adult? Never, never – like life itself
which never matures, forever green ...[1]

Writing about youth in Pier Paolo Pasolini's work means, in a sense, writing about his entire oeuvre. He was, after all, the poet who popularized the phrase *"la meglio gioventù,"* or "the best of youth," which television and cinema audiences, in Italy and twenty-seven other countries, now associate with the popular 2003 miniseries by Marco Tullio Giordana. Pasolini did not invent the expression, but Italianized a verse from a World War I song from Friuli, the region of his maternal family, in northeastern Italy. He chose the phrase, which in the song mourned young lives lost to the war, as the title for a collection of poems in Friulian dialect. The "best of youth," in those poems, was celebrated as an idyllic condition, lost or inaccessible to the poet, and invariably tinted with nostalgia. The collection contained Pasolini's early poems, several composed before he was twenty years old. That premature nostalgia for lost youth marked the beginning of a literary and cinematographic career characterized by a persistent idealization of youth. The literary construction of adolescence as a natural force, uncorrupted by civilization, and in constant flux, shaped Pasolini's poetics and provided a subject for identification.

However, Giordana's miniseries, which claims to tell "the story of a generation," namely of Italians who came of age during the 1960s, also evokes, without direct quotation, Pasolini's most famous pronouncement about young protesters in 1968: a verse libel in which he polemically sided with the young policemen who had clashed with protesting students at the University of Rome.[2] Pasolini's controversial position with respect to the student movement, still remembered by many Italians over four decades later, introduces the opposite pole of his interest in youth: the social subject that gained great visibility in the 1960s.[3] As a social observer, Pasolini was deeply aware of the attention devoted to adolescents in modern Italy. He dedicated many articles and interviews to analysis of young people, their habits, and their political aspirations. Having grown up during Fascism, he had also experienced firsthand the translation of a cult of youth into social and cultural policies aimed at controlling the young. The generational discourse, which had shaped his own coming-of-age, reappeared twenty years later when he addressed the young protesters as "sons" and "daughters." The intersection of those two concepts of youth – a cultural construction and a specific historical subject – which can be traced in many of his works, structures this study.

Youth, both as a socio-historical cohort and a literary ideal, with its changing connotations, influenced Pasolini's poetics, critical position, and self-perception. He identified with the infinite potentiality and transformational energy of adolescence, and positioned himself critically outside of a patriarchal order, which would be questioned by young people in the 1960s. He related ambivalently to generational discourse, particularly when it intersected with literary and ideological genealogies. On the one hand, he flourished in his youth, adopted models of youthful self-creation from Romantic and Symbolist literature, and embraced the non-conformist and anti-authoritarian stances that we associate with modern adolescence. His confessional style, as a poet and essayist, established in his work the "authority of the personal," which Patricia Meyer Spacks describes as a central feature of adolescence in literature.[4]

As the verses quoted in the epigraph exemplify, immaturity was a privileged position for Pasolini, though he developed an early sense of himself as an artist, identified a poetic lineage that he wished to enter and alter, and established a distinctive, mature, presence in the Italian literary world (if only to question that acquired authority whenever possible). Following the configurations of youth in Pasolini's works, consequently, provides a lens onto the creation of a critical subject, which converses with both literary tradition and contemporary society. Youth offers a space for identification, self-invention, or projection of desires. Since its appropriation for symbolic purposes long predates Pasolini, he relies on a familiar metaphor and subverts its significance by changing the context. Frequently, adolescence offers a space for resistance: the interstitial position occupied by young people – or particular subgroups – in the social order represents a crucial feature in Pasolini's attention to youth. Adolescence embodies the author's critical position, questioning universal models of development and modernization. Finally, Pasolini often chose young people as interlocutors, even though, increasingly in later years, the dialogue turned into a monologue, and the *"maestro mirabile"* into a slightly pedantic pedagogue.[5]

Besides exploring the multiple ways in which youth, real or imagined, shaped Pasolini's poetics, this book also looks at Pasolini's oeuvre as a source for representations of young people, mostly Italians, in a key period for the formation of a new national identity. There are no doubts about the partiality of such representations. As Stephen Burt claims, "Poets do not, as a rule, react to cultural changes by striving to represent them fairly and comprehensively. Rather, poets react to changes that move them, to what they see in their locales and in their social strata (often, urban, educated elites), or else to popular impressions of a changing culture."[6] Pasolini is no exception. His descriptions of young people, in any media, are always coloured by his subjective mood, be it nostalgia, delight, or frustration. However, rhetorical and stylistic choices foreground his subjective stance, and I read his impressions within a broader discourse of youth produced in other media and analysed by social and cultural historians. On the other hand, his sustained interest in the particularity of regional cultures leads to acute observations of changing youth styles and behaviours, both locally and nationally.

The focus on Italian youth in this book – which excludes Pasolini's representations of the young people he encountered in his frequent travels to Africa and Asia – is also, indirectly, a focus on Italy's self-creation between the 1940s and the early 1970s. This period begins with Fascism, which elevated youth to a political myth, and ends with the neo-capitalist era he referred to as "new Fascism," due to its disastrous effects on young people. Through the examination of adolescence as a sociological and ideological signifier permeating his work, *Fictions of Youth* highlights the crucial role played by Pasolini, both as a witness and a participant, in the contradictory mythologizing of adolescence that pervades Italian culture in the twentieth century.[7]

From his university years in Bologna, the city where he was born in 1922, to his last days in Rome, where he was murdered in 1975, Pasolini occupied a variety of positions in the Italian cultural world: he was a poet in dialect and in Italian, an experimental novelist, a literary critic, a playwright, and a filmmaker.[8] He edited journals and poetry collections, wrote essays on a range of subjects from linguistics to film theory, held columns in popular magazines and newspapers, translated classical drama. His novels and films received prestigious awards, but more frequently were charged with obscenity or religious offence, requiring frequent appearances in court and gaining him the reputation of a controversial, or even scandalous, intellectual. He often embraced that reputation, and nourished it with the relentless "introspection and experimentation" which, as Robert S.C. Gordon observed, set the boundaries of his work.[9] His homosexuality, which was the cause for his first trial and expulsion from the Communist Party, instigated prosecution and the sense of exclusion that informs many of his writings.[10] Despite a passionate defence of Communism, his re-evaluation of irrationality as a critical tool alienated him from the cultural politics of the Italian Communist Party in the post-war years. Considered and self-identified as a Gramscian intellectual, committed to the ideal of culture as a means for political emancipation, he believed, more than he was willing to admit and more than Antonio Gramsci did, in the value of "high" culture.[11] However, he also appreciated "popular" culture in the sense of folk and oral traditions (*cultura popolare*, as opposed to "pop"), and lamented its erosion due to neo-capitalism in the 1960s.

Adolescents populate the pages and screens of Pasolini's work: street urchins in Roman slums, peasant *giovinetti* in the Friuli countryside, proud and ancient youths in Persia, American flower children and Italian Teddy boys are recurrent protagonists of his fiction and non-fiction, of his written as well as cinematographic works, creating what French theorist Michel Foucault defined as a "great saga of youth."[12] One of the few elements of continuity in his eclectic and multidisciplinary production, adolescence is invested with a symbolic meaning that is peculiar to the author's aesthetics, but at the same time strongly influenced by changing cultural models. From the early journalism in Fascist youth organizations, to the unfinished pedagogical treatise published in the weekly *Il Mondo* a few months before his death, the discourse of youth was the arena in which the author negotiated, with readers, viewers, institutions, and other intellectuals, his assessment of the substantial changes taking place in the country. Beyond the pedagogical passion and erotic desire usually cited, Pasolini's attention to adolescence can be traced to a wider debate in which young people embody, or directly express, the hopes and fears of a young nation.[13]

Because Pasolini's life coincided with the culmination of what historian Patrizia Dogliani called "the long century of youth," the configuration of adolescence in his works partakes in a multifaceted discourse that includes literary *topoi*, historical and cultural changes, and media representations.[14] As adolescence acquired importance in both the historical landscape and collective imagination, its symbolic connotations became progressively unstable. Throughout the "long century," youth stood for innocence and vitality, anti-authoritarianism and rejection of traditions, rejuvenation and revolution. Increasingly, however, youth also connoted fluidity and uncertainty, potentiality and incompletion.[15] Thanks to its ambiguity, youth could thus become synonymous with both opportunity and danger, and be appropriated as a mobilizing myth at opposite ends of the political spectrum. Modern notions of youth, both compelling and ambivalent, became available to Pasolini through an official Fascist education and a cultural "anti-Fascist" self-education via poetry: school and the extra-curricular activities for the young imposed by the regime promoted the qualities of vitality, strength, and courage, as an antidote to bourgeois decadence; the writings of Rimbaud, the Symbolist poets, and Dostoevsky offered young Pasolini the myth of youth as self-discovery, singularity, and self-creation.[16] Keenly self-aware as a young man, likely encouraged by the practice of writing about youth in Fascist journals, Pasolini found a space for identification in the polyvalent concept of youth, which shaped his critical stance and poetics early on.[17] The aura of exceptionality and the values projected onto adolescence by modern society gave him a sense of mission, which ought to be carried out both individually and collectively. He depicted himself and his peers as endowed with a special task: to renew the poetry of tradition by running it through an "anti-traditional filter" available to the young. Stylistic innovation combined with an underlying ethical purpose, which would soon acquire pedagogical overtones, characterized his identification with youth thereafter.[18]

More prominently, perhaps, adolescence in Pasolini's work often functions as a correlative of the poet's self-exclusion from the locus of power. Characterizations of Pasolini in terms of marginality are by now canonical, and they have been since his 1954 poem "Le Ceneri di Gramsci" (The Ashes of Gramsci) offered a concise and powerful self-identification via contradiction: "tra i due mondi, la tregua, in cui non siamo" (2.1; between the two worlds, a truce not our own).[19] The two worlds of bourgeois consciousness and proletarian life are experienced from the outside, as the struggle between conflicting allegiances forces the poet into a liminal position, from which poetry issues. The expression of the poet's alienation from the middle class of his birth, his feeling of being "del paterno stato traditore / - nel pensiero, in un'ombra di azione" (4.4; a traitor to my father's station / in my mind, in a semblance of action), yet "ad esso attaccato nel calore degli istinti, dell'estetica passione" (4.6–7; bound to it in the heat / of my instincts and aesthetic passion), set the paradigm for reading most of Pasolini's creative work. His attraction to the proletariat due to "la sua allegria, non la millenaria / sua lotta: la sua natura, non la sua / coscienza" (4.10–12; its joyousness, not its millennial / struggle – its nature, not its / consciousness), provided a lens through which his 1950s poetry, his Roman novels, and many of his films could be interpreted as celebrations of lower-class existence outside of history.

Beyond his expressed attraction to proletarian life, the poet identifies with a young Antonio Gramsci, "non padre, ma umile / fratello" (20–1; no father, but a humble / brother). His confinement, in death as in life, transforms the political theorist into an alter ego for the poet and a fraternal interlocutor. The poet addresses him informally – "tu giovane" – as he recalls Gramsci's role in shaping the Resistance ideals, and mourns their betrayal in the decade of post-war reconstruction and political restoration (1.16). Nothing has come of the ideal outlined by his "slender hand" but deadly peace (1.21–2). Gramsci's premature death, which fixes him in eternal youth, and his continued exclusion from the city, through interment in the Protestant Cemetery, configure him as a permanent exile.[20] Unlike the "fathers," who have entered history and betrayed the ideal, the forever young Gramsci created by Pasolini remains *in limine* and identifies youth as a marginal condition from which poetry issues.[21] The poet, young Gramsci, youth, poetry: all are situated outside the patriarchal order of adult society.

The young working-class life introduced in "Le ceneri di Gramsci," and the Roman sub-proletarian adolescents portrayed in the novels *Ragazzi di vita* (1955; *The Ragazzi*) and *Una vita violenta* (1959; *A Violent Life*) reiterate the romantic notion of youth as existence outside the rational order of adult society. Applied to a narrative genre that typically charts the progressive socialization of a young bourgeois man, that view of youth challenges the idea of development in the *Bildungsroman*. Becoming adult in traditional coming-of-age novels means adopting bourgeois codes of conduct that limit freedom and thus restrict youth's infinite potentiality in a productive, socially acceptable compromise.[22] Instead, in Pasolini's novels, becoming adult implies conforming to a normalizing social order and distancing oneself from an authenticity found in forms of life that are closer to nature. While the nineteenth-century bourgeois novel celebrates upward social mobility as a material sign of the possibility of self-improvement, Pasolini questions the universality of those models of development with narratives that celebrate youth in its impermanence. Challenging the adoption of pre-existing parameters of maturity as normative, he also casts doubt on the alleged coming of age of Italy as a modern, democratic nation in the 1950s. With their focus on the vitality and volatility of a specific form of youth, the Roman novels depict the transformation of post-war Italian society while highlighting the losses implicit in the advertised development.

Becoming adult in Pasolini's view always meant conforming to a pragmatic and rational order, which had no space for poetry. Thus, the choice of youth as a subject corresponds to the adoption of irrationality as a critical tool and of poetry as a means of expression.[23] Ever since he defined his generational mission as that of renewing poetic tradition by filtering it through modernity, Pasolini saw youth and poetry occupying analogous spaces in contemporary society: connected to the past but containing the potential for innovation. He envisioned poetry as the language of youth, but at the same time ancient, rooted in local traditions, and constantly evolving. His experiments with dialects and linguistic pastiche can be read as attempts to capture the specificity and infinite variability of adolescence through an expressive language, which also exposes the layered meanings of youth in literary tradition. His preoccupations with Italian language and Italian youth became further intertwined when he saw both being challenged by the cultural homogenization produced by neo-capitalism.

Considering Pasolini's oeuvre through its relationship with youth helps understand his search for, and later rejection of, Style. If for the young poet the search for an original form was an expression of the exceptionality of youth, the mature poet renegotiated his allegiances by setting immaturity as a goal for an incomplete, uncertain, unfinished poetry. The importance of irrationality as a balancing force for Marxism became particularly evident in his critique of the *Sessantotto*, the protest movement of the late 1960s. In that discourse of protest, which Pasolini envisioned as an expression of youth, creativity and irrationality ought to play a more prominent role than they did in Italy. His critical and creative contribution sought to address that imbalance. Coinciding with his reflections on the mutation of the Italian language, his critique of the pragmatism of the *sessantottini* produced a poetic response in visual form: the cinema of poetry.

Youth, in its multiple connotations, embodies Pasolini's unorthodox, anti-authoritarian ideological stance, and his stylistic experiments. Pasolini's works also provide a window onto changing configurations of adolescence as a social subject in twentieth-century Italy. He observed and wrote about young people as he saw them in his time: during Fascism; in the years of the economic miracle and the modernization of Italy; in the course of the student protests and social upheaval of the sixties; and at the beginning of the period of political violence known as the *anni di piombo*. His letters, articles, poems, novels, and films described, celebrated, and often criticized specific forms of adolescence: university students in 1940s Bologna, young farmers in the countryside of Friuli during the war, young inhabitants of the *borgate*, the slums on the outskirts of Rome, in the 1950s, Italian Teddy boys in Milan, young Communists in Friuli, young filmmakers in Pesaro, young protesters, young policemen, and so on. Lifestyles, clothing, and pastimes of young people of different classes and geographical origins come to life in his novels and film, providing us with snapshots of changing youth culture. Despite his unabashedly subjective point of view, Pasolini's oeuvre offers unique portraits of modern Italian youth and of contemporary perspectives.

Most of these portrayals focus on young men, and arguing otherwise would be impossible. Whether he reflected on himself and his friends as young intellectuals, or depicted the Roman *ragazzi* that he sought during nightly cruises in his sports car, or reminisced of the young strikers in late 1940s Friuli, Pasolini wrote more frequently about young men than young women. This is, to a certain extent, the expression of his erotic desire, which may never be separated from his interest in youth. Homosexual desire shapes all of Pasolini's poetry, both textual and visual, and changes in his own aging body undoubtedly affected his self-perception, and consequently his relationship with young men in the late 1960s. Several books explore the relationship between erotic desire, pedagogy, and ideology in Pasolini's work: Enzo Golino's *Pasolini: Il sogno di una cosa. Pedagogia, eros, letteratura dal mito del popolo alla società di massa*; Sam Rohdie's *The Passion of Pier Paolo Pasolini*, Sergio Parussa's *L'eros onnipotente*, Barth David Schwartz's *Pasolini Requiem*, to name only a few.

There can be no doubt that the author's homosexual identity was a factor in his frequent portrayals of male youth. Although subjective, however, Pasolini's view of youth also revealed a gender imbalance in Italian culture, and particularly the way in which youth was valued and elevated to myth in the twentieth century. Both his personal experience of youth (as a young member of Fascist-sponsored cultural organizations, a young poet, a young Communist in the 1940s) and the literary and cultural models shaping his aesthetics (coming-of-age novels, Rimbaud's poetry, among others) were predominantly male. Pasolini's frequent identification of youth with young men is also a product of cultural constructions, which, across centuries, defined youth and assigned values to it according to primarily male roles. He adopted those models and made use of the assumptions more often than he questioned their gender bias.

In the 1960s, when young women acquired greater social visibility, they appeared in Pasolini's social analyses and films: he criticized them as much as their male peers for falling prey to consumerism or the illusion of sexual liberation, but at that point the generational gap separating him from both "daughters" and "sons" seemed to prevent any dialogue. Occasionally, however, he recognized that young women still inhabited that liminal space, outside the patriarchal order, which he had chosen as the locus of youth and poetry, and which young men had relinquished, he thought, with their politics. My discussion of young women within various incarnations of "the best of youth" (in *Il sogno di una cosa*, *Comizi d'amore*, and *Teorema* specifically), and of Pasolini's distinction between daughters and sons after 1968, highlights contradictions in both his view of women and contemporary debates on youth: a comprehensive study of women in Pasolini's work would have to go beyond contemporary Italian youth to include maternal and mythical figures, for instance. Colleen Ryan-Scheutz's *Sex, the Self, and the Sacred: Women in the Cinema of Pier Paolo Pasolini* offers an in-depth discussion of this topic, which is clearly beyond the scope of this book.

Granted that Pasolini's interest in adolescence depends mainly on its indeterminacy, a few clarifications are in order. Besides the already introduced distinction between a cultural construction (and the variable qualities connoting it: innocence, vitality, energy, instability, rebelliousness, danger) and a social subject (young people who live at a specific time in a specific place), a few more working definitions are necessary. Discussions of youth in generational terms, such as the ones I propose for Fascist youth and for the *Sessantotto*, rely on a notion of generation as a distinctive historical cohort characterized by shared formative experiences, which produce a sense of collective identity.

Generational conflict may thus be the expression of the "natural" defiance of youth, (although that too has been proven to be more the product of sociocultural conventions than psychological processes),[24] as well as attitudes and aspirations that characterize a specific historical cohort. The former guarantees continuity between subsequent generations while still allowing for the projection of regenerative ideas on the young. The latter presumes a generational gap, which hinders the transmission of values and qualifies the younger generation as truly revolutionary.

Pasolini's celebration of youth was based on a Romantic notion of an ephemeral life phase, unstable and uncontrollable, but also steady from generation to generation. These positive qualities were enhanced by conditions of marginality, which underscored both the adolescent's exclusion from a restrictive social order, and intergenerational continuity. Nourished by this literary ideal, his interest in adolescence struggled at times to come to terms with young people's actions, which seemed to reduce that "pure transformational energy" he had found in Rimbaud's youth.[25] Pasolini's reaction to youth shifted from trust in a pattern of repetition, based on the assumption that the experience of youth did not change from cohort to cohort, to the realization, later in life, that each generation shared experiences which were unique to that group and not recognizable by other cohorts. Pasolini's negotiation of his relationship with youth at different times of his life reflects this shifting view.[26] In undertaking political action, as many did in 1968, young people both embodied the rejuvenating capacity assigned to them by modern society, and betrayed the marginal position on which that capacity largely stood, at least in the poet's mind. As actual young people failed to live up to the literary ideal, the best of youth, for Pasolini, remained for the most part a product of his imagination: a lost condition that could be accessed only in memory, or through poetry. Although deeply personal, Pasolini's ambivalent relationship with adolescence also makes explicit a paradox underlying its modern conceptualization: the enduring projection of hope for renewal on youth, and the concomitant displacement of the younger generations from positions of power.

The book consists of six chapters, arranged chronologically. Each chapter is centred on a paradigm of youth, explored in several genres, and analysed in the context of the contemporary discourse. The first chapter, "*Giovinezza*, or The Best of Youth," examines Pasolini's early work in relation to the ambivalent interpellation issued to young people by Fascism. Pasolini's activity as editor and contributor to Fascist youth journals, his correspondence with friends, and the collection of Friulian poetry *Poesie a Casarsa* provide powerful illustrations of his ability to formulate alternative definitions of adolescence without openly questioning the eternal youth of the *Duce* and the nation. Adolescence becomes synonymous with continuous transformation, a locus of indeterminacy and contradiction observable only from a self-imposed distance. His desire to connect to youth, from which he feels alienated at an early age, becomes a generational call to his peers as heralds of a new culture, which finds expression in poetry. The second chapter, "Being Young: *Bildung*, Development, and Growing Up *Ragazzi*," reads the young protagonists of the Roman novels as Pasolini's most explicit response to both the symbolic use of youth in European coming-of-age novels and the discourse of emancipation produced by the Italian Communist Party and promoted by neorealist film and fiction. The critique of *Bildung* as individual evolution entails a parallel critique of the model of development embraced by Italy in its own coming-of-age as a democracy. Youth as a marginal condition is observed as an ontological state. While the fluidity and dynamism of the urban spaces in the novels mirror the transience of youth, the linguistic pastiche of Roman dialect and literary Italian captures the specificity of adolescence while preserving its otherness. In the third chapter, "Looking Back in Longing: Lost Youth, Teddy Boys, and *Il sogno di una cosa*," Pasolini's contribution to the discourse of youth as opportunity and peril in the late 1950s and early 1960s is analysed through popular magazines and a nostalgia novel. At a time when adolescents begin to claim a distinct generational identity, and left-wing parties worry about their diminished political militancy, Pasolini steps in as unlikely conciliator. He reflects on contemporary young people in the pages of the weekly *Vie Nuove*, but invokes romantic notions of youth to justify their actions. He responds to a growing anxiety towards young people among adults by turning a retrospective gaze onto the Friuli of his past, and presents youth as a trans-historical signifier of innocence and unthreatening innovation in his fiction.

As the 1960s progress and the results of the "economic miracle" become evident in Italian society, so does the generational conflict between the children born after the war and all paternal authorities, including Pasolini. Both chapters 4 and 5 address the discourse surrounding the *Sessantotto*. A complex shift occurs at this time, which induces Pasolini to renegotiate his relationship with youth, in light of his age and fame, and of their actions. Chapter 4, "Revolutionary Youth: From the Page, to the Streets, to the Screen," examines the screen presence of young people in the interviews conducted by Pasolini in *Comizi d'amore* (1963–4; *Love Meetings*), a *reportage* on the sexual habits of Italians, and in the poetic fable *Uccellacci e uccellini* (1965; *The Hawks and the Sparrows*), where the father-and-son archetype is explored in the moment of transition between modernity and post-modernity. Pasolini's exploration of alternative forms of participation in students' actions, inspired by the creative approach of the American counterculture, provides a model for his interpretation of the Italian protest. Chapter 5, "Fatherless Youth: Fathers, Children, Orphans," explores Pasolini's multifaceted reactions to the generational discourse introduced by the *Sessantotto*, initiated by his infamous libel against Italian student protesters. On one hand he reflects on his critical position towards the young, and the type of commitment that their actions require of him. On the other his cinema of poetry, exemplified by *Teorema* (1968; *Theorem*) reassigns to youth the poetic space they lost by undertaking action. The critique of a young generation, whom he finally sees as historically different from his own, continues in chapter 6, "*Giovani Infelici*: Consumer, Disobedient, Unhappy Youth." His 1970s "pirate writings" and the film *Porcile* (1969; *Pigsty*) are read for their analysis of young people as consumers and forced disobedients in the all-encompassing realm of neo-capitalism. Young people are victims of a new power, which does not allow for ambiguous stances, and Pasolini issues another generational call to his peers, now cast as fathers, inviting them to take responsibility for the unhappiness of youth. The author's distance from the young people of his time becomes explicit in the creation of the imaginary pupil Gennariello in the eponymous pedagogical treatise, which remains unfinished. Few pictures of youth's unhappiness could be more powerful than the ones provided in Pasolini's last film *Salò, o Le 120 giornate di Sodoma* (1975; *Salò, or The 120 Days of Sodom*). The epilogue, "Coming of Age as Sadists: *Salò* and the Repudiation of Youth," shows how Pasolini's last film brings the discourse of youth to an unambiguous conclusion.

Writing a book in English on the intersections of youth discourse with Pasolini's work inevitably implies dealing with a very basic problem: vocabulary. The semantic field of youth presents a variety of words in Italian that have no exact correspondent in English. The Italian word *giovane* (pl. *giovani*) functions both as an adjective (*young*) and as a noun (*young person*, often *young man*, as in the phrase *"un bel giovane"* (also, *"un giovanotto"*). The plural form of the noun, *i giovani*, is frequently, and economically, used to refer to the social group (*young people*), as in the phrase *"i giovani d'oggi"* (literally, "the young people of today") frequently found in newspaper headlines of the 1950s and '60s that first addressed the emerging generational gap with alarm or excitement. The diminutives *giovinetto* and *giovinetta*, frequently found in Pasolini's Friulian poetry, refer to a boy and a girl, respectively, between twelve and eighteen years of age. Technically, the word means "adolescent," as both an adjective and a noun, but its literary connotations may suggest the English nouns "lad" and "lass." The noun and adjective *adolescente*, whose present participle morphology implies the transitory condition it refers to (from the Latin *adolescens*, present participle of *adolesco*, "I begin to grow up"), do not enjoy the same popularity in Italian as their equivalent "adolescent" does in English-speaking countries. The term is associated with the social sciences, which have few points of contact with literary and historical discourse in Italy. Significantly, the discussion of *"adolescenza traviata"* ("misled adolescence") appears in this study in the context of Pasolini's 1960 dispute with psychologists and sociologists on the alleged crisis of Italian youth. I use the terms "adolescent" and "adolescence" in English as synonymous with "young" and "youth" for the sake of lexical variety. While Pasolini's Friulian poetry of the 1940s is populated with *giovinetti* and *fanciulli* (< Lat. *infantiolus*, alleged diminutive of *in-fans*, child, literally, "not speaking"), innocent boys between childhood and adolescence, with an established literary history, his Roman novels introduce *ragazzi* on the literary scene.[27] The noun *ragazzo* (< Lat barb. *ragàzium*, connected to *raga* = Gr. *ràka*, "ragged clothes," an epithet applied to the children of servants, then by extension to young people in general) is the most common Italian word to refer to a young man. The scraggly boys described in the 1955 novel, *Ragazzi di vita*, come close to the word's etymological root. This seems to support the translator's foreignizing choice to maintain the source language term *"ragazzi"* in the English title (*The Ragazzi*), thus condensing in the Italian noun the idiomatic phrase *di vita*, which refers to street life and prostitution. In the narrative, the word *ragazzo* is variously translated as "boy" or "kid." The feminine *"ragazza"* never appears: a linguistic signal that young women did not inhabit the transitory space occupied by their male peers in the world view proposed by that novel.

The word "youth" corresponds in Italian to both *giovinezza* and *gioventù*. Both nouns refer to a phase of life, but the latter is also a collective identifier of the social group. Although they were used interchangeably until the beginning of the twentieth century, the cult of youth in Italian Fascism seems to have historically and politically connoted *giovinezza* thereafter. The slight decline in use of the term in post-war Italy may be explained as a reaction to the official anthem of the National Fascist Party, called in fact "Giovinezza," which was sung at every public appearance of Mussolini, and officially banned after the country's liberation. Thus, the Fascist youth journal in which Pasolini publishes his first theoretical reflection on youth in 1942 presents itself as a *rassegna di giovinezza* (youth review). However, to define more personally the ambivalent view of youth that emerges from a Fascist education but is also removed from its centres of power, he chose the phrase *La meglio gioventù* (the best of youth), the Italianized verse of a WW1 song in the Friulian dialect. The mere existence of such lexical variety in Italian, and in many dialects, suggests a proliferation of discourse on youth that goes well beyond the social sciences, in a culture in which the adjective *giovanile* remains a beloved compliment, unlike the English *juvenile*, and *giovanilismo*, the behaviour of someone who wants to appear young, is a practice so common as to warrant a specific noun.

1 *Giovinezza*, or The Best of Youth

Largo ai Giovani! **Youth and Fascism in the 1940s**

Pasolini's earliest writings on youth emerged in the context of the debates over the younger generation's role within Fascist society that occupied Italian intellectuals in the 1930s and '40s. Proclaiming itself a revolutionary force that would create a new Italy and new Italians, Fascism hoped to appeal to the young: to their youthful desire for glory and excitement through its militaristic rhetoric, and to their idealism and ethical principles with its plan for social justice.[1] Benito Mussolini had always made the cult of youth one of the central components of his political discourse. However by the late twenties, much of the press registered a growing sense of apathy or dissatisfaction among young people and, by the thirties, the party press referred to an alarming *problema dei giovani*.[2] The regime responded with increased efforts to mobilize the younger generations and a painstaking organization of their education and leisure activities. School reform and the regulation of after-school programs by the *ONB* (*Opera Nazionale Balilla*) were aimed at shaping perfect Fascist men and women. The creation of Fascist University Youth groups (*Gioventù Universitaria Fascista*, or *GUF*), the establishment of patronage programs within state institutions, and a relative easing of censorship on youth journals were among the measures adopted to favour the formation of a young intellectual elite that would lead Fascist Italy into the future. When Minister of Education Giuseppe Bottai's initiatives to "make way for youth" (*far largo ai giovani*) were gradually turned into policies, young intellectuals had platforms on which to express their views on Fascism as a revolutionary force and their own role in the announced renewal of society.[3]

Having attended Italian public schools since the late 1920s, Pasolini was in a way a product of the Fascist education reforms. His apprenticeship was intertwined with the initiatives of official Fascist culture, even though later recollections, by Pasolini and by his friends, prefer to draw attention to the seeds of an anti-Fascism that became explicit only after the war. As a university student in Bologna, he was a member of the local *GUF* and participated proudly in the *Littoriali della Cultura e dell'Arte*, the competitions organized to showcase the literary and artistic accomplishments of the young generations.[4] He played in the university soccer and basketball teams and took part enthusiastically in ski trips organized by Fascist youth organizations (Gioventù Italiana Littorio (GIL) and the above-mentioned GUF), although he commented ironically, in his correspondence to friends, on the expectation that young men be "virili e guerrieri" (virile and warlike).[5] In the same years, he envisioned his role as a member of that young intellectual elite through individual and group projects, involving his friends Franco Farolfi, Francesco Leonetti, Roberto Roversi, and Luciano Serra. As he attended university courses that would distinctively shape his aesthetic outlook, particularly art history lectures by Roberto Longhi and conversations with his assistant Francesco Arcangeli, Pasolini prepared a monograph on contemporary Italian art to be published through the GIL. While he read voraciously and attended film screenings organized by Renzo Renzi at the Cinema Imperiale, he staged group readings of modern plays at his house. In the same period, he composed poetry and, with the same friends, conceived of a literary review that would renew the great tradition of Italian literature by running it through the filter of modernity. Meanwhile he published his first articles in the journals sponsored by the GUF and the GIL, and contributed to the debate on the role of youth in Fascist society that had been a recurrent feature in youth publications for at least a decade.[6]

In the reviews that sprang up in Rome, Florence, Milan, and other cities in the early 1930s, "taking to heart Mussolini's promises to bring social justice to Italy, younger men and women produced blueprints for antibourgeois mass societies that would embody the principles of gender equality, corporativist economics and social revolution."[7] They shared a belief in Fascism as the fitting political movement for the diverse and changing conditions of modernity, and in corporativism as a valid alternative to both Communism and capitalism. The proposed vertical organization of corporativist society promised to eliminate class conflict and reconfigure the relationship between the individual and the state.[8] From many of these journals issued a generational discourse, which corresponded to the awkward experience of the young men born too late to participate in World War I and in the March on Rome. The dissatisfaction and inadequacy that these young men felt in a regime that defined identity and masculinity on the basis of military practice were channelled in cultural debate, and often produced conflict with the older generation over the plan for the new Fascist world.[9] Animated by the ideal of Fascism as the Italian way to modernity and social change, they expressed anti-capitalist and anti-bourgeois positions that were at odds with the regime's intent to project the image of a youthful and innovative political force while in fact maintaining the status quo.[10] On the other hand, in criticizing the older generations, young writers upheld the ideal of youth as continuous revolution that the government wanted to project, thus fulfilling Bottai's project.

Young people's ambivalent relationship with a regime that had chosen youth as a mobilizing myth can be understood in light of the distance between the ideal of the continuous revolution and the practical measures applied to regulate the expressions of young intellectuals. The difficulty in reconciling youth as a cultural construction with the actual experience of young people in the present, not exclusive to the *Ventennio*, became particularly significant in a discursive regime that invested so much of its self-definition in the notion of *giovinezza*.[11] However, the gap also shows the conflation of sociological and historical ideas about generations, and consequently of different conceptualizations of youth. The specific life experiences shared by one young generation, the WWI *arditi* and the *squadristi*, who were the protagonists of the March on Rome, created a unique generational identity. The early Fascists encapsulated their shared values of action, revolution, courage, and violence in the concept of youth, following an equation that was common to early twentieth-century avant-gardes. That ideal of youth, born out of specific historical experiences, combined with trans-historical connotations of vitality, fertility, and innocence, was subsumed into a trans-historical paradigm, which could be imposed on following generations. Inevitably, despite the numerous efforts by the regime to produce virtuous, virile, and courageous "new men" out of Italian boys, the second generation could hardly relate to the experiences that had shaped their fathers or older brothers. On the other hand, the ideal of permanent revolution, also associated with youth, was less appealing to aging Fascists who had settled in positions of power in the established regime. The freshness, ardour, vitality of youth, still an antidote to the poison of bourgeois liberalism and Communism, was thus cast as an absolute condition detached from biological age. Perpetual youth was a key component in the cult of the Duce and, through the identification of the Fascist nation with its leader, of the new Italy. The well-known prohibitions against publicizing Mussolini's birthday, mentioning any illness, or announcing the birth of his grandchildren in the press, and his own habit of shaving his head were only a few signs of a conscious effort to hide the passing of time, in order to uphold the myth of the eternal youth of the *capo*, and by extension of the nation.[12]

The coexistence of these conflicting notions of youth within Fascism is comparable to the contradictory interpellation issued to women. As Barbara Spackman observes, the Fascist regime "at once excludes women, depriving them of rights they never had and fixing them in the role of wife and mother, and calls them loudly to participate in political life."[13] While apparently contributing to the perceived incoherence of Fascist ideology, the coexistence of a divided interpellation, Spackman shows, also produces responses that exploit this ambiguity to their advantage. The interpellation issued to young people shows a similar, perhaps more blatant contradiction: the Fascist regime at once celebrates youth, elevating it to a mythical status, and excludes young people from the exercise of power. This contradiction is implicit in the *"largo ai giovani"* policies, which institutionalized youth's participation in the regime through the *Littoriali* and the GUF press, without real danger for the totalitarian system. In this light one can understand how alternative definitions of youth could be formulated within, and even thanks to, the Fascist discursive regime. Pasolini's first articles in the journals sponsored by Fascist youth organizations in Bologna exploit, to their advantage, the ambiguity of the terms sustaining official youth discourse. The article "I giovani, l'attesa," which appeared in the first issue of *Il setaccio* in November 1942, represents, together with "Cultura italiana e cultura europea a Weimar," published a few months earlier in *Architrave*, Pasolini's earliest contributions to the debate on youth. Despite the apparently different topics, the two articles outline a notion of youth that will recur, in slightly different shapes, throughout Pasolini's oeuvre: the identification of a cultural locus of indeterminacy and contradiction, which will come to coincide with the poet's subjective stance, but that, at this early stage, joins in the current debate on the subject.

Pasolini and Fascist University Youth: *Architrave* **and** *Il setaccio*

In 1942, when young Pasolini contributes to *Architrave* and *Il setaccio*, the debate on youth and its contradictory conceptualization is still crucial to both journals' self-definition. Described in its first issue as a "youth journal" but "not necessarily a journal against old people," *Architrave*, the review of the Bologna *GUF*, is expected to "be young" without offending the older officials who sponsor and censor the publication.[14] In the words of the editor-in-chief, its mission seems rather that of a mentor: "Essa sceglie, accoglie, guida i giovanissimi e li affianca in disciplina ai giovani più maturi e agli uni e agli altri vuol servire di palestra e di laboratorio." (It chooses, welcomes, guides the very young and it matches them up with more mature youths for discipline, and to both it wishes to serve as a gymnasium and laboratory.)[15] Youth, often combined with the adjective "virile," is thus vaguely defined as "passione, entusiasmo, conquista, tirocinio, lavoro" (passion, enthusiasm, conquest, training, work), and becomes a vehicle for the promotion of revolutionary ideals against the fossilization of the institutions.[16] Several contributions present youth as the necessary antidote to a Fascism "more form than substance." For instance on March 1, 1941, in a first-page article titled "Noi, i giovani," Agostino Bignardi argues that the Fascist revolution cannot be limited to one generation, and claims for his generation the mission to pursue and extend it, "sempre naturalmente permanendo un 'costume' fascista di fronte ai problemi storici, costume che noi giovani prendiamo direttamente dal vivo dell'esperienza squadrista" (always of course maintaining a Fascist "approach" to historical problems, an approach that we, young people, take directly from the experience of *squadrismo*).[17] Based on a relationship of continuity with the fathers (or at least with the *squadristi* among them) and on a real identity between word and action, the mission envisioned for the young is "continuazione della rivoluzione in tutti i settori con un'intransigenza accanita; compimento dell'esperienza corporativa in una nuova socialità integrale, stroncando ogni forma di supercapitalismo pseudocorporativo; valutazione in pieno della purezza nella vita collettiva" (continuation of the revolution in all fields, with dogged intransigence; completion of the corporative experience in a new comprehensive social structure, crushing all forms of pseudocorporative supercapitalism; full evaluation of purity in collective life).[18]

For this generation of intellectuals raised within Fascism, culture continues to have the compensatory function it had for the youth of the 1930s, even if the war now in progress offers an opportunity for self-definition unavailable to the young intellectuals of the previous decade. Presenting a view of the war as a continuation of the Fascist revolution, the editors and contributors of *Architrave* emphasize the role of university students in defining the civilization that will emerge from the conflict, the new thought that will be one with the new actions.[19] The role of youth as an anti-bourgeois force, however, can be fulfilled by the young generations only if they take the teachings of their elders to the next level:

> Una generazione di giovani può affermare valori nuovi solo se nasce da un tormentato studio dei valori tradizionali, cioè di quelli delle storiche maturità e, insieme, da un sofferto distacco dai medesimi. Se manca lo *studio*, l'assimilazione dei valori tradizionali, una generazione si nutre di vento: se manca il *distacco* una generazione continua l'altra in un grigiore senza primavere.
>
> A generation of young people can affirm new values only if it starts from an excruciating study of traditional values, that is, of the values arrived at by past generations and, simultaneously, from a painful detachment from those same values. If such study, and such assimilation of traditional values, is lacking, a generation feeds on wind: if the detachment is lacking, a generation follows in the footsteps of the previous one in a greyness where spring never comes.[20]

Running parallel to this generational view, however, is the view that youth remains a question more of attitude than of age. As the author who writes under the pseudonym *La Scolta* (The Scout) powerfully reminds the readers in a brief article in July 1941, youth is separate from biological age and coincides with a "spirito schiettamente rivoluzionario, la sua chiara visione delle mete da raggiungere, l'instancabile coraggioso e – perché no? – audace sforzo di intransigenza e di onestà" (a frankly revolutionary spirit, its clear view of the goals to reach, the tireless, courageous and – why not? – bold effort of intransigence and honesty).

The first public definition of youth offered by Pasolini coincides with the position of the journal hosting his debut, but also advances some personal positions. In "Cultura italiana e cultura europea a Weimar" (*Architrave*, August 1942), the young intellectual reflects on his recent encounter with his peers from other European countries at two gatherings of Fascist youth.[21] He recognizes the important role his generation must play in guaranteeing the fundamental freedom of poetic creation from propaganda, and its necessary closeness to "contemporary political, social, and economic movements."[22] Generational change is as important as the continuity advocated by previous *Architrave* articles: "I semi gettati in tutta Europa dalla generazione che ci ha preceduti sono stati feracissimi; soltanto hanno dato in noi frutti diversi da quelli previsti" (ibid., 6; the seeds sowed all over Europe by the generation that preceded us were extremely fruitful; however, they produced in us different fruits than were expected). The relationship with tradition is envisioned as a rapport of "continua e infinita trasformazione, ossia antitradizione, scandita da una linea immutabile, che è simile alla storicità per la storia" (ibid.; continuous and infinite transformation, that is, antitradition, marked out by an immutable line, which is similar to historicity for history). The new culture, expression of the younger generations, is born out of an interaction between tradition and modernity: "una tradizione passata attraverso il filtro dell'antitradizione, una tradizione studiata sui poeti nuovi" (ibid., 7; a tradition that has been run through the filter of anti-tradition, a tradition based on the study of the latest poets). Young poets find their style in a creative re-elaboration of their masters' style, but it is in youth that tradition can best find expression: "Ed ecco la tradizione, tanto cara agli stessi mediocri ed agli interessati, eccola risolta nella migliore gioventù, e amata, come se fosse nata di nuovo, nuovamente vergine, intatta, interamente da scoprirsi e godersi" (ibid; and here is tradition, so dear to the same mediocre and interested parties, here it is, worked out in the best of youth, and loved, as if it were reborn, virgin once more, completely there, ready to be discovered and enjoyed). Generational change is ineluctable, Pasolini claims, just as dawn anticipates the day to come: "Questo, almeno, avviene in potenza, è, almeno, l'origine di una prossima condizione culturale, come equilibrio tra cultura e vita sociale, che, adesso, appare a noi giovani come l'incerta luce dell'alba che è tuttavia una certezza del giorno" (ibid., 6; this, at least, happens potentially; it is, at least, the origin of a future cultural condition, like the balance between culture and social life, which, now, appears to us, young people, as the uncertain light of dawn, which is nevertheless the certainty of the day). Recasting the relationship between past and present in cultural terms, Pasolini defines his generation as the heir of a great tradition that becomes significant in its dialectical relationship with modernity. The conceptualizations of youth and poetry go hand in hand: the tension between literary tradition and modernity is analogous to the conflict between, on one hand the notion of youth as an experience that is repeated unchanged generation after generation and, on the other, the accounts of his generation as something unique.

Il setaccio, to which Pasolini directs his energies soon after his debut in *Architrave*, takes a similarly polyvalent stance in the definition of youth. In its inaugural issue the journal is defined a *"Rassegna di giovinezza"* (Youth Review), and presented by its editor, Giovanni Falzone, as an example of *"stampa dei giovani,"* a publication by the young, rather than simply *"per i giovani,"* for the young. Young people are the agents, but not necessarily the sole target of the journal, which functions as a springboard and testing ground for *"la grande stampa"* (major publications): "Ragazzi, quindi che si elevano già dalla massa e che sentono il diritto di esprimersi, sia pur contenuti dalla vigile guida di qualche anziano capace di comprenderli e di indirizzarli verso una coesione capace di frutti insperati" (Young people, that is, who already stand out from the mass and feel they have the right to express themselves, albeit contained by the watchful guide of an elder, who is able to understand them and direct them towards a synthesis that can produce unexpected fruits). In the same issue, in a response to the alleged crisis of Italian theatre, Carlo Manzoni laments insufficient attention to what he calls *"teatro dei giovani,"* defined in terms of its attitude towards experimentation rather than the biological age of its practitioners. "Non è contro gli anziani di età che protestiamo, bensì contro gli anziani nello spirito. Se, poi, questi coincidono con quelli la colpa non è nostra." (It is not against the elderly in age that we protest, rather against the elderly in spirit. If, however, these two coincide the fault is not ours.)[23] Youth as a moral condition that could restore society to health is invoked in defence of Italy's participation in the war. One recognizes this view most prominently in Riccardo Castellani's article "Sui concetti di 'fede' e 'giovinezza,'" in which he defines youth as the age of faith and spirituality, when moral concerns triumph over material ones.[24] For Castellani, the attitude coincides naturally with young age, but may be preserved in one's heart into maturity. When applied to nations, this notion of youth distinguishes Fascist Italy from its enemies in the war. Fascism, born on the ruins of a decaying organism, "fu il germoglio nuovo che, per virtù di un'idea, seppe trovare la via alla luce e ricominciare una nuova vita, fresca di energie e di calore vitale" (was the new sprout that, thanks to an idea, could find its way to the light and start a new life of fresh energy and vital warmth). Fascism has channelled the spiritual energy of youth, and demands of young people "la difesa della loro stessa giovinezza contro i mali e i vizi che la insidiano" (the defence of their own youth against the evils and vices that undermine it).[25] Defining youth in a way that goes beyond limits imposed by age and envisioning their work in a relationship of continuity with their elders, the editor and contributors of *Il setaccio* reflect the contradictory position that youth occupies in Fascism.

A similar recognition of the continuity between generations is evident in Pasolini's article "I giovani, l'attesa."[26] Rejecting an openly Fascist notion of youth as *"gagliardia"* (vigour), his debut article in *Il setaccio* describes youth as a transitory state, which can only be defined by approximation, as the apposition in the title suggests. Recalling the "painful awakenings" of Ungaretti's verse quoted in the epigraph, youth is compared to dawn, a passing moment that inexorably becomes full daylight:

> Al risveglio è simile la giovinezza, e come il giorno a poco a poco consuma l'alba, che inerte si abbandona al mutamento, così nelle generazioni dei giovani, che a una a una passano, gridano, giungono alla meta, e, giunte, si volgono stupite a guardare chi senza scampo viene a sostituirle, grava un gelo indifferente di silenzio.

> Youth is like waking up, and as the daylight little by little consumes dawn, which inertly yields to this change, there hangs over young generations, which one by one pass, cry out, reach their goal and, once they have reached it, look back amazed at those who inexorably have come to replace them, a cold, indifferent silence.[27]

Generations follow one another with the certainty of hours in a day, and even lacking the direct experience that anchored their elders to history, the author and his young peers are the cultural heirs of their predecessors:

> sia in sede politico-economico-sociale, sia in sede di cultura, succediamo immediatamente a un riscoprimento sulla cui strada dobbiamo proseguire, non già meccanicamente, ma con intenso e lucido approfondimento, che verrà a discriminare nella eredità affidataci – nel nuovo sentimento dell'esistenza – quanto c'è di realmente nuovo e quanto è rimasuglio, avanzo o malafede.

> Both for what concerns the political-economic-social aspects, and for culture, we come immediately upon a rediscovery on whose path we must pursue, not mechanically, but with intense and lucid analysis, which will allow us to discern within the inheritance entrusted to us – as part of a new feeling for life – what is really new, and what is residue, a leftover, or bad faith. (Ibid., 12)

With the peremptory statement "ora è la nostra volta" (now it is our turn), the young author claims a right to define the role of youth in his time. The responsibility of such heritage and the awareness of their "unripeness" place young people in a state of *attesa*, a painful wait for a future that will inexorably determine youth's end. Only in memory will youth, now a conflicted condition, appear clearly to those who look back to it from afar: "Così noi abbiamo valicato, ormai, i luoghi della nostra giovinezza, e, da lontano, la contempliamo, commiserando la sua condizione di dolorosa attesa." (Ibid. 11; So we have passed over by now the space of our youth, and we contemplate it from afar, pitying its condition of painful waiting.) Within the ambivalent discourse of youth created by Fascism, Pasolini affirms the value of adolescence as an uncertain, suspended state, full of unarticulated potentiality.

Suspended between past and future, defined mostly through negatives, adolescence is thus the transitional status par excellence. Rather than trying to affirm one notion of youth over another, the young Pasolini acknowledges the liminality of the condition, "suspended in heroic hiatus between a past which must be suffered and a generational coming to fruition vaguely denoted as 'l'attuazione' (realization)."[28] In so doing, he assigns value to unripeness and to the soul-searching, which is a trope of modern adolescence. Behind the inflated rhetoric of the period and the venue, the seed of Pasolini's own mythology of youth stands out clearly in this article. Surprisingly, the twenty-year-old author, who identifies with the collective subject of his peers, also defines his relationship with youth as detachment. "I giovani, l'attesa" expresses in preliminary form the dichotomy of youth as a specific and collective subject, acknowledged through the "we" in the article, and an indeterminate, polyvalent idea nourished by literature and social policy.

Generational Identity, Personal Exclusion: *Eredi*, Exile, Nostalgia

The young generation for whom Pasolini speaks in "I giovani, l'attesa" has a more explicit referent in the school and university friends with whom he shares intellectual and creative goals: Francesco Leonetti, Roberto Roversi, Luciano Serra, and Franco Farolfi. Their correspondence in the years 1940–2 confirms that Pasolini's considerations on youth, poetry, and tradition, rhetorically expressed in the Fascist publications, were a recurrent personal preoccupation in this period. A cluster of ideas on youth recurs in the letters and in the poems that they contain: youth is an exceptional condition, blissful and ephemeral; it is a group experience, which Pasolini cherishes, but from which he also feels detached. The generational *"noi"* of the articles is replaced by a more specific subject particularly in the letters addressed to the first three and dedicated to the planning of the review *Eredi* (*Heirs*). Although the very format of the letters, which Pasolini sends to Serra but that are addressed to all three friends, already testifies to the collective nature of the relationship, Pasolini also often reminds his friends that "davanti a *Eredi* dovremo essere quattro, ma, per purezza, uno solo" (Where *Eredi* is concerned we must be four but in purity only one).[29] Individual creation will be the expression of a common project and be jointly supported, through critiques of poems in draft and shared publication expenses. The main project that draws the four young intellectuals together, the planning of *Eredi*, also shows their self-identification as the "unexpected fruits" of past generations, as Pasolini theorized in "Cultura italiana e cultura europea a Weimar." Epistolary discussions show that the title chosen for the review "doveva rappresentare la continuità della poesia classica filtrata nella poesia moderna di Ungaretti, Montale, Sereni" (ought to represent the continuity of classical poetry filtered through the modern poetry of Ungaretti, Montale, Sereni).[30] Their expressed desire to enter and alter their precursors' lineage and the communal quality of the project are two equally important aspects of their agenda. The encounter of tradition with modernity, a position that Pasolini defined *"eredismo,"* is a prerequisite for the expression of youth.[31] In positioning themselves in a relation of continuity with their poetic forefathers, both in critical and creative endeavours, the *eredi* embody the best of youth as envisioned by Pasolini in his Weimar article.[32]

The group identity is as important as it is transitory. When faced with the necessity of postponing publication, Pasolini is optimistic but cautious and, in entreating his companions to be patient and continue writing, he also warns them of the changes that each will undergo: "Se esce fra due anni io e Serra saremo professori e guadagneremo; avremo tutti e quattro una propria personalità almeno 15 volte più sviluppata; pensate in due anni (o anche, uno) quale sviluppo possono avere delle culture adolescenti come le nostre!" (If it comes out in two years Serra and I will be teachers and will earn a living; we will all four have our own personalities at least fifteen times more developed. Think, how much an adolescent culture like ours can develop in two years (or even in one!)[33] The group dynamic highlights the fleetingness of a time that Pasolini often experiences as escaping him.

28 Fictions of Youth

The letters to Franco Farolfi, a high school friend who had moved from Bologna to Parma, offer another window onto Pasolini's conflicting thoughts on youth. He recounts the progress of his literary and artistic apprenticeship in passionate terms (his avid readings, participation in the pre-*Littoriali* competitions, enthusiastic plans for the review); and then describes intense personal experiences, like a late night escapade in the hills with a group of friends, in an idealized light:

> Allora ho pensato come sia bella l'amicizia, e le comitive di giovani ventenni che ridono con le loro maschie voci innocenti, e non si curano del mondo intorno a loro, continuando per la loro vita, riempiendo la notte delle loro grida. La loro maschilità è potenziale. Tutto in loro si trasforma in risa, in risata. Mai la loro foga virile tanto chiara e sconvolgente appare come quando sembrano ridiventati fanciulli innocenti, perché nel loro corpo è sempre presente la loro completa e ilare giovinezza. Anche quando parlano di Arte o Poesia.
>
> Then I thought how beautiful friendship is and the groups of twenty-year-old youths who laugh with their innocent male voices and take no notice of the world around them, continuing along their lives, filling the night with their shouts. Theirs is a potential masculinity. Everything in them turns to laughter, to bursts of laughter. Never does their virile energy appear so clear and overwhelming as when they seem to have become once more innocent children because their complete and joyous youth is still present in their bodies. Even when they are talking about Art or Poetry. [34]

The energy and potential of youth is cast in a nostalgic glow, as if observed from a distance, even though the reminiscence is only a few days old. Specific friends and conversations become archetypical twenty-year-olds, young male voices, "complete and joyous youth." Their separation from the outside world, accentuated by the repetition of the third-person pronouns, is also a separation from the narrator, who only at the end of the passage acknowledges that he was in that group: "Ho visto (e me stesso vedo così) giovani parlare di Cézanne, e pareva parlassero di una loro avventura d'amore, con uno sguardo scintillante e turbato. Così eravamo noi quella notte" (ibid.; I have seen – and see myself in the same way – young men talking about Cézanne and it seemed they were talking about one of their love affairs, with a bright and troubled look. That is how we were that night). At other times, nostalgia is explicitly acknowledged, with the awareness that the object of longing is a past not too far removed: "una violenta nostalgia per il nostro passato (il bel tempo che ritorna, gli alberi che mettono le foglie, i tavolini dei caffè all'aperto, i ragazzi che vanno in giro sulle biciclette che sembrano nuove) tutto mi ricorda le nostre antiche (ma non tanto) fini-scuole" (ibid.; violent nostalgia for our past [the good weather coming back, the trees putting on their leaves, the small tables outside of cafes, the boys riding around on what look like new bicycles] – everything reminds me of our long ago [but not so long ago] last days of school).

Other letters to his "dearest companion" Farolfi communicate the paradox of the young man's keen self-awareness: sensitive to the potential implicit in his youth, articulated in centuries of art and literature, Pasolini feels incapable of enjoying the present. From Casarsa, in August 1940, he describes his tendency to displace into the future the enjoyment of the present moment: "Casarsa mi ha deluso, ma del resto ogni cosa mentre è qui mi delude e quando è passata la rimpiango ... E quanto rimpiangerò quest'inverno le presenti giornate, come sempre mi accade!" (Casarsa has disappointed me, but then everything disappoints me while it is there and when it is past I regret it ... And how much I shall regret these present days next winter – as always happens with me!)[35] But at the end of the summer the intense awareness of experiencing a special time in his life elicits a more complex reflection:

> È molto triste la partenza da qui; è finita un'altra estate e un altro periodo della mia vita; sono impaziente di rivedere un'altra volta le cose che lascio e nello stesso tempo spero che quel momento sia molto lontano perché deve intercorrere un anno della mia vita, e voglio sperare che sia il più lungo possibile perché i diciannove anni non torneranno più.

> Leaving here is very sad – another summer is over and another period in my life; I am impatient to see once more the things I am leaving, and at the same time hope that moment may be very distant because in between there must come a year of my life, and I very much hope that it will be as long as possible because one's nineteenth year will not come back.[36]

Split between the desire to extend the fleeting time of youth and the sense of potentiality inscribed in his future, nineteen-year-old Pasolini expresses in more personal form the ideas on youth that underly contemporary articles. The sense of an ending, the present quickly receding into the past, the tension towards the future: adolescence generates an ambivalent relation to time that he will define as "nostalgia for the present time" ("nostalgia del tempo presente").

A series of poems included in these letters from Casarsa articulated this nostalgia as the predominant mode of his experience of youth. The rural birthplace of his mother's family and summer destination from an early age, Casarsa della Delizia, in Friuli, was near and dear to Pasolini's heart. As Colleen Ryan-Scheutz has shown, "it was the place where the combined experiences of his intellectual growth, political action, sexual freedom, and linguistic experimentation formed the basis for a lifelong poetics concerned with recovering what was genuine and authentic in human life."[37] Casarsa signified departure from the intellectual life of Bologna and return to the maternal land, removal from the beloved university companions and sexual discovery. Just as he later elevated Casarsa to "primo luogo della vita," in many recollections, despite it not being his actual birthplace, in his early poetry he identified Friuli with his adolescence: a state of being as well as a state of mind. He attributed to each an uncertain, suspended quality, which translated into infinite potential. However, he also experienced both as a form of exile. Like exile, adolescence for Pasolini is a suspended state, characterized by the double impossibility of departing and returning. All experience remains at the stage of potentiality, present before the eyes of the young man, but somehow unattainable, removed. Adolescence can be the object of reflection and writing only inasmuch as it is beyond reach, receding into the past or vanishing into the future. [38]

Fundamentally dialectical in nature, youth as exile both constricts and liberates writing; it constitutes a limit but also an incentive for poetic expression.[39] The link between writing and exile is made explicit in the epigraph of "Nostalgia del tempo presente," the first of four poems devoted to the subject: "Super flumina Babylonis, illic sedimus / et flevimus, dum recordarmur tui, Syon. / In salicibus, in medio eius, suspendimus organa nostra" (Psalm 137: vv. 1–2). The biblical reference to the lament of the exiled Israelites in Babylon, and the subsequent definition of Casarsa as "lost Zion," anticipate the poet's future removal from Casarsa, and from youth. The sense of loss, which precludes the singing in Babylon, sparks poetic activity in the universe of young Pasolini. The dialectical tension between past, present, and future, made explicit in the title, structures the poem, which has echoes of Foscolo, Pascoli, and D'Annunzio, all poets that Pasolini read in school:

> Celeste errore sono i miei passi, e oscuro
> senso le mie parole a chi d'altri luoghi
> mi sa. Presso le siepi, bianche per lontananza,
> intoccabile fuoco arde il mio corpo
> a chi è fanciullo, e da lungi mi guarda.
>
> Celestial error are my footsteps, and obscure
> is the sense of my words to those who know me
> from elsewhere. Near the hedges, white in the distance,
> untouchable fire burns my body
> to one who is a boy, and looks at me from afar.

Immersed in an indistinct landscape in what should be the present, the poet distances himself from gestures and words that define him. He embraces the gaze of another, a young boy who watches from a distance, in order to express the sexual energy of youth ("intoccabile fuoco arde il mio corpo"). Through the Proustian echo of the white hawthorn hedges physical distance morphs into temporal removal. In the projected memory, the poet is transfigured into the natural elements that suddenly materialize:[40]

> Ed a me stesso, spirito vivente
> sotto le azzurre viti e arboree ombre
> sarò, quando straniato, perso, lontano,
> mi terrà nuova vita e nuovo giorno.
>
> And to myself, living spirit
> under the blue vines and treeline shade
> I shall be, when drifted off, lost, distant,
> new life will hold me and a new day.[41]

The town ("il mio paese") is also suspended ("sospeso sull'azzurro / di nebbie piano"), as the embodiment of the present floating self ("sperduta effige in questo sogno di vita") and sharing the self's dialectical relation to time: "e sarà antico / al tempo, che, fermo, si consuma" (and it shall be old / to time which stands still and is consumed). In this prefigured removal from the locus of youth, Casarsa mirrors the poet's otherworldly wandering, his retracing his footsteps while moving away:

> Perduta Elèusi (*Syon*), Casarsa, al mio cammino
> che ritorna sull'orme, e s'allontana.
>
> Lost Elysium (Zion), Casarsa, on my path
> which turns back on its footsteps and goes away.[42]

The anticipated loss of youth inspires poetry, and Casarsa as its embodiment becomes the object of nostalgia in a present that is both immutable and already vanishing. The link between exile and nostalgia is further explored in subsequent poems, which refer to a similar tension between past and future. "Paesi nella memoria" (Places in Memory) also predicates present poetic activity upon the certainty of future silence:

> Quando rievocherò, sospeso il canto,*
> i lenti giorni e la mite solagna
> di codesti compiuti, intatti e trapassati
> gesti d'uomo che vive, ed ai richiami
> di nostalgia ritorna alla memoria,
> mesti con lui verranno, onda di pianto,
> i miei paesi, nel calante inverno e nelle diacce
> nevi, caldi di perenne estate
> fioriti, tra l'arboree morti!
> * Suspendimus organa nostra
>
> When I shall invoke once more, my song suspended,*
> the slow days and the gentle solace
> of these deeds accomplished, intact and past,
> of a living man, summoned
> by nostalgia he will come back to memory,
> sadly with him will come, a flood of tears,
> my places, in the waning winter and in the icy
> snows, heats of perennial summer, blossoming among the dead trees!
> * Suspendimus organa nostra

The certainty of a future "hanging of the harps," which the accompanying footnote links to the Babylonian exile of the previous poem, imposes the present expression of a unique condition: summer vacation, a topos of modern coming-of-age narratives, is a stand-in for the exceptionality of youth, and the return to the city for its passing. The splendour of summer is filtered through the nostalgia that the distance will cause. Nostalgia connects the present and future selves in a projected exile, which both suspends and elicits poetry. Cast into a future recollection, the time and places of youth are displaced into a "perennial summer" accessible only from afar. It will bring serenity and clarity to a winter defined by tears, missteps and jumbled voices:

> Dentro il mio pianto ed i supini errori
> e le scomposte voci, sempre più sereno
> a me stesso sarò, sempre più chiara
> questa mia vita.
>
> Inside my tears and the supine errors
> and the jumbled voices, more and more serene
> to myself I will be, clearer and clearer
> this life of mine.[43]

Summertime in the countryside, and Casarsa as the locus of youth, will remain fixed, unaffected by space and time: "vedo che non lo spazio fine / t'impone, e non il tempo" (I see that space imposes no limit / on you, nor does time). Poetry imposes and expresses the removal, requires and alleviates the exile. In "Seconda elegia" the displacement of the present is conveyed in the first line: "Agosto è sul morire e non è nato / ancora" (August is at the point of death and is not born / yet). The presentment of the end of summer transfigures it into the end of life; "Non lungi è il cimitero" (The cemetery is not very far), and the loss of friends: "Benché vi guardi e senta ancora, al tempo / vi rapiscono il freddo e gli oscuri presagi ed il pensiero / che qui non cesserà la vita (Although I still see you and hear you, the cold / and obscure forebodings and the thought / that life will not end here steal you away). The anticipation of loss and consequent nostalgia are made explicit in this invocation:

> Oh nostalgia
> del tempo presente! Amici, con voi cammino,
> e già tremate, larve, in fondo alla memoria.

> Oh nostalgia
> for the present time! Friends, I walk with you
> and already you tremble, ghosts, in the depths of memory.[44]

Simultaneously present and removed, youth is the object of writing inasmuch as it escapes any firm definition. Poetry attempts to capture adolescence in its dynamic tension between past, present, and future. However, the immortalization effected by poetry stops time and amplifies the longing. The end of the summer in Casarsa evokes death also in the fourth and last poem of the series, "Severina nell'aria buia" (Severina in the Dark Air). Here the suspension between past and future takes the shape of a dark cloud foretelling a thunderstorm:

> La morte (è vero) come questo
> sospeso rombo di tuono,
> te sovrasta che vivi
> e me che ti contemplo.

> Death (it is true) like this
> interrupted rumble of thunder,
> hangs over you who are alive
> and me who is contemplating you.

In the opposition between daylight and darkness we recognize the juxtaposition of action, represented by Severina cleaning up after the storm, and contemplation, embodied in the poet who fears "il male sordido della vita che ricomincia" (sordid evil of life that begins again).[45] Self-exiled from life, and specifically from youth, the poet finds relief in the writing that crystallizes the moment of longing and fear, expressed in the Ungaretti-inspired lines: "Strappar / pavento dai rami foglie" (To wrench / I fear leaves from branches). Contemplation and writing require removal from direct experience, while poetry conveys a fear of the future and of the inevitable maturity. In the accompanying note, Pasolini traces the common inspiration connecting this poem to "Seconda Elegia," "Nostalgia del tempo presente," and "Paesi nella memoria" as a "'timore del futuro' che si può identificare, appunto, nell'espressione 'nostalgia del tempo presente'" ("Fear of the future," which can be identified, as it were, in the expression "nostalgia for the present time").[46] While poetic isolation is necessary for the expression – and celebration – of youth, the experience of adolescence seeks articulation in order to be shared by a community.

The condition of "nostalgia for the present time" in these early poems reveals the tension between present, future, and memory, which Pasolini identifies with youth. Experienced as exile, youth both liberates and confines the poet: it inspires him to express its uniqueness, but requires him to anticipate its loss.[47] Removal from the present – youth, the summer, Friuli – is necessary in order to write about it. The dualism of Casarsa and Bologna, or of summer and winter, visualizes that loss. In youth as in more conventional forms of exile, however, writing also rests on another dialectic: the isolation that constitutes its premise, and the communion with peers that demands a sharable text.[48] The young poet's desire to capture adolescence, not only as an indefinite, suspended state, but as an audience for his poems, is explicitly manifested in a poem titled "Il flauto magico" (The Magic Flute). Shared with Franco Farolfi as "rimpianto della fanciullezza perduta ed esaltazione della giovinezza violenta e sensuale" (a lament for lost childhood and the exaltation of violent and sensual youth), it is loosely based on the legend of the Pied Piper of Hamelin.[49] All traditional dark undertones removed, the narrative is transposed into a luminous Arcadia, where "conduca il sole per mano primavera, / rami agitando e frondosi peschi!" (may the sun lead spring by the hand, / waving branches and leafy peach-trees!). Identifying explicitly with the young piper, glowing with erotic energy, the poet wishes that his music and his adult-child body could prove irresistible:

> Così dolce suoni, e così bello vada
> il mio corpo di fanciullo adulto,
> che non indugi la stirpe dei ragazzi,
> non sprezzanti né ostili, ad inseguirmi
> con incerto passo ...
>
> May my adult child body sound so sweet and move so beautifully / that the boyish tribe will not hesitate, / neither scornful nor hostile, to follow me / with uncertain steps ...[50]

It is arguably the earliest poetic manifestation of a desire that characterized all of Pasolini's oeuvre: the desire to capture youth, meaning both to express its essence and to gain their attention. Initially these goals coincided: finding a way to express his own ambiguous position (already nostalgic not only for "lost childhood," but for a youthful condition that was still present, suspended between past and future, "heir" of a tradition that could only be authentically lived when filtered through modernity) meant finding a common language to share with "the boyish tribe": "Cantino poi con me / le melodie, danzino poi con me tutti fioriti / di cinte e serti …" (ibid.; let them sing with me / the melodies, let them dance with me festooned / with wreaths and chaplets …). Later, the task of "enchanting" young people would take a secondary position to the renewed effort to express the essence of an ineffable, constantly mutable condition. For the moment, sharing the experience with his young peers was as important as establishing their position in the literary genealogy.

Poesie a Casarsa: The Very Best of Youth

The struggle for expression focused not only on thematic concerns but also on stylistic ones: it was the search for an adequate form for youth, which could reflect the generational identity of the *eredi* (the "unexpected fruits" of tradition), and the permanent alienation experienced by the young poet. In celebrating the uncertainty of adolescence, young Pasolini was also finding his voice in the arena of Italian letters. Becoming adult meant "breaking the chains which tie one to the past by an act of pure will," even if it required "kill[ing] a sick and hypersensitive adolescent who tries to pollute my life as a man as well."[51] With regard to tradition it meant dismissing "this university culture which consists of dust and palimpsests," as Pasolini defined it in a letter to Farolfi, in favour of a more personal approach to culture that the *eredi* were articulating at this time.[52] Finding a voice for youth meant writing in a language that did not obscure its complexities. Pasolini found it in the dialect of Friuli, more specifically that of Casarsa: ancient yet lacking a written tradition, familiar yet artificially appropriated by the young poet, Casarsese mirrored the dialectical nature of youth as exile. The dialect of Casarsa, a marginal linguistic reality elevated to poetry for the first time, offered the material presence of "lost Zion" on the page. Its adoption by twenty-year-old Pasolini was the first conscious step in a search for the perfect form for youth that would characterize his entire career.

In his early Friulian poems, first published in the little volume *Poesie a Casarsa* in 1942, and later expanded as *La meglio gioventù* (*The Best of Youth*), Pasolini found his own voice, and delved into the dialectics of youth as exile that he had introduced in the "nostalgia" poems.

Consistently with the title chosen for the later collection, a verse taken from a WWI song of the *Alpini*, the crack, fast-moving, mountain-climbing infantry troops of the Italian army, *"la meglio zoventù la va soto tera"* (the best of youth goes underground), the dominant theme is the celebration of lost youth ("il vivi pierdùt," in dialect).[53] In the song, war deprives young men of youth; in Pasolini's poems the best of youth is lost when he casts it into an inaccessible space, once again identified with his maternal hometown. *Poesie a Casarsa*, the first published volume, offers the young poet's ode to lost youth. Just like the choice of Casarsa as place of origin is artificial, a posteriori, a displacement with respect to the birthplace Bologna, this early expression of youth is mediated by literary conventions. As the dedication anticipates, through the topos of the "aga fres-cia" (fresh water), the distinctive feature of youth in these poems is pastoral: the Friulian countryside offers the ideal backdrop for an idyll. The green fields and poplars, blue sky, dark blue violets, the sunlight, water as rain, dew, rivers, canals, all serve both as the background and the protagonists of these poems. The natural elements embody youth, and the young characters populating this world are physically part of it. Emerging from nature, or blending in with the natural elements around them, the boys shine with sunlight, have violets for eyes, and alder trees for hips; they feel the warm earth and the cool sky in their bodies and see their reflection in the water of the ditches. The celebration of youth is a celebration of Friuli as a comforting maternal land, but also of a mythical time.

The defining images in "Il nini muàrt," the luminous evening, the water, the sound of the church bells, set the scene and the tone for the entire collection:

Sera imbarlumida, tal fossàl
a cres l'aga, na fèmina plena
a ciamina pal ciamp

Jo ti recuardi, Narcìs, ti vèvis il colòur
da la sera, quand li ciampanis
a sùnin di muàrt.

Sera luminosa, nel fosso cresce l'acqua, una donna incinta cammina per il campo.
Io ti ricordo, Narciso, avevi il colore della sera, quando le campane suonano a morto.

> Radiant evening, water rises / in the ditch, a woman with child / walks in the field. / I remember you, Narcissus, you were the colour of evening when the bells / tolled the knell.[54]

The water is rising in the ditch, a pregnant woman walks in the field in the shimmering evening, the bells sounding the death knell recall Narcissus, the colour of the evening. All the *loci* of Pasolini's poetic Friuli are present in these two tercets: the field, the luminous sky, the water and the implicit reflection, the ringing bell, the boy-Narcissus and the mother, all transfigured by memory. Assonances and alliterations (imbarlumida-fossàl, ciamina-ciamp-ciampanis, recuardi-quand-muàrt) link together the coexisting opposites: the light and the evening, the unborn child and the dead boy, movement and stasis, life and death. Past and present coexist as well: Narcissus belongs to memory ("Jo ti recuardi, Narcìs"), but the bell sound and the rising water make his reflection resurface, and the glimmering light of the evening blurs the lines between memory and present experience. The first figure of identification with youth for the poet is created in this poem: immaterial, but projected upon the natural elements of an idyllic landscape.[55]

The protagonist of the idyll is the *giovinetto* in his various incarnations: *nini, donzel, frut, fantassùt, fì, zòvin, soranèl*. Invoked as an earlier incarnation of the poetic self or as its timeless narcissistic reflection, the *giovinetto* functions as the poet's interlocutor and as an embodiment of Friuli. Just as Provençal troubadour Peire Vidal's Provence, offered as a model by the verse of the epigraph, Pasolini's Friuli and the *giovinetto* are fused into a single object of desire.[56] The poet is far away and nostalgia for the region is intertwined with longing for his own youth. The *donzel* is part of the landscape, and of Casarsa, which thus becomes once again identified with youth. The relationship between youth, memory, and place becomes clear in the comparison between two versions of "O me donzel." In the earlier version, published in *Poesie a Casarsa* (1942) as "O me giovanetto!," memory is born from the scent which rain stirs from the earth:

> O mè donzel, memòrie
> ta l'odôr che la plòja
> da la tière 'a sospìre,
> 'a nas. 'A nàs memòrie
> di jèrbe vìve e ròja.

O me giovanetto, memoria nasce dall'odore che la pioggia ravviva dalla terra. Nasce memoria di roggia ed erba viva (*Poesie 1*, 171; Oh me, a boy, memory is born from the scent that rain revives from the earth. Memory of a ditch and live grass is born).

In the later revision, in *La meglio gioventù*, Pasolini completes the identification of his younger self with Friuli:

O me donzel! Jo i nas
ta l'odòur che la ploja
a suspira tai pras
di erba viva ... I nas
tal spieli da la roja.

O me giovinetto! Nasco nell'odore che la pioggia sospira dai prati di erba viva ... Nasco nello specchio della roggia (*Poesie 1*, 13; Oh me, a boy! I am born from the scent that the rain exhales from the fields of live grass ... I am born from the mirror of the ditch*)*.

In the water, the image of the *giovinetto* blends with the flickering reflection of Casarsa: "In chel spieli Ciasarsa / - coma i pras di rosada - / di timp antic a trima. In quello specchio Casarsa – come i prati di rugiada – trema di tempo antico." (In that mirror Casarsa – like the dewy fields – trembles of ancient times.) The identification of Casarsa and Friuli as the locus of youth through the *giovinetto* is further developed in "Ploja tai cunfins" (Rain on the Boundaries), where the rain dissolves the contours of the village into the rose-and-honey face of the boy: "Fantassùt, al plòuf il Sèil / tai spolèrs dal to paìs, / tal to vis di rosa e mèil / pluvisin al nas il mèis. Giovinetto, piove il Cielo sui focolari del tuo paese, sul tuo viso di rosa e miele, nuvoloso nasce il mese (*Poesie 1*, 11; Boy, the Sky rains down on the hearths of your town, on your rose and honey face, cloudy rises the month).

Although the portrait of youth provided in these poems seems generally detached from contemporary discourse, the poem "David" constitutes an exception. Displaying the reference in its original title, "Per il 'David' di Manzù," the poem addresses the sculpture by Giacomo Manzù, which significantly breaks with the classic iconography of the Judeo-Christian hero. Rather than a virile warrior, in Manzù's 1939 interpretation David is a thin adolescent, squatting on a rock, his back curved forward, his arms hanging between his bent legs, and his head tilted sideways. The torsion confers dynamism to his body, which appears as if it was captured the instant before throwing the stone he holds in his hand, but the posture and the slight body, with big ears protruding from his head and vertebrae showing through the skin on his back, suggest frailty.[57] Pasolini's poem reflects the ambiguity of this modern interpretation of a classic icon of youth: the thin David becomes a Friulian *giovinetto*, identified with his hometown, its exhaustion reflected in the boy's posture:

> Di fadìe, fantàt, l'è blanc il tò paîs,
> tu vòltis fèr il ciâf,
> pasiènt ta la tò ciâr lutàde.

> Amico, di stanchezza sbianca il tuo paese; tu volgi fermo il capo, paziente nella tua carne tentata. (*Poesie 1*, 172; My friend, your town fades away from fatigue; you look back slowly, patient in your tempted flesh.)

The repetition of the sound "cia" in the words *ciâf* and *ciâr*, paired with "paîs" at the end of the line, recalls the implicit "Ciasarsa" and identifies the thin scrawny boy with that town, as it recedes in memory. The alliteration *fadìe-fantàt* links fatigue and friendship, and both with desire through the assonance *fantàt-lutàde*. The second tercet transforms David into a Dionysian creature, through the image of a bull conducted to sacrifice by a smiling youth:

> Tu sôs, David, come il tòru in di d'Avril
> che ta li mans d'un fi c'al rît,
> al va dòls a la muàrt.

> Tu sei, David, come il toro in giorno d'aprile, che, nelle mani d'un fanciullo che ride, va dolce alla morte (*Poesie 1*, 17; Sartarelli, 63; You, David, are like a bull on an April day / in the hand of a laughing boy, / gently bound for slaughter).

While the second tercet remains substantially unchanged, the first changes in the revision for *La meglio gioventù*: the friend becomes more explicitly Narcissus, a "poor boy" bent over a well, but turning sideways to look at the poet:

> Pognèt tal pos, puòr zòvin,
> ti voltis viers di me il to ciaf zintìl
> cu'un ridi pens taj vuj.

Appoggiato al pozzo, povero giovane, volti verso di me il tuo capo gentile, con un greve riso negli occhi (*Poesie 1*, 17; Sartarelli, 63; Leaning on a well, poor lad, / you turn your graceful head towards me, / with a solemn smile in your eyes).

The reflection in the well replaces the vanishing image of Casarsa, and the poetic "I" is explicitly introduced in the equation. Manzù's David enters more explicitly in the gallery of *giovinetti* who embody both Friuli as the locus of youth and the poet's desire.

The later section "Suite furlana (1944–49)" fully explores the theme of Narcissus. Five of the eight poems in the second subsection, "Danze," are dedicated to the archetypal young man. In "Suite furlana," Narcissus, not satisfied with his reflection, looks behind the mirror "to see if that shape is a body" (*Poesie 1*, 63; par jodi s'a è un cuàrp chè Forma; per vedere se è un corpo quella Forma). His search only stops when the glimmer in the mirror comes to coincide with the glimmer of life in the infancy of the mother/Madonna. The narcissistic relationship is not complete until it includes the mother, and particularly the child-mother, the only other inhabitant of this idyllic landscape. In "Dansa di Narcìs," the title announces the identification of the poetic "I" with the dancing Narcissus, as he arises from the violets at dawn. The reflection is a "spirit" that casts a shadow on the grass with the glimmer of his curls (66). The play of light and darkness returns in the next "Dansa di Narcìs," where the "I" defines Narcissus through opposites: a violet and an alder.

Jo i soj na viola e un aunàr,
il scur e il pàlit ta la ciar

Io sono una viola e un ontano, lo scuro e il pallido della carne (*Poesie 1*, 67; I am a violet and an alder tree, the dark and the pale of the flesh).

The play of opposites ("il scur e il pàlit," "il neri e il rosa," "il sec e il mòrbit," "il frèit e il clìpit") establishes the image of an inevitably split self. The reflection, in the second movement of the poem, is internalized: "a si spièglin ta l'azùr fun / da laga dal me còur avàr; e si specchiano nell'azzurro fumo dell'acqua del mio cuore avaro" (68; and are mirrored in the blue smoke of the water of my greedy heart). The two opposites, the violet and the alder, are reflected in the water of the poet's miserable heart. The same colour scheme, the pale face with the dark eyes, introduces the narcissistic presence in the third "Dansa di Narcìs":

o me pàlit
volt cu'l neri da li violis

o mio pallido volto col nero delle viole (*Poesie 1*, 69; o my pallid face with the dark of the violets).

The identification of the violets with the poet's eyes furthers the contrast between the dark eyes and the pale skin of the face, on which the previous poem was constructed: "il veri dal me neri / vuli spàvit come un flour" (il vetro del mio nero occhio, pavido come un fiore; the glass of my dark eye bashful as a flower). The reference to the bashful look and the play on the phonetic similarity between "vuli" and "violis" at the end of the poem flesh out the identification eyes-violets that was introduced in the first stanza. The dark eyes serve as a reflecting surface for the sunlight, but no figure is reflected in them (ibid.). In "Pastorela di Narcìs" the poet's look is no longer directed at himself but at a young woman harvesting grass, and the secret gaze generates a fantasy of substitution: "I olmi platàt ... / e al so post i soj jo; Spio di nascosto ... e al suo posto sono io (I spied her unseen ... / and in her place I saw / myself). The protagonist's eyes, no longer violets, are "i vuj di me mari/ neris coma il fons dal stali; gli occhi di mia madre, neri come il fondo della greppia" (my mother's eyes, / dark as the bottom of a manger); her chest is shiny in the new dress and her hand, which was kept "in sacheta" (in the pocket) in the first stanza, touching the "cuàrp cialt di belessa; corpo caldo di bellezza" (body hot with beauty), is now gently resting in her lap (trans. Sartarelli, 79). The object of Narcissus' desire is both himself and his mother, as in "Suite furlana" (70–1).

In "La not di maj" the narcissistic subject is an old man ("ma tu veciu") with "an eye that looks like a frozen tear" (cun chel vuli ch'al par/ na àgrima inglassada); he looks at his reflection in the water and sees "un fantassùt" singing. The boy is so handsome that he could be his son. Life was taken away with the body, and the subject, who was once a son, has suddenly become a father: "Vita sensa distìn, / puartada via cu'l cuàrp; / di fi doventàt pari/ dal spolèr al sgivìn; vita senza destino, portata via col corpo: da figlio diventato padre, tra il focolare e la zolla" (*Poesie 1*, 54–5; life with no destiny, taken away with the body: the son becomes father, between the hearth and the clods).

Composed in 1945 and published in a longer version in the Friulian review *Ce fastu?* in December 1946, this reflection on aging shows a premature nostalgia for youth on the part of the 23-year-old poet. The return of the dead man portrayed in "Ciants di un muart" reiterates the sense of exclusion from life and youth: "Jo i torni da l'ombrena / dai muàrs; Io torno dall'ombra dei morti (I come back from the shadow of the dead). Announced by the death knell ("A bat na ciampana / I soj muart") and conveyed through the repeated contrast between outside and inside ("four" and "drenti"), between the cold of death ("neif") and the warmth of life ("vif"), the exclusion of the poetic subject ("Four, e no drenti") from everything but the memory of sensory experience is further rendered through the past tense of "i sintevi il senoli, i nasavi il fen" (sentivo il ginocchio, odoravo il fieno; I felt the knee, I smelled the hay) juxtaposed to the negative form of the present in "i no sint il zenoli / nè il cialt dal me cuàrp; non sento il ginocchio né il caldo del mio corpo" (I don't feel the knee or my warm body). The identification of the poet with the dead man, and of the latter with his former self, Stefano, observed as he performs everyday activities, enhances the sense of loss: "Vuei al era / un dì ch'i vevi di no essi! Oggi era un giorno che non dovevo essere!" (*Poesie 1*, 47–51; Today was a day when I wasn't supposed to be here!).

Friuli and its landscape (rivers, canals, poplars, blue skies, snow, but particularly the combination of water and light, in numerous variations) become synonymous with youth, even more poignantly when that landscape really emerges from the geography of memory. This is particularly true after 1950, when the scandal of the Ramuscello events forced Pasolini to leave Casarsa for Rome.[58] Through removal and nostalgia Friuli is immortalized as "the best of youth":

un Friùl ch'al vif scunussùt
    cu la me zoventùt
di là dal timp, ta un timp
sdrumàt dal vint

un Friuli che vive sconosciuto con la mia gioventù, al di là del tempo, in un tempo rovesciato dal vento (*Poesie 1*, 93–5; a Friuli that lives unknown, beyond time, in a time turned upside down by the wind).

From the vantage point of Rome, youth in Friuli becomes synonymous with holidays: the county fair, communal dances, and boys in their

Sunday best. This festive mode is assigned to the past and to the realm of nostalgia in a poem significantly titled "Lùnis": Rome is the supreme Monday to Casarsa's Sundays, a perennial weekday ("a e lùnis / e a no'l finirà mai pì; è lunedì, e non finirà mai più"; it is Monday, and it will never end), coming after holidays that are now beyond time. In the "light forever alive of a dead day, of an empty feast" the poet acknowledges that "a è dut finìt, dut; tutto è finito, tutto" (everything is over, everything). The experience of youth is crystallized in the realm of Friuli, a time and place inaccessible to the poet, except through memory.[59] The poem "De loinh" completes this reflection on adolescence. The Provençal expression aptly summarizes the relationship binding the poet to his maternal land: it is love from afar for an idealized object of desire.[60] Further removed in space than the distance separating Casarsa from Rome, and further in time than the few years that presumably passed since his departure from Friuli, youth is turned into myth. The repeated word "adès" (now) at the beginning of each stanza reiterates the peremptoriness of the present, in a crescendo of emotions that range from blind fear to the urge to cry, to the bursting into a death lament ("plant di muàrt") at the thought that the blue of Friuli belongs to "dis no pierdùs, / ma doventàs di un altri; giorni non perduti, ma divenuti di un altro" (days not lost but belonging to someone else): not removed to the timeless dimension of lost youth, but immersed in time and thus subject to change. Those Sundays in Friuli that were the triumph of adolescence hum in another young man's ears now: "e ch'a businin li sagris / ta li me orelis come ta ches di un altri ... ; e ronzano le sagre nelle mie orecchie come in quelle di un altro" (*Poesie 1*, 96–7; the festivals buzz in my ears as if in the ears of someone else). *De loinh*, from afar, describes Pasolini's love for Friuli, his maternal country, but also for youth: idealized and removed from time, from history, from change, Friulian youth is the perfect poetic subject. Youth embodies this contradiction: an extremely transitory state, which poetry elevates to an absolute condition.

In the volume "Romancero (1947–52)," the elegiac, solipsistic poetry of *Poesia a Casarsa* opens up to different voices, and youth becomes a more historically specific experience.[61] While a variety of speakers and dialects seem to offer different perspectives on the experience of youth, regular metre harmonizes those voices.[62] The poem opening the section, "Spiritual," directly inspired by Langston Hughes' "Brass Spittoons," introduces youthful subjects who speak from the margins. The African-American experience of Hughes' poem, its urban working-class setting and religious theme are transcodified into the specific experience of youth in rural Friuli in the mid-1940s: "cine, sgnapa e messa, /e fèminis di Sabo; Cine, grappa e messa, e donne di Sabato" render the Friulian equivalent of Hughes' "babies and gin and church / and women on Sunday." The repetition of a refrain, "Hèila, bocia! Li barghèssis, / la maja, i supièj, i supièi da l'Anzul; Hei, ragazzo! I calzoni, la maglia, i sandali, i sandali dell'Angelo" (Hey boy! Pants, sweater, sandals, the Angel's sandals), reproduces the syncopated rhythm of the American poem, while its "spiritual" element, the transfiguration of the shiny spittoon into an offering to the Lord, is replaced in the Friulian by a shiny sickle, "pai siòrs na stela / dismintieada da mijàrs di sècuj; per i ricchi una stella dimenticata da migliaia di secoli" (*Poesie 1*, 107–8; for the rich a star forgotten for thousands of centuries). A series of portraits of youth follows, a gallery where the frame restricts and embellishes each portrait. The use of *terzina lirica*, a rare metre that, like the better-known *sestina*, is structured on the repetition of rhyme-words, imposes a recurrence of key terms that set the overall mood. Words like "ligrii" (cheerfulness) and "sogni" (dreams), "seda" (silk) or "veudo" (velvet), "timp" (time), and "piardùs" (lost) define a form of youth that is still pastoral, like the one found in *Poesie a Casarsa*, whereas the repetition of "thento franchi" (a hundred lire) or "operajo" (worker) as rhyme words identify a more historically specific form of youth. The unusual metre ties together the different voices and varying dialects in a collective expression, made explicit in the poem "I dis robàs (I giorni rubati)" (The Stolen Days). Here the plural speaking subject "nos" conveys the transience of the "timp / de zoventùt (tempo di gioventù)" (time of youth): young people are "pavèjs ch'a no àn mai vut belessa muartis ta la galeta dal timp; farfalle che non hanno mai avuto bellezza, morte nel bozzolo del tempo" (*Poesie 1*, 113; butterflies that were never beautiful, dead in the cocoon of time).

Finally, the sixteen-year-old voice of "El testament Coràn" is the victim of Nazi reprisals in a small Friulian town in 1944. The boy tells his story post-mortem in a style reminiscent of the epitaphs in Edgar Lee Masters' *Spoon River Anthology*. His testament is a celebration of the joys of youth and of the courage of the underprivileged, recounted in nine narrative stanzas, each composed of two quatrains.[63] The protagonist is "the ideal missing link between the early magic Friulian boys and the future '*ragazzi di vita*' of Roman slums: he still has the characteristics of the former, but reconfigured in a lively, highly original realism.

He is a live, pulsating character, a young farmer, the first realistic *character* in Pasolini's work."[64] Sunday dances, *bocce* games, bicycle rides in the countryside, group fishing trips, singing and card games in the fields are all activities that characterize him as a rural youth, while a reference to the fear and pleasure "of loving the sickle and hammer" ("de amà la falth e e l martièl") situates those timeless activities in a more specific historical frame. "La mare e il pare a eri muarti; la madre e il padre erano morti" (The mother and father were dead) seems a metaphorical statement, rather than a literal one, a revelation of the young man as a free agent. "La compagnia dai fiòj; la compagnia dei ragazzi" (the company of boys), with its nighttime gatherings among the poplars, does not preclude desire for Neta, a young shepherdess who seems to come out of a pastoral poem:

E na sera mi ài vist la Neta
in tal lustri da la boscheta
ch'a menava a passòn la feda.
Lena co la sova bacheta
a moveva l'aria de seda.

E una sera ho visto la Neta, nella luce del boschetto, che conduceva al pascolo la pecora. Con il suo ramoscello essa muoveva l'aria di seta. (*Poesie 1*, 119–22; And one night I saw Neta, in the light of the woods, who led the sheep to pasture. With her small bough she was stirring the silk-like air.)

The rite of passage represented by the first sexual experience with Neta is the preamble to the boy's violent death:

Tal paese desert coma un mar
quarto todèscs a me àn ciapàt
e thigànt rugio a me àn menàt
ta un camio fer in ta l'umbrìa.
Dopo tre dis a me àn piciàt
in tal moràr de l'osteria.

Nel paese deserto come un mare quattro tedeschi mi hanno preso e gridando rabbiosi mi hanno condotto su un camion fermo nell'ombra. Dopo tre giorni mi hanno impiccato al gelso dell'osteria. (*Poesie* 1122; In the deserted town, a desert like the sea, four Germans took me and shouting angrily led me to a truck parked in the shade. After three days they hung me from the mulberry tree at the inn.)

Violence interrupts the boy's coming-of-age, and the "Testament" celebrates the sacrifice of youth: "Coi todescs no ài vut timòur / de lassà la me dovenetha. Coi tedeschi non ho avuto paura di lasciare la mia giovinezza." (With the Germans I was not afraid to leave my youth behind.) Despite the straightforward populism of the last lines, "Viva el coragiu, el dolòur / e la nothentha dei puarèth; Viva il coraggio, il dolore e l'innocenza dei poveri" (ibid.; Long live the courage, the sufferings and the innocence of the poor), the testament is most successful as a celebration of lost youth. Significantly, what he left behind is expressed as *giovinezza*, the term for youth that the Fascist regime had chosen as its emblem. The word, ubiquitous during the Fascist era, would be less commonly heard after 1944, when the official song by that name was banned. The alternative word *gioventù* remained in use, even though the monopoly on youth exercised by Fascism led anti-Fascists to avoid generational discourse, when not openly rejecting it.[65] Pasolini, however, who had experimented with critical and poetic definitions of adolescence early in the context of Fascist cultural institutions, would continue to do so.

In both poetry and prose, in the published works as well as his correspondence with his closest friends, Pasolini's early production showed his keen awareness of the polyvalence of the category of youth in modern society. Nourished by a fertile, if contradictory, public discourse favoured by the Fascist regime, and benefiting from the numerous stimuli offered to the young intellectual by his readings and his mentors, Pasolini's notion of adolescence became the foundation for his reflections on literature, and also on the role of intellectuals in society. The dichotomy and frequent intersections of a cultural construction, imbued with politically expedient meanings, and the life experience of young people under specific circumstances, already transpires in his early reflections. The frequently conflicting needs of innovation and recognition, of poetic isolation and communication, of originality and solidarity, were explored first through the debates on youth's role in contemporary society, and the definition of young poets' relation to their poetic forefathers. The *Eredi* project, with all the accompanying conversations, and the poetic experiments through which young Pasolini defined for his companions his relationship to youth as "nostalgia for the present time," offer a window on the centrality of those issues in his apprenticeship. The poems of *La meglio gioventù*, with the celebration of lost youth and the use of a familiar dialect transposed to verse, provided the first response in the quest for a form that could adequately express youth. The best of youth, as it were, was found and already lost in Friuli.

2 Being Young: *Bildung*, Development, and Growing Up *Ragazzi*

Come il Partito e l'organizzazione giovanile comunista hanno mutato, in questo decennio, la mente e il cuore di tante migliaia di ragazzi e di uomini; come i ragazzi di Roma, nati in luoghi dove la millenaria civiltà non ha gettato neppure la sua ombra, pur cresciuti nella fame e spinti ai margini della vita sociale, hanno conservato una grande forza morale; come essi hanno saputo resistere sani, fieri, decisi, animati da una volontà di riscatto quando tutto li spinge a cedere, a cercare nel vizio la strada più facile e immediata per uscire dalla loro inumana condizione: ecco una vera cronaca da cui può nascere opera d'arte, ecco una "storia italiana" che attende ancora il suo narratore.

How the Communist Party and its youth organization have transformed, in the past decade, the mind and heart of several thousand adolescents and adults; how young people in Rome, born in places where ancient civilization hasn't even cast its shadow, though starved and marginalized, have preserved great moral strength; how they have resisted healthy, proud, resolute, moved by a will for redemption, while everything pushed them to give up, to seek in vice the easiest and most direct way out of their inhuman condition: here is a true account from which art can be created; here is an "Italian story" that is still waiting for its narrator.

(Giovanni Berlinguer, *l'Unità*, July 29, 1955)[1]

Whereas his early poetry provided Pasolini with an arena in which to explore youth as a trans-historical condition, in novels he problematized its symbolic significance in an increasingly modern society. He drew both on genre conventions and contemporary debates on realism to debunk universal notions of development. The marginalized boys of *Ragazzi di vita* and *Una vita violenta* resisted the transformation demanded by classic coming-of-age stories. Their sub-proletarian life in 1940s and '50s Rome appeared incompatible with the emancipatory narrative structuring the classic *Bildungsroman* and the bourgeois culture in which the genre had originated. By centring both novels on adolescents, and disallowing their coming of age, Pasolini highlighted how models of development that were assumed as universal were in fact class-specific. Furthermore, as realist novels depicting the life of an underprivileged group in post-war Italy, *Ragazzi di vita* and *Una vita violenta* provided a commentary on the implications of realist aesthetics as a medium for progressive discourse. The neorealist search for an anti-rhetorical language that would not distract the reader from "the reality of the 'others,' be they persons or things," presupposed universal humanistic values which, Pasolini showed, obscured the subjects' otherness.[2] What's more, the ethical imperative underlying neorealist fiction and film implied confidence in the perfectability of the world depicted, a notion that Pasolini's essentialist portrayal of the Roman sub-proletariat demystified. The combined choice of realist narratives and young protagonists in the two novels exploited the potential for transformation implicit in the genre to critique the bourgeois model of emancipation embraced even by fellow left-wing intellectuals.

Being Young: *Ragazzi di vita* as a Reversed *Bildungsroman*

Published as a volume in 1955, *Ragazzi di vita* initially met with moderate success, until the publicity caused by its forced removal from the stores on charges of pornography and the subsequent trial propelled the novel and its author to celebrity.[3] Critical reception on both ends of the political spectrum focused on the hopelessness of the sub-proletarian lifestyle as an aberration: for conservative Catholic critics, moral reprehension translated as "pornography"; Communist critics codified moral outrage in literary and ideological terms as a refutation of the national-popular consciousness that the Partito Comunista Italiano (PCI) had been working so hard to develop.[4] The "Italian story" which, according to Marxist critic Giovanni Berlinguer, quoted above, was to celebrate everything that the Communist Party had done to change the condition of youth since the end of WWII, had not been written. Neither had a novel that highlighted the moral strength of underprivileged young people, their unwavering wish for redemption, and their noble efforts to leave behind the "inhuman" condition of the slums.

However unfavourable, Berlinguer's review of *Ragazzi di vita* serves as a useful point of reference in defining the novel's accomplishments with respect to the discourse of youth in the 1950s. It is particularly in relation to the rhetoric of change and emancipation promoted by the PCI in the post-war period that *Ragazzi di vita* acquires significance as a reversed *Bildungsroman*. Questioning the conventions of the genre, *Ragazzi di vita* does not celebrate the mobility of a young man and his ultimate socialization, but rather shows the limitations of that model of development.

Ragazzi di vita centres on adolescence as a marginal and fleeting condition to debunk its symbolic use in classic coming-of-age novels. At the same time, its popular setting and mimetic approach to the life of the subaltern converses with contemporary neorealist narratives and challenges the optimism of leftist intellectuals in post-war years. The age limitation of the chosen subgroup allows Pasolini to celebrate the vitality of the lower classes, following a bourgeois literary *topos* that he never denies; it also highlights the transience of such vitality and of the values associated with it. While acknowledging the literary genre that traditionally celebrated youth as the promise for the renewal of society, Pasolini replaces its conventional individualism with a group identity that is both opportunistic and short-lived. To the novel of social mobility he responds with a circular narrative that frustrates progress. And he counters the discourse of change promoted by the Communist Party, and particularly by its youth organization, with a portrayal of youth that shows the underside of emancipation.

Set in Rome between 1943 and 1950, the novel follows the adventures of several sub-proletarian boys living in the slums located on the outskirts of the city, the so-called *borgate*. Episodic in structure, it is composed of eight chapters, each self-standing and connected to the others in subtle and complex ways, which often do not become evident to the reader until the end of the novel.[5] The choice of young men as a central subject is affirmed right from title. The lens directed at the Roman sub-proletariat focuses primarily on that specific category of *borgatari* that are teenagers, that is, *ragazzi*. The qualifier *"di vita"* announces to the Italian reader the protagonists' adoption of a lifestyle that is not traditionally associated with boys in novels of apprenticeship: prostitution, and more broadly life on the streets.[6] The protagonists, all aged between twelve and eighteen, live by their wits. Legitimate work, although not completely absent, is less likely to feature in their daily activities than petty theft, robbery, gambling, street scams, and prostitution. Their identity, and significance as characters, is found in their age, social class, and actions. Riccetto, Marcello, Alduccio (Aldo), Lenzetta, Genesio, among others, often identified exclusively by their nicknames, wander around the city looking for quick ways to make money and, subsequently, equally quick ways to spend it. Likewise they shift in and out of focus, alone or in groups, often without introductions. Their actions are apparently aimless or at best determined by short-term goals – procuring money or pleasure, avoiding punishment – and they lack the intentionality that could justify seeing their life as a trajectory towards a goal. The boys' circular movement, from lack of money, to appropriation, to loss of money, returns them to the original condition and disproves change as a result of experience, the essential theme of coming-of-age narratives. Their obvious failure to learn from their mistakes belies the very notion of youth as a learning process. Instead of the bourgeois "teleology of individuality" that typically underlies literary apprenticeship, *Ragazzi* offers an epistemology of street education observed through multiple, often interchangeable, subjects.[7] The lack of intentionality in the boys' actions and the short-term perspective that characterizes their lives show their freedom from bourgeois and proletarian codes of behaviour that equally define youth in relation to clear goals. Simultaneously, the plurality of points of view debunks the univocal notion of young protagonists of coming-of-age narratives as universal examples.

Although closer in structure to a picaresque novel than a *Bildungsroman*, *Ragazzi* benefits nevertheless from being read in the framework of the classic coming-of-age narrative for both its contribution to a discourse of youth heavily shaped by this genre, and the assumptions that this interpretation highlights regarding the discourse of development in 1950s Italy. If a protagonist can be singled out by virtue of sheer stage presence, it is Riccetto, the boy who appears on both the first and last page. His significance as alternative *Bildungsheld*, repeatedly challenged by frequent shifts in point of view, and further questioned by his disappearance from the narrative for two full chapters, becomes evident only in the last chapter.[8] Riccetto is introduced directly in the opening lines of the novel:

> Era una caldissima giornata di luglio. Il Riccetto che doveva farsi la prima comunione e la cresima, s'era alzato già alle cinque; ma mentre scendeva giù per via Donna Olimpia coi calzoni lunghi grigi e la camicetta bianca, piuttosto che un comunicando o un soldato di Gesù pareva un pischello quando se ne va acchittato pei lungoteveri a rimorchiare.

Being Young 53

It was a very hot July day. Riccetto, who was going to make his First Communion and be confirmed, had been up by five o'clock, but as he went down by the Via Donna Olimpia in his grey long pants and his white shirt, rather than a first communicant or a little soldier of Jesus, he looked like a a kid roaming around down by the Tiber, trying to make a pickup.[9]

Any assumptions the readers might make regarding this boy, who is up early the morning of his first Communion and Confirmation day are immediately pre-empted by the narrator, who warns us that appearances can deceive. In the narration that follows, Riccetto wanders around various neighbourhoods, meets friends, participates in the looting of the *Ferrobeton* factory, watches other boys play soccer in front of an elementary school, swims in the Tiber with Marcello, meets other friends who play soccer in front of the same school, steals piping from a nunnery with them, plays cards with older boys, swims and rents a boat with Marcello and Agnolo at the Ciriola's bathing barge on the river. In the second chapter, while Riccetto is at the beach enjoying the money he stole from a Neapolitan hustler, Marcello goes looking for him at home: "Riccetto abitava alle scuole elementari Giorgio Franceschi" (43; 50; Riccetto lived in the Giorgio Franceschi elementary school building). Not only was the information about the protagonist's home life, central to coming-of-age narratives, delayed; the repeated mention of the school building in the previous chapter and the exclusion of that important detail draw attention to the partiality of the narration. The shifting of a point of view that the readers assume stable becomes even more evident in chapter 3. The opening scene focuses on two boys pushing a cart: "Sul cavalcavia della stazione Tiburtina, due ragazzi spingevano un carretto con sopra delle poltrone" (58; 65; on the overpass by the Tiburtina station, two boys were pushing a cart loaded with armchairs). The subsequent description highlights the contrast between the teeming crowd filling the bridge and the sidewalks with movement and sound, and the boys slowly pushing the cart to a stop, lying down on the armchairs, and peacefully sharing a cigarette. Generic descriptors follow: "i due ragazzi" (the two boys), "uno ..., l'altro" (one ..., the other), "quello con la maglietta nera si issò sopra una delle due poltrone ... con le gambe larghe e la testa tutta riccioletti appoggiata sulla spalliera" (59; 66; the boy in the black shirt hoisted himself onto one of the two armchairs in the cart and stretched out, his legs apart and his curly head resting on the chair's back). When two more boys pushing a cart full of garbage catch up with them, the boy in a black T-shirt mocks one of them:

> "Che, te sei fatto pecoraro, a cuggi'?" chiese al primo quello della maglietta nera, senza spostarsi d'un centimetro da come si trovava sbragato sulla poltrona con le mani sulla pancia e la cicca incollata al labbro inferiore. "Vaffan..., a Riccè," gli rispose quello. Il Riccetto – era proprio lui quel fijo de na mignotta sulla poltrona – corrugò astutamente la fronte e appannò lo sguardo, calcando il mento contro la gola, con aria di saperla lunga.

> "Since when are you herding sheep, cousin?" the boy in a black shirt asked the handsome boy, not shifting an inch from his position, sprawled on the armchair with his hands on his belly and the butt sticking to his lower lip. "Fuck you, Riccè," said the other. Riccetto – for it was the little bastard himself – wrinkled his brow meaningfully, tucking his chin into his throat with a know-it-all look. (60; 67)

By observing Riccetto as if for the first time in this situation, after having assumed his role as protagonist of this story for the previous two chapters, we become aware that any pretence of a linear development underlying traditional coming-of-age narratives is, in fact, a pretence. The strategy mirrors Riccetto's and his friends' inability to connect present to past situations in order to make wise decisions, that is, to learn from their mistakes.

Chaotic urban life and rapid transformation contribute to the sense of impermanence in the novel. The boys' freedom to wander the streets provides a narrative vehicle for the exploration of Rome as it transforms from capital of the Fascist empire to centre of the new democratic state. The city, a shambles after the war and undergoing rapid reconstruction as the novel progresses, reflects the transience of its young inhabitants. Comprehensive historical introductions are absent from the narration, which begins *in medias res* and is characterized by an elliptical style. However, brief allusions to the occupation of the city by German troops, and to the subsequent arrival of Americans, scattered in the text, remind the reader of the rapid turnover of authorities in the background of the frequently shifting main characters. Numerous references to the changing condition of houses, streets, or entire neighbourhoods provide material examples of the fluid urban space in which the characters move. Buildings are shut down, reopened, repurposed. After the collapse of the school building where Riccetto's family lives, among many refugees and squatters, the victims are buried, the survivors relocated in other makeshift shelters, the rubble is heaped on one side so as to free the passage, and "un due domeniche dopo la vita era tornata come sempre" (53; 59; a couple of Sundays later, life was going on as usual). Road construction is promised, started, and not always completed. Manhole covers and piping fall prey to thieves. Garbage, when not accumulated in heaps along the roads, floats freely down the Tiber, where the boys often swim, connoting the permeability of boundaries in the Eternal City.

The *borgate*, where the boys grow up, are geographically and culturally interstitial entities: located at the margins of the city, they embody the transition between urban and rural space in the coexistence of tall buildings of recent construction (*i Grattacieli*), still lacking roads or courtyards, small houses "piccole come dadi o come pollai, bianche come quelle degli arabi, e nere come capanne" or "villaggi di tuguri ammucchiati nelle aree da costruzione" (93; 99; little dwellings like cubes or henhouses, white as Arab buildings or black as mountain cabins ... groups of hovels piled up together in construction lots) among dusty fields, ravines, garbage dumps. The variety of residents reflects its mixed and temporary nature: refugees from the war and squatters, old-time Romans and recent immigrants, "cafoni pugliesi o marchegiani, sardegnoli o calabresi" (93; 99; peasants from Apulia, the Marche, Sardinia, or Calabria). Rather than trying to impose a rational order on the geo-historical chaos that characterizes life on the outskirts of Rome, the novel attempts to reproduce it, underscoring both its vitality and the artificiality of any order imposed upon it. Construction sites, piles of trash, muddy streets, or sun-beaten dusty fields constitute the space that the boys navigate, and that helps define their identity.

Their homes, non-traditional in many ways, are far from the familiar place that protagonists of conventional *Bildungsromane* leave in order to establish their own identity. Rather, as far as the kids' relationship with them goes, homes are equivalent to public spaces. For instance, Riccetto's family lives in a school building which, we are told, hosted a variety of residents in previous years: "c'erano stati lì prima i Tedeschi, poi i Canadesi, poi gli sfollati e da ultimo gli sfrattati, come la famiglia del Riccetto" (43; first the Germans had been there, then the Canadians, then the refugees, and finally the squatters, like Riccetto's family).[10] However, the first mention of the school in the novel, in the opening chapter, makes no reference to the special function it serves for

Riccetto's family. At this point, in the description of his daily activities, the building features only as the background to the boys' soccer games:

> Oppure andavano a giocare a pallone lì sullo spiazzo tra i Grattacieli e il Monte di Splendore, tra centinaia di maschi che giocavano sui cortiletti invasi dal sole, sui prati secchi, per via Ozanam o via Donna Olimpia, davanti alle scuole elementari Franceschi piene di sfollati e di sfrattati.

> Or else they went and played ball in the empty space between the Grattacieli and the Monte di Splendore, hundreds of boys playing in the back lots invaded by the sun, in the dried-up fields around the Via Ozanam or the Via Donna Olimpia ... in front of the Franceschi elementary-school buildings, filled with hookey players and dropouts. (8; 14)

The leisure activities outside the school building are more important in defining Riccetto's identity than his family, whom the reader only meets in marginal observations scattered throughout the novel. Riccetto's family's status as squatters determines that they live not even in classrooms, as the refugees do, but in a hallway subdivided by partition walls. The little rooms adjacent to one another, and each shared by an entire family, are so interchangeable that when, in chapter 2, Riccetto wants to talk to his new Neapolitan friend without his mother meddling, he goes to the next room, where his friend Agnolo lives with his family, and sits down on Agnolo's bed (26–7; 32). When Agnolo's mother returns, and Riccetto advances a feeble excuse for trespassing, she does not even respond. Later, after the school has collapsed and killed Riccetto's mother, his family relocates to another *borgata*, next door to his aunt's family. Riccetto's indifference to his home is made explicit when, with the prospect of unexpected earnings, he states:

> "E chi ce torna ppiù a casa," ... Tanto la sua era una casa per modo di dire: andarci o non andarci era la stessa cosa, magnà non se magnava, dormì, su una panchina dei giardini pubblici era uguale. Che era una casa pure quella? Intanto la zia il Riccetto non la poteva vedere: e manco Alduccio, del resto, ch'era figlio suo. Lo zio era un imbriacone che rompeva il c... a tutti l'intera giornata. E poi come fanno due famiglie complete, con quattro figli una e sei l'altra, a stare tutte in due sole camere, strette, piccole, e senza nemmeno il gabinetto, ch'era giù abbasso in mezzo al cortile del lotto?

"And who's going to go home again after that?" Calling it home was a manner of speaking. To go there, not to go there – it all came to the same thing. As for eating, nobody ate there. As for sleeping, you could sleep just as well on a park bench. Call that a home? Besides, Riccetto couldn't stand his aunt, or her son Alduccio either. His uncle was a lush who was always breaking balls. And then, how were two whole families supposed to manage, one of them with four kids, one with six, all in two narrow little rooms, without even a toilet – that was downstairs in the centre of the courtyard. (62; 69)

His "manner-of-speaking home" does not offer him any reasons to return: a park bench is just as good a bed, and the unexpected earnings can be used to update one's wardrobe: drainpipe trousers, trendy shirts, and black-and-white pointed-tip shoes can be bought cheaply at the flea-market in Campo dei Fiori. The casual relationship the boys have with their homes and their life on the streets, it must be noted, is not presented as a direct consequence of a conflict with their parents. When Caciotta runs into two kids from his neigbourhood on a crowded bus, in a nostalgic recollection of their childhood, he remembers how they used to run away from home:

> Di tanto in tanto, non avevano nemmeno otto anni, se ne andavano di casa, e se ne stavano fuori per qualche settimana, digiunando o mangiandosi qualche cipolla o qualche persica fregata ai mercatini, oppure un po' di cotiche sfilate dalla borsa di qualche comare. Scappavano di casa, così, per nessuna ragione, perché gli piaceva di divertirsela.

> Every now and then – they were hardly eight years old at the time – they used to leave home and stay away for weeks, starving or else living on onions or peaches hooked from the vegetable stalls, or stuff that dropped from housewives' shopping bags. They ran away for no reason, just like that, to have some fun. (79; 85)

Apparently casual remarks like this remind the reader that the *ragazzi*'s unstable circumstances, although geographically and historically identifiable, are not presented as a social problem to be solved. Their existence as young *borgatari* does not participate in historical change: both their youth and their social class, albeit inherently transitory, are meaningful as conditions, not as processes.

Fatherlessness, however, aligns these *ragazzi* with many protagonists of traditional *Bildungsromane* who are subject to change, from Wilhelm

Meister to David Copperfield. The marginality or complete absence of paternal authority, which in those novels signals the young characters' opening to autonomous development, in *Ragazzi* confirms the centrality and privileged condition of youth. Far from being models to imitate or reject, fathers mostly hover in the background, drunk and violent, authority figures that have lost all real authority. Riccetto's father is mentioned only indirectly, by his mother, as the unsuccessful enforcer of discipline on the boy. Genesio and his brothers vow to kill their father as soon as they are old enough. Alduccio's father gets an explicit critique in a passage that highlights both the physical signs of old age, prematurely brought about by alcohol abuse, and his son's indifference towards him. Riccetto's sister, by now living with them, walks in "carrying another Riccetto in her arms," and is promptly turned away. Aldo, who constantly argues with his mother, completely ignores his father, even when he returns home drunk at dinner time, tries to hit his wife, and then collapses on the bed while his son gets dressed for an evening out:

> Il padre, dopo qualche minuto di raccoglimento, riuscì a articolare un po' la voce e, in seguito a due o tre tentativi, riuscì a dire qualcosa come: - Sta sempre a baccajà, sta disgrazziata! - Si alzò all'impiedi, e ondeggiando indietro e avanti, fece una specie di ragionamento tutto coi gesti, portò due tre volte la mano dall'altezza del petto all'altezza del naso poi fece con le dita una piroetta come per indicare un'idea tutta sua che gli passava per la capa: infine, correndo per non cadere, andò nella camera dove Alduccio si stava vestendo, e si buttò vestito sul letto alla supina. Il vino che aveva bevuto per l'intero dopopranzo l'aveva fatto diventare bianco come un lenzuolo e gli aveva come intostato le tre dita di pellaccia rasposa di barba intorno alle froce del naso e agli angoli della bocca, scura umida e rugosa come quella dei cani. Era tutto spiovente, spioventi le braccia distese sul copriletto, spiovente la bocca semiaperta, spioventi le ganasce e le fessure degli occhi, spioventi i capelli ancora neri e lucidi di sudore che pareva di brillantina. La lampada accesa che pendeva sopra il letto gli illuminava a una a una sulla faccia le macchiette color cacao della vecchia zella miste con le recenti crostine di polvere e di sudore sotto la fronte; mentre la ragnatela delle rughe gli si spostava su e giù per conto suo sopra la pelle, tirata e imbolsita dal vino, gialla per chissà quali vecchie malattie di quel fegataccio insaccato dentro le sue quattr'ossa coperte di panni vecchi. E qua e là si vedevano le ombre delle ammaccature, color marrone nel

centro con intorno una coroncina di lenticchie, ch'erano botte prese forse quand'era ragazzino, o in gioventù, quando faceva il soldato o il manovale, cent'anni prima. E tutto come fuso dal grigiore del digiuno e del vino, più quello dei ciuffi di barba di quattro giorni.

Aldo era ormai pronto, coi calzoni a tubo e la maglietta a righine col collo aperto e le falde fuori dai calzoni. Ancora si doveva pettinare. Andò davanti allo specchietto in cucina e, col pettine bagnato al rubinetto, cominciò a aggiustarsi i capelli, stando con le gambe larghe, perché lo specchio era troppo basso per lui.

The father, after some moments of reflection, managed to get his voice working again, and after a couple of tries managed to say something like, "Always yapping, that tramp!" He stood up, and delivered an address all in gestures, weaving back and forth, lifting his hand two or three times from breast-level to his nose, then making his fingers do a pirouette as if to indicate that some highly original idea was going through his mind. At last, running so as not to fall down, he went into the bedroom where Alduccio was dressing, and fell flat on the bed, fully clothed. The wine he had been drinking all afternoon had made his face as white as a sheet and seemed to have singed the two inches of bristly whiskers, dark, damp, and rough as a dog's, beneath his nose and at the corners of his mouth. He was completely limp – arms stretched out on the bed, half-open mouth, slack jaw, and drooping eyelids, and lank hair, still black, and shining with sweat as if with brilliantine. The lighted lamp which hung over the bed showed up each separate chocolate-coloured stain of ancient grime on his face, together with newer incrustations of dust and sweat upon his forehead; the web of wrinkles shifted about upon his face, stretched and swollen with wine, yellow from God knows what kind of liver disease hiding somewhere in that frame draped with old rags. Here and there were the shadowy traces of wounds, dark-colored, encircled by little spots, that went back to his childhood, perhaps, or his young manhood, when he had served as a soldier or worked as a day laborer, ages ago. And over all that was a grayness that came from going hungry and drinking wine, plus the stubble of a four-day beard.

By now Alduccio was dressed, sporting his pegged pants and his striped shirt with the open collar, the tails hanging outside his pants. Now he had to comb his hair. He went to the mirror in the kitchen, and after wetting the comb under the faucet, he began to primp, standing spread-legged because the mirror was set too low for him. (186–7; 190–1)

The insistence on the adjective "spiovente," (literally "sloping," in this context, "drooping," or as the translator has it, "limp") in reference to several parts of the man's body underlines the lack of energy, the passivity of a body that has long ago stopped being young: the skin is yellow, puffed up, and crossed by a web of wrinkles; the frame is weak, barely filling the old rags that cover it. Even the bruises are old, sole remnants of a young age that seems to have happened "ages ago." The man's condition, described in such grotesque detail, appears so habitual as to not even interrupt the son's grooming routine, which instead emphasizes his own youth: the drainpipe trousers, the untucked polo shirt, and the slicked back hairstyle define Aldo as a young man of his time.

The condition is emblematic, here as in traditional coming-of-age stories, of a crisis of paternity, but while in those novels the crisis is strictly related to the rise of individualism in Germany and England, and "the impulse towards self-determination that, encouraged by nature itself, prompts a youth at some point to resist his parents, especially his father," in *Ragazzi di vita* fatherlessness doesn't translate into freedom to decide how to shape one's future.[11] From this perspective, the *ragazzi* are not "modern youth" as are the protagonists of eighteenth- and nineteenth-century coming-of-age novels, who are concrete signs of innovation embodying the era's dynamism and instability.[12] The social mobility presented to those protagonists is not accessible to Riccetto, Genesio, and their peers. Despite their geographic fluidity, the *borgate* are a socially self-enclosed space in this novel, and as such they reflect a paradoxical view of youth: intrinsically fluid, yet crystallized under the lens of the observer. So if on the one hand the novel celebrates adolescence as a transitory condition, its continuous becoming is suspended in a specific moment and its social status is never questioned. Denied social mobility, the protagonists of this anti-*Bildungsroman* also lack the interior exploration that the possibility of social change engenders.[13] Hopes, dreams, projections of these characters are not available to the reader, who must rely exclusively on actions and simple dialogue to understand them. The lack of introspection, which in itself subverts the genre conventions, also precludes the identification of reader with character that would allow the coming-of-age experience to be shared.[14] The reader of *Ragazzi* is not expected to undergo a vicarious growing up, or re-growing up, alongside the novel's protagonists. In a broader perspective, *Ragazzi* questions the universality of the coming-of-age process, and the status of the *Bildungsheld* as Everyman, which was implicit in the classic incarnation of the genre. Riccetto and his friends are not stand-ins for "Every Young Person," and certainly not for the projected reader.

Alternative Lessons in the Streets of Rome

The Roman *borgate* in the mid-1940s were a world in which coming-of-age experiences for an adolescent boy like Riccetto only minimally overlapped with those of his peers in the centre of the city. From the very beginning Riccetto is presented as a liminal figure in a transitional world. He embarks on his first adventure by walking among "palazzine in costruzione ... valanghe d'immondezza, case non ancora finite e già in rovina, grandi sterri fangosi, scarpate piene di zozzeria" (2; 8; garbage piles, unfinished houses already in ruins, great muddy excavations, slopes heaped with junk). Mirroring the mood of this unusual coming-of-age story, the landscape fluctuates between construction and decay. The traffic is deafening, engines and horns create a single roar that fills the air: "Tutta Roma era un solo rombo" (2; 8; all Rome was one droning rumble). Dressed up for his First Communion and Confirmation, yet hardly convincing as an altar boy, Riccetto provides an immediate introduction to one of the key themes in the novel: the alternative coming-of-age available to young *borgatari*. As Enzo Golino argues, the formative experiences of a *ragazzo di borgata* go well beyond church and school. These two institutions play little or no role in the education of Riccetto and his friends. Completely absent from the protagonists' everyday experience, the only school mentioned in the novel, the already mentioned *scuola elementare Franceschi*, is repurposed as a house for refugees and squatters. Their contacts with the church, besides Riccetto's hasty sacraments at the beginning of the novel, are limited to emergency situations: Riccetto and Caciotta, "bianchi per la fame" (pale with hunger) go to a soup kitchen run by friars, "del Sacro Cuore o della Beata Vergine, uno di quei nomi lì" (73–4; 80; of the Sacred Heart or the Blessed Virgin – one of those names). Their reaction to the friar's request that they give their "particulars" (*generalità*) signals the distance of the church from their everyday life:

> "Le che?" fece il Riccetto, sorpreso ma tutto servizievole. Quando seppero che cavolo erano queste "generalità," le diedero false, e, in compenso, presero rispettosamente dalle mani del frate il tagliando.

"Our what?" asked Riccetto, surprised but agreeable, and ready to cooperate in any way required. When they found out what the hell particulars were, they gave false ones, and respectfully took the ticket from the friar as a reward. (74; 81)

The boys' disconnection from the church as an educational institution is evident also in the choice of sports as pastimes for the young guests of the refectory. At the church, boys who are waiting for their free lunch play basketball, "e si vedeva benissimo che lo facevano tanto per far contenti i frati" (73–4; 80; and you could tell that they were playing just to please the friars). Passionate soccer players like most *ragazzi* their age, Riccetto and Caciotta are always ready to pick up a game: "si misero a giocare senza conoscere per niente la pallacanestro, ch'era un gioco che non avevano sentito mai" (75; 81; [they] started to play without knowing the first thing about basketball, a game they had never heard of). Unknown to most of the guests of the refectory, basketball indicates first of all the separation between these *ragazzi* and their peers in other social milieux, where the sport had been known since the 1920s.[15] From a wider perspective, the promotion of basketball in churches in Rome shows the changing landscape of youth leisure activities in the post-war years and the use of supervised sports as a technology of social control over the bodies of adolescents.[16]

Rather than in churches and schools, the *ragazzi*'s unorthodox education occurs in alternative locales: streets, movie theatres, and prisons. Theft, robbery, and deception are the tricks of the trade that a boy quickly learns and practises alongside the odd legitimate job, and acts of bravado guarantee the affirmation within the peer group.[17] Movies, watched even twice in an afternoon, provide not only much anticipated excitement (as when Riccetto and Caciotta fight over the newspaper to check the theatre listings), but fantasies that help the boys transfigure their everyday life. The squalid landscape of a factory courtyard becomes, in Riccetto's eyes, "una prateria recintata" (a fenced prairie).[18] As he takes part in the looting of the "Ferrobedò" factory, Riccetto finds a horse attached to a cart, and a deposit of weapons nearby, "e s'era messo un mitra a tracolla e due pistole alla cintola. Così armato fino ai denti montò in groppa al cavallo" (3; 9; [he] slung a submachine gun over his shoulder and stuck two pistols in his belt. Armed to the teeth, he got up on the horse's back). When Marcello joins the crowd, he finds himself in front of the tar sump: "Stava per caderci dentro, e affogarci come un indiano nelle sabbie mobili, quando fu fermato da uno strillo: 'A Marce', bada, a Marce'!'" (4; 10; He was just about to fall in, and drown like an Indian in quicksand, when a yell stopped him in his tracks: "Hey, Marcè! Look out! Hey, Marcè!"). It is Riccetto, who transfigures the looting into an assault on the fort from a Western movie, in which he and his friends are starring. Similarly, at the end of the first chapter, when a group of older kids jump on the rented rowboat that Riccetto and his friends took out on the river, the prank is quickly transformed into a pirate attack from an adventure movie, reminding the readers of both the childish playfulness of the characters and the influence exercised by popular culture on their everyday life.[19] Riccetto is lying in the boat pretending to be at sea when his fantasy materializes in the sudden appearance of a pirate: "'Ecco li pirata!' gridava con le mani a imbuto sulla sua vecchia faccia di ladro uno dei trasteverini, in piedi in pizzo alla barca." (23; 29; One of the group from Trastevere, who had the face of an old thief, cupped his hands into a megaphone, and standing up in the bow yelled, "Here come the pirates!"). Public spaces and peer groups replace schools as places of apprenticeship for the *ragazzi*, while popular movies shape their imagination.

While the absence of schools indirectly points to an institutional failure with respect to education, such malfunction is explicit with regard to prisons. Although socially recognized as a rite of passage, which gives the newly released Lenzetta bragging rights with younger boys, time in prison has no tangible effect on his life, other than to convince him that "ormai per questo gli si doveva una certa considerazione" (113; 119; [he] henceforth rated a certain amount of respect). The chance of rehabilitation through correctional facilities is inconceivable. A stint at Regina Coeli, the main city prison, may at best have damaged his brain through beatings: "Boh, si vede che era rimasto un po' sonato per le botte che gli avevano dato prima in camera di sicurezza e poi a bottega" (112; 118; Well, he must still have been punchy from the beating he'd got, first at the police station and then in jail). Having survived in prison only thanks to the respect commanded by his older brother, "uno dei ladri più autorevoli a Regina Coeli" (112; 118; one of the most influential cons in Regina Coeli), Lenzetta is released on parole after a couple of weeks and goes back to the same life. The rehabilitation methods adopted in juvenile correctional facilities are openly mocked in a passage about the thefts the boys periodically organize at their favourite hangout, the Bar della Pugnalata. They take advantage of the good nature of the owner, who doesn't report them, and justify their actions as follows:

> Siccome che il Lenzetta e qualcuno degli altri era già stato a Porta Portese, sapevano i metodi d'educazione "moderni" che ci volevano con dei discoli come loro erano fieri e compiaciuti di considerarsi: e allora, siccome la sorella del padrone li trattava male, per scusarsi e mettere a posto le loro coscienze – non che gliene fregasse niente, ma perché avevano comodamente il modo di farlo – dicevano che quei colpetti li organizzavano perché lei non li sapeva prendere, per castigarla ...

> Since Lenzetta and some of the others had already done time in Porta Portese, they knew all about the "modern" methods for straightening out young delinquents – which they were pleased and proud to be. So, because the owner's sister gave them a hard time, and in order to absolve themselves and keep their consciences clear – not that they gave a good goddamn but because they had a convenient way of doing it – they used to say that they got up those little ruckuses so as to punish her because she didn't know how to deal with them. (143–4; 148)

Not only have the "modern methods" used at Porta Portese to reform young criminals had no effect on these rascals, perversely, they become the justification for the perpetration of crime.

The boys' unsurprisingly problematic relationship with the prison and the church shows their existence in a world outside the reach of institutions of social control.[20] However, while the boys' indigence is never questioned, it is never really used to justify their illegal activities. As Ward clearly explains, Pasolini "does not want us to think of the *borgatari* as deviant products of a society whose glue is coming unstuck. He is less interested in pointing out how contemporary society produces monsters as in using the *borgatari* to suggest the kind of vital life we could live if we succeeded in severing all our ties with a castrating social order."[21] This potential is emphasized through the focus on young *borgatari*, whose failure to conform to bourgeois models of education mirrors the fluid lifestyle characterizing the *borgate* and their underlying principles: survival, freedom from both bourgeois and proletarian codes of conduct, and enjoyment.

Challenging the bourgeois and proletarian work ethic, the *ragazzi*'s rejection of regular work is another manifestation of their existence outside conventional codes. Temporary jobs are only acceptable insofar as they provide opportunities for theft and scams. The drudgery of work is succinctly expressed by the friends whom Caciotta meets on the bus:

"Che, nun lo vedi," fece uno, con aria abbacchiata, e i panni che puzzavano d'officina, "che tornamo dallo sgobbo?"
"'O vedo, 'o vedo," disse il Caciotta.
L'altro continuò amaro: "Mo se n'annamo a casa, magnamo, e annamo a dormì, e domattina n'antra vorta ar risgobbo!"

"Can't you see we've just knocked off work?" one of them said in a dejected voice, his clothes stinking from the factory.
"I can see all right," said Caciotta.
The other went on bitterly, "Now we go home, eat, go to sleep, and tomorrow morning get up and sweat all day again." (77–8; 84)

The mothers' refrain "Chi nun lavora nun magna" (113; 119; you don't work, you don't eat, right?) has no bearing on the young men, who are proud of their freedom from work. Riccetto and Alduccio drag their feet around, "mettendo in mostra però con aria fanfarona la loro fiacca di paraguli" (114; 120; making a big thing all the same out of their young hoodlum indolence) until the day they play the part of fine young fellows (*bravi ragazzi*) to impress two girls, the daughters of a poor man who helps them during a robbery. In that spirit, Riccetto introduces himself for the first time with his real name, "Mastracca Claudio" (see 131; 139).[22] This gesture anticipates the radical change determined by the combination of a steady relationship – with the youngest daughter of that man – and the stable job he consequently acquires – helping a fishmonger at the Maranella market. His transformation into a straight-up guy is discussed publicly at the Bar della Pugnalata and requires him to buy new clothes to play the new part (141–2; 146). The tension between old and new life, which leads him to participate in small crimes even as he holds a regular job and spends Sundays with his girlfriend, is temporarily resolved when Riccetto is arrested and sent to Porta Portese for three years, ironically, "per imparargli la morale" (154; 158; to teach him to behave).

Taking place primarily in the streets, the *ragazzi*'s alternative coming of age questions both the humanistic notion of education as the shaping of an individual self and the identification of distinct phases within that process. The geographical and social fluidity of the world in which the boys live matches the unpredictability of their transition between domestic and public space, periphery and centre, familiar and unfamiliar territories. Riccetto and his peers move in and out of these spaces without any apparent reaction or change in behaviour. Their education, consequently, cannot be defined in terms of evolution. Rites of passage, albeit present, are often void of the meaning traditionally attached to them in the context of coming-of-age stories: religious confirmation, sexual initiation, or loss of a parent, for instance, do not mark significant changes in the boys' life.[23] Riccetto's sexual encounter with the prostitute Nadia, who steals all of his money, highlights his immaturity more than any crossing of important thresholds. The death of his mother in the collapse of the school building receives no explicit mention, except as "la disgrazia delle Scuole" (the tragedy of the school building), which causes Riccetto's relocation in a room next door to his aunt and uncle's, that is, Alduccio's family (62).[24] In a way, Riccetto and his peers are *ragazzi* precisely because they resist traditional rites of initiation.

The choice of adolescents as protagonists of this novel is not dictated by an interest in one especially gifted youth who can exemplify his class and, by extension, his world. Adolescence is characterized as a group experience and its collective identity can only find representation through multiple characters, moving in and out of the foreground and challenging any linear progression towards a specific goal. It is not the boys' growing up that is significant, but rather their *being* young. Fleeting and undefinable, youth is interesting as an ontological status, as an indicator of difference: it is the liminal position *par excellence*, enhanced by the interstitial geography of the *borgate* and by the period of historical transition, for the city and the nation. It is at this threshold that youth embodies its potential for resistance.[25] Change can only corrupt it, because it upsets the precarious balance between rationality and irrationality that adolescence embodies, and inevitably aligns the young protagonist with a discourse of emancipation and self-improvement.

The detrimental effects of change on an individual are observed in Riccetto through a double comparison, which paradoxically confirms his role as protagonist of this reversed *Bildungsroman*. Although seemingly caught in a circular path and incapable of learning from his mistakes throughout most of the narrative, Riccetto reappears in the final chapter to show how socialization, consisting in regular employment and a romantic relationship, has made a new man out of the *ragazzo*. His encounter with Genesio and the latter's little brothers on the banks of the Tiber parallels Riccetto's own adventure on the river in the opening chapter, and offers a tangible measure of the time elapsed since the beginning of the novel. As a young version of Riccetto, Genesio offers an opportunity for evaluating Riccetto's transformation. There is a touch of nostalgia – and introspection, even – in his recollection of "quand'era come loro ... disprezzato e ignorato da tutto il mondo" (248; 251; when he was like them ... and everybody ignored him or scorned him), but his practical preoccupation to get back to work and collect his wage immediately corrects it. When Riccetto jokingly threatens to report the boys to the police for a crime they didn't commit, their genuine fear reveals that they perceive him as an authority figure. No longer one of them, in the eyes of the new *ragazzi*, Riccetto is associated with fathers and policemen. The subsequent death of Genesio, who drowns attempting to swim across the river while Riccetto watches from the shore, is senseless but functional to the economy of the novel. Riccetto's decision not to jump in, which he poorly rationalizes with the justification that "gettarsi a fiume lì sotto il ponte voleva proprio dire esser stanchi della vita, nessuno avrebbe potuto farcela" (253; 255; to jump in there beneath the bridge would just mean you were tired of living; nobody could get away with it there), marks the irreversible change he has undergone since the day, narrated in the first chapter and just recollected, when he had jumped into the water to save a swallow (see 23–4; 30–1). In growing up he has developed an interest in self-preservation that aligns his behaviour with bourgeois individualism: "Io je vojo bbene ar Riccetto, sa!" (253; 256; I got to look out for Riccetto). Although some ambiguity remains as to Riccetto's feelings, the narrative parallel points clearly to the fact that his decision is the product of a transformation, rather than his innate instinct of self-preservation. Maturity, before instinctive cowardice, dictates his behaviour.[26] Paradoxically, Riccetto's status as modern *Bildungsheld*, challenged throughout the novel, is confirmed at this moment, when his individual development, his sense of self, is better defined than ever. When he reveals the negative effects of growing up, Riccetto's behaviour becomes exemplary: rather than the exception, his transformation must be viewed as the standard outcome of a process of individuation, which distances youth from itself.[27]

In Riccetto's encounter with Genesio the ephemeral nature of youth, which the novel celebrates, becomes tragically visible. While Riccetto's failure to jump to Genesio's rescue shows the dark side of maturity, the younger boy's death appears as its only alternative. As the *ragazzo* drowns (Genesio, and young Riccetto with him), the new man walks off, unnoticed, into an almost unrecognizably empty city: "sia nella campagna che si stendeva intorno abbandonata, verso i mucchi di casette bianche di Pietralata e Monte Sacro, sia per la Tiburtina, in quel momento non c'era nessuno; non passava neppure una macchina o uno dei vecchi autobus della zona" (254; 256; in all the lonely countryside stretching as far as the white jumble of houses in Pietralata and Monte Sacro, and on the Via Tiburtina, there wasn't a soul around at that moment. There wasn't even a car going by, or one of the old buses that ran through that section). "Youth doesn't last forever," Franco Moretti reminds us, indicating the inherently contradictory nature of the coming-of-age novel, which must balance the opposing needs of dynamism and finality.[28] The shape of *Ragazzi di vita*, just like that of traditional novels of apprenticeship, is based on an intrinsic tension between the form-lessness of youth and its inescapable boundaries. However, unlike the novels through which Moretti defines the genre, *Ragazzi di vita* is not regulated by either its ending or the transformation that leads to it. Its necessary conclusion, which is also the end of youth, does not grant the narrative a "teleological rhetoric," which according to Moretti confers meaning on events only insofar as they lead to a specific goal.[29] Conversely, the emphasis on the open-endedness of the process does not deprive the ending of significance.[30] Youth is not "subordinated to the idea of maturity" in *Ragazzi*; it does not "'make sense' only because it leads to a stable and 'final' identity." Its significance depends, largely perhaps, on its protean and impermanent nature. Yet, that final revelation shapes by contrast the notion of youth conveyed by the novel: the formlessness of youth appears even more valuable when compared with this portrayal of maturity.

The socialization that marks the completion of the apprenticeship in traditional coming-of-age novels is exposed as loss, rather than achievement. However, in the novel's circular structure, the loss of Riccetto is not as tragic. One could paraphrase an Italian proverb and say, *"morto un Riccetto se ne fa un altro,"* literally, "one Riccetto dies, another's born." Although the Riccetto we had come to know dies with Genesio, another little Riccetto, will soon, in turn, be ready to step in: Riccetto's little brother, or perhaps one should say Claudio Mastracca's little brother, who had appeared briefly, held by his child sister, in the previously discussed father scene at Alduccio's home (186; 190). That minor appearance, otherwise inexplicable, acquires significance when the end of youth, ineluctable and undesirable, confronts the reader. A cursory recognition of the existence of "another Riccetto" recasts the impermanence of youth as part of a cyclical system. The idea of youth prevails over each individual embodiment, even the quasi-protagonist of a reversed *Bildungsroman*.

Far from being excluded from the educational project underlying any traditional novel of apprenticeship, the readers of *Ragazzi* are its subjects: the novel takes them on a journey outside their familiar sphere and helps them articulate a new *Weltanschauung*.[31] However, the apprenticeship is predicated as much on an acknowledgment of the unknowability of the Other as on the discovery of its existence. The readers leave the bourgeois or proletarian world of familiar realist novels and venture out in the sub-proletarian world of Riccetto and his peers; they come into contact with a linguistic and cultural reality that they recognize as alien, attempt to familiarize themselves with it, only to discover that such familiarity is ultimately unattainable.[32] Despite its apparent failure, this project adheres more faithfully to the conventions of the genre than one might expect. The process of encountering the sub-proletarian world of the *borgate* is significant even though it does not lead the reader to a complete socialization. Considering the greater emphasis on the process than on the result of the readers' apprenticeship, one could say that the "transformation principle" prevails over "classification," in Moretti's distinction: "What makes a story meaningful is its narrativity, its being an open-ended process. Meaning is the result not of a fulfilled teleology, but rather, as for Darwin, of the total rejection of such a solution." Based as it is on a rejection of the teleological notion of youth, the novel consistently proposes for the readers a model of *Bildung* as process.[33]

The ethical imperative underlying *Ragazzi di vita*, the readers' apprenticeship and its limitations, is articulated both through the choice of young sub-proletarian protagonists and the use of dialect. A novel about the lower classes set in mid-1940s Rome and published in 1955 obviously confronted both stylistic and moral expectations established by a decade of neorealist film and fiction. Furthermore, the focus on young people in an urban setting would immediately evoke the hopeful and exemplary children of De Sica's and Rossellini's movies, embodiment of the virtuous underclass and promise of social and political change in post-war Italy.[34] In adopting the perspective of young men, however, Pasolini emphasized a subjective rather than the presumedly objective stance guaranteed by the child-as-witness.[35] Consistently with the subjective viewpoint, in encouraging the readers to explore an unfamiliar world through a language that draws attention to itself, the novel takes issue with the anti-rhetorical strategies adopted by recent realist narratives, and with their supposed objectivity. The use of Roman dialect expresses the specificity of the chosen youth group, and free indirect discourse gives the readers an insider's look on the universe explored. These stylistic choices respond to the desire, later theorized in the essay "New Linguistic Questions," "at first of knowing and then of making known a psychological and social world unknown to the nation."[36] The local dialect, which required readers to refer to the glossary included in the novel, brought to light the fragmented linguistic reality of Italy. As a result, it exposed the use of a "neutral" national language as the imposition of a bourgeois *lingua media* onto the working-class, rural, or sub-proletarian classes portrayed in neorealist narratives, a choice that effectively obscured their diversity.[37] Through free indirect discourse the third-person narrator regresses to the linguistic and cultural level of the characters, observes the world through their eyes, and expresses it with their dialect. However, because the readers' exploration of the *borgate* can never become full integration, the regression is never complete. The narrator moves in and out of the characters' point of view, and descriptions retain a cultural filter, which draws attention both to the difference between observer and observed and to the subjective perspective of each. The readers of *Ragazzi* are thus both immersed in the new cultural and linguistic reality and remain aware of the difference, in a mode consistent with the alternative ethical choice.

A complete identification of reader with character, on which the readers' second-hand apprenticeship is predicated in traditional *Bildungsromane*, is unattainable in *Ragazzi*. That impossible relationship, which parallels the *ragazzi*'s resistance to the code of individual development established by the genre, constitutes perhaps the most important aspect of the *Bildung* envisioned for the readers: a vicarious journey into unknown territory, which debunks certainties and questions assumptions. The novel exposes as loss, rather than achievement, the socialization that marks the completion of the *Bildung* in traditional coming-of-age novels. The man who walks away from the river in the last page of the novel has little in common with the *ragazzi* whose adventures allow the readers to explore a new social milieu. However, the true apprenticeship happens for readers, while following those boys and observing the specificity of their world.

The depiction of young men in the *borgate* shows not only how the notion of youth is context bound, but also how the innocence and insight attributed to children in neorealist narratives is a projection of progressive optimism. The *ragazzi* are not innately moral creatures that can embody the coming-of-age of a democratic nation. They embody, instead, the irreducible aspects, the difference that such projected national coming-of-age obscures. Against a model of evolutionary development, *Ragazzi* highlights the liminality of youth, while at the same time denying the visionary qualities this status affords in neorealist narratives. Although the apprenticeship can never be completed, making the readers aware of its impossibility is the ethical imperative proposed by this novel.

Redeeming the *Ragazzi: Una vita violenta*

The authentic "Italian story" of Roman boys inspired to join the PCI by a "healthy" desire for redemption and self-improvement, a story that according to Communist critics like Giovanni Berlinguer was still waiting to be written, was later recognized in *Una vita violenta* published in 1959.[38] In this more conventional novel, Pasolini seems to follow the suggestions of his harshest critics and allow for the possibility of change in the conditions of the Roman sub-proletariat.[39] Consequently, whereas *Ragazzi di vita* focused on being young as an ontological condition, from its very title *Una vita violenta* broadens its scope to a parable of errors and lessons learned.[40] *Vita* resembles a standard coming-of-age narrative whose protagonist, Tommaso Puzzilli, evolves from a sub-proletarian *ragazzo di vita* moved only by self-interest to a prudent, hard-working man, willing to sacrifice his life for the life of others. Whereas the plot of the earlier novel followed multiple circular trajectories, mirroring the boys' inability to learn from their mistakes, Tommaso's development is more linear. Animated by a desire for redemption lacking in his peers from the earlier novel, the young man seeks emancipation through work, stable relationships, and a series of political allegiances: first the neo-Fascist MSI (Movimento Sociale Italiano), then the Christian Democrats, and finally the Communist Party. Tommaso's parable is evidently offered as an exemplary path from instinctual life to political consciousness.

Initially, Tommaso is immersed in a densely populated environment and participates in several group adventures similar to those depicted in *Ragazzi di vita*. Yet his status as protagonist is never questioned: the third-person narration focuses consistently on him, and frequent moments of introspection confirm his role as *Bildungsheld*.[41] From the first chapter, aptly titled "Chi era Tommaso," this narrator, unlike the one of *Ragazzi*, guides the readers into the life of the young protagonist, putting his situation into the broader context not only of life in the *borgate*, but of post-war Italian history. Roman dialect and sub-proletarian jargon confer specificity to the dialogue and colour to descriptions, but the linear structure and background information facilitate the reading experience. Mobility and interiority, the key components of the modern coming-of-age novel, are both defining elements of *Una vita violenta*. Initially living in a shack on the bank of the Aniene River, Tommaso and his family eventually relocate to a newly built housing project. Although theft and occasional prostitution remain part of his lifestyle, he has a steady income from a job at the fish market and claims to aspire to a better position. Friendship with other *borgatari* guarantees him group support for petty crime and romantic serenades, but Tommaso also seeks the companionship of the "*studentini figli di papà*" (preppy students) with whom he brushes sleeves at the fussball table. He tries on new identities as easily as other *ragazzi* acquire new clothes after a successful scam, and the intentionality of his actions is never in doubt. His self-awareness becomes accessible to the readers through frequent, if sketchy, reflections that open up his interior landscape: anger for a failed scheme, pride in his new girlfriend, and shame for time spent in prison are among the feelings explored.

Traditional educational institutions have a more prominent position in *Vita* than in *Ragazzi*, even though their effect on the protagonist remains ambiguous. Whereas in the earlier novel the school building functioned exclusively as makeshift shelter for refugees and squatters, the opening description of *Vita* suggests that school attendance plays an important part in the boys' life: the book bags piled on the side of the pitch during the lunch-break soccer game, the bustle of the *borgata* stopping for a couple of hours in the afternoon, when all the students are in class, the cleaning chores for which students take turns staying after class (see 3–6; 11–13). However, Tommaso's attempt to take the place of his classmate in the after-school cleaning routine, and in the concomitant sexual encounter with their teacher, casts an ambiguous light on the educational role played by this school authority. Tommaso's vengeful report to the police when his plan fails procures him the scorn of his classmates and the nickname "spy."[42] This awkward emancipatory attempt through sexual activity sets off Tommaso's apprenticeship as a process that distances him from his peers. Even less effective than school, the penitentiary has lost the rite-of-passage status it had in *Ragazzi*. Tommaso's short prison sentence does neither improve his standing as a *borgataro*, nor rehabilitate him. It appears more as a brief detour on the path to respectability than a decisive factor thereof. More influential is the stay at the Forlanini sanatorium, where Tommaso embraces the cause of patients' rights and thereby attains the political initiation that will lead him to the Communist Party.[43] The confinement within the city offered by the long-term care institution facilitates the path to individuation: removed from his everyday environment and confronted with his own mortality, Tommaso gains self-consciousness and recognizes the need to engage in political struggle.[44]

Although partially shaped by educational institutions, Tommaso's individuation and upward mobility advance mainly through imitation of particular behaviours he recognizes as socially advantageous. He joins a neo-Fascist group because he wants to consort with students and middle-class adolescents, whose preppy outfits and velvety lawns in front of their villas identify them as models of respectable life (see 37; 43–4). As a romantic suitor and *"bravo ragazzo"* he tries to impress Irene by explaining his professional ambition: "Io m'adatto a fà er commesso. Ma ho fatto er secondo avviamento, a Tiburtino, e mo' spero d'avè un posto mejo. Sto a aspettà 'na risposta ..." (84; 88; "I've been doing a bit of clerking. But I've been going to technical school, at Tiburtino, and now I'm hoping to get a better job. I'm waiting for the answer to my application now ..."). The relationship with Irene, in turn, sets him apart from his fellow *borgatari*, at least in his mind: "c'aveva da fare, lui, mica come quei due nullafacenti senza speranza del Zucabbo e del Zimmìo, buoni solo d'andare a bilancino, che se non rubavano o non facevano qualche impiccio, non gli si faceva giorno" (102; 106; he had things to do, not like those hopeless bums Zucabbo and Zimmìo, who could think only of pulling off some job). His significant absence from the choral scene of the police raid in his neighbourhood described in the chapter "La battaglia di Pietralata" offers him the opportunity to practise with his new *"bravo ragazzo"* identity: he has dinner with his family, exchanges pleasantries with the neighbours, goes to bed early (see 122; 126). If the repeated accent on mobility implies a successful transition from the margins to the mainstream, from the *borgate* to the working class, this performance and the sentimental epiphany that concludes it suggest that any attempt to cross that ontological chasm between the two worlds is an act. Development is not equivalent to change.

Urban Development and Neorealism: The Tiburtino Quarter

If youth in *Ragazzi di vita* embodied the interstitial life of the *borgate*, in constant flux yet perceived by Pasolini as an ontological condition, unrelated to historical causes, Tommaso's development mirrors that of the *INA-Casa* project in the Tiburtino quarter, where his family relocates while he is in prison. A government-funded initiative for the construction of public housing in various Italian cities after WWII, *INA-Casa* projects (*Istituto Nazionale Assicurazioni*) responded to the double demand for unskilled employment and low-income housing.[45] In its idea of rehabilitating the lower classes through urban development, however, the *INA-Casa* showcases both the idealistic and paternalistic sides of post-war politics. On the one hand, the project provided material evidence of the State's efforts to promote economic development and modernization, and of its welfare concerns. On the other, with its stated goals of educating the residents to behave like homeowners in the responsible administration of housing projects, the literature justifying the *INA-Casa* outlines an ideological mission for the creation of good citizens.[46] The construction of civic identity through the sense of private ownership implied a projection of the bourgeois values of the planners onto lower-class residents. These values were reflected also in stylistic choices, particularly those made for the Roman quarter featured in the novel, the Tiburtino.[47]

Designed in 1949–54 by a group of architects led by Mario Ridolfi and Ludovico Quaroni, the Tiburtino is a perfect example of Italian neorealist architecture, the post-war style that aimed to transcend Fascist monumental classicism and avant-garde modernism by combining the ideas of European Rationalism with location-specific considerations. As John David Rhodes shows in his study of *INA-Casa* projects in Pasolini's cinema, the parallel between cinematic and architectural neorealism is based on the rejection of classical stylistic solutions in favour of an "appropriation of real life."[48] What cinematic neorealism strived for, through location shooting, non-professional actors, and plots based on real-life events, its architectural counterpart attempted through a preference for local, pre-industrial materials, artisanal details, and traditional construction techniques. In particular, it countered the rationalist hierarchies of Fascist modernism through the combination of eclectic elements. In the Tiburtino, this intent translated into a picturesque appropriation of various components from rural Lazio architecture and their irregular arrangement aimed at reproducing the look and feel of discontinuous, unplanned development. The creation *ex-novo* of a "village-like atmosphere" was meant to offer the residents, many of whom had relocated from rural villages, a living experience comparable to the one they had left behind. In this shift from the original village to the village-like quarter, one recognizes the neorealist shift from the representation of "the way things are" to "the way things ought to be," based on neorealism's faith in art as a determinant of the world it records.[49] The confidence in architecture as an instrument for inspiring social change, which clearly animated the designers of the Tiburtino, is the object of critique in *Vita*. As a young sub-proletarian with aspirations of upward mobility, Tommaso exemplifies the human project implicit in the urban plan.

The distance between the architects' idealistic intent and the imagined assignees' perception of the organic architecture of the Tiburtino, highlighted in several instances in the novel, anticipates a critique of its premises. A flashback to the Puzzillis' life before their arrival in Rome, odd when compared to the essentialist vision of the *borgate* offered in the earlier novel, provides both background information on the family and a description of their previous dwelling:

> Torquato era padrone d'una casetta, magari messa su coi tufi, in mezzo alla campagna, a un chilometro da isola Liri, che gli era rimasta dalla madre: intorno c'era un po' di metri di terra, che se li lavorava, e c'aveva messo le stalle pei maiali, le pecore e le galline.

> Torquato had been the owner of a little house, probably made of slabs of tufa, in the midst of the countryside half a mile from Isola Liri, which he had been left by his mother: around it were a few square feet of land that he worked, and he had built a shed for the hogs, the sheep, and the hens. (165; 167)

Paradoxically, while the architects' plans for the Tiburtino quarter meant to offer the inhabitants a familiar environment, reminiscent of their home villages, the finished product has none of the envisioned familiarity to the prospective residents:

> ... le case cominciarono a spuntare, sui prati, sui montarozzi. Avevano forme strane, coi tetti a punta, terrazzette, abbaini, finestrelle rotonde e ovali: la gente cominciava a chiamare quei caseggiati Alice nel Paese delle Meraviglie, Villaggio Fatato, o Gerusalemme: e tutti ci ridevano, ma tutti

quelli che abitavano nelle borgate in quei paraggi, cominciarono a pensare: "Aaaah, finalmente anche a me me danno un harem!

... the blocks of housing began to sprout on the fields, on the little hills. They had strange shapes, pointed roofs, little balconies, skylights, round and oval windows: the people began to call those buildings Alice in Wonderland, Magic Village, or the New Jerusalem, and everybody laughed, but all the people who lived in those slums began to think: "Aaaah, at last they're gonna give me a [harem]!" (166; 168, trans. modified)[50]

The incredulity of the Puzzilli family at being assigned an apartment, after years of applications and prayers, and the superstitious gestures with which they meet the news, confirms the new houses' unreality. It also reveals that the improvement of the Puzzillis' material conditions is only a drop in the ocean, since there is another family ready to purchase their shack:

Chi se lo sarebbe mai creduto? Uno degli appartamentini dell'INA Case fu assegnato a Torquato Puzzilli. Mannaggia! S'era stancata la sfortuna di corrergli appresso col bastone! Contento che cantava, il sor Torquato offrì da bere a tutti quelli delle baracche, sfasciò per scaramanzia un po' di cocci vecchi, altri li distribuì ai vicini, e alla fine contrattò pure con uno per vendergli la bracca: cinquanta brandoni, mannaggia, e quando li aveva visti mai!

Who would ever have imagined such a thing? One of the INA-Case apartments was assigned to Torquato Puzzilli! Jeezus! Old lady Bad Luck had got tired of running after him with her cane! Singing with happiness, Sor Torquato bought wine for all his neighbours in the shacks, broke a few old plates as a precaution against the evil eye, distributed other stuff among his friends, and in the end even made a deal, selling his shack: fifty thousand, goddammit, more money than he'd ever seen at once! (167–8; 169)

As a young man driven by the desire to improve his position, Tommaso welcomes the move to the Tiburtino quarter as the beginning of his "new life" after two years in prison. He is surprised at the completion of a project that "la gente cominciava a guardare con ironia, perchè fin da allora si capiva quello che doveva uscirne fuori" (172; 174;

people looked at with irony, knowing what was going to come of it). The encounter takes the form of a vision:

> Adesso era lì, tutto bello pronto, con intorno una specie di muretto di cinta sui praticelli ch'erano rimasti quelli che erano, pieni di zozzeria. Le strade nuove nuove entravano in curva in mezzo alle case, rosa, rosse, gialle, tutte sbilenche esse pure, con mucchi di balconi e abbaini, e sfilate di parapetti. Arrivando con l'autobus, a vederlo, quel quartiere pareva davvero Gerusalemme, con quella massa di fiancate, una sopra l'altra, schierate sui prati, contro le vecchie cave, e prese in pieno dalla luce del sole.

> Now it was there, all nice and completed, with a little wall around it, on the fields that had remained what they were before, full of filth. The brand new streets curved in among the pink, red, yellow houses, also curved, with lots of balconies and skylights and rows of railings. Arriving with the bus, looking at it, you really thought that quarter was Jerusalem, with its mass of cement flanks, one above the other, serried in the fields, against the old quarries, and struck directly by the sun's light. (172; 174)

Despite his initial scepticism, Tommaso recognizes the completed project as a dream come true: the multicoloured and variously shaped houses stand out brightly against the untouched dirty fields surrounding them, glimmering in the sun like a mirage, or like the Holy City in the eyes of a pilgrim. As if confirming the intent of the *INA-Casa* designers, the sense of ownership of the new home and quarter transforms Tommaso, who suddenly feels shame at the prospect that his new neighbours might find out about his recent incarceration: "È vero che in conclusione non c'era stato nemmeno due anni, e adesso usciva che ancora puzzava di libertà. Ma però gli rodeva che la gente del quartiere nuovo dove adesso abitava lo venisse a sapere" (173; 174–5; It's true that, in the end, he hadn't been in for anything like two years, and now he was coming out with the stink of freedom still on him. But he was worried all the same that the people in the new neighbourhood where he lived now might find out about it).

The description of Tommaso's arrival at his new neighbourhood shows both the stylistic eclecticism sought by the architects and the desired reaction on the part of a new resident:

> C'erano sei o sette palazzine, storte, di sguincio, con file di finestrini tondi, dipinte di rosa scuro, con delle porte dove ci s'arrivava facendo cinque o

sei scalini, e tante balaustre a zig zag che le univano fra loro: poi dietro a queste la strada finiva di colpo, contro un'altra strada senza case, tagliata nel tufo. E tutt'intorno, i prati.

There were six or seven little dark-red buildings, set at a slant, with rows of round windows, five or six little steps up to the doors, and lots of zig-zag railings joining them all: then, behind these buildings the road ended abruptly in another road, without houses, cut from the tufa. Then fields, all around. (173; 175)

The variety of architectural details, combining modern and traditional features, is noticeable but well integrated in the surrounding landscape, and the general atmosphere recalls that of a village, as the architects had desired: women singing at the windows, children playing ball in the street, teenagers playing soccer, one kid singing "come un fringuello, nell'aria dolce dolce una nuova canzone ch'era uscita in quei mesi e che Tommaso non conosceva" (173; 175; like a finch in the mild air, a new song that had come out during these past months, a song Tommaso didn't know): "Oi Lazzarella..."[51] The situation described in the song, a young love between the well-off student Lazzarella and the more modest narrator, anticipates Tommaso's desire, and the opportunity offered by the residential proximity, to mingle with the better-off students who also live in the Tiburtino. However, just like the Lazzarella of the song, the *"studentini figli di papà"* are not easily approachable. Tommaso is well aware of the economic and social distance between the two categories of people housed at the *INA-Casa* projects:

Da una parte impiegati dello stato, ferrovieri, tranvieri, che avevano avuto casa attraverso le loro aziende: e tra loro c'erano anche ragionieri, geometri e gente per bene di quella pasta. Dall'altra parte c'erano quelli che avevano abitato nei tuguri e nelle casette, a cui il comune di tanto in tanto assegnava qualche casa, e che era tutta gente morta di fame o della mala.

On the one hand the government employees, railwaymen, tram conductors, who had been assigned houses through their departments, and among them there were even bookkeepers, surveyors and high-class people like that. On the other hand there were those who had lived in caves and dumps, to whom the City assigned new houses every now and then, all bums or petty crooks. (179; 180-1)

Landscape and man do seem to mirror one another, just as neorealist architects and filmmakers had envisioned.[52] Tommaso's intentions to leave behind his wild ways and settle down are sustained by a self-image that is determined by his new residence. The shift from "Tommaso as he is" to "Tommaso as he ought to be" is brought about by the change of scenery. "Vojo cambià da come che so': nun vojo più esse' Tommaso!" (195; 197; "I want to change from what I am, why I don't wanna be Tommaso any more!") he declares to his girlfriend Irene when he proposes to her. The civic apprenticeship that failed in prison could succeed at the Tiburtino, encouraged by the sense of ownership and pride in the new quarter. However, the "stink of freedom" that set Tommaso apart in prison still does when he enters the new neighbourhood: during his detention, the briefness of his sentence, and the suspicion it aroused among his fellow convicts that he was an informer, tainted Tommaso's credibility and prevented him from integrating in the prison community; outside, his condition barely qualifies as freedom, since his incarceration makes him feel different from his neighbours. Caught in-between, Tommaso is never fully integrated in either of the communities that are supposed to encourage change. The *puzza di libertà*, which gives this chapter its title, signifies Tommaso's ironic embodiment of the new man envisioned by the *INA-Casa* designers. This liminal position belies the development implicit in the Tiburtino project: the creation of a new cohesive community through the appropriation and combination of disparate elements from authentic villages. Tommaso's transformation into a model citizen reproduces the stages of a coming-of-age process as bourgeois architects and lawmakers imagined it. Just like the layout of the Tiburtino quarter projects upon his residents an image of their supposed desires, as envisioned by its architects, Tommaso's coming-of-age as an honest, socially committed citizen reflects the progressive ideals of the left-wing intellectuals who demanded, as Berlinguer did in his review of *Ragazzi*, a narrative depiction of the lower classes' desire for redemption.

Although Tommaso's material circumstances have undeniably changed for the better, Pasolini's particular attention to the transformations the new house triggers in the young man suggests that the material improvement comes at a cost. The death of Tito and Toto, his toddler brothers, immediately following the family's relocation had already cast a shadow of doubt regarding the possibility of real change or its desirability (see 168–9; 170–1). Tommaso's illness recasts the doubt more directly. While showing the "healthy" desire for change, the will for redemption from inhuman life conditions that Communist critics wished to see in contemporary youth, fictional and not, the young protagonist is struck by an illness that both accelerates his transformation and cuts his life short. Pasolini uses the metaphoric connotations of tuberculosis to characterize Tommaso, to give him depth, following a rich literary tradition of young heroes spiritualized by the experience of TB. Susan Sontag shows how throughout nineteenth-century literature, "TB is a disease of time; it speeds up life, highlights it, spiritualizes it":

> It is with TB that the idea of individual illness was articulated, along with the idea that people are made more conscious as they confront their deaths, and in the images that collected around the disease one can see emerging a modern idea of individuality that has taken in the twentieth century a more aggressive, if no less narcissistic, form.[53]

TB definitely speeds up Tommaso's coming-of-age, accelerates his political development, and ultimately leads him to a self-sacrificing/suicidal gesture, which elevates him above his peers.

The course of his illness accompanies his new life step by step. The first symptoms significantly appear when he reconnects with Irene after being released from prison, as they proudly walk in the centre of Rome, imagining their possible social advancement through hard work. His individuation becomes evident when, sitting in a movie theatre, Tommaso looks at other young people with superiority: "appetto a loro si sentiva una persona superiore" (194). The symptoms intensify as his new life grows steady: he shows off the *INA-Casa* quarter to Irene, grinds away at his job at the market, and becomes worried when the mysterious "weakness" affects his sexual performance. As a clear sign of its significance in the young man's coming-of-age, the illness is diagnosed at the military hospital, when Tommaso undergoes an important rite of passage: the medical examination on admission to the military service. Following the diagnosis, the sanatorium replaces the army as his initiation into manhood. In the forced confinement and democratic socialization imposed by the hospital, Tommaso finds his path to political consciousness.

The exile at the Forlanini hospital, with its combination of *otium* and isolation, develops Tommaso's interiority well beyond the recurrent bouts of frustration that characterized his healthier self. In the modernist tradition of Thomas Mann's *The Magic Mountain*, the need to look inside the patient's body creates the need to look into his mind. An intricate dream, featuring Tommaso's family and friends, reveals subconscious desires and guilt feelings with unprecedented detail. Without suggesting a relation between his unconscious or repressed feelings and his disease, Tommaso's transformation in the sanatorium reproduces the romantic notion that illness exacerbates consciousness. The epiphany that follows shortly after the dream shows the exacerbation:

> Poi qualcosa cambiò: si sentiva che fuori non era più scuro, che un po' di luce, leggera, stava sbiancando l'aria. ... Ma ecco che, piano piano, delle campane cominciarono a suonare. ... Era un suono che Tommaso non aveva inteso mai: o forse l'aveva inteso da ragazzino, e non se ne ricordava. Pareva venisse su dal fondo della terra, o da qualche punto del cielo, di sopra le nuvole della prima mattina, dove c'è un po' di luce che si colora appena, e pare già quella d'un giorno bello e felice. Era il suono del Mattutino. Ancora non risultava bene s'era un segno di festa, per il giorno che tornava, oppure se annunciava un lutto, una disgrazia. Forse erano tutte le due cose mischiate insieme, e mischiandosi si annullavano, e quel suono era un suono soltanto, che si ripeteva, fiacco ma continuo. Tommaso non riusciva a capire che volesse dire, perché non aveva né il modo né le parole per capirlo, non c'aveva fatto caso mai a queste cose, né qualcuno gliene aveva parlato mai, come non ci fossero nemmeno. Ma ora c'era, e forte, quel suono, don don don don, che passava attraverso tutti quei quartieri ancora addormentati, quell'aria vecchia, che, appena appena, si cominciava a rischiarare, dal di dentro, come da se stessa, diventando grigia e pulita, ritrovandosi con tutte le cose in mezzo, muri, piante, caseggiati, strade. E per qualcuno doveva per forza suonare: per il prete, che lo faceva fare, per il sagrestano, per qualche vecchietta, per gli operai che andavano a un lavoro notturno, e a quell'ora staccavano, per quelli che dovevano prendere il treno e partire.
>
> Ma, come dire, sembrava che quelle campane, quel don don don don misterioso che riannunciava la vita d'ogni giorno, dicesse invece che no, che era tutto inutile, che tutti erano vivi ma già morti, sepolti, anime sperdute. E nel tempo stesso l'odore di fanga, di pioggia, di caffelatte che, come portato dai rintocchi di quelle campane, cominciava a farsi sentire tutt'intorno, dava un senso di calma e di freschezza.

> Then something changed: he felt that outside it wasn't all dark any more, that a faint light was whitening the air ... But then, slowly, some bells began to ring ... It was a sound Tommaso had never heard: or maybe he had heard it when he was a little kid, and now he didn't remember.

It seemed to come up from the bottom of the earth from some point above the early-morning clouds, where the sky is just taking on colour and already seems the light of a good and happy day. It was the sound of Matins. It still wasn't clear whether it was a sign of celebration for the returning day or whether it was announcing a misfortune, a death. Maybe it was both things mixed together, cancelling each other out as they mingled, and that sound was only a sound, repeated, faint but constant. Tommaso couldn't make out what it meant because he had no words for it, no way of understanding; he had never paid any attention to these things, nobody ever talked to him about them: it was as if they didn't exist. But now it was there, and loud, that sound, dong dong dong dong, passing through all those sleeping neighbourhoods, that old air which was beginning to brighten, barely, from within, as if from itself, becoming grey and cleansed, rediscovering all the things around: walls, trees, buildings, streets. And it had to be ringing for someone: for the priest, who made it ring, for the sacristan, for some old woman, for the workers on some night-time job, coming off work at that hour, for those who had to catch a train for somewhere.

But ... how to say it? ... it seemed that those bells, that mysterious dong dong dong dong that re-announced the life of every day, were saying instead no, that everything was in vain, that all were alive but already dead, buried, lost souls. And at the same time the smell of mud, of rain, of coffee, as if borne by the tolling of those bells, began to be perceptible all around, giving a sense of calm and of freshness. (226–7; 226–7)

The subtle and detailed interior monologue shows both the young man's deepened sensitivity and his awareness of the novelty of such experience. Introduced after only one day at the sanatorium, the reflection clearly accelerates the process of interior exploration that leads to self-knowledge in narratives of illness and confinement.

The individuation presented in this monologue functions as a premise to the chance discovery of the red flag in the office of the hospital workers' union. Both moments of epiphany in the style of modernist psychological novels, they stage Tommaso's conversion to Communism as an irrational choice. Illness and its attendant condition of isolation, produce the change that the active, hard-working, socialized experience of his healthy self did not attain. The selflessness that earns him the recognition of the Communist Party is thus a symptom of the illness that accelerates his *Bildung*, but also interrupts his life. The melodramatic finale, containing many of the figurative elements of "romantic" TB, confirms this: the "disease of liquids"... and of air, of the need for better air" regains control of Tommaso's body after the flood that washed away part of his old *borgata*.[54] He carries a woman, then two children to safety, trailing through the mud and water, exhausted, shouting "Don't choke me!" to the child clutching him tightly around his neck. The next morning, the cough and the blood on his shirt make outwardly visible the real change in Tommaso's body. As he fulfils the promise of youth outlined by the classic *Bildungsoman* – mobility, interiority, and individuation – and reinhabits an emancipatory paradigm advocated by both conservative institutions and left-wing intellectuals, Tommaso only develops his potential in the illusory vitality of impending death.

Both *Ragazzi di vita* and *Una vita violenta* problematize the optimistic views of development, which, according to Pasolini, were shaping post-war reconstruction and modernization in Italy. By adopting realist narrative forms centred on adolescence and setting the novels in interstitial spaces on the outskirts of the capital, he focused on the transitory quality of youth and the ongoing transformation of the country. Pasolini's critical eye concentrated on the loss implicit in coming-of-age narratives, be they individual or national, and brought to light the resistance to change he saw in sub-proletarian adolescents. Both novels demystify the teleological view of education inherent in the bourgeois notion of youth, and projected upon the lower classes through a variety of institutions, including schools, prisons, hospitals, and urban planning. While *Ragazzi di vita* celebrates youth as a condition – being young rather than becoming adult – it also foregrounds the specificity of adolescence in the Roman *borgate*. In so doing it challenges bourgeois models of coming-of-age that are assumed as universal, and paradoxically provides an alternative apprenticeship for the readers. The critique of hopeful post-war realist narratives of national development takes the form of a thwarted coming-of-age in *Una vita violenta*. Here the parallel between individual and collective models of emancipation becomes explicit, and the tragic ending provides Pasolini's response to critics who wanted *ragazzi* to grow up.

3 Looking Back in Longing: Lost Youth, Teddy Boys, and *Il sogno di una cosa*

The ambivalent relationship between Pasolini and the changing discourse of youth in twentieth-century Italy became particularly evident in the 1960s, the decade that most clearly saw the emergence of young people on the sociopolitical scene and the diffusion of the double notion of youth as infinite opportunity and uncontainable danger. Pasolini's contribution to the discourse of youth in this decade was rich and varied, encompassing all of the genres in which he expressed himself. From the vantage point of the sixties, his gaze was directed at various geographical and historical configurations of adolescence: at the young people he met during his frequent travels in India, Africa, and America, who became the protagonists of essays or travel journals, both in writing and as film; at contemporary adolescents in Italy, who populated the pages of newspapers and magazines with new tastes and habits that both worried and excited adults; and at the young Friulian peasants of his past, whom he recaptured in a nostalgic operation in the novel *Il sogno di una cosa*.[1] These explorations created a multifaceted portrait of youth as both alarming and reassuring; a mirror image of a society that was undergoing a rapid transformation and fluctuated between exhilaration, moral panic, and longing for an authenticity that was more imagined than lost.

After his Roman novels had challenged the representational principles of neorealism and responded to the emancipatory ideals of left-wing intellectuals, particularly regarding young people, Pasolini enjoyed sufficient consideration in literary and political circles to be frequently consulted in discussions on changing adolescence. Particularly after the success of *Una vita violenta*, his unorthodox Marxism and interest in maladjusted adolescents appeared as attractive features to a party worried about declining youth activism and looking to mobilize the young. His collaboration with the Communist weekly *Vie Nuove* between 1960 and 1965 (although occasionally even in 1959) provided a venue for his active participation in the debate on contemporary youth, which was prominent in all mass media. In articles and responses to readers' letters, Pasolini mostly defended young people, minimizing their alleged dangerousness and shifting attention to broader transformations in Italian society, which could be blamed for adolescents' worrisome behaviour. *Il sogno di una cosa*, published in 1962, must then be read in the context of that debate, as a creative response to the widespread anxiety towards youth: the novel expresses a renewed faith in young people and proposes a reassuring notion of adolescence, in which innovation and tradition are not at odds, and different generations collaborate in political action.

Giovani, Giovani, Giovani: Youth and Mass Media in 1960

The desire to re-establish faith in adolescence as a positive social force was particularly significant at a time, the early 1960s, when Italy manifested anxiety and fear regarding its younger generations. As the country transitioned from a rural to an industrial economy, learning to appreciate consumer products and international pop culture after years of war and Fascism, a distinctive youth culture emerged. The phenomenon was part of a general change of lifestyles involving Italians of all generations, but new youth pastimes and interests became privileged subjects of media attention and sociological literature. Young people reacted with both exhilaration and discomfort to the new values promoted by the so-called "economic miracle," and their ambivalence worried parents, teachers, scholars, and journalists. In newspapers and magazines, the multiplication of the word *"giovani"* in headlines signalled a greater interest in youth, both in the choice of subject matter, and the editorial angle chosen for book, film, and music reviews. This same literature, however, produced a sense of alarm among adults about behaviours that appeared inexplicable.[2] In the proliferation of inquiries, *reportages*, and studies that tried to examine and explain the new young people, youth became "a metaphor of social change, a territory on which the fears and resistances of adults [could] be measured," and the construction of "deviant and dangerous youth ... the lost youth of the post-WWII years [was] an epiphenomenon of an experience of youth that was being redefined."[3]

In the years 1959–60, numerous newspaper articles focused on changing relations between adolescents and their parents, new configurations of friendship among teens, or new pastimes that captivated the young. They also gave prominence to young film directors and singers, and to books and movies that depicted adolescents. Whether in accounts on the European Festival of Youth, reviews of the young directors of the Nouvelle Vague, reports on the Gerovital anti-aging treatment, or letters to the editor from young readers, the persistent use of the words *"giovani"* and *"gioventù"* in headlines and articles revealed an unprecedented degree of interest in youth in magazines as diverse as the Communist *Vie Nuove* and the progressive newsweekly *l'Espresso*.[4] Several articles described the new lifestyles of Italian adolescents, English teenagers, French *blousons noirs*, American students, and German *halbstarken*.[5] *L'Espresso*'s famous investigative reports brought into focus the various configurations of youth in different countries and different social milieux.[6] Many *Vie Nuove* readers wrote to the editor about the so-called "youth question": topics ranged from general malaise to the proposed legal measures to address the alleged increase in juvenile delinquency and the phenomenon of "Teddy boys."[7]

Book and film reviews and promotional ads provide additional examples of the proliferating discourse of youth at that time. The movie *Ragazzi del juke-box* warranted an explanation of an innovative singing style: "Perché urlo: Le più note voci del juke-box riunite a Roma per un film" (Why I shout: The most famous juke-box voices gathered in Rome for a movie).[8] Marcel Carné's film *Les Tricheurs*, distributed in Italy as *Peccatori in blue jeans* was advertised as "un film che è un grido d'allarme" (a movie that is an alarm signal), portraying the "sinners in blue jeans" as "gioventù più sperduta che pervertita" (youth more lost than perverted). The viewers would have to decide whether the sinners could be saved. Not surprisingly, reviews of Pasolini's works occasioned discussion on youth behaviours as well: Mauro Bolognini's film *La notte brava* became "La Notte dei Teppisti (The Night of the Hooligans)" in the review of *l'Espresso*, and its protagonists became "I Ragazzi della Notte Brava" in the title of a *Vie Nuove* interview with Pasolini, who had written the screenplay.[9] The comic film *Totò, Fabrizi e i giovani d'oggi*, advertised in *l'Espresso*, signalled the popularity of inquiries on the youth condition through a direct quotation of the RAI (Radiotelevisione Italiana) documentary *Giovani d'oggi*, directed by Carlo Alberto Chiesa, which was itself reviewed in a previous issue.[10] Broadcast on Thursday nights after the popular show *Campanile Sera*, the eight-episode inquiry covered topics like family relations, school, and leisure activities, and tried to understand the reasons for youth malaise.[11] It considered new musical genres and pastimes drawing young people together and away from their parents as especially dangerous. The episode about leisure activities drew a direct connection between pinball machines, undesired friendships, and crime among adolescents. Likewise, articles in *l'Espresso* linked jukeboxes and pinball machines with the decline in religious practices and political activity among adolescents. Other articles presented alarmed reports on the violent Italian Teddy boys and French *blousons noirs*.[12]

Many articles magnified disturbing youth behaviour and attributed it to foreign sources.[13] In a lengthy article on Teddy boys in Milan (*Vie Nuove*, August 22, 1959) "Teddy boys di serie A e di serie B," the reporter Renato Nicolai contributed to the wider debate on juvenile delinquency by offering individual profiles of the members of a gang who had attacked a jewellery store. Predictably, he pointed to absent and ineffective parents, and a desire for quick material gain as the possible causes for their behaviour. However, among the bad influences were comic books ("in ogni piega del fatto "teddy-boys" vien fuori evidentissimo il peso di questa influenza"; every aspect of the "teddy-boys" phenomenon reveals the strong weight of this influence) and "the wildest Americanism" popularized by "a certain kind of" cinema, press, and television. The impact of these factors appeared stronger in the large urban areas of northern Italy, where "the most extreme contradictions of modern civilization become explicit and profoundly affect individual lives, people's thoughts and feelings."[14] On the other hand, when a letter from a *Vie Nuove* reader explicitly attributed the change in youth habits to the "Americanization" of Italy, to the introduction of bikinis and blue jeans, pinball machines and jukeboxes, "cannibalistic dances" and "mad motorization," comic books and gangster movies, the editor responded that while those superficial changes were not related to delinquency, American individualism and materialism were. The editor offered an essentially optimistic image of young Italians, but also confirmed that youth was the social group that needed to be observed, studied, and understood. (September 26, 1959).

The growing interest in young people's conduct between the end of the 1950s and the early 1960s produced numerous *inchieste* and reports. *L'Espresso* published a "Rapporto internazionale sul comportamento amoroso della gioventù," which included reports from the United States ("La rivoluzione della Flaming Youth"), England, Sweden, and France.

In the same period, *Vie Nuove* launched its own inquiry on youth: it was based on sixteen questions, which covered topics ranging from relationships with parents and aspirations for the future, to the role of Italy in the Cold War détente, and the application of constitutional rights for all Italian citizens. The answers, collected by interviewers in different parts of the country, or sent in directly by readers, were then compiled in ten instalments, commented on by journalist Miriam Mafai, and published between the end of January and the beginning of April 1960. Young interviewees showed a widespread anxiety about the future, especially job and career opportunities, and a general dissatisfaction with educational institutions, but did not envision a political role for themselves. Politics was a profession that the average student or worker did not imagine choosing, and traditional party organizations were viewed as foreign. However, according to Mafai, the survey offered an "exceptionally favourable" overall impression of Italian youth even though, or perhaps because, the interviewees expressed often critical views of their world: "Con la presa di coscienza di se stessi, del proprio mondo interiore, si fa il primo passo decisivo verso una matura comprensione della realtà." (With the awareness of oneself, of one's inner world, one takes the first decisive step towards a mature understanding of reality) (February 13, 1960, 20). In the survey's closing remarks Mafai observed that young people were:

> figli di una rivoluzione che non si è ancora tutta compiuta, che noi abbiamo iniziato ma il cui corso è stato interrotto e in parte deviato da forze politiche e sociali diverse contro le quali la parte migliore del nostro paese, e noi stessi, continuiamo a batterci. C'è tuttavia un margine di sfiducia, di amarezza, di delusione anche in noi, e che, forse involontariamente abbiamo trasmesso a coloro che hanno oggi venti anni. Se questo è vero, la *loro* crisi è in realtà la *nostra* crisi. Ed è inutile gridare allo scandalo quando la leggiamo nei loro occhi. Imbalsamarci nel ricordo di una "nostra" giovinezza che sarebbe stata migliore di quella del 1960, è un modo di non capire le cose.

> children of a revolution that has not been completed yet, that we began, but whose course was interrupted and partly diverted by various political and social forces against which the best part of our country continues to fight, as we do. However, there is a margin of mistrust, of bitterness, of disappointment in us too, which, perhaps involuntarily we have passed on to those who are twenty years old today. If this is true, *their* crisis is actually *our* crisis. And it is pointless to make an outcry when we read it in

their eyes. Embalming ourselves in the memory of a form of youth, "ours," that was allegedly better than that of 1960, is a way of not understanding the issue. (April 2, 1960, 44)

Beyond the alleged "youth question," the most urgent problem facing her readership, in Mafai's view, was the incomplete democratic renewal that had begun with anti-Fascist Resistance. In the completion of that project, she claimed, "non possono esistere divisioni di compiti tra giovani e anziani" (44; there cannot exist any division of tasks between young and old). Thus, if to many sociologists and journalists youth appeared as a problem, for Communist intellectuals young people represented also the hope for change in a social asset that did not fulfil the expectations of the Resistance. Generational issues took second place to class and political questions, as the PCI tried to revive an interest in militancy among young people.

An attempt to re-establish this continuity between young and older readers motivated Maria Antonietta Macciocchi, the editor, to invite Pasolini to write a regular column in *Vie Nuove*. In introducing the new column, she described him as "uno dei pochi scrittori italiani che sia legato da migliaia di fili ad un pubblico popolare" (one of the few Italian writers who is linked by thousands of threads to a popular audience). In particular, she justified Pasolini's appointment with his close bond with young readers:

> si tratta, in genere, di un pubblico giovane che va a sentirlo, come quello che siamo abituati a pensare riunito attorno ai juke-box, sui campi di calcio, nelle sale da ballo di periferia e che avverte come nel mondo che Pasolini descrive, brutale, carico di vizi e di magagne, intervenga poi come fatto risolutivo quel momento della *coscienza* e della *speranza* che garantisce l'avvento di un mondo nuovo.
>
> It is generally young people who listen to him, like those we usually imagine gathered around jukeboxes, in soccer fields, or in the dance halls of the periphery, and who understand how, in the world that Pasolini describes, brutal, burdened with vice and imperfections, there intervenes as a crucial event that moment of *consciousness* and *hope* that guarantees the advent of a new world. (*Vie Nuove*, May 28, 1960, 6)

If the choice to hire Pasolini as a youth magnet for a Communist weekly sounds surprising, the explanation provided offers an image of the author that is unique to this period. Linking the jukebox adolescents to the ideology of hope and emancipation of the PCI through a critic of party orthodoxy became conceivable shortly after the publication of *Una vita violenta*, the novel that had shown to Marxist critics that the *ragazzi* could attain political consciousness, albeit in an unconventional way.

Even before beginning his regular collaboration with *Vie Nuove*, Pasolini's remarks on youth were largely aligned with the editor's goal of decriminalizing adolescence. When, in the previously mentioned interview granted upon the release of Bolognini's *La Notte Brava*, Pasolini was asked whether the kind of stories and characters he created represented, in his opinion, a "danger for society," he answered:

> Un pericolo per la società sono alcuni rotocalchi che, facendo di alcune banali imprese giovanili (qualche scazzottata qua e là, in un paese di cinquanta milioni di abitanti, non sono nulla) un mito, deformano, con i mezzi più adatti – la superficialità di giudizio, l'asservimento all'opinione pubblica, la facilità della fama, ecc. – la mentalità dei ragazzi, soprattutto appartenenti alla piccola borghesia, scontenta e annoiata.

> A danger for society are some magazines that, by turning some banal youthful actions into myth (a few brawls here and there, in a country with fifty million inhabitants, are nothing) distort, with the most effective means – superficiality of judgment, subjection to public opinion, easy celebrity, etc. – young people's mind, especially those belonging to the unhappy and bored petit bourgeoisie. (*Vie Nuove*, September 12, 1959, 28)

A month later, commenting on a recent symposium on "Adolescenza traviata" (Misled Adolescence), he once again shifted attention from the presumed problem onto its spectacularization:

> Da questo congresso è risultato chiaro perché esistono i teddy boys, voglio dire non dai lavori e dalle discussioni del congresso, ma dal congresso stesso, dalla sua presenza: tanta presunzione pedagogica, tanta cecità reazionaria, tanto sciocco paternalismo, tanto represso sadismo non possono che giustificare in molte città italiane l'esistenza di una gioventù insofferente e incattivita.

> This conference made it clear why Teddy boys exist, I mean not the work and discussions of the conference, but the conference itself, its presence: so

much pedagogical presumption, so much reactionary blindness, so much silly paternalism, so much repressed sadism cannot but justify in many Italian cities the existence of an irritable and nasty youth.[15]

If as part of his polemical stance towards such presumptuous pedagogues Pasolini admitted to the existence of malaise among young Italians, when explicitly asked to comment on the alleged "crisis of Italian youth," he counterbalanced the historically specific definition by asserting his belief in the fundamental goodness of young people. In typical Pasolinian fashion, he paradoxically maintained, on the one hand, the impossibility of defining youth in a consistent manner, while on the other he identified a core set of distinctive qualities that justified his optimism: "Non c'è niente di più labile del periodo della giovinezza" (Nothing is more fleeting than the time of youth), but despite this intrinsic transience and the stratification of Italian society that made youth virtually indefinable, it was clear "che i migliori italiani sono i giovani, dai sedici ai vent'anni: di gran lunga i migliori" (the best Italians are the young, between sixteen and twenty years old: by far the best). Free, uncorrupted, and open-minded adolescents were still the embodiment of hope for the future. "Non può esistere una crisi della gioventù: l'unica sua crisi è una crisi di crescenza." (There cannot exist a crisis of youth: its only crisis is a crisis of growth.)[16]

Where Is the Best of Youth?: Timeless and Contemporary Adolescence in *Il sogno di una cosa*

The publication of *Sogno* in 1962 responds in a more creative way to the alienation from young people that Pasolini perceived among contemporary adults. The novel visualizes the paradox, expressed in the *Vie Nuove* column, that youth is fleeting and historically defined, but also eternally familiar and incorruptible. To celebrate youth in both its promise and its impermanence, *Sogno* portrays lovable, well-meaning, non-threatening adolescents, who are poised between continuity and innovation, between faith in the older generations and desire for change; between century-old rural traditions and popular culture introduced by Hollywood movies and celebrity magazines. The boys ride bicycles, not motorcycles, but they enjoy boogie-woogie as well as traditional Friulian folk songs, and are willing to protest alongside their fathers for a more democratic society. The girls read *Grand Hotel* and try to assert their independent views within the family, but their alternative to a failed romance is still the convent. Even considering the gender disparity, the adolescents represented in the novel have little in common with the maladjusted rock-and-roll maniacs that many *inchieste* describe.[17] Removed in space and time, the young protagonists of *Sogno* stand at the crossroads of innocence and subversion, which epitomizes perfect youth as the middle class imagines it. A careful combination of timeless symbols and generational markers opens up the world of his characters to 1962 readers, but their removal from the present smooths off the edges and confers on youth a familiar and welcoming glow.

In its depiction of adolescence in rural Friuli at the end of the 1940s, *Il sogno di una cosa* is both a recollection of Pasolini's own coming-of-age and a celebration of youth in general, as the title originally assigned to the novel, *La meglio gioventù*, indicated.[18] The novel weaves together the friendship and romance storylines involving Nini, Eligio, and Milio, on one hand, and Pia, Cecilia, and her sisters on the other, with a political-historical plot centred on the sharecroppers' protest against the landowners to request the application of the *lodo De Gasperi*.[19] Coming-of-age rituals available to the boys identify this generation as a transition between a rural familial system and a nascent industrial world: participation in political protest, immigration to Yugoslavia and Switzerland, and, upon return to Friuli, employment at the local factories. The young women's traditional rites of passage, however, which include courtship and marriage, or entry into religious life, are only marginally influenced by the modernization investing their rural world. In any case, plot is secondary to atmosphere; the narrative details less important than the recreation of an Arcadia in which youth is the perfect balance of eternal pastoral and historical rebelliousness.

In the early 1960s, when adolescents are claiming a distinct identity, ontologically different from that of other age groups, and adults project upon them the apprehension accompanying social change, *Il sogno di una cosa* offers an image of youth as a trans-historical signifier of innocence and a positive force of innovation. While young people in the news worry and alarm adults with their rebellious conduct, causing psychologists and sociologists to speak of antisocial behaviour, the boys and girls in *Sogno* are generally in perfect harmony with their elders. The nostalgic tinge of the novel, however, assumes significance beyond the personal elegy of lost youth that critics have identified.[20] Looking back on the Friuli of his past, Pasolini responds to the growing anxiety about young people in the present, and offers nostalgia as a healing process. Through an imaginative recovery of a key formative period, in both personal and national history, he presents a comforting and hopeful vision of youth.

Published in 1962, the novel is presented as an early prose work, only recently recovered and prepared for publication; a unique opportunity to see the author's youthful approach to a subject that would become a constant factor in his oeuvre. Pasolini himself thematizes this in his presentation of the novel, on its back cover:

> Scritto nel 1949–50 ... questo romanzo può essere sostanzialmente considerato il primo tentativo di prosa di Pasolini. Se lo scrittore si è oggi deciso a presentarlo – debitamente tagliato, restaurato, verniciato, e incorniciato – è perché ritiene sempre operanti le ragioni che allora l'avevano messo in piedi: quelle di una partecipazione diretta e tenace ad una realtà in cui gli istinti lirici iniziali si sono venuti via via concentrando in un incontrastato impegno morale.
>
> Written in 1949–50 ... this novel can basically be considered Pasolini's first attempt at writing prose. If the author decided to present it now – appropriately cut, restored, varnished, and framed – it is because he believes that the motivations that produced it then are still relevant: a direct and firm participation in a reality in which the early lyrical instincts gradually coalesced to form an undisputed moral commitment.[21]

Although the "tormented elaboration" of this manuscript, the result of several rewritings and additions over a period of fourteen years, is well documented in the *Collected Works*, both the history of composition and its presentation as juvenilia confirm its status as nostalgic text.[22] It is a mature work that deliberately imitates an earlier style, and also a nostalgic reconstruction of the past that passes itself off as a contemporary narrative. *Il sogno di una cosa* finds its significance in this intrinsic contradiction. Alongside material written in the 1940s and early 1950s, the novel includes, in fact, new sections written just a few months before publication, which Pasolini defines as an interesting experiment of "imitazione del me stesso di allora" (imitation of my older self).[23] This deliberate imitation of a conventional form, quite unlike the linguistic experiments with Friulian dialect and Roman slang that made Pasolini famous, supports the stylistic definition of *Sogno* as a nostalgic text. Vera Dika's description of nostalgia films as "reconstructions of dead or dismantled forms, genres that are now returned after a period of absence or destruction" can be applied to other types of texts, which "are thus better understood as copies whose originals are often lost or little known."[24] The conventional narrative seems therefore consistent with the novel's recreation of 1940s youth culture. It is a copy of an earlier genre, mimicking the style of a 1940s novel as 1960s readers might expect it, with a matching reconstruction of an outdated view of youth. Shaped by his adult views on youth rather than by his youthful inexperience, the novel is thus a "fantas[y] of the past determined by needs of the present."[25]

If the deliberate imitation of a conventional style serves the artificial recreation of a1940s narrative, the backdating through which the mature author passes off as juvenilia a text that he crafted much later is not only functional to the author's manneristic reconstruction of his literary apprenticeship.[26] When the composition date is moved back to the time of the events narrated, the nostalgia for a lost world that informs the narrative becomes intrinsic to that world, rather than an effect of recollection. In presenting the text as the product of his younger self, the author not only draws attention to his early interest in the social and symbolic function of youth, but also projects his mature awareness of its fugacity onto his experience as a young man. The doubling of the author implicit in the operation – the young author who narrates events as he is experiencing them and the mature author presenting the old text to the public – maintains the ambivalent position with respect to youth that the Roman novels achieved through free indirect discourse.[27] The author is at once immersed in the world he is depicting and removed from it. His proximity to Friulian youth, guaranteed by the stated date of composition, allows him to bring the readers closer to that world; his removal at the time of publication allows him to project upon that world the wished-for experience of youth that is both eternally innocent and intrinsically transient.

Late 1940s Friuli, perceived through the lens of nostalgia, offers the ideal setting for the performance of perfect youth: the green fields and luminous sky, the idyllic landscape and rural customs, transfigured according to century-old poetic and pictorial traditions, reflect youth's timeless innocence and regenerative powers. The opening sequence, an image of country roads filling with young people attending the Easter Monday festival introduces a trans-historical performance of youth:

> Fin dal mattino, se la giornata è serena, la strada provinciale e i viottoli campestri che conducono a Casale, si riempiono di gente che va alla sagra del Lunedì di Pasqua. Un po' alla volta le immense radure, d'un verde

ancora invernale, freddo e leggero, colorato qua e là da qualche ramo rosa di pesco, formicolano di gente che passeggia, si diverte, gioca, corre; i cavalli sciolti dalle carrette trottano pascolando lungo i fossi, cavalcati da qualche ragazzo vestito a festa; i bambini corrono agitando le loro spade di rami scortecciati, tra i grandi depositi delle biciclette, e le bambine con le loro bluse arancione, viola o verde, giocano tranquille sotto i sambuchi appena ingemmati.

From early in the morning if it is a fine day, the main road and the paths through the field leading to Casale become full of people going to the Easter Monday fair. Little by little the immense open spaces – they are still a wintery green, at once cold and light, tinged here and there by the pink branch of a peach tree – are swarming with people, walking along, enjoying themselves, playing, running. The horses, unyoked from the little carts, trot and graze along the ditches, youths in their holiday best astride them. The little boys run about waving their swords of peeled branches among the great bicycle enclosures and the little girls in their bright orange, purple, or green blouses play peacefully under the elder trees, which are just beginning to bud. (9; 3)

In rural communities the *sagra*, the village festival, is the traditional social occasion when, as anthropologist Daniel Fabre argues, "'youth will be youth.' A formal or implicit delegation of authority gives the young people the duty and the right to act publicly, to produce a festival for everyone while making the singularity of their own status known."[28] The local festival, better than other social practices, deploys the apparently contradictory elements of youth as they work together: they comply with traditions, which guarantees the future of the community, but also introduce novelties and claim independence, regardless of social status: "There are no student, artisanal, or worker ways of 'doing youth' ... Despite sometimes perceptible differences in wealth and status in the village, when it comes time for the festival, there is only one 'youth'" (ibid., 64). The *sagra*, supporting the ahistorical, pastoral notion of youth, allows young people to define themselves with respect to, and in respect of their elders. Its traditions, renewed year after year, include activities organized by and for youth. These set adolescents apart as a social group, even transcend class divisions, but do not violate social norms established by adults.[29]

The adolescent protagonists of *Sogno* are integrated into the timeless world of the *sagra*, although their clothes, means of transportation, and musical tastes suggest the beginning of a historical transformation that could challenge the very existence of that world. Nini and Milio ride into town on their bicycles, the former with a hawthorn branch on the handlebar ("un ramo di biancospino"), the second carrying an accordion across his back. Milio is part of a group of snappily dressed boys: "una compagnia di ragazzi dai quindici ai venti anni, con la giacchetta sulle spalle e le maglie dalle grandi striscie colorate intorno al petto" (10; 4; a company of boys ... of between fifteen and twenty years of age with their jackets on their shoulders and jerseys with big coloured stripes on their chests). The casual clothing style, which replaces the traditional suits typically worn by men of all ages on holidays and weekends, identifies a new generation that distinguishes itself from its elders. Nini and Eligio attempt a similar distinction: "volevano sembrare anch'essi qualcosa di meglio che contadini; il Nini indossava infatti una camicia alla cow-boy, e Eligio una americana dello stesso celeste dei suoi occhi" (14; 6; they too wanted to be better than the peasant boys. In fact Nini was wearing a cowboy shirt and Eligio an American one of the same sky-blue as his eyes). While clothing clearly locates the boys in a historically specific moment, defined by the influence of American popular culture on their sense of self, other visual elements remove them to the realm of the timeless pastoral. Flowers, in particular, a universal feature in the pastoral genre, play an important role in defining adolescence in trans-historical terms.

The hawthorn, by virtue of its complex symbolism and rich literary history, represents the ambivalence of youth while being of the novel's nostalgic mode.[30] First of all, it draws together several important influences on Pasolini's poetic education – Provençal troubadours, Giovanni Pascoli, and Marcel Proust primarily – and thus honours his own literary coming-of-age.[31] In poetic tradition the hawthorn blossom has bittersweet connotations: the joy and promise of spring and the pain inseparable from it; the anticipation of youth and the pang of memory.[32] The spring flower, which in the poem "Ab la dolchor del temps novel" by Guilhem d'Aquitaine is the metaphor for love's enduring hope even in sorrow, carries similar double-edged meanings in Pascoli's poems. It is the bittersweet and momentary innocence evoked by the *prunalbo* in "Novembre": an instant of spring, yet carrying the bitterness of the season's end within. Similarly, the *biancospino* is a harbinger of youth and spring renewal in "Valentino," but also a source of pain to the child's naked feet; and through those feet it evokes the innocence of youth that "non sa / ch'oltre il beccare, il cantare, l'amare / ci sia qualch'altra felicità" (doesn't know / that beyond pecking, singing, loving / there is any other happiness).[33] The flower's early appearance in *Sogno* anticipates the complex notion of youth embodied in the text: its promise and a premature nostalgia for its passing. The hawthorn crowns the new friendship between the young men and, through that, marks a new beginning:

> Il Nini, Eligio, Milio avevano tutti l'età in cui una fisarmonica è una cosa importante: fu così che si conobbero, per mezzo della fisarmonica di Milio, che, sotto due cespugli di biancospino, stava suonando tra i suoi compagni, e il Nini era già lì con le mani in tasca che stava a sentirlo.
>
> Nini, Eligio, Milio were all at the age when an accordion is a thing of importance. It was thus that they got to know one another – through Milio's harmonium, which he was playing among his mates under two hawthorn bushes and Nini was there already with his hands in his pockets, standing and listening to him. (11; 4)

However, it also predicts the passing of this brief and perfect moment: the age in which an accordion is an important thing does not last forever. The awareness that this moment is unique rests on the knowledge of its passing. From the perspective of the adult author looking back, this idyllic scene contains the signs of its imminent loss.

The hope and promise of youth, embodied in the hawthorn blossom and the *sagra*, is visualized through a more historically determined symbol in the political protest demanding the application of the *De Gasperi* law: the red flag of revolution. Crowning the heads of young people before the rally, as the hawthorn had crowned them at the opening of the *sagra*, the flag helps them articulate their position with respect to their elders and the cause: unrolling, shaking, and almost wearing it over their heads, the youngsters cry "Evviva la nostra bella bandiera" (Long live our beautiful flag). The white hawthorn blossom and the beautiful red flag epitomize the *sagra* and the political protest, the pastoral and the historical. The same excitement, energy, anticipation that precede the day of the *sagra* are also present in the preparation for the rally. People of all ages gather in the tavern to discuss the plan of action:

> come a San Giovanni, così in tutti i paesi del mandamento, c'era la stessa animazione, lo stesso inconsueto brillare di luci. Come Eligio e Jacu a San

Giovanni, così Milio era andato alla riunione nella sua sezione di Rosa, e il Nini a Ligugnana, dove, si sarebbe detto che tutti fossero in piedi, come alla vigilia di una festa piena di preparativi.

As in all the villages of the district, there was the same stir, the same unusual shining lights. Like Eligio and Jacu in San Giovani, Milio too had gone to the meeting at his Party branch in Rosa and Nini in Lingugnana, where it seemed as if everyone was up and about as if it were the busy eve of some festival. (94; 54)

Although the unions and the local cell of the Communist Party organized the protest, Pasolini's narrativization of the events draws attention to the degree of spontaneous participation of young people under the benevolent eyes of the older generations. The red flag replaces the hawthorn in defining the political rally as a collective rite of passage. The boys' avant-garde opens the demonstration. The red handkerchiefs they wear around their necks recall the flag carried by Onorino, one of the youngest: in the piazza "c'era quasi la ressa del giorno della sagra della Madonna: centinaia di giovani, quasi tutti coi fazzoletti rossi al collo..." (99; 57; there was almost as big a crowd in the square of the Madonna: hundreds of young people, almost all with red scarves round their necks...). The association between the strike and the festival is important, not inasmuch as it diminishes the political significance of the protest, as Ward suggests, but because it characterizes the struggle as an event in which young people are protagonists.[34]

The *sagra*, the political rally, and the Resistance converge in one image, which summarizes the nostalgic and utopian spirit of the novel: "In tutte le strade che portavano al centro, si vedevano gruppi di ragazzi, con le tute e i fazzoletti rossi, o antiche divise di partigiani coi berrettini mimetizzati, e i calzoni e gli stivali presi ai tedeschi e agli americani." (100; 57; in all the streets leading to the centre one could see groups of boys in overalls and red scarves or old partisan uniforms with camouflaged berets and the socks and boots taken from the Germans and the Americans). The energy introduced by the presence of young people among the protesters renews the promise of youth inherent in the *sagra* and evokes the idealism of the Resistance, another locus of projected harmony in Pasolini's poetics.[35] The nostalgic gaze on youth allows for the creation of a myth that is both regressive and utopian. The adolescents of Friuli in the late 1940s, seen from a comfortable distance, are reassuringly cooperative and optimistic. They show none of the malaise that adults see in 1960s youth, but also little of their independence. However, the image of Nini and his friends as new partisans, wearing the pants and boots left behind by American and German soldiers, red handkerchiefs tied around their necks, redefines a coming-of-age ritual. In the utopian dimension of nostalgia, the young rebels fight to complete the project of democratic reconstruction initiated by their elders.

Albeit utopian, the nostalgic gaze on youth offered by the novel contains the sense of its loss. The potential and impermanence of youth, visually embodied by the hawthorn, resonate in music. The sound of Milio's accordion marks the beginning of the protagonists' friendship, under the hawthorn bushes, as we have seen. It also accompanies the youth-defining moments of the holiday: the boys' arrival into town, the late night drinking and singing at the tavern, the bicycle rides home across the countryside. The latter summarizes in musical terms the timelessness tradition of "doing youth" at the *sagra*. Eligio gives Milio a ride home: "Finalmente Eligio la spuntò dicendo che mentre lui lo portava, Milio avrebbe potuto suonare l'armonica. Allora Milio si sedette sul manubrio, appoggiò il capo sulla spalla del nuovo compagno e cominciò a suonare" (21; 10; at last Eligio brought it to an end by saying that while he gave him a ride Milio could play the accordion. Then Milio sat on the handlebars, leant his head on the shoulder of his new mate and began to play). The repertoire includes dance tunes, religious hymns ("intonò un *Te Deum* a passo di marcia"), and political songs: "E quando furono in piazza, Milio, sempre appoggiato addosso a Eligio e seduto sul manubrio, li fece star tutti zitti un momento, con un grido, e con la sua fisarmonica attaccò: 'Avanti popolo...' E tutti gli andarono dietro urlando" (23; 11; and when they were in the square, Milio, still leaning on Eligio and sitting on the handlebar, quietened them all for a moment with a shout and on his accordion struck up "The Red Flag..." And they all followed him shouting). Milio's accordion defines the young age of the protagonists as unique and inherently passing: the accordion that is so important at their age will not be so for long. The boys' musical repertoire, in fact, shows some of those Americanizing influences lamented by sociologists in the 1960s already in place more than a decade earlier.

The notion of a transnational youth culture existing alongside local traditions even in the 1940s becomes evident during the young men's emigration. On the beach in Fiume, after a disappointing encounter with the local girls has dampened their spirits, Nini, Eligio, and their friends resort to familiar songs to alleviate their nostalgia. One of them starts singing "una delle loro più care canzoni di Ligugnana: 'Forse l'ultimo incontro d'amore, forse l'ultimo bacio sarà....'" The "beloved song from Ligugnana," however, is not a Friulian song, but rather the Italian version of "Red River Valley," the American folk song presumably popularized in Italy by the movie *The Grapes of Wrath* (*Furore*, 1940), released in 1947. The boys gladly sing along, and only later do they switch to traditional *villottas*.[36] The diffusion of American cultural products among Italian youth, unquestioned here, is highlighted elsewhere through Eligio's boogie-woogie performances:

> Era un ritmo di boogie, che Eligio cantava proprio come un negro: tving, ca ubang, bredar, lov, aucester, tving tving, morrou thear ... Non si riusciva a capire che cosa cantasse, se fosse uno scherzo o una cosa da pazzo, comunque non finiva mai, e lui rideva sempre battendo con le dita sulla scopa un ritmo perfetto, e cercando chissà dove le parole e il motivo: den bredar tuinding fear...

> It was a boogie rhythm that he sang – just like a Negro: *tving, ca ubang, bredar, lov, aucester, tving, tving, morou thear* ... It was impossible to understand what he was singing – whether it was a joke or some crazy idea – but at all events it never ended and he kept on laughing beating out a perfect rhythm on the broom and finding, from goodness knows where, words and tune: *den bredar tuinding fear...* (18; 8–9)

Using a broom as a fake guitar and making up "English" words for the lyrics, Eligio enthralls an audience at the tavern. The foreignness of this musical genre is signalled both by the language, which he mimics without understanding, and by the very characterization of the singer's performance, "just like a Negro." In clear counterpoint to the accordion, the guitar evokes, particularly in 1962, the youthful rebellion of rock and roll.[37] The contrast of tradition and rebellion becomes particularly visible during another performance, which Eligio offers, on the day of the protest, at the Faedis', a large peasant family related to Milio. The conflict between the paterfamilias' resigned acceptance of his fate, "Noi siamo nati per lavorare e sacrificarci: è inutile avere idee per la testa!" (124; 73; We are born to work and wear ourselves out, there's no use having any other idea in your head!), and Nini's revolutionary ideas is accompanied by a mixed soundtrack that reflects the cultural hybridity: on one hand Gufa, the Faedis' neighbour, sings a traditional folk song;

on the other Eligio repeats his "negro" performance on a broom and makes everyone dance and laugh. Although the red handkerchief tied around Nini's neck, "gli dava un'aria quasi da bandito" (125; 73; made him look almost like a bandit), the music re-establishes the harmony temporarily lost in the ideological debate:

> Tutti si misero a ridere, come prima, con le facce scottate dall'allegria e le bocche aperte, piegandosi sulla vita: i figli più forte dei grandi, approfittando della loro buona disposizione, e i grandi più forte dei figli, approfittando di quel momento di tregua dai pensieri e dalle preoccupazioni.

> Everyone began to laugh as before, their faces burning with merriment and their mouths open, leaning forward from the waist, the children more loudly than the grown-ups, taking advantage of their good humor, and the grown-ups louder than the children, enjoying this moment of respite from their thoughts and cares. (126; 74)

The palpable energy emanating from the young men's performance overcomes the generational clash and affects even the outcome of the rally:

> Quel po' di sole che era spuntato sul mezzogiorno tra le nuvole, era di nuovo scomparso, e intorno era tutto nero. Ma non nel cuore dei ragazzi.
> Pedalarono a tutta velocità verso Gruaro, cantando.
> A Gruaro era tutto pieno di gente, già pronta alla lotta: non si era mai vista tanta gioventù tutta insieme. Era come se, tre quattro anni prima, fossero venuti giù dai monti tutti i partigiani.

> That litte bit of sun which had peeped out at midday through the clouds had disappeared once more and it was black all round. But not in the boys' hearts.
> They pedaled towards Gruaro at full speed, singing.
> Gruaro was full of people all ready for the fight; no one had ever seen so many young people all together. It was as if, three or four years earlier, all the partisans had come down from the mountains. (126–7; 74)

The collective effort that follows, involving both young and old, women and men, is victorious: "...non c'era niente da fare, quel giorno, con la forza del popolo" (127; 74) ...there was nothing that could be done that day against the power of the people).

The Boys with the Striped T-Shirts

Punctuated by such populistic comments, and presenting young people so harmoniously integrated in adult society, *Sogno* seemed anachronistic in 1962. However, the publication of this nostalgic and utopian novel responded both to the pervasive discomfort regarding new youth lifestyles and to the hope instantly revived in left-wing parties by the protests against the Tambroni government, which sprung up in several Italian cities in the summer of 1960. The adolescents who had been causing concern for their political apathy only a few weeks before were suddenly applauded as protagonists of political demonstrations, echoes of which can be found in the rallies described in *Sogno*. Their group identity signalled by the striped T-shirts they wore, *i ragazzi dalle magliette a strisce* dominated the news and once again stirred debate: "Perché così giovani (Why so young)" was the title of the *l'Espresso* reportage on the demonstration held in Genoa on June 30, 1960, to protest the imminent congress of the neo-Fascist Movimento Sociale Italiano (MSI). One article reported how "swarms of young people took to the streets in Genova," and interpreted their presence alongside the old anti-Fascist leaders as giving new meaning to the event. A parallel was drawn between these youths and Italians who came of age in 1935–40, both generations expressing a gap between the modernization of the country and the senility of the institutions. (*l'Espresso*, July 10, 1960). The key role played by adolescents in opposing the MSI congress was further expressed in another article in *l'Espresso* through the headline "Balilla l'ha impedito (Balilla stopped it)," a reference to the Genoese boy who, according to a famous legend, had initiated a revolt against the Hapsburg troops in 1746.[38] The iconic striped T-shirts singled out the numerous young people who participated in the demonstrations in other cities in the following week: "Dovunque magliette a strisce"(*l'Espresso*, July 16, 1960; striped T-shirts everywhere), in Reggio Emilia and Palermo, Rome and Catania.

Although *l'Espresso* applauded young men who stood their ground more firmly than older protesters when the police asked them to disperse, ("there was no restraining the striped T-shirts" (July 10, 1960), *Vie Nuove* interpreted the presence of a young avant-garde in the protest mainly as a sign of unity between generations: "Anche a Palermo i giovani in prima fila" (Young people in front in Palermo as well) (July 9, 1960). By rekindling the opposition to Fascism, the summer events of 1960 were seen as the emergence of a "New Resistance," as

Miriam Mafai had wished in her closing comments on the survey on youth a few months earlier. Along the same lines, Pasolini restated his belief in generational continuity in his response to yet another letter from a reader asking for his opinion on the alleged disaffection of youth: "Sono convinto che il nuovo entusiasmo antifascista, la 'Nuova Resistenza' è un fatto generale, che include vecchi, anziani, giovani e giovanissimi" (*Vie Nuove*, July 30, 1960). He then added some comments, referring to his recent participation in a conference on "the anti-Fascist unity of intellectuals for the renewal of Italian society" organized in Reggio Emilia by the Unione Goliardica Italiana, a left-wing university student association. In his opinion, the importance of the Resistance in the political education of contemporary youth could not be underestimated:

> Che cos'hanno alle spalle, da che cultura provengono, i giovani di oggi? Hanno alle spalle la Resistenza, provengono dalla cultura che è stata definita "impegnata." Non c'è niente da fare: nelle scuole si può ignorare o mistificare, l'informazione ufficiale della radio, della televisione, dei giornali può essere reazionaria fin che vuole: ma il "reale" riferimento storico per un giovane è la Resistenza e la sua cultura. E la realtà si potrà nascondere: non la si potrà mai sopprimere.
>
> What is behind young people of today? What culture do they come from? The Resistance is behind them, they come from a culture of "commitment," as it has been defined. There is no way around it: schools may ignore or mystify it, radio, television, and newspapers may provide reactionary official information as much as they desire: but the "real" historical point of reference for young people is the Resistance and its culture. You can hide reality: you can never suppress it. (Ibid.)

The enthusiasm animating youths with striped T-shirts in the streets, and the "rational, critical, and methodological rigour" he had admired in young speakers at the Reggio Emilia convention, were the fruit of the continuity between three generations whose representatives had taken turns at the podium, "all sharing the same anti-Fascist and progressive spirit" (ibid.).[39] Despite the continuity, or perhaps because of it, the young anti-Fascists of 1960 could not be confused with their predecessors of 1940, in Pasolini's view. Rather, they were contemporary *eredi* to past generations, who had built on the "desperate and sometimes confused" struggle of their elders. Just as young Pasolini and his friends in the early 1940s saw themselves as heirs to an important tradition that ought to be filtered through modernity in order to shine forth, the young anti-Fascist intellectuals of 1960, according to Pasolini, owed their remarkable "maturity, ... consciousness, and their superior critical and rational spirit" to the earlier struggle that became "cultural legacy and tradition for today's youth" (ibid.).[40]

Viewed in the optimistic context of the "New Resistance" of 1960–1, *Il sogno di una cosa*, with its hopeful youth carefully poised between tradition and innovation, appears less surprising as a 1962 novel.[41] The combination of the eternal promise of youth, the political tradition of class struggle passed on from one generation to the next, and the spirit of the Resistance coming to the foreground again in the actions of those who were too young to have participated, is the expression not only of a nostalgic gaze on youth forever lost, but also of the utopian dream of the 1960s. In Pasolini's interpretation, a genealogy connected the partisans to the boys with the striped T-shirts. As *eredi* of the anti-Fascist movement of the 1940s, the striped T-shirts embodied the hope for a completion of the project left unfinished by their elders. Nini, Eligio, Onorino, and the other young men protesting for the De Gasperi law in the novel appeared thus as a midway link between the Resistance and the New Resistance. It is to this interpretation of youthful militancy that Pasolini would return on several instances in his interpretation of student movements later in the 1960s, as will be shown in the following chapters.

Second Best? Portraits of Young Women in the 1940s

The formula *"boys* with striped T-shirts," describing young representatives of the New Resistance, reflects the persisting gender imbalance in the discourse of youth of the early sixties.

Even though inquiries on youth revealed that gender relations had been changing since the end of the war, and that young women had begun a process of emancipation, which reduced both practical and representational discrimination, newspaper reports and photographs of the events of summer 1960 presented youth as an apparently gender-neutral (*giovani, ragazzi*) but, in reality, predominantly male experience.[42] The choice to privilege boys in the discourse of youth in *Sogno* reflects that imbalance. Throughout the novel, young women participate in the common rituals of adolescence that are associated with local festivals, Sunday dances, and carnivals: like boys, they put on costumes, dance, or wave almond blossom branches on the way to the *sagra*. Gender-specific practices, however, seem to exploit readers' expectations, often shaped by movies, regarding representation of young women in a rural environment at the end of the 1940s. Thus, young women embody the rural simplicity and idealized moral virtues, frequently identified with the notion of *popolare* in Italian culture, which contributed to the success of the *maggiorate* in 1950s Italian cinema.[43] The sisters from Gruaro, who appear at the beginning of the novel, evoke that popular model:

> Erano belle e ben accomodate: con le loro capigliature castane con la permanente di moda due o tre anni prima; abbondanti, del resto, fin sulle spalle; bei seni altrettanto abbondanti, sotto i vestiti leggeri, uno turchino e l'altro marrone, indossati per la prima volta il giorno precedente che era Pasqua, e ancora immacolati come sulla tavola della sartoria. Le sarte, anzi, erano esse stesse, e infatti le loro mani non erano arrossate e nel comportamento avevano qualcosa che le rendeva diverse dalle contadine.
>
> They were pretty and well got up with their chestnut hair and the permanent wave that had been the fashion two or three years earlier; well built, too, including their shoulders, with beautiful breasts under their light dresses, one turquoise and the other maroon. They had worn them for the first time the day before, which was Easter, and they were still as immaculate as they had been on the dressmaker's table. In fact, they themselves were the dressmakers and indeed their hands didn't look red and in their bearing they had something which set them off from the peasant girls. (14; 6)

Dark flowing hair, pretty faces, simple but neat dresses that highlight the curvaceous bodies connote a feminine model, popularized by Gina Lollobrigida and Sophia Loren, which condenses the stereotypes of an Italian national popular identity: "Buxom bodies are ... immersed in rural landscapes. They express the values of an idealized archaic society, in which poor but happy people bustle about: women whose eroticism is uncontainable but pure, and men who are inveterate but fundamentally harmless seducers."[44] Just like Nini and Eligio who approach them, the sisters from Gruaro bear the physical and cultural signs of the peasant world that produced them, but also traces of a change that is slowly infiltrating even rural communities after WWII. The bright spring dresses, kept neat and worn two days in a row speak of peasant frugality and common sense, while the hair, permed in the style of a couple of years before suggests the influence of imported fashion, accessed through magazines or movies. Their job as dressmakers sets them apart, by taking them out of the domestic sphere and into an environment that was central to the production of a gender- and age-specific subjectivity.

While the adoption of stylistic features of popular 1950s cinema regarding women contributes to the construction of a reassuring image of youth, less stereotypical representations show the limits of the coming-of-age of a nation that identifies itself with its young men. The women whom Nini and his friends meet on the beach near Fiume, during their immigration to Yugoslavia, present an alternative model of femininity that threatens Italian masculinity. Beautiful, statuesque, shining in the sun, the *fiumane* attract the desiring gaze of the Friulian boys, like *divas* on a screen, but keep them at a distance: "Pareva che fossero completamente felici, che non avessero bisogno di nulla, che non si potesse nemmeno toccarle" (49; 28; It seemed that they were completely happy, that they needed nothing, that one could not even touch them). They play with a beach ball, swim, or read under umbrellas, regardless of the attention of the young Italians. The superiority of the beautiful *fiumane* is confirmed when swaggering Nini tries to impress a girl who seems hesitant to dive into the waves:

> Il Nini si avvicinò a una di esse, e in italiano, con la sua pesante pronuncia friulana, le gridò allegro: "Mi aspetti, signorina, se no si annega." La ragazza gli diede un'occhiata inespressiva, poi rivolta alle compagne scoppiò a ridere. "Cosa vuole questo mulo!" gridò: e tutte insieme si gettarono verso il largo battendo perfettamente il crawl, e si allontanarono in direzione del molo. Il Nini non si fidava a andare dove non si toccava, Eligio e Germano sapevano nuotare solo a cane, e Basilio non sapeva nuotare per niente. Restarono vicino alla riva a sguazzare un po' tra le onde, poi riguadagnarono scornati la spiaggia; ma le mutande di tela, di cui già tanto si vergognavano, ora zuppe com'erano, restavano tutte incollate addosso più ridicole che mai.

> Nini approached one of them and called out cheerfully to her in Italian with his thick Friulian accent: "Wait for me, signorina, or else you'll drown!" The girl gave him an indifferent glance then turned to her companions and burst out laughing. "What does this donkey want?" she shouted; and together they made for the open sea doing the crawl with a perfect rhythm and swam away towards the mole. Nini dared not go out of his depth.

Eligio and Germano could only paddle like dogs, and Basilio could not swim a stroke. They stayed near the shore splashing about in the water then went shamefacedly back up the beach; their cloth pants, which had already made them feel ashamed, were soaked and clinging to them more ridiculously than ever. (50; 28)

The women's "fare franco e spigliato" intimidates Nini and his friends, for whom women's independence clearly represents a novelty. The *fiumane*'s athletic prowess puts the men to shame, mocking their virility. Unlike the Italian *divas* Gina Lollobrigida and Sophia Loren, unlike Silvana Mangano in *Bitter Rice*, whose sexually charged but non-threatening young bodies denote the rural and archaic landscape that became the "privileged locus for refounding national identity after the fall of Fascism," the young *fiumane* in *Sogno* embody a contested site of Italian identity.[45] Fiume's century-old struggle for independence and the importance of its annexation in nation-building rhetoric since WWI are reflected in the alternative model of femininity the women propose. Completely unprepared for a relationship with young women outside the codes inherited from previous generations, Nini and his friends reveal the limits of their own modernity and of their country's. Their nostalgia for Friuli and for Italy, manifested on this occasion, involves a desire for familiar feminine models that allow them to prove their masculinity: "'Avere qui la Onorina, o la Ines,' disse Eligio. 'O la Gemma ...' continuò Basilio. 'O quella p ... della Regina,' aggiunse il Nini, 'vi ricordate di quella festa che l'ho accompagnata dentro il suo orto?'" (52; 29; "'Just to have Onorina here – or Ines,' said Eligio. 'Or Gemma,' Basilio went on. 'Or that whore, Regina,' added Nini. 'Do you remember that fair when I went into her orchard with her?'"). As a glimpse into Italy's coming-of-age, this encounter shows how the models for change in young women's codes of behaviour lie just outside the national border, within reach, but not quite appropriated yet.

The second part of the novel, focusing more specifically on young women and their rituals, is a rare occurrence in Pasolini's fiction. While the importance of the female sphere in the author's own coming-of-age helps explain the central position women gain in a novel set in Friuli, such centrality does not correspond to an equal part in the generational portrait of the "best of youth."[46] Unlike the sisters from Gruaro and the *fiumane*, the Faedis sisters are neither reassuring *maggiorate* nor threatening independent women. Their engagement with the changing youth culture of their time is limited, as are their possibilities for arriving at a gender and age-specific identity. Only a few social occasions allow them to define themselves collectively as young women. While volunteering at the local convent to prepare the annual children's pageant, the Faedis sisters are "overjoyed" at the prospect of wearing angel costumes for the carnival. The reason for the girls' exhilaration becomes clear when Ilde sighs "Ah ... avere la permanente!" and "nessuna, neanche le più sagge, protestarono a quel sospiro. Pensavano tutte a come sarebbe stata bene la stella in fronte con una pettinatura all'angelo, o alla Giovanna d'Arco" (193; 115; "Ah ... to have a perm!" ... No one, not even the best behaved, protested at that sigh. They were thinking how good the star would have looked on their brows with their hair done like an angel's or Joan of Arc's). Rather than a religious experience, the girls view the pageant as an occasion for dressing up together, as if for going to a dance. They dream of permed hair, hairstyles modelled after movie stars, and proper mirrors in which to admire themselves instead of simple window panes:

> e ridevano per il compiacimento di vedersi, benché così diafane contro il vetro, vestite a quel modo, tanto che stentavano a riconoscere nelle proprie immagini il colore di fragola delle loro guancie, che loro consideravano volgare, la goccia di luce del loro occhio allegro, i seni gonfi e dritti mal nascosti dalla tela ruvida.

> And [they] laughed to hide their pleasure at seeing themselves dressed like that in the glass, even if it were so diaphanously that they could scarcely make out their own images of the strawberry color of their cheeks, which they considered vulgar, the spot of light in their merry eyes, their breasts swollen and hard and scarcely hidden by the thick material. (194; 115)

No longer identifiable by their regular dresses, which mark their social or familial affiliation, they are now simply young women and can behave as such. The costume frees them from their usual restraint and allows them to behave more freely:

> un contegno così libero e allegro da riuscire anche un pochino offensivo nei confronti degli altri, se non fosse stato per la loro espansiva giovinezza. "Benedetta gioventù" aveva l'aria di dire il parroco prendendo dal vassoio un amaretto, o bevendo una sorsata di liquore.

> [They behaved] so freely and gaily that it might have been a little offensive to the others but for their expansive youth. "Bless the young people!" the

parish priest seemed to be saying as he took an almond biscuit from the plate or sipped at the liqueur. (194; 116)

Their youth is brought forward by the adults as an explanation for their otherwise inexcusable conduct. The episode presents the girls' activity at the convent as an excuse to be girls, to dress up and be someone else for a few hours, with the blessing of the adults. The young women's gaze upon each other and upon themselves as others in the reflection on the windowpane facilitates, in a Lacanian framework, the construction of a young female subjectivity. The group dress-up experience can be seen as an early form of that process of self-identification through photography and film that accelerates and expands the construction of young feminine identity in the 1950s.[47]

The not-so subtle juxtaposition of Cecilia and Pia, the most prominent female characters in the novel, as alternative partners for Nini, suggests that their functionality with respect to his identity prevails over a characterization of the young women *per se*. They embody opposite models of femininity, which Nini must reject or negotiate in order to affirm his own version of "the best of youth." The shy and pious Cecilia represents the rural familial order and traditional church values that young men like Nini are challenging. She wears her blonde hair in a braid, goes to vespers on Sunday afternoon, and feels guilty when she briefly looks at the dance floor on her way to church. With her "occhi di agnellino" (126; lamb's eyes) she stands for the pastoral notion of youth that connotes innocence and unawareness. The failed relationship between Nini and Cecilia signals the clash between different views of youth and social organization: the rural family, a patriarchal structure in which, as Mitterauer shows, young people are defined by their dependency on adults, whose work is autonomous; and the factory, where all workers are paid and subordinate regardless of age, and young people can have a more independent voice.[48] While for the Faedis "le cose non erano cambiate e erano rimaste sempre uguali, ... casa e chiesa casa e chiesa" (161; 94–5; things had not changed but remained the same ... home and church, home and church), Nini has changed his status. He works at the local powder factory, dresses well, and sports an air of superiority, like a city boy: he is a "giovanotto progredito," who finds authority in his age and aspires to improve his station.

Beautiful and restless Pia, on the other hand, is explicitly presented as a product of that process of identity formation through "the gazes that young women directed at images, shot in public and private spaces, of themselves and others."⁴⁹ A brunette with long, sleek hair flowing on her back, a "sly air of *femme fatale*" (aria sorniona e fatale), and eyes that "guardavano da sotto in su, imploranti o ingenui, come quelli delle attrici" (185; 110; looked up, imploring or naive, like an actress's eyes), Pia has an exotic look and a mysterious past:

> ...Pia era partita per la città, proprio il contrario di quello che facevano tutti, che dalla città sfollavano verso la campagna. Ma lei aveva una zia, a Padova o a Mestre o a Verona, e là sperava di sistemarsi, dicevano. Cosa avesse poi fatto non si sapeva. C'erano delle chiacchiere, in giro, ma nessuno poteva dire niente. Adesso Pia cantava, la domenica, con l'orchestrina di una sala da ballo, a Pordenone.
>
> ... Pia had left for the city, which was the very opposite of what everyone else was doing, for people were evacuating the cities to come to the country. But she had an aunt in Padua or Mestre or Verona and hoped to set herself up there – or so they said. What she had done then no one knew. There was gossip going about but no one could say anything. Now Pia sang on Sundays with the little orchestra in a dance-hall in Pordenone. (169; 99)

While Cecilia is ashamed to dance on Sundays, Pia sings in a dance hall, reads *Grand Hotel*, and allows Nini to be the modern young man he wants to be:

> Sale da ballo, orchestrine, cantanti: figurarsi! Erano tutte cose che erano come una luce dentro di lui: la luce che lo aveva sempre fatto diverso dagli altri ... Era sempre stato a quel modo: un cittadino, non un contadino. Come Pia. E così cominciò a parlarle di tutte quelle cose lì, coi gomiti sul bancone, e il boccolo nero sulla fronte: sale da ballo, orchestrine, cantanti...
>
> Dance-halls, orchestras, singers – imagine that! They were all things that were like a light inside him – the light which had always made him different from the others ... He had always been like that, a town boy not a peasant boy. Like Pia. And so he began to talk about all these things with his elbows on the bar and the black lock on his forehead: ballrooms, orchestras, singers... (170; 100)

He spares her the details of his political activity "perché le donne di solito non vogliono sentir neanche parlare di politica" (172; 101; because usually women don't want to hear any mention of politics), but she responds "graciously" (con grazia): "Eh, andrà su il socialismo!" (172; 101; eh, socialism will be on the up and up!), thus perfectly playing the part of the emancipated yet non-threatening woman that suits the "giovanotto progredito" Nini thinks he is. Not unlike Silvana, the rice harvester played by Silvana Mangano in *Bitter Rice* (Giuseppe De Santis, 1949), Pia appears as an ingénue whose perception of reality, and her relationship with Nini in particular, is mediated by the photo-romances she reads: "Pia accettava quel rapporto con aria un po' sognante, come se si trattasse di una cosa che succedeva non a lei, ma a una delle ragazze dei suoi romanzi: e posava continuamente, muta e buona" (186; 110; Pia accepted their relationship with a slightly dreamy air as if it was something happening not to her but to one of the girls in her romantic stories and was constantly silent and well-behaved).[50] Thus thematized, such mediation is exposed as inappropriate, but no alternatives are available to her besides posing as either *femme fatale* or wide-eyed child. She initially mystifies Nini, but soon becomes a victim "of his and of her own weakness" (188; 139; di lui e della propria debolezza), and recedes into the background after her pregnancy and consequent marriage.

Two Weddings and a Funeral: Rites of Passage

Nini and Pia's marriage, prompted by her pregnancy, does not constitute a defining act in the way marriages do in many traditional *Bildungsromane*, marking the end of a process and bestowing meaning on the events that lead up to it.[51] Consistently with the novel's celebration of the ephemerality of youth, coming-of-age is frustrated and the traditional rites of passage are devalued. In general, becoming adult is presented in terms of loss. Rather than signalling the successful completion of a *Bildung* process, Nini's marriage announcement to his friends underscores his defeat. Walking behind the carnival floats, a group of young men exchange wisecracks, unrecognizable inside the giant heads of the costumes they are wearing, "due o tre metri di diametro, che ballonzolavano contro il cielo, sulle gambette di chi li portava: con le bocche spalancate che ridevano, gli occhi fissi circondati di rughe, e i pomelli lustri" (198; 118; two or three metres in diameter, which bobbed against the sky on the little legs of the persons who wore them, with gaping, laughing mouths, staring eyes surrounded by wrinkles and red, shiny cheekbones). Taunted by his friends, in a drunken haze, one of them admits to his imminent shotgun wedding. Only when the speaker removes his balloon-head to unzip his trousers and join his friends urinating in a field do we discover his identity: "era il Nini, ubriaco morto, bruciante di sole e di vino" (199; 119; it was Nini, dead drunk, burnt up by the sun and the wine). The anticlimactic announcement, overheard by the readers alongside heartbroken Cecilia, expresses the failure of the promise of youth.

Cecilia's consequent decision to enter the novitiate, the rite of passage traditionally assigned to unmarriageable young women, is also presented as a renunciation of life. Her bride-like departure on a horse-drawn cart, amid the glorious summer nature, functions as the counterpoint to the Easter Monday scene opening the novel: there, young women and men rode into town singing and waving blossom branches, in joyful anticipation of the *sagra*; here, in the silent summer afternoon, "in mezzo a quel gran mare di verde, coi fiori campestri rossi e azzurri a frane pei prati" (203; 121; in the midst of the great sea of green with red and blue wild flowers split over the fields), only two sounds can be heard: "il canto di un usignolo, tra le fratte, e il pianto sommesso di Cecilia" (the song of the nightingale among the thickets and Cecilia's low weeping). In contrast to the springtime celebration of youth opening the novel, the magnificent ripeness in this scene is an anticipation of death.[52]

Eligio's death, which concludes *Sogno*, is as necessary as Genesio's drowning in *Ragazzi di vita*. The coming-of-age, devalued in Nini and Pia, painfully self-inflicted by Cecilia, is reversed in the case of Eligio, whose illness causes a regression to childhood: "Non era Eligio quel ragazzo disteso nel lettino della corsia. La faccia consumata, i capelli lunghi, le spalle che sporgevano dal lenzuolo, parevano quelli di un bambino di tredici anni." (207; 123; it was not Eligio, this boy lying in the little bed in the ward. The ravaged face, the long hair, the shoulders sticking out of the sheets, seemed those of a child of thirteen). Thus transformed, he is unrecognizable to Nini and Milio, who cannot connect that childlike body with the young man whom they had met only a year before:

> il sorriso di quella sera ... quando si era messo a cantare in inglese, con la scopa per chitarra, inventando le parole, o quella sera quando aveva strappato la bandiera dal suo angolo dietro l'armadio e l'aveva agitata sulle teste dei compagni.
>
> The smile of that evening ... when he had started to sing in English with the broom for a guitar, inventing the words, or that evening when he had

seized the flag from its corner behind the cupboard and had waved it over the heads of the comrades. (155; 125)

The key moments in which youth appeared as promise – the Easter Monday festival, the boogie-woogie, the rally – are definitely lost. Eligio's death thematizes the impossible reconciliation of that view of youth with any sort of coming-of-age. Genesio's drowning, in *Ragazzi*, highlighted Riccetto's inevitable maturation as a loss of the prerogatives of being young, in the constantly changing world of urban peripheries; Eligio's death seals the utopia of youth as a culturally hybrid experience, in which tradition and modernity coexist in the realm of memory. His funeral replaces the wedding as the rite of passage that concludes many conventional coming-of-age novels and marks the protagonist's socialization. When Eligio and his friends, carrying his casket, step out of the narrative, there are no younger clones of Nini to take their place, as there had been a little Riccetto. Unlike the *gioventù perduta* who alarmed adults in the late 1950s, the lost youth of *Sogno*, presented as unique and ephemeral, produces nostalgia. Like the striped T-shirts in the summer of 1960, the political engagement of young people alongside their fathers could give hope to the Communists who wanted to believe in the possibility of a "New Resistance."

As a contribution to contemporary discourse on youth, the novel reflects the ambivalence of adults towards younger generations: the mix of fear and exhilaration that met the display of new cultural forms, the projection of desires and aspirations onto the heirs of an unfinished revolution, the sense of loss inherent in any recollection of one's past. Precisely in this ambivalence lies youth's ultimate attraction for Pasolini: the synthesis of eternal pastoral and rebelliously new, the coexistence of individual memory and generational call, and the recognition of a genealogy based on a disidentification with received authority. As a reconstruction of young people's experience in a past era, *Sogno* both explicitly relies on the author's personal recollections, tinted with nostalgia, thereby forsaking any pretence at objective historiography, and acknowledges the role of other texts in creating our understanding of the past.[53] The latter is especially true of the representation of women, which is explicitly mediated by popular film. The distance between the world depicted and the time of publication is not completely erased by the desire to recover that perfect notion of youth. Instead, the novel tries to bring readers affectively closer to a historically specific experience of youth, while keeping us aware of both its distance from the present and the subjective nature of our relationship with the past. *Sogno* expresses in prose form the "amor de loihn" that Contini had recognized in the poems of *La meglio gioventù*: an affection that is nourished by distance.[54]

As a nostalgic reconstruction of adolescence in 1940s Friuli, *Sogno* offers a myth that is both regressive and utopian: youth, as eternal signifier of innocence and as historical subject of subversion, is imagined in the past because it cannot be projected in the future. The nostalgic operation that posits loss – of personal youth and of the sense of harmony projected upon the past – as intrinsic and necessary, "can be perceived as a way of coming to terms with the past, as enabling it to be exorcised in order that society, and individuals, can move on. In other words, while not necessarily progressive in itself, nostalgia can form part of a transition to progress and modernity."[55] In foregrounding the subjective nature of historical recollection, this nostalgia novel draws our attention to the conflicting desires to identify an unalterable essence of youth and to posit it as the embodiment of innovation.

4 Revolutionary Youth: From the Page, to the Streets, to the Screen

As the 1960s progressed, and young people assumed a more prominent role in the social and cultural transformations taking place in Italy, Pasolini's evolving interest in youth reflected ideological, aesthetic, and personal changes. The tension between youth as a literary ideal and an increasingly defined social subject became more evident, as Pasolini seemingly tried to understand young people's actions through poetic symbols. The multiplication of means of expression available to him, which came to include, most prominently, cinema, provided newly effective ways to convey the dynamism of youth, its revolutionary force, and its powerful impact on consumer society. Just like the dialect of Casarsa in the poems of the 1940s, and the Roman slang in the novels of the 1950s, cinema allowed the poet to capture youth in its specific "reality" in a way that written poetry no longer could. Representing youth meant allowing young people to speak for themselves on screen, as they did in the documentary *Comizi d'amore*, but also reflecting on issues of representation, when the paradigms of narrative realism became outmoded. In *Uccellacci e uccellini*, the core of such reflection, the hybrid quality of youth that shaped all of Pasolini's oeuvre, was embodied in the boy/character Ninetto. He pushed the boundaries between reality and fiction, thus exemplifying that unresolved tension.

The Generation of 1968

In Italy, as in many Western countries, young people became the protagonists of unprecedented collective action in the late 1960s. The Italian movement that entered national memory with the name of its peak year, the *Sessantotto* (1968), found its origins in the social and cultural changes that had started at least a decade earlier. A substantial economic growth, favoured by Italy's opening to international markets, technological advances, and low cost of labour, had generally improved the standard of living for large segments of the population, albeit with enduring geographical differences. The consequences of the so-called "economic miracle," that is, increased per capita income, significant urbanization, geographical and social mobility, and access to new pastimes, favoured the development of a youth culture and generational identity, which transcended regional specificity. A long-awaited school reform, in 1962, extended free and compulsory school attendance to age fourteen, and increased the number of students who pursued higher education. Combined with growing access to television, these economic and cultural changes also prompted the first actual linguistic unification of a country that had debated a *questione della lingua* since the sixteenth century.[1]

The *sessantottini*, as the young protesters were called, were the first generation of Italians to grow up in a republic: they had no direct knowledge of either the war or the Fascist regime, and only a second-hand memory of the Resistance – a defining experience for their parents – which they acquired either through oral history, specific institutional initiatives, or movies.[2] They were growing up in the forward-looking optimism of the reconstruction, among the opportunities for economic and social advancement made available by the "boom." Thanks to greater access to education and employment, they had more chances to socialize with peers than had been available to past generations.[3] Direct encounters between young people of different backgrounds through increased geographic mobility and indirect communication through mass media favoured the creation of a distinct youth culture, which prevailed over regional and national specificities, and of a generational identity that transcended class and nationality.[4] Many young people manifested discomfort with the individualism and consumerism that sustained the "economic miracle," and found in peer groups the venues for expression of alternative lifestyles. They were likely to experience inequalities related to too-slow changes in gender relations, or discrimination when mass south-north immigration brought into close contact cultures that had no previous experience of cohabitation. Many recognized the shortcomings of a university which, having remained unchanged since the 1920s, was ill-equipped to respond to the needs of the more diverse student population entering it in the 1960s. However, the protest soon went beyond personal experience and trauma, beyond the specifics of curricular choices and union demands, to question the foundations of the society in which this generation grew up: materialism and consumerism as the new idols of post-war prosperity; the family as an institution that reproduced at the cellular level the age and gender imbalance existing in society at large.

Ambivalence towards parental figures, both on the Left and on the Right, played a crucial role in the culture that the new generation wanted to establish. Although parents – militant Catholics, Communists, anti-Fascists – sometimes provided the values that nourished the children's sense of justice, their culture demanded "a non linear emancipation, for it must be a double emancipation, from society and from the family."[5] Whether they reacted to conservative or progressive biological fathers, young people expressed their position as a rupture with the past. In questioning fathers they questioned male, church, state, and party authority. The historical parties of the Left, the PCI and PSI, were among the parental figures, with which the young maintained an ambivalent relationship. Although Marxist interpretation of the economic transformation of Italy saw a comeback, particularly in reviews like *Quaderni Rossi* and *Quaderni piacentini*, the reformist approach of the PSI and "integrated opposition" of the PCI were perceived as other "fathers" complicit with the corrupt political system. The Socialists' decision to enter a coalition with the Christian Democrats contributed to that image, while the Communist Party drew criticism for being strongly hierarchical and unresponsive to the substantial changes that massive immigration and urbanization had caused in the composition of the workers' movement. Relationships between the emerging youth movement and the PCI were also complicated by the party's resistance to the growing importance of popular culture in the 1960s: "Deeply suspicious of what they considered to be the conservative agenda lying behind mass culture," the party insisted on "high culture" as the instrument for cultural emancipation.[6] This approach, which had enhanced the cultural formation of young people in the previous decades, proved less suitable for a generation that had greater access to public education and mass cultural products.

The fact that the emerging student and workers' movement also had strong generational identity complicated its relationship with the historical Left. The rhetoric whereby youth had been elevated to political myth and symbol of the Fascist regime prevented its becoming a founding myth of the anti-Fascist Resistance. Although many of the partisans were indeed young men and women, as a reaction to the Fascist *"giovinezza,"* the anti-Fascist movement adopted a more inclusive discourse, which emphasized brotherhood and community rather than youthful initiative. Even in post-liberation years, the need to contain the generational conflict between returning servicemen and younger people competing for jobs encouraged the two major political parties, the Christian Democrats and the Communist Party, to limit initiatives celebrating youth as an intrinsic value, while trying to attract younger generations to inclusive activities. The generational identity that sustained the *sessantottini*, which appeared stronger than other allegiances, took older generations by surprise. In an attempt to reach out to the young, the PCI and PSI resorted to cultural representations of the Resistance.

Encouraged by the participation of young people in the anti-Fascist rallies of July 1960, older members of the PCI and PSI saw elements of continuity between the protest taking shape in the mid-1960s and a revolution that they had not been able to complete twenty years earlier. The passionate and collective nature of a movement that seemed to cross class boundaries rekindled the spirit of the Resistance, at least in the eyes of the older generations. "The Resistance continues with you," declared the "one-time Resistance prime minister" Ferruccio Parri in April 1966 to a protest gathering at the University of Rome after the death of Paolo Rossi, a student of architecture who had been attacked by neo-Fascists while distributing political leaflets.[7] The younger generations, however, would soon distance themselves from that legacy and question the outcomes of what many perceived as a failed revolution. This view, held by many young people in the non-Communist Left, inspired a rewriting of history that, David Forgacs argues, challenged "the main legitimating narrative of the post-war state, that of the Italian Republic as the product of the Resistance (1943–45)."[8] Young activists contested the inherited narrative of the Resistance as a cohesive phenomenon and either highlighted its failures or reread its accomplishments as the product of specific groups, which had been silenced in those inclusive accounts, such as Communists, or women.[9] While the older generations were trying to claim continuity between the young protesters and themselves in the name of the Resistance, the young sought to establish their project as alternative to that legacy, while drawing attention to the links between Fascism and post-war anti-Fascism.

A New Poetry of Youth: New Linguistic Questions and the Cinema of Poetry

The irreverent critique of authority on the part of young people could be expected to find a natural ally in Pasolini. As shown in the previous chapter, he had demonstrated a positive interest in the "youths with striped T-shirts," when they appeared in anti-government rallies during the summer of 1960. On the one hand they could be considered as the early representatives of a movement which, by the mid-sixties, more and more frequently manifested youth's dissent through strikes and occupations. On the other, the cultural continuity perceived or projected upon the young protesters of 1960 by older generations could not as easily be recognized in the *sessantottini*. Pasolini's changing relationship with youth in the course of the sixties was therefore characterized by an ambivalence similar to that experienced by other paternal authorities. That he could be counted among the "fathers" was both a factor of his advancing age and of political and cultural formation. Having turned forty in 1962, Pasolini belonged, chronologically, to the fathers' generation. Despite the evident physical fitness and contemporary dress style, he was deeply aware of aging, particularly after an ulcer hemorrhage forced him to stay in bed for a month, in the spring of 1966: "Certi mattini, al risveglio, il pensiero dell'età è come una folgore. Mi sono sentito vecchio per la prima volta." (Certain mornings, upon waking up, the thought of aging is like a thunderbolt. I felt old for the first time.)[10] His belief in humanistic culture as an instrument of emancipation and his renewed faith, albeit practiced in unorthodox form, in the PCI, aligned him with the cultural authorities that the *sessantottini* questioned. However, his ideal identification with youth continued to characterize his work. His intense intellectual activity in the mid-1960s – shooting movies, writing film scripts, treatments, verse tragedies, essays on literature, linguistics, cinema, plans for a new literary review – suggests a high degree of energy and a desire to renew the intellectual's mandate with new critical and creative instruments. Moreover, his desire to continue representing the alterity of youth in a form appropriate to the new cultural landscape motivated his experimentation with cinema.

Pasolini interpreted the radical transformation that Italy was undergoing in the "economic miracle" as a bourgeois coming-of-age, which homogenized a young linguistically and culturally diverse country according to a foreign model of modernity and development.

His assessment of the country's *Bildung* process, like his critique of bourgeois models of development in his Roman novels, focused on the inherent losses. Improvement of material conditions came at the price of standardization of experience, reduction of regional diversity, and linguistic homogenization. He promptly recognized the younger generations as protagonists of this process: embracing innovation and peer identity they distanced themselves from cultural models inherited from their parents, thus accelerating the disappearance of century-old regional traditions. Their new position with respect to neo-capitalist society imposed a new conceptualization of youth for the author, who identified with adolescents' existence outside the social order. By participating in consumer society, and then more specifically by undertaking action to change that social order, they lost the marginality that guaranteed their redemptive power in Romantic and bourgeois notions of adolescence. Ceasing to embody difference, they became signifiers of conformity in Pasolini's analysis of contemporary Italy. As social agents in a bourgeois system, they perpetuated its pragmatic and rational order, instead of subverting it. Pasolini's change of poetics in the 1960s constituted an attempt to redefine his relationship with youth, given the changed conditions in which both he and young people could impact society. Cinema, poetry, and essays offered different and complementary ways to advance the "saga of the young" in the decade of youth.

The transformation of young people into social agents and the erosion of regional differences, both products of the nation's modernization in post-war years, were equally significant factors in the redefinition of Pasolini's poetics in the 1960s. His reflections on the spreading of a national language focused on the consequences of that standardization on literature. The 1964 essay "New Linguistic Questions" outlined how Italy's *de facto* trilingualism, that is, the coexistence of a national literary language, a bourgeois language of common use, and a myriad of locally spoken dialects, used to guarantee numerous possibilities for writers' experimentation. Expressiveness, in Pasolini's view, could be found in the poetic contamination of high and low, of earthy and sublime, particularly through the use of free indirect discourse, as exemplified in his novel *Ragazzi di vita*. At the beginning of the 1960s, however, the layering of sublime, humanistic, and popular languages was challenged by a new linguistic phenomenon, which exercised a homogenizing power over the existing strata. He described that as a "new technological language" radiating from the economically and culturally hegemonic centres of the North to the rest of Italy. Since "the guiding spirit of language [was] no longer literature but technology," its emphasis was on communication rather than expressiveness.[11] According to Pasolini, the linguistic standardization facilitated by education reforms, increased circulation of newspapers and magazines, and particularly the influence of television, reduced the expressive possibilities of literary language. The polysemy available to the poet in a stratified language in which centuries of literary usage coexisted with regional and class-specific modes of expression, could no longer be found in a national language which, in aiming for exactitude, reduced regional and class difference.

Perceiving youth's specificity as no longer a factor of social or linguistic marginality, Pasolini tried to capture it through an expressive medium that was not affected by language homogenization: film. While he deplored a crisis of humanistic values and a progressive distancing of Italian language from its literary origins, he advocated an expansion of the notion of language to include cinema: "Cinema is a language ... a language which compels the enlargement of the concept of language."[12] In the essays "The Cinema of Poetry" and "The Written Language of Reality," Pasolini outlined a theory of cinema as a new poetic language for the neo-capitalist era. While a rapidly changing social reality was outrunning traditional, humanistic language, cinema expressed "reality with reality." It was "nothing more than the 'written' manifestation of a natural, total language, which [was] the acting of reality" (l'agire nella realtà).[13] Cinema could thus achieve that physical, visceral contact with youth that Pasolini had established in the 1950s through a controlled immersion in the linguistic reality of the Roman *ragazzi*. Unlike the new national language, which aimed for exactitude, cinema could both appropriate contemporary reality and maintain its polysemy. Since "life [was] unquestionably drawing away from the classical humanistic ideals and [was] losing itself in pragmatics," cinema could be the "written language of this pragmatism. But it may also be its salvation, precisely because it expresse[d] it – and expresse[d] it *from the inside*, producing itself from itself and reproducing it."[14] Pasolini's growing interest in cinema was thus, as Maurizio Viano claims, "among other things, an attack on humanist ideology," but an attack conducted in the name of a renewal of the poet's mandate.[15] Pasolini assigned to cinema the poetic function that words were unable to sustain in a neo-capitalist world. Through complementary cinematic theory and practice, he explored the expressive possibilities and critical potential of this medium. He also reaffirmed the critical function of poetic discourse with respect to the bourgeois world, even when traditional humanistic culture was challenged by neo-capitalistic materialism. Film allowed him to express effectively the new reality and establish a channel of communication with the subjects of the new power. In order to continue to exercise his critical function, the poet was forced to create a new kind of poetic discourse. The cinema of poetry, with its intrinsic ambiguity, carried out that task.

Thanks to its expressive possibilities, cinema became a new means for Pasolini to critique the transformation that Italy was undergoing. It also allowed him to assign a critical role to youth, alternative to the actions undertaken by young people in the streets, which he frequently criticized in articles and poems in the same period. Their physical presence was the transgressive gesture that could throw a wrench in the conformist machinery of the new "technological" language. If, in the context of Italy's development in the 1950s, street kids had led readers through an alternative coming-of-age, in the framework of emerging neo-capitalism young people on the screen became the last bulwark against the advance of conformity.

Although his movies were in all likelihood not conceived specifically for a young audience, Pasolini associated movie-going with his own cultural apprenticeship. Admittedly, he had cultivated an interest in film during his youth in Bologna, where he attended screenings organized by the *CineGUF*, the film section of his Fascist University Group, and followed the recommendations of his art history professor Roberto Longhi, a film enthusiast. In Rome, the intense activity at *Cinecittà* studios in the 1950s and '60s provided him with work as a screenwriter.[16] However, when he started shooting his first film, he did so without any technical training. The vision of the young *borgatari* in *Accattone*, inspired by fifteenth-century painting, translated onto film the lessons learned in Longhi's art history courses.[17] After *Accattone*, which he presented at the Venice Film Festival in 1961, and until his death in 1975, Pasolini wrote and shot at least one film a year. He wrote additional screenplays for films that were never made, and elaborated a cinematic theory.[18] Most of his twenty-two films focus on young protagonists: the *ragazzo di vita* Ettore in *Mamma Roma*, the innocent son Ninetto in *Uccellacci e uccellini*, young Oedipus in *Edipo Re*, Riccetto in *La sequenza del fiore di carta*, the divine guest in *Teorema*, the young cannibal and the bourgeois rebels in the intertwined narratives of *Porcile*, and the boys and girls who were victims of the libertines' desires in *Salò, o le 120 giornate di Sodoma*. Even when youth is not ostensibly the main subject of a film, as in *Il Vangelo secondo Matteo* or the *Trilogy of Life*, narrative and casting choices focus the viewer's attention on young people. Through cinema he created a "saga of the young," as French philosopher Michel Foucault later defined Pasolini's cinematographic opus, highlighting with this definition both the sustained presence of young people in film after film, and the celebratory approach characterizing their representation.[19]

Coming of Age on Screen: *Comizi d'amore*

Even though young men (and some young women) are central to all of Pasolini's cinema, it is particularly when the films comment on the neo-capitalist transformation of Italy that their screen presence expresses different issues from the previously explored individual and national coming-of-age. In other words, while *Accattone* (1961) and *Mamma Roma* (1962), set in the Roman *borgate*, for the most part reproduce in visual form the concerns addressed in the Roman novels, the 1963 documentary *Comizi d'amore* (*Love Meetings*) inaugurates a mode of representation of youth that is more specifically suited to the *giovani* of the sixties. *Comizi d'amore* marks in fact the first screen appearance of modern youth in Pasolini's films, and arguably represents the only attempt on his part, albeit minimal, to let the young speak for themselves. Despite the scarce success it had in the theatres, it is also of particular interest in a study of Pasolini's relationship with youth because it foregrounds the tension between youth as a symbol for the author's concerns about society and young people as subjects who resist his pedagogical impetus.

In all likelihood inspired by the numerous *reportages* on various aspects of Italian life, which, as seen in the previous chapter, populated magazines and television programs between the late 1950s and early 1960s, *Comizi d'amore* takes the form of an inquiry. Through a series of interviews conducted by Pasolini himself, people of different ages, geographic origins, and social backgrounds share their views on sexuality. Conversations with psychoanalyst Cesare Musatti and novelist Alberto Moravia, and with journalists and writers Camilla Cederna, Oriana Fallaci, and Adele Cambria, inserted among street interviews, offer intellectual analyses of the commoners' responses. The interview format corresponds to the stated intent for the film: to collect opinions, experiences, points of view from a variety of Italians, as a preliminary step in a pedagogical project that Pasolini defines as a "lotta contro i 'mostri,' ossia l'ignoranza, le aberrazioni della ragione" (a fight against "monsters," that is, ignorance [and] the aberrations of reason) and "aiuto terapeutico ... a chi soffra, direttamente o indirettamente, del peso dell'ignoranza, dell'inibizione ipocrita, o, più largamente, dei pregiudizi che regolano i rapporti sessuali" (therapeutic help for those who bear, directly or indirectly, the brunt of ignorance, of hypocritical inhibition, or, more broadly, of prejudice regulating sex).[20] The survey is apparently sustained by what Foucault would define as the "repressive hypothesis," a way of speaking about sex in terms of repression, which provides those who break the silence with the so-called "speaker's benefit": "If sex is repressed, that is, condemned to prohibition, nonexistence, and silence, then the mere fact that one is speaking about it has the appearance of a deliberate transgression."[21] However, despite the stated intent, the most revealing information comes from meetings, physical encounters between viewers and interviewees, rather than from the mere content of their answers.[22]

Unlike the French documentary *Chronique d'un été* (Chronicle of a Summer; Jean Rouch, Edgar Morin, 1961), a sociological and ethnographic project that provided a model of *cinéma-verité*, the interviews in *Comizi d'amore* do not allow viewers to get to know the subjects or explore their lifestyles. Instead, Pasolini meets interviewees in the streets, outside factories, or at work in the fields, questions them point-blank, and prods them, often seemingly more intent on exposing their ignorance than on collecting information. He begins by asking rather abstract questions: "Is sexuality an important problem for you?" "Do you think that sexual problems should be discussed openly?" "Does the thought of having a sex life give you happiness or anguish?" "[Miss,] why did you choose the path of honesty instead of prostitution?" Answers are unsurprisingly vague, until questions eventually become more specific: "Do you think that young people today enjoy greater freedom than when you were young?" "What would you do if you discovered that your son has some sexual anomaly?" "Are you for or against divorce?" The announced topic of "love" is extended to include power relations between men and women, the importance of virginity, the function of prostitution with respect to marriage and society. Predictably conservative constituencies, like Calabrian farmers or Sicilian men, maintain traditional views on marriage, the role of women, and virginity. Predictably more emancipated groups, like Bologna university students, resolutely state that they have no sexual taboos.

Men and women of different ages and geographical and social backgrounds invariably condemn homosexuality. Women are sometimes reluctant to speak in front of the camera, but their nuanced answers show a keener awareness of social and sexual mores as problems than do statements by men. Given the enlightenment project declared as the premise for the film, "un dialogo tra chi sa e chi non sa" (a dialogue between those who know and those who don't), it is not surprising that the answers collected depict a country in need of education: Pasolini wants to show the viewers that Italians are not as liberated as they think they are, or as the image of "modern Italy" projected by mass media may imply.

However, as Foucault noted in his 1977 review, more significant than the line separating men and women, rural and urban dwellers, northerners and southerners, is the gap between "'the young' and the others."[23] Adults – older people – discuss the erosion they are witnessing of an established system of values, and the consequences that social and cultural change is having on individuals and families; the young demand attention, and don't shy away from the camera, whether to declare their emancipation or to complain about a lack thereof. Pasolini explicitly acknowledges his "pleasant surprise" at the frankness and openness of younger interviewees, particularly, of young women. The presence of young people in front of the camera is more eloquent than any answer they might give. They fill the screen with their bodies: they lean on one another, seek each other's support when facing the camera, or smoke nonchalantly as they watch one another speak. They participate in the interview with a group of peers – as in Bologna – or among people of all ages – as in Sicily – thus revealing varying degrees of independence and different intergenerational relations. We meet young women as they walk out of a factory in Milan chatting casually with their male colleagues; they talk with equal nonchalance to Pasolini and give the viewers a visual sample of social interactions among twenty-something, working-class women and men. In the countryside near Modena, a teenage girl, sporting a 1960s-style short haircut, contradicts her farmer parents who are standing next to her. She feels freer than they declare she is, and her demeanour supports her words: smiling, not intimidated by either her parents or the interviewer, she answers looking straight at the camera. In Sicily, women's participation in the survey is solicited and carefully overseen by men, who try to prove to the interviewer their wives and daughters' emancipation. This variety of reactions and physical interactions with the camera and with Pasolini as interviewer go beyond the pedagogical project from which the meetings originated. Although not strictly a youth film, since it is not designed to investigate specifically the conditions of young people, *Comizi d'amore* nevertheless provides a revealing portrait of youth in 1963 Italy.

The movie also contributes to youth discourse in at least two other ways. First, by investigating sexuality, a key component of the coming-of-age experience, and the connected issues of family and gender relations, the film depicts social mores that younger generations were beginning to question, precisely at the time when that change was happening. Second, through the interview format, the documentary makes explicit a condition of representation of young people that underlies all of Pasolini's oeuvre. The unevenness of change in gender relations and sexual habits is evident throughout *Comizi d'amore*, and the reflections of interviewed intellectuals highlight, beside obvious geographical differences, the permanence of class distinctions. The confident answers and casual demeanour of young factory workers in Milan show the explicit effects of economic and social emancipation afforded to women and young people by the industrialization of large cities in the North. Conversely, when a young Sicilian man explains the continued practice of the *fuitina*, the consensual elopement of a young couple traditionally used to force marriage consent from families, now used as a practical way of avoiding expensive wedding receptions, the social changes in small southern communities appear less dramatic. The image of Italy emerging from this survey is that of a country unevenly affected by modernization, but more importantly in Pasolini's view, ideologically ill-equipped to understand the ongoing transformation. It is presumably these Italians – "those who don't know" – that the movie addresses, as a preliminary step in their education. However, while the editing and captions draw attention to an alleged "state of confusion" of the interviewees, which justifies the pedagogical project, young people appear lucid, certain of their expectations and aspirations, or willing to acknowledge the limits of current systems. They do not fit the repressive model of the country envisaged as the premise for the film. Conceived as an invitation to Italian audiences to recognize their own ignorance and prejudice in the interviewees' contributions, the film in fact allows viewers to witness a series of conversations in which young people resist the filmmaker's pedagogical project.

Besides exploring issues that are central to the emergence of young people as a socially distinct group in the sixties, *Comizi d'amore* shows Pasolini's relationship with youth as it is challenged by young people.

Since the days of *Eredi*, when the young people he encouraged to express themselves were his peers, Pasolini's desire to establish a channel of communication with youth shaped much of his work. That intention is realized and foregrounded through the interview format in *Comizi d'amore*: the author puts a microphone in front of young people and offers them a chance to speak their mind. His physical presence on screen as interviewer, however, also reveals the ultimate limit of that intent: the young interviewees see him as the forty-year-old he is, and the age gap inevitably affects the conversations, even when the author, for once, is not speaking for youth. In this sense *Comizi d'amore* explicitly stages, albeit unwittingly, the limit of youth representations in cultural artefacts produced by mature artists.

The interview format sets up a conversation, which the author can only partially control. The prologue, which deals with children, makes most explicit a dynamic that runs through interviews with adolescents and young adults in a subtler way. When asked if they know where babies come from, groups of Neapolitan and Sicilian eight- or nine-year-olds resort to stock answers: "the stork brings them," or "they grow among cauliflowers," or "Jesus delivers them." Facing an adult, they provide the answers that they think are expected of them. Their looks to the camera, however, tell another story, as Foucault observed:

> With their smiles, their far-off tone, their silences, their glances that dart from left to right, the answers to these questions from adults have a perfidious docility. They reserve the right to keep to oneself what one likes to whisper. The stork is a way to make fun of the "grown-ups," a way of paying them back in their own counterfeit money. It is the ironic, impatient sign that the questioning will go no further, that the adults are prying, that they shall not join the game, and that the child will keep the "real story" for himself.[24]

The inconsistency between the words uttered into the microphone and the expression of the children's faces reflects the gap between what they know and what they have learned to say as appropriate in conversations with adults. Pasolini sounds like the patient and engaged teacher he had been twenty years before in Friuli, trying various approaches to elicit an answer from easily distracted pupils. Their verbal compliance acknowledges their recognition of that relationship – "If you answer correctly I'll reward you," he says – but the camera captures also what remains unsaid, namely the tension between the interviewer's authority and his invitation to speak "freely."

A similar interaction takes place when Pasolini interviews students from the University of Bologna, his *alma mater*. Students gather in front of the camera and take turns diligently answering Pasolini's questions, with the earnest confidence of young intellectuals aware of the importance of their words. Like the children before them, the twenty-year-olds seem to recognize the interviewer as an authority, who expects a certain kind of answer from them. In this case he is not perceived as the teacher who requires polite responses, but the left-wing intellectual who is testing the modernity of the country. Their answers show a compliance with the perceived goal of the interview, which surprises Pasolini. If the stated purpose of the documentary is to violate the law of silence surrounding sex, or to show that such law is still in effect, an act that in and of itself qualifies as transgressive, the students subvert the expectations of the interviewer with their effortlessness answers. Far from refusing to talk about sex, or being at a loss for words as Pasolini and Moravia expected them to be, these young educated bourgeois willingly respond to the invitation to transform sex into discourse. A perfectly coiffed young woman in a formal skirt suit confidently states that she feels "equally free" in all areas of her existence, including sex, and that the moral principles regulating her life are not imposed on her, but the result of free choice. After her, two clean-shaven young men wearing jackets and ties promptly subscribe to the ideal of a modern, sexually liberated country by stating that they feel no inhibitions whatsoever. A bearded student in a corduroy jacket affirms his independence from the traditional model of Italian masculinity (which the documentary otherwise recognizes as still prevailing), by declaring that his sex life is inseparable from his love life. These are not outwardly rebellious young people who wish to *epater les bourgeois*, and yet their confident answers show their familiarity with a discursive mode that does not organize itself exclusively in terms of repression or liberation.

The students in Bologna, but also the farmers' daughter in the countryside near Modena, the young women in Sicily, and the boys and girls on the beach near Rome are quite comfortable with the camera. They resist Pasolini's effort to speak of sex in terms of repression, but they agree to speak of it in other forms. For instance, discussions of the Merlin Law passed in 1958, which decreed brothels illegal, and of prostitution in relation to marriage and family, involve people of all ages and find both young women and men willing to express their opinion. While older interviewees confirm Pasolini's impression that sexual habits haven't changed much during the economic miracle, or that the changes that have occurred are not organic to the society that adopted them, young Italians present to the interviewer and the audience a new subjectivity. The young men and women on screen not only resist the pedagogical intent implicit in the movie, but the culture that produced it. They show signs of a different relationship between power and discourse. The mere fact of being asked for their opinion, of being on screen, introduces them to a power network that relies on visibility. Power structures are changing in this period of economic and social transformation in Italy, and 1963 was also the time, Foucault remarks in his review, "when almost everywhere in Europe and the U.S. the variety and multiplicity of the forms of 'power' began to be questioned" (74). As the struggle for civil rights in the United States gained national and international attention with the March on Washington, the continued process of decolonization led to the independence of several African countries, the publication of Betty Friedan's *The Feminine Mystique* relaunched the women's movement, young people in Europe and the United States identified common causes in the struggle against all forms of imposed authority and made their presence visible and heard in various forms. Although *Comizi d'amore* sets out to prove that Italy is in fact only marginally involved in these radical changes in power structures, and most of its verbal results apparently confirm that point, the visual component of the project tells a slightly different story. Young people in particular resist Pasolini's pedagogical approach and show him that giving a microphone to them could produce unanticipated results.

Somewhat unexpected in *Comizi d'amore*, the opportunity to hear young Italians speak for themselves does not present itself again in Pasolini's films. His need to renegotiate his relationship with youth, however, which transpired from *Comizi d'amore*, would shape his films in the following years. It was complicated by a cultural crisis that affected both his role as a committed intellectual and the modes of representation available to him. "Marxism has gone out of style," he declared in the essay "The end of the avant-garde" and with it a "vast operation of cultural diffusion" underwritten by the PCI in the 1950s, which created "consumers of films and books that the PCI and left-wing culture considered committed."[25] Old ideologies proved inadequate to make sense of the new social and cultural reality emerging from the economic boom, and the very notion of reality as an object of representation was being questioned. In fact, critical theories focusing on processes of signification and on the opacity of language challenged the primacy of the referent in post-war fiction and film. Although Pasolini's earlier movies and novels had questioned the supposed transparency of language assumed in neorealist texts, the issue of "reality" and how to maintain a grasp on it with reduced linguistic tools at his disposal remained central to his critical reflection throughout the 1960s. More specifically, the PCI's loss of power in the cultural sphere caused an identity crisis in intellectuals like Pasolini, committed to an emancipatory view of culture, and now confronted with the growing popularity of "lowbrow" cultural products quite different from their own. Pasolini's reflection on the end of an era and his exploration of alternative modes of representation and intellectual *impegno* are depicted in *Uccellacci e uccellini*.

Moving beyond Pedagogy, One Step at a Time: *Uccellacci e uccellini*

Uccellacci e uccellini (1966; *The Hawks and the Sparrows*) marked the beginning of a second phase in Pasolini's filmmaking, which he characterized as *cinema d'élite*.[26] In this second period, he abandoned, by his own admission, the "Gramscian" approach underlying his early films, and addressed more difficult, provocative topics through intensified formal experimentation. *Uccellacci* reflects on this shift and on the social, ideological, and aesthetic crisis that imposed it.[27] Specifically, the movie references the end of 1950s Marxism, of national popular art as the mandate for committed intellectuals, and of realism as its primary mode of representation.[28] This meditation becomes the explicit subject of the movie, through an anti-realistic *mise-en-scène*, pedantic lectures delivered by a talking crow and a story-within-a-story that reduplicates the open-endedness of the main narrative. The self-conscious intellectual, who has lost confidence in his pedagogical role towards the lower classes, remains an effective storyteller, particularly in the episodic mode of the picaresque narrative. The result is a hybrid movie, which combines a biting metanarrative and an amusing fable."[29] The reflection on commitment in a post-ideological society also implicates youth. Specifically, the representation of youth in the movie epitomizes the crisis of realism and explores its implications.

Totò (Totò) and Ninetto (Ninetto Davoli), father and son, walk on a deserted road towards an unknown destination. A talking crow soon joins the travellers and interrogates them on their lives and their plans. To entertain and teach them a lesson he narrates a medieval fable, which is embedded in the main narrative. It is the story of Brother Ciccillo and Brother Ninetto, also played by the main actors, two monks whom St. Francis orders to evangelize two types of birds at war with one another: the hawks and the sparrows. After months of self-denial and unsuccessful attempts, the friars finally devise a language for communicating with each set of birds. However, despite Brother Ciccillo's exhortations to peace, the hawks continue killing the sparrows. Brother Ciccillo despairs, but in the end consents to St. Francis' entreaty that he start again. As we return to the main plot line, after listening patiently to the fable, Totò and Ninetto become bored with the loquacious crow, who offers unrequested comments and lectures on the various encounters the travellers make on the road. Hungry and tired of the preaching, the two men kill the bird and eat it. Ironically, they follow his teachings: "Professors should be eaten in a spicy sauce!" he had told them. But whether they digest the professor and "become a little professors themselves" is doubtful. The road in front of them is as long as it was at the beginning of the movie.

A road movie of sorts, *Uccellacci e uccellini* promises to explore the changing geographical and social landscape of Italy in the early 1960s. However, unlike Dino Risi's *Il sorpasso* (1962; *The Easy Life*), a paradigmatic road movie showing the signs of the economic boom, *Uccellacci* does not deliver images of a mobile, modernized, and pleasure-seeking country.[30] Quite the contrary: there are no automobiles or motorcycles in Pasolini's film and freeway overpasses under construction allude to an incomplete modernization, and one in which the protagonists are not participating. The only mechanized means of transportation appearing briefly on the screen are two buses, which the characters run after and miss.

"Dove va l'umanità? Boh!" ("Where is mankind headed? Hmph!), announces an intertitle at the beginning of the movie, quoting an interview with Mao by Edgar Snow. If mankind is headed somewhere, these two specimens are either unaware or in no hurry to get there. Not only is their destination unknown; references to their location, in both space and time, are vague and inconsistent. Contradictory street signs indicating distance to Istanbul or Cuba offer no help in orientation. The opening dialogue between father and son, encompassing references to ocean tides, new dentures, and spraying of DDT, oscillates between the contemporary and the timeless. The meaning of this journey may not be found in the destination, but it does not seem to be in the process either. Encounters and adventures along the way are not trials through which the protagonists learn a lesson, following the logic of a traditional quest. Even the story-within-a-story, a fable whose moral we expect to apply to the main characters, is similarly open-ended. Crossing the boundaries between genres, the film is simultaneously a timeless fable and a contemporary road movie, a didactic treatise and a series of humorous sketches, a lament over political failure and a celebration of the new possibilities available to those who acknowledge and overcome superseded ideologies.

The film's depiction of youth, in particular, exemplifies the ideological and representational crisis. Consistently with the hybridization of different genres and narrative styles, several literary and extra-literary adolescents are evoked in the first part of the movie, as if in a medley of Pasolini's previous work: Ninetto's dark curly hair and distinctive accent immediately recall the *ragazzi* of the Roman novels; the teenage girl dressed as an angel for the kindergarten pageant evokes the Faedis sisters in *Il Sogno di una cosa*; the group of young men dancing to a jukebox tune in the "Bar Las Vegas" visualize the new pastimes often discussed in the articles and letters published in *Vie Nuove*. After this quick typology, the viewers' attention is focused on Ninetto, who is both an adolescent of his time and an eternal youth. When Ninetto brags to the girl about test-driving a brand new Fiat 600, or dances in front of the jukebox, we see him as a 1960s teenager. However, this historical and cultural specificity, sustained also by his clothing, is counterbalanced by eternal features: according to the sung opening credits, he is *innocente* e *furbetto*, a guileless child and a wily teenager. A particular sequence symbolically establishes him as the archetypal youth: a shot of Ninetto running in slow motion is cross-cut with a long shot of the periphery of Rome accompanied by strings as lyrical counterpoint. The countryside appears in the foreground, while new residential buildings in the distance recall the Tiburtino quarter featured in *Una vita violenta*. An ancient Roman bridge cuts diagonally across the two horizontal halves of the frame. Underscored by the visual analogy with the constantly changing Eternal City, Ninetto's carefree run embodies a synthesis of contemporary and timeless youth.

Ninetto makes the timeless features of his youthful identity explicit in his self-introduction: "Io invece so' Ninetto, di Innocenti Totò e Semplicetti Grazia." (I, on the other hand, am Ninetto, son of Totò Innocenti and Grazia Semplicetti.) "Those are religious qualities," states the rational crow, who claims he is the child of "Mr. Doubt and Mrs. Conscience." The child of innocence, grace, and simplicity also defines himself in relation to his father, thus confirming a generational continuity that many of his contemporaries were beginning to reject. Thus, while his jeans and embroidered team jacket situate Ninetto firmly in the 1960s, they actually dress a young man who does not question paternal authority. Intergenerational continuity, often reaffirmed by his enthusiastic "Sì, papà!," is however removed to the fictional framework of the fable, with a Chaplinesque clown for a father and a talking crow as a teacher. However, while this removal casts the reassuring Ninetto as an antidote to contemporary generational conflicts, the father-son-teacher trinity introduces a shift in Pasolini's reflection on youth. His focus is increasingly on the relationship between different generations, and on issues of authority that affect his identification with youth.

Pasolini's review of his relationship with youth at this transitional time is reflected in the characterization of the crow as his alter ego: a pedantic intellectual who shows an interest in the lower classes and complains about being obsolete in the contemporary world, the talking bird is a rare example of Pasolini's self-irony. Introduced on the notes of "Fischia il vento," a famous Resistance song, the crow addresses Totò and Ninetto by saying "Non mi volete come compagno di strada, eh?" (You don't want me as a fellow traveller, do you?) Using the well-known Trotsky phrase, "fellow traveller," the voice of Francesco Leonetti (a member of the *Eredi* group and co-founder of the review *Officina*) openly acknowledges the loss of status of committed intellectuals, even those who, like Pasolini, inhabited an eccentric position in the party.[31] Although the father and the crow are both "ageless" figures, consistent with the story's surreal setting, the crow's ambivalent authority resonates with the contemporary crisis of social commitment, or *impegno*. Clearly, the crow's didactic approach has no impact on the pupils, but the embedded story adds a level of ambiguity to the teacher's failure. Because Totò and Ninetto also play the protagonists of the Franciscan tale, we may immediately look for a parallel with the father and son in the main story. The parable, apparently illustrating the value of patience, humility, and faith, does not however appear to have any specific applicability to the condition of the listeners. Instead, there is a stronger analogy between the friars in the story and the teacher who tells it, with a reversed bird-to-human communication problem. Brother Ciccillo and Brother Ninetto's failure to create harmony among the birds mirrors both the crow's failure to communicate effectively with Totò and Ninetto, and the Marxist intellectuals' inability to bridge the gap between their bourgeois culture and that of the new working class.

This is the message that the crow keeps repeating, in more or less explicit form: old ideologies are no longer relevant, and intellectuals must explore alternative ways of expressing their message: "The time of Brecht and Rossellini is over." The double *mise en abyme* of a failure of communication – because Totò and Ninetto validate the crow's ultimate fear – thematizes the film's own self-awareness. No effective channel of communication exists between teacher and pupils, and the author can no longer identify with either of them.

As a transitional movie, *Uccellacci e uccellini* also marks the introduction of Ninetto, a unique embodiment of the hybridity of youth in Pasolini's oeuvre. A seventeen-year-old whom Pasolini had met three years before on the set of *La Ricotta*, and who had played a minor part in *Il Vangelo secondo Matteo*, Ninetto Davoli made his cinematic debut as co-protagonist in *Uccellacci*. Alongside Totò, an actor chosen for his "double nature: on one side the Neapolitan sub-proletarian, on the other the clown" and for his bringing to the movie "who he really was," Ninetto Davoli becomes the hybrid Ninetto: a character who never ceases to be a real boy, a boy who never leaves his characters behind.[32] His physical and cultural traits, encapsulated in an often quoted verse from a Pasolini poem included in the 1965 volume *Alì dagli occhi azzurri*, combined historically determined and ahistorical characteristics of youth, cheerful and subversive at once: "Ed ecco che entra nella platea un ossesso, con gli occhi dolci / e ridarelli, / vestito come i Beatles" (And suddenly he walks into the theatre like a madman, with sweet and cheerful eyes, dressed like the Beatles).[33] Centring its meta-fictional reflection on such a composite character, *Uccellacci* establishes Ninetto as the archetypal youth, who exists in a liminal space between fiction and reality. As Marco Bazzocchi convincingly showed, "the character Ninetto never leaves behind the real Ninetto. A typically Pasolinian tautology recurs in him: reality is reality. Ninetto, from film to film, plays a different character, but he always remains Ninetto."[34] Never completely lost in the characters he plays, and never completely outside them, Ninetto embodies the paradox of youth that shaped Pasolini's work, simultaneously poetic notion and *ragazzo in carne ed ossa* (flesh-and-bone boy).

The unique position of Ninetto in Pasolini's life and work, which challenged Pasolini's entire erotic and expressive system, also helps explain a significant shift in his representation of youth. Introduced as a messenger in the previously quoted poem, Ninetto maintains that role throughout the films of the late 1960s: in *Edipo Re* (1967) he is Nunzio, the mediator between the city and Oedipus; as Angelino, the dancing mailman, he announces the arrival of the divine Guest in *Teorema* (1968); and in *Porcile* (1969) the double character Ninetto/Maracchione crosses over between the two storylines, bearing witness to the violence perpetrated on the young protagonist of each story. His crucial, albeit marginal, role in those films signals the irruption of a peculiar form of youth in worlds where its authenticity has become unrecognizable. A main feature of such authenticity, Ninetto's existence between different levels of reality, as a character and a real boy, embodies a form of youth that could only be adequately captured by cinema.

Thus, while *Uccellacci e uccellini* bid farewell to neorealism and showed the limits of a pedagogical approach to political commitment, it simultaneously explored alternative forms of representation and styles. The humility of Brother Ciccillo and the cheerfulness of Brother Ninetto, willing to experiment with different languages in order to talk to the birds, and ready to use their bodies when their words were not sufficient, suggested to contemporary intellectuals the necessity to adjust the mode of expression to the changed conditions. The "religious" qualities which, according to the pedantic crow, make up Ninetto's lineage – simplicity, innocence, and grace – revived in Pasolini an interest in an alternative form of engagement that could go beyond Marxist and bourgeois rationalism and find expression in the language of cinema. *Uccellacci e uccellini* set up the possibility for a creative approach to social change, one that Pasolini would look for in the student movements of the late 1960s and attempt with his cinema of poetry.

Flower Power and Flower Shops: A Brief Encounter with Counterculture

Since *Uccellacci e uccellini* allowed Pasolini to start exploring new forms of expression and social critique, it seems appropriate that he would come into contact with what he perceived as a creative revolution while presenting that film in the United States. His enthusiasm for the American New Left and the civil rights movement, surprising when considering his political allegiance and classical education, shows the hope of a poet and intellectual who had identified with the anti-bourgeois potential of youth. Pasolini idealized young American protesters as new partisans of an imaginative movement that involved poets and artists. Unlike their Italian counterparts, limited by rational discourse and practical goals, young Americans subverted the bourgeois code through irrationality.

Visiting New York City for the first time in 1966, Pasolini shared his first impressions in an interview with Italian journalist Oriana Fallaci for the prominent weekly *L'Europeo*. He was struck by the overwhelming beauty of the city, which appeared to him as "a blinding light at the end of a tunnel..., Jerusalem appearing to the eyes of the Crusader." To the filmmaker's eye, the modernist architecture presented a challenge for the camera: "Maybe it is not filmable. Seen from far away it is like the Dolomites, too photogenic, too wonderful, and it irritates you. From up close, from inside it, you can't see it: the lens can't contain the beginning and the end of a skyscraper." Besides its aesthetic uniqueness, however, New York attracted Pasolini for its youthful atmosphere: "But what matters isn't only its physical beauty. It's its youth. It's a city of young people, the least crepuscular city I have ever seen" (*SPS*, 1599).[35] Fallaci's introductory description of the interviewee highlights his youthfulness: "dressed like a college boy. You know, those slender, athletic types, who play baseball and make love in their cars. A light brown sweater, with a leather breast pocket, light brown corduroy pants, slightly slim-fitting, suede rubber-soled boots. He really doesn't look forty-four" (*SPS*, 1597). Wearing a similarly casual outfit he appears walking on Seventh Avenue in the photos accompanying the interview, which complete the portrait of "A Marxist in New York" as a disenchanted Communist seduced by American idealism and youth.[36] It is a note of shock that Fallaci seems intent on striking with her interview. In the introduction, after describing his youthful looks and moralizing on his nighttime escapades in "the darkest streets of Harlem, of Greenwich Village, of Brooklyn ... looking for the dirty, unhappy, violent America that suits his problems, his tastes," she confesses: "I am really curious to know if this committed Marxist, if this angry Christian, if Pasolini that is, likes America" (ibid.). Perhaps surprisingly, he does. The palpable energy of the city inspires the forty-four-year-old intellectual, who wishes he had visited twenty years earlier: "New York is not an escape: it is a commitment, a war. It makes you feel like acting, facing things, changing them. You like it in the way that you like things, say, when you are twenty" (*SPS*, 1598).

Unlike Africa, a frequent travel destination for Pasolini in the 1960s, which he often described as an escape from Italian modernization and consumerism, New York inspired a renewal of political commitment. This impression was connected to his appreciation for the activity of young members of the Student Nonviolent Coordinating Committee (SNCC), whose dedication to the struggle for civil rights recalled the absoluteness of early Christians: "They are neither Communist nor anti-Communist, they are mystics of democracy: their revolution lies in taking democracy to its extreme and almost crazy consequences" (*SPS*, 1601).[37] More generally, however, Pasolini's enthusiasm for the city arose from the everyday performance of youth he observed in the streets:

> And how elegant young people are, here ... They have a fabulous taste: look at how they dress. In the most sincere, the most non-conformist way possible. They do not care about petty-bourgeois or popular rules. Those gaudy sweaters, those cheap jackets, those incredible colors. They don't get dressed, they put on costumes ... And so dressed up they go along, proud, aware of their elegance, which is never absolute or innocent. (*SPS*, 1599)

In the colourful outfits worn like costumes, Pasolini recognized the non-verbal expression of a spirit of disobedience that was stronger than any slogan. The imaginative clothing externalized a generational difference, setting young people apart from their elders. In their refusal to conform to sartorial norms set from above, young Americans set up an existential resistance to a universal bourgeois system comparable to that embodied by the Roman *ragazzi* he had portrayed in his 1950s novels. The analogy, and the positive connotation it carried for Pasolini, became explicit in his description of the population of New York as the encounter of sub-proletarians from different backgrounds, whose lack of class awareness produced a *de facto* classless society: "An explosion of races, all assimilated and made similar by the same system, by the same origin: the sub-proletariat" (ibid.). Despite an oversimplification that may strike American readers as superficial, if not naive, Pasolini's perception of America as classless underscored the revolutionary impact of a group whose collective identity was based on age. Similar to *ragazzi* of the Roman *borgate*, young New Yorkers embodied a radical alterity to a bourgeois system of values that Pasolini saw as universal.

Their physical expression of non-conformity, their fundamental difference with respect to the bourgeois mainstream, qualified their form of resistance as "sacred." He had words of praise for the civil rights movement in the United States even when, upon his return to Italy, he clarified his thoughts in an article, published in the Communist newspaper *Paese Sera*, in response to the letter of a concerned reader who had expressed surprise at Pasolini's keen appreciation for the American Left. He recalled breathing an atmosphere of hope and anticipation, in

New York, which induced him to describe America as the place where "everything seems to be about to begin" and where "one lives ... as if on the eve of great things."[38] The various events he witnessed in New York, including a peace rally, the meeting of a black labour union, a gathering of progressive intellectuals, and even a demonstration in favour of the Vietnam War, gave him the sense of a "great human experience," whose visionary quality was perhaps more important to him than its immediate political content. In the same article, perhaps to reassure other similarly concerned Communist readers, he compared the American New Left to the Italian Resistance: "The clandestine climate of conflict, of revolutionary urgency, of hope," and "the creation of an "anti-community [in the breast of the American community]" were comparable, he said, only "to the great days of Hope of the Forties."[39] Comparable was also the bonding of participants: "Those who belong to the New Left (which does not exist, it is only an idea, an ideal) are recognizable immediately, and among them is born that kind of love that tied the partisans together."[40]

The visionary approach to protest in America– "the protest, the pure and simple confrontation, the rebellion against consumerism" – allowed also for a more direct and creative participation of poets. In the United States, intellectuals played a fundamental role in providing class consciousness to a country without a Marxist tradition:

> Class consciousness, to make way in the head of an American, needs the long, contorted road of an enormously complex operation; that is, it needs the mediation of – let's admit it – the bourgeois or petit-bourgeois idealism which gives meaning to the life of every American and which he absolutely cannot leave out of consideration. There they call it spiritualism.[41]

This "intelligent spiritualism" determined forms of dissent which, instead of being based on class conflict, were typically non-violent and pacifist. Pasolini admired the active role played by poets and artists in creating a new language of protest for the American counterculture. This became particularly evident in his brief encounter with American poet and countercultural icon Allen Ginsberg, who was idolized by both American and European students. Although admittedly not an admirer of American literature, Pasolini declared in several instances to have found a brotherly spirit in Ginsberg's poetry.[42] They met for the first time in 1966, during Pasolini's first trip to New York, and crossed paths again when Ginsberg was in Milan the following year. His Italian translator, Fernanda Pivano, facilitated the conversation, which concerned, among other things, their roles as revolutionary poets and their relationship with social protest in their respective countries.

While a few years earlier *Vie Nuove* had presented Pasolini as a "youth magnet" for the magazine, one of the few Italian writers who naturally attracted young readers, by the time he met Ginsberg Pasolini was critical of the emergent Italian student movement and would soon be publicly labelled as a student hater.[43] Ginsberg, on the other hand, regularly led rallies and sit-ins against the Vietnam War, in San Francisco's Bay Area, in New York, and even in Europe. In Prague, the year before, he had been crowned King of May and young people had carried him through the streets in a rose-covered chariot. In London, seven thousand students had welcomed him at a poetry reading at the Royal Albert Hall.[44] Even in Italy, where his poetry had been translated and made popular by Pivano, his reputation among young people was by now that of a leader of the Flower Power movement.[45] Ginsberg was obviously *with* the students, while Pasolini was apparently *against* them. However, Pasolini saw Ginsberg's position and his own as analogous, inasmuch as the object of their critique was the bourgeoisie and their critical instrument was poetry. The encounter with one of the poetic leaders of student protest in the United States gave him the opportunity to compare that movement with its Italian counterpart, a comparison on which he reflected again in a letter to Ginsberg:

> Caro, angelico Ginsberg, ieri sera ti ho sentito dire tutto quello che ti veniva in mente su New York e San Francisco, coi loro fiori. Io ti ho detto qualcosa dell'Italia (fiori solo dai fiorai). La tua borghesia è una borghesia di PAZZI, la mia una borghesia di IDIOTI. Tu ti rivolti contro la PAZZIA con la PAZZIA (dando fiori ai poliziotti): ma come rivoltarsi contro l'IDIOZIA?

> Dear, angelic Ginsberg, last night I heard you say everything that came into your mind about New York and San Francisco, with their flowers. I told you something about Italy, (flowers only to be found in flower shops). Your bourgeoisie is a bourgeoisie of INSANE people, mine of IDIOTS. You rebel against insanity with INSANITY (giving flowers to policemen): but how can one revolt against IDIOCY?[46]

The half-joking tone of the letter does not detract from the sharpness of an analysis which, within a couple of pages, outlines the differences in the social and historical structure of the two countries and illustrates the role played by such apparently different poets as Ginsberg and Pasolini in the critique of the bourgeois establishment. Although Pasolini's appraisal of Ginsberg's poetic and political role is occasionally superficial, it is nevertheless revealing: the idealization of Ginsberg seems to correspond, in Pasolini, to an admission of his own limits and frustrations, while the acknowledgment of Ginsberg's poetic achievements indirectly sheds light on Pasolini's own redefinition of the poet's mandate in relation to student protest.

Pasolini recognized Ginsberg's advantage in the freedom, which was afforded to him by a society devoid of class consciousness, to invent a new "revolutionary" language:

> Perché tu, che ti rivolti contro i padri borghesi assassini, lo fai restando dentro il loro stesso mondo ... classista (sì, in Italia ci esprimiamo così) e quindi sei costretto a inventare di nuovo e completamente – giorno per giorno, parola per parola – il tuo linguaggio rivoluzionario.
>
> Since you rebel against the bourgeois assassin fathers by staying within their ... class-conscious world (yes, that's how we speak in Italy), you are compelled to invent your revolutionary language anew and completely – day by day and word by word.[47]

Ginsberg, in Pasolini's view, was able to both create an alternative critical instrument through poetry and to engage in creative protest alongside young people. Political discourse in the United States at this time was dominated by the Vietnam War and Ginsberg ran a poetic campaign against the war, as well as directly participating in political demonstrations. In both fields, he exposed and denounced the absurdity of the conflict and of institutions supporting it, through the creation of an alternative discourse: he recycled the language used in war propaganda to compose poetry against the war; he organized peace rallies and encouraged protesters to offer flowers to policemen, which spoke not only against physical violence (the kind exercised by the police upon protesting students and the violence of the war), but also against the psychological violence implicit in mass society.[48] Flowers, just like the rallies themselves, gathering thousands of flamboyantly dressed young people, introduced a visual spectacle in a war discourse that was mainly verbal. They exposed the "insanity" of what was presented as logical – the necessity of attacks in Vietnam – through a creative "insanity." It was this kind of creativity that Pasolini admired in

Revolutionary Youth   141

the American students' movement and that he saw missing among Italian youth: in Italy, flowers remained in flower shops, and the students protesting in the streets were unable to invent their own language of protest.

Instead of inventing a new revolutionary language, Italian protesters adopted a language inherited from their fathers:

> Noi qui invece (anche quelli che hanno adesso sedici anni) abbiamo già il nostro linguaggio rivoluzionario bell'e pronto, con dentro la sua morale. Anche i Cinesi parlano come degli statali. E anch'io - come vedi ... Chi ha fornito a noi – anziani e ragazzi – il linguaggio ufficiale della protesta? Il marxismo, la cui unica vena poetica è il ricordo della Resistenza, che si rinnovella al pensiero del Vietnam e della Bolivia.
>
> We here, instead (even those now sixteen years old) already have our revolutionary language, prefabricated, and with its own ethics behind it. Even the Chinese speak like civil servants. Who provided us – both young and old – with the official language of protest? Marxism, whose only poetic vein is the memory of the Resistance, now recalled by the thought of Vietnam and Bolivia.[49]

Marxism still dominated the language of protest in Italy, and it had lost the "poetic vein" it had in the Resistance. That was the only time, according to Pasolini, in which revolutionary discourse had gone beyond the practical goals of the conquest of power and embraced existential issues: the goal was not simply to overturn Fascism, but rather to reconstruct society on a different basis, to redefine democracy. A similar "poetic vein" was present, in Pasolini's view, in the peace rallies and civil rights movement in the United States: young American protesters were conducting an attack on the establishment that went beyond immediately political goals, and questioned the very notion of rationality. The "bourgeois fathers" against whom young protesters struggled, in both countries, were the ones who had based their hegemony on the language of "Practice and Reason." Young Italians, however, struggled in vain against those bourgeois fathers, in Pasolini's view, because they used a language of protest that was, itself "always practical and rational": the discourse of class struggle.

Pasolini's concise analysis underscored the common origin of liberalism and Marxism in the discourse of the Enlightenment, and showed the potential of any discourse of protest that could overcome the limits of rationality. The equation of rationalism and democracy, in European critical discourse, had demonized irrationalism as preparing the ground for Fascism: "Povero Wagner e povero Nietzsche! Hanno preso tutta loro la colpa. E non parliamo poi di Pound!" (Poor Wagner and poor Nietzsche! They have taken on all the guilt. And let's not speak of Pound!)[50] The association of irrationality with Fascism excluded *a priori* the possibility of an irrational, spontaneous, "poetic" discourse:

> And therefore everyone – from the divine Rimbaud to melting Kavafy, from the sublime Machado to the tender Apollinaire – all poets who have struggled against the world of pragmatism and reason, have done nothing else but prepare the ground, like prophets for the god War whom society invokes.[51]

In recognizing a genealogy of poets who challenged the "reasonable and practical" approach of the "bourgeois fathers," Pasolini was suggesting that a possibility of genuine innovation, at this point in history, may very well depend on the ability to step out of that binary opposition of democracy and irrationalism, and see beyond the pragmatic limits of Marxism, even in the "left of the PCI" version adopted by student protesters. Evidently, he placed Ginsberg among those challengers of rational discourse, both for his poetic approach to politics, and for his ability to recognize, and lead, young people's creative spirit. Unlike those poets, whom, he said, bourgeois society destined to self-destruction, Ginsberg and the representatives of "the other America" found a way to use the creativity of poetic language to dissent from the bourgeois establishment.

Despite his fascination with the "stupendous mysticism of the Democracy of the New Left" and his partiality to the non-violent approach of American students, Pasolini was also aware of its possible limits: "But, at the same time, to renounce, besides Holy Violence, also the idea of the conquest of power on the part of the just, signifies leaving power in the hands of the Fascists who always and everywhere hold it. If these are the questions, I wouldn't know how to answer. And you?" (ibid.). He still doubted whether renouncing the conquest of power would not mean giving up the possibility of effecting change, but he seemed willing to see the outcome of a great social and cultural experiment and to discuss alternative possibilities with a fellow poet. The isolation he felt in Italy made him look to a movement based on the cooperation between poets and young activists with keen interest. Pasolini's analysis of Ginsberg's poetic and political activity in the context of the 1960s was therefore an occasion for reflection on his own poetics and on his relationship with the Italian student movement.

The Written Language of Action: Poetry and Cinema

Pasolini's re-evaluation of poetry as a critical instrument in a neo-capitalistic society, which underlay his enthusiastic reaction to the American student movement, proceeded simultaneously with the theorization of cinema in the late 1960s. Ongoing cultural changes questioned the aesthetic and ideological premises of his earlier poetry. As a civic poet, his aesthetic pursuit was never separate from an ethical concern. His preoccupation remained that of finding an expressive language that could not only adequately represent, but also have an impact on, the new reality. Unlike the *Neoavanguardia*, whose stylistic experiments remained, in Pasolini's view, in the realm of the literary, he still championed a performative view of poetry. Poetry occupied for Pasolini an ambiguous space between being and doing, analogous to the position that he assigned to youth in society. Poetic discourse introduced alterity in a homogenous cultural landscape, where literary and regional particularities were being supplanted by a "technical" mode of communication. No longer finding an adequate instrument in the new national language, Pasolini expanded the notion of poetic discourse to include cinema.

In the essays on language, literature, and cinema written between 1965 and 1967 and collected in *Empirismo Eretico*, definitions of poetic and cinematic language intersected. On one hand, the advent of audio-visual techniques questioned the "identification between poetry ... and language." Poetry was thus defined as a translinguistic action: "Every poem is translinguistic. It is an *action* "placed" in a system of symbols, as in a vehicle, which becomes *action* once again in the addressee.[52] The conditioned reflex associated with poetic discourse, that is, the response that produces action, is based on the expressiveness of the "vehicle," which allows the action to be transmitted to the addressee. Such expressiveness, hardly attainable with a verbal language that had lost its stratification, could instead be achieved in cinema. Like poetry, cinema is an aesthetic operation that confers new meanings on linguistic signs. However, while the writer can count on an established system of signs and has only an aesthetic task, the filmmaker, in Pasolini's view, performs a linguistic action before an aesthetic one. Due to the lack of an established dictionary of images, he claims, the filmmaker must choose his images from the infinite language of action, establish their primary meaning, and then perform an expressive operation on them. Capturing action, "the first language of men," cinema reproduces reality analogously to how writing reproduces oral language: it is the written moment of a "total language of action."[53]

Cinema was thus defined as the "written language of action": a malleable medium, which allowed the poet to establish a physical contact with reality while simultaneously reshaping it through montage. Although pro-filmic choices are also significant in establishing the dictionary of images at his disposal, it is particularly in the editing room that the filmmaker can "denaturalize" images: "[He] either consecrates or desecrates them violently, one by one: [he] does not bind them in a correct flow, [he] does not accept this flow. But, [he] isolates them and adores them, more or less intensely, one by one.[54] Editing establishes the relationship between the two languages which, in Pasolini's theory, coexist in a film: the language of prose and the language of poetry, the narrative convention and the irrational elements. Through montage the "irrational, enteric, elementary, and barbaric elements [that] were forced below the level of consciousness" of film are allowed to emerge and create a tension with the "surface" film.[55] The "hypnotic *monstrum*" flowing underneath the narrative film that we see regularly shows language as such, as an opaque entity, and expresses the point of view of the author. The language of prose that appears in the surface film, and the language of poetry that constitutes its foundation, are inseparable in cinema, creating more or less tension depending on the stylistic choices of the author. In the editing process, the filmmaker can thus achieve the expressiveness which for Pasolini stimulates action.

Pasolini's combined reflections on poetry and cinema explain his choice of film as a critical and creative act at a time when social transformations and students' actions required intellectuals, directly or indirectly, to take a stand. At a time of cultural change, when the Italian language seemed to be losing diversity, the cinema of poetry could renew the performative function that he had previously confided to linguistic contamination: that of expressing difference and challenging assumptions of naturalness.[56] Pasolini, who traditionally associated the critical function of his poetry to the creation of a new language, saw in cinema a wider spectrum of expressive possibilities. However, his redefinition of poetic discourse to include cinema also drew attention to the qualities of poetry that made it "translinguistic." In establishing an analogy between cinema and poetry, Pasolini underscored their intrinsic dynamism and ambiguity: the qualities that he also ascribed to youth. Youth, poetry, and cinema remained part of his critical discourse because of these characteristics, even when young people took a more definite position with respect to the social order.

Although at this time he assigned to cinema the performative function of poetic discourse, he continued to write poetry, if only to expose its weaknesses. Poems became mainly investigations on the possibility of poetry, on the act of writing, and on action in general: not *poesia* as a finished product, but *poetare* as an action, ongoing and unfinished. This interrogation is evident in the poems collected in 1971 in the volume *Trasumanar e organizzar* (To Transfigure and Organize), which were composed in the six preceding years. The tension between the two verbs of the title announces the effort to maintain a balance between aesthetics and ethics in a post-ideological world. The neologism "*trasumanar*," created by Dante to express the transcending of human limits, which challenges words ("Trasumanar significar *per verba* / non si poria"), is juxtaposed to the practical "organize," with a parallel elision to underscore a difficult balance.[57] The challenge for contemporary poetry is no longer the sublime, but linguistic homogenizaton, which reduces its expressive possibilities. On the other hand, action remains the opposite extreme of the poet's *impegno*, as the Dantean genealogy of civic poetry suggests. Aesthetics and ethics remain equally important for Pasolini, particularly at a time when young people appear to be sacrificing the former for the latter. While cinema acquires both the aesthetic and ethical function that poetry used to have in the era of the "strong word," poetry becomes written action, the act of writing as a sign of non-capitulation. On the other hand, while montage confers expressive power to cinematic images, words on the page often seem to have eluded editing.

The poems in the collection are not organized in a definite structure and the section division does not seem to respond to a precise necessity, beyond pointing to an order and a self-sufficiency that are no longer there. Section titles underline poetry's loss of autonomy: "Commissioned poems," or "Limping poems," for instance. The poems' provisional titles and unfinished appearance suggest both a struggle to express meaning through words that have become inadequate, and a renunciation, on the part of the poet, of his own discriminating duty. Described by Enzo Golino as a type of "action writing" comparable to Jackson Pollock's "action painting" for the "calculated stylistic nonchalance" with which the poet seems to hurl words at the page and then let them flow and compose long verses, the poetry in *Trasumanar e organizzar* calls attention to its unfinished form and makes the language shortcomings explicit.[58] Doubting the function of poetry in a world increasingly focused on productivity, the poet declares his intention to "resist against any temptation of action-literature or intervention-literature: through the stubborn, and almost solemn, assertion of the uselessness of poetry." As a polemical gesture, rather than insisting on the importance of poetry as an instrument of social change, he redefines his activity as amateurish and useless, thus nominally freeing himself of all duties connected with being a committed intellectual: "Io non ho più il sentimento / che mi fa avere ammirazione per me. / Non considero il fondo delle mie parole / come un fondo prezioso, una grazia, / qualcosa di speciale e di particolarmente buono." (I no longer have the sense / that I'm anything special. / I don't consider the substance of my words / to be a precious substance, a grace, something out of the ordinary and particularly worthy.)[59] He presents poetry alternatively as a craft that the poet uses only when commissioned, or a practical instrument for dealing with current events. Even in these limited capacities, however, poetry often falls short of completing the task it sets for itself. In the latter case, the shortcomings are revealed by titles that document the repeated attempts to tackle a certain topic: "The Restoration of the Left," "More on the Restoration of the Left," "The Restoration of the Left (III)," "The Restoration of the Left and Who," for example. Several poems present themselves as works in progress: "Plans for Future Works," "Notes for Works to be Realized," "Resolution to Write a Poem titled 'The First Six *Canti* of Purgatory,'" "Notes for a Meaningless Harangue," "Remaking of the Harangue," and numerous other remakings and notes. Some other poems set their task in practical terms: "Press Release," "Job Application," "Lines from a Testament." The inadequacy of words and the poet's difficulty in establishing a channel of communication with his audience are visible in such titles as "Trembling Hand," "First Phatic Then Emphatic Verses."

In presenting his poems as work in progress, the poet in *Trasumanar e organizzar* relinquishes his authority, but does not completely renounce poetry's essential dynamism. Instead, he involves the readers more actively in a process of signification, analogous to the one he envisions for readers of screenplays:

> The author of the screenplay asks his addressee for a particular collaboration: namely that of lending to the text a "visual" completeness, which

Revolutionary Youth 147

it does not have, but at which it hints. The reader is an accomplice immediately ... and his representational imagination enters into a creative phase mechanically much higher and more intense than when he reads a novel.[60]

Like a screenplay, which Pasolini defines as a "a structure that wants to be another structure," poems in *Trasumanar e organizzar* ask the readers to take part in a dynamic relationship with the text and with the poet. The poems are constellated by gaps, repetitions, further attempts at expression that frustrate the construction of meaning. Frequent references to famous people and personal acquaintances, to historical as well as current events, invite the reader on a quest that might never be concluded. More than on finding answers, on defining poetry in new terms, the poet seems intent on raising questions for which no immediate answer exists. The essential dynamism of poetry, on which its critical function depends, must then be considered in a broader perspective: as an action set by the poet in a system of symbols, which becomes action again in the reader, poetry involves more than the words on the page. It is a total action, of which the words are simply the vehicle. Readers are called to decipher the poems, thus completing the act of signification that will return to poetry its inherent performativity.

In redefining poetic discourse, in both visual and verbal form, Pasolini focused primarily on its performative quality. This preoccupation, which had shaped his poetics in the past, became particularly relevant in the late 1960s, when young protesters started questioning forms of engagement and dissent that did not translate into action. Conversely, Pasolini's critique of the *Sessantotto* hinged on what he perceived as an excessive pragmatism on the part of young Italian protesters, as he expressed in his comparison with American flower children. The possibility to carve out a space for creativity and irrationality in political discourse had rekindled his hope for a new form of commitment: an ethical engagement that did not exclude aesthetics, even in neo-capitalism. No longer an expression of the transformative power of youth in the bourgeois world, verbal poetry now manifested its link to adolescence in its lack of autonomy. The features previously embodied by youth became a goal for the poet, who claimed to be uncomfortable with authority: fluidity, incompletion, unripeness. The poet's resistance to the values attached to maturity translated into a kind of poetry that spoke from the transitional space previously assigned to adolescence: "a voice which speaks from the place of youth rather than ventriloquizes it, and the impossible notion that youth might not have to come to an end."[61] The analogy with Rimbaud, to whom this description originally referred, might be said to function more in terms of aspiration than realization. However, the French poet was admittedly one of the strongest influences on Pasolini's sense of himself as a poet and intellectual, and the ideal of a form of poetry "rebellious, unstable, immature" as Rimbaud's poetry is typically read, became even more appealing for mature Pasolini than it was in his youth. In his twenties, he had aspired to enter and modify the genealogy of great poets of the tradition; in his forties, he rejected expressions of maturity and recast poetry as the "liminal zone of adolescence."[62] Even as young people were articulating their position clearly in the streets, the poetry of *Trasumanar e organizzar* reflected the "unfinished, uncertain, or unstable attitudes that characterize adolescence, as adults continue to imagine it."[63]

5 Fatherless Youth: Fathers, Children, Orphans

Ugly Verses for Spoiled Children: "The PCI to the Young!"

Pasolini's enthusiasm for the American student movement and their use of an alternative form of protest, based on visuality and irrationality, helps understand his disapproval for its Italian counterpart. While the representatives of "the other America" were able, in his opinion, to create a new revolutionary discourse that could effectively undermine the logic of the establishment, he saw Italian students adopt a discourse of protest that they inherited from their fathers and that, in his view, could no longer change a neo-capitalist society. He expounded this opinion in the famous poem "The PCI to the Young!" published in 1968, one year after his Milan encounter with Allen Ginsberg. In that year, the student movement had gained strength and was met by violent repression. Although the material and cultural origins for the protest could be traced back to the early 1960s, and the first signs of tumult had been visible already in 1966, university occupations started in the fall of 1967 in Trento, the site of Italy's first school of sociology. Soon students occupied the Catholic University in Milan, and then Palazzo Campana, at the University of Turin. Students questioned outdated curricula and pedagogical approaches, and demanded a more direct involvement in the decisions regarding their education. The protest gained momentum in Turin, the city symbol of the "economic miracle," where a high concentration of young factory workers had already favoured the formation of a "workerist" movement (*operaismo*), an alternative to traditional union and party organizations. The workerist movement, and the young Marxist-Leninist intellectuals who gathered around the review *Quaderni Rossi* in Turin, were both instrumental in creating the basis for the collaboration between students and workers that characterized the Italian protest.[1] Equally important was the alternative academic experience of the sociology students in Trento.[2] By early 1968, the movement had spread to universities throughout Italy and many high schools, and reached its apex in the spring. The so-called "Battle of Valle Giulia," in which students clashed with the police at the School of Architecture in Rome on March 1, 1968, marked a decisive moment in which violence – hundreds of injured students and policemen – made its appearance in a movement that had until then been largely peaceful.

The "Battle of Valle Giulia," became a paradigmatic event in the debate over the *Sessantotto* also thanks to the dispute generated by the poem "The PCI to the Young!," which Pasolini composed on the occasion. Clearly meant as a provocation, the long free-verse poem mocks the students' revolutionary aspirations in the face of their bourgeois background. Students, the poem maintains, are young bourgeois who protest a system that reveres them, and in so doing, rejuvenate it. They do not really understand the conditions of working-class youth, even though they claim to speak for everyone. If they did, they would also understand that the only effective instrument for fighting the bourgeois system is the Communist Party. Students should take over, destroy the bourgeois residues of the party, and through its resources organize a true revolution. The argument is presented via a series of provocations, the most famous of which, persisting over forty years later as the emblem of Pasolini's position with respect to the *Sessantotto*, sets him openly against the students: "Quando ieri a Valle Giulia avete fatto a botte / coi poliziotti, / io simpatizzavo coi poliziotti!" (When yesterday at Valle Giulia you fought with the policemen, / I sympathized with the policemen!). The provocation worked, aided also by a shrewd editorial strategy: lines from the poem, leaked from the press agency to major newspapers, were quoted and criticized days before the anticipated "early" publication of the poem in the weekly *l'Espresso*, and weeks before the official publication of the "ugly verses," supplemented by a prose "Apology," in the literary review *Nuovi Argomenti*, which Pasolini co-edited at the time with Alberto Moravia and Alberto Carocci. *L'Espresso* accompanied its publication with a debate between Pasolini, Vittorio Foa, the secretary of CGIL (Confederazione Generale Italiana del Lavoro), the union affiliated with the Communist Party, and Claudio Petruccioli, the national secretary of the youth organization of the PCI (FGCI). The discussion, moderated by journalist Nello Ajello, was part of a continued *reportage* on the student protest, which the magazine had run for weeks. Invited representatives of the student movement refused to participate in a debate held in a newspaper office. They only read two prepared statements, basically inviting Pasolini to get to know young people better by meeting them on their ground, and then left. Despite his claimed admiration for American intellectuals who "threw their body into the fight," Pasolini did not accept the invitation. He, and fellow intellectuals, continued to talk *about* young people and *to* them, more than *with* them.

The generational discourse is evident throughout "The PCI to the Young!," particularly in the poet's choice to address the students as *"figli."* "Avete facce di figli di papà / Vi odio come odio i vostri papà. / Buona razza non mente." (You have the faces of spoiled children. / [I hate you like I hate your daddies. / Good blood doesn't lie.)[3] These verses, quoted and requoted even out of context, offered the headlines for articles on Pasolini, the "student-hater," in various newspapers: from the banner headline "Vi odio, cari studenti" (I hate you, dear students) given to the debate in *l'Espresso*, to "Pasolini in versi contro gli studenti," (Pasolini in verse against the students), and "Infuriati gli universitari per una poesia di Pasolini" (University students infuriated due to a poem by Pasolini), to "Poesia di Pasolini contro i filocinesi" (Pasolini's poem against the philo-Chinese) and "Pasolini contro i 'cinesi'" (Pasolini against the "Chinese"). Those memorable lines identify protesting students as *figli di papà* (papa's boys, literally), spoiled bourgeois children, who demand only that which is due to them, that is, their fathers' position in power. Although the protest rhetoric is based on a discourse of class struggle, Pasolini argues, there is no actual class conflict when bourgeois children attack their bourgeois fathers: "You are their children, / their hope, their future; if they reproach you / they are certainly not preparing a class conflict / against you! If anything, / the old civil war." Students appear to be unaware that the power structure they are allegedly fighting needs and welcomes their protest: "Now the journalists of all the world (including / those of television) / kiss (as I believe one still says in the language / of the Universities) your ass. Not me, friends."[4] In what is perhaps the most important argument in the poem, as he points out in debates, Pasolini distances himself from fellow intellectuals, "middle-aged flatterers," who embrace the student movement in order "to feel young and to create a blackmailing virginity."[5]

Although he criticizes these middle-aged intellectuals who side with the students, but also does not recognize himself in the bitter "student hater" of newspaper headlines, Pasolini does clarify his position towards youth in this poem. The expression *figli di papà* – young people who receive everything from their fathers – allows the poet to reintroduce the contrast between Italian students, who employ an inherited revolutionary discourse, and the creative protest of the American "flower children," or *figli dei fiori* in Italian:

> Look at / the Americans, your adorable contemporaries, / with their foolish flowers, they are inventing / a "new" revolutionary language! / They invent it day by day! / But you can't do it because in Europe there already is one: / can you ignore it? / Yes, you want to ignore it (with great satisfaction / of the *Times* and of *Tempo*.) / You ignore it going, with the moralism of the deep provinces, / "more to the left." Strange, / abandoning the revolutionary language / of the poor, old, official Communist / Party of Togliatti, / you have adopted a heretical variant of it / but on the basis of the lowest jargon / of sociologists without ideology (or of the bureaucratic daddies).[6]

The contrast indicated by Pasolini in his letter to Allen Ginsberg is here addressed directly to the students. Pasolini presents flower children as a model, only to conclude that his interlocutors cannot, and should not, disregard the continuing importance of class discourse in Italy. While American students can invent a new and creative revolutionary language, because their society does not know class struggle, Italian students must consider not only the existing Marxist discourse, but the impact of class on the experience of youth. The only form of class conflict in the Italian student protest was absurdly revealed at Valle Giulia where, says Pasolini, middle-class students were fighting against working-class policemen: "At Valle Giulia, yesterday, we have thus had a fragment / of class conflict; and you my friends (even though on the side / of reason), were the rich, / while the policemen (who were in the / wrong) were poor. A nice victory, then, / yours!"[7] For this reason Pasolini controversially sides with the young policemen, *figli di poveri* (children of poor families), against the bourgeois students, *figli di papà*.

By labelling protesting students as *figli di papà* Pasolini not only reintroduced the notion of class struggle in different terms from those assumed by the protesters. He also reduced the protest to an Oedipal conflict that ultimately diminished its importance as a radically new, and global, event. In claiming that students remained bourgeois despite their spontaneous identification with working-class youths, he rejected the same idea that allowed young Italians to embrace the case of young

Americans drafted in the Vietnam War, of young South American revolutionaries, and so on: a generational identity that transcended class and cultural specificity. As Lorenza Mazzetti commented in her column in *Vie Nuove* soon after the publication of the poem in *l'Espresso*:

> Pasolini has an Oedipal view of today's young people. He sees them as children who kill their fathers in order to sit on their thrones and claim the power and the crown ... Pasolini sees them in a generational war, adults against youth who, like anthropophagous creatures, cannibals, fight each other. But Pasolini does not realize that this is precisely how the newspaper *Il Tempo* sees them, as it tries to turn into an Oedipal and generational struggle what is a Promethean struggle for the end of all authority of any generation over any other.[8]

Although he highlighted the father-son continuity to underline the class difference between students and young workers, an undeniable reality of the movement, Pasolini's interpretation was based on the assumption that the experience of youth repeats itself from cohort to cohort. Not allowing for the possibility that this generation was radically different from the ones that preceded it, because it had been shaped by unique historical experiences, this position disregarded a notion of youth that was both the product and the condition of the *Sessantotto*. A cartoon by Roberto Galve succinctly summarized the outcome of this debate: in the first frame, a boy and a girl meet a second boy, who is wearing a helmet and carrying a baton. "And who are you?" the first boy asks. "I am the policeman's son," answers Helmet Boy. In the next frame, the first boy keeps asking: "And what are you gonna be when you grow up?" "A policeman," answers Helmet Boy. In the third frame, Helmet Boy is gone. The girl asks coyly "What are you thinking about, my love?" Her pensive friend answers "About Pasolini." Affirming the existence of a father-son continuity within classes was not in itself a groundbreaking statement. It was no secret that the majority of university students in 1968, and also many high school students, were still bourgeois, and that their privilege could not be overlooked, as the material needs of working-class youth could not be forgotten. Yet, in the context of 1968, Pasolini's *figli di papà* statement sounded outrageous because it disregarded the shared belief that a Promethean struggle could prevail over any class-specific generational turnover. And although it was a position shared by many conservative critics of the student movement, it became specifically associated with Pasolini, who was otherwise supportive of youthful initiative.

As Pasolini's "official" interpretation of the student movement, "The PCI to the Young!" brought to the surface an unresolved tension between different concepts of youth coexisting in his oeuvre. The celebration of *gioventù* in all of his writings is based on a romantic notion of youth as a fleeting life phase, fluid, and in permanent transition, but which can be expected to recur similarly generation after generation. The inherently positive qualities of adolescence are enhanced by socially marginal conditions, but, as he repeatedly reassured readers of *Vie Nuove* worried about a supposed crisis of Italian youth in 1960, "the only crisis is growing up." The cultural construct influenced his social critique, allowing him to question, for example, the imposition of coming-of-age models developed by and for bourgeois youth onto other classes, as he did in the Roman novels. However, his basically steady generational view (youth is in flux, it repeats itself, and it is always good) clashes with his essentialist view of social class, and the latter always prevails. Youth can express difference within a class system, but somehow its disruptive force is class-specific and cannot cross social boundaries. In fact, the enthusiasm he had felt for youthful countercultural demonstrations in New York was linked to their being expressions of a society that he perceived as classless.

When a new historical cohort had started to challenge generational continuities at the beginning of the 1960s, Pasolini had defended them invoking an intrinsic "goodness" of youth as a life cycle. He had projected a desired harmony between young and old Communists onto the fictionalized recollection of political struggle in late 1940s Friuli, and portrayed young people leading the rallies against landowners as new partisans. Once again, in 1968, young people must be the avant-garde of a multigenerational struggle, in Pasolini's opinion. Like in the novel *Il sogno di una cosa*, if they do not wear flowers, they must enthusiastically carry red flags: "But instead, children, go attack Federations! / Go invade Cells! / Go occupy the offices of the Central Committee! Go, go / camp out in Via delle Botteghe Oscure! / If you want power, at least take over the power / of a party which nevertheless is in the opposition."[9] Revolutionary discourse in Italy must deal with Marxism, even though its rationalism, which Pasolini always felt as a strong limitation, appeared out of touch with contemporary reality. Given the specific situation, young Italians ought to engage in a radical renovation of the Communist Party, and contribute to the completion of a revolution that had been started in the forties. However, the series of rhetorical turns concluding the poem casts an ironic light on the whole argument:

> In any case: the PCI to the young! / .... / But ah, what am I suggesting to you? What am I / recommending? Towards what am I pushing you? / I repent, I repent! / I have taken the road which leads to the lesser evil, / may God damn me. Don't listen to me. / Ahi, ahi, ahi, / blackmailed blackmailer, / I was blowing the trumpets of common sense! / I stopped barely in time, / saving at the same time, / fanatic dualism and ambiguity... / But I have reached the edge of shame... / (Oh God! must I take into consideration/ the eventuality of fighting the Civil War alongside you / putting aside my old idea of Revolution?)

The rapidly changing stance in the final lines makes the poet's ambivalence towards youth protest explicit and anticipates the debate that the poem would cause. Pasolini was clearly aware of his readers' expectations and of the effect that his taking a public stance on the movement would have. Given his well-known interest in youth, he might be expected to support the *Sessantotto*, and the apparent endorsement of the PCI given in the poem was likely to surprise the readers familiar with Pasolini's critical attitude towards the party. The prose "Apology," which accompanied "The PCI to the Young!" when it was published in *Nuovi Argomenti*, defined the poem as ironic and self-ironic: "Everything is said *in quotation marks*." The poet's polemical stance, his sympathy for the "poor policemen," and the final recantation of his statements should be read as a provocative way of exposing a complex problem confronting young protesters:

> Through neo-capitalism the bourgeoisie is becoming the human condition. Those who are born into this entropy cannot in any way metaphysically be outside of it. It's over. For this I provoke the young. They are, presumably, the last generation which sees workers and peasants; the next generation will only see bourgeois entropy around itself.[10]

Neo-capitalism was transforming the bourgeoisie, and "the petit bourgeois of today is no longer the one who is defined in the classics of Marxism, for example in Lenin." Consequently, even a civil war fought by the bourgeoisie against itself could not lead to a revolution. Young protesters, Pasolini claimed, demanded a democratization of society that was already happening through neo-capitalism. They should instead focus on the false emancipation of ever-larger segments of the population to a petit bourgeois lifestyle, a form of "Development" (*Sviluppo*) that did not equal real "Progress" (*Progresso*). His provocation tried, thus, to raise awareness of the diversity being lost in the bourgeois transformation of Italy and of the necessity to consider different approaches to this new condition.

At the most immediate level, Pasolini's complex and contradictory relationship with the Italian student movement reveals a discomfort with the emergence of global youth culture. He saw the globalization of generational interests and values as a loss of specificity that weakened the cultural importance of youth within a specific community. This generation was the last that could count on a direct connection to pre-economic boom Italy, through their biological and ideological fathers. The invitation to invade cells and federations, even if ironic, can be read as a desperate attempt to restore that lineage. More broadly, his critique of the *Sessantotto* indicates a concern with the transformation of society and his own poetic and political role therein. Italy was modernizing following a model of development that was imposed from the outside, rather than organic to its specific culture. Since the younger generations demanded not simply to participate in the modernization of the country, but to lead its democratic transformation, he offered them suggestions for acquiring a better awareness of the "bourgeois evil." Young people should "get rid of the horrible classist definition of students and become intellectuals" and "implement the last possible choice in favor of what is not bourgeois ... by substituting the force of reason for the traumatic and personal reasons to which I alluded." Most importantly, they should find their instruments of analysis "outside of sociology as well as the classics of Marxism."[11] This suggestion, which takes issue with the analyses conducted by the Trento students and the Marxist-Leninist groups around *Quaderni Rossi* and *Quaderni Piacentini*, is part of a broader cultural critique of the *Sessantotto*, which occupied Pasolini beyond the provocation he launched with "The PCI to the Young!"

In a collective counter-response addressed to those who had commented on the poem, he elaborated on the idea that in rejecting humanistic culture, students were depriving themselves of important critical instruments, which they could apply to neo-capitalism: "In their extreme and negative position (which, as such, is very attractive to me), students bundle together (in order to throw them out), all "humanist intellectuals," who until now have led the labour aristocracy and farmers' masses in revolutions, or simply in "Resistances."[12] The bourgeois condition, which was becoming universal, produced its own internal conflicts, in order to perpetuate itself. Young people fulfilled the traditional role of rejuvenators of society while propagating bourgeois values: "neo-capitalism, in its totality, refusing and overcoming classic capitalism. New culture, technical and urban, overthrowing old culture, humanistic and rural."[13]

Free of the provocation that shapes "The PCI to the Young!," this article contains an articulated analysis of the relationship between the young protesters and the historical Left. Three options confronted the young members of the student movement, suggested Pasolini: they could stay what they were, that is, "something fluid and indescribable" although "extraordinarily democratic and fascinating"; they could position themselves "left of the PCI" and compete for its constitutency, the workers' masses; or they could take over the PCI.[14] Refusing to help them choose, he declared that he was "tempted on the one hand by perpetual revolt, on the other by his love for the working class, which requires cautious steps and common sense."[15] He declared his fascination with the youthful approach to the protest ("What they did in these months was beautiful," "they are strong of a strength, which is also youth"), but what was conceived as "free and informal" needed to take a definite shape ("prendere forma") if it wanted to effectively involve the workers. The students' movement embodied the tension between being and doing, central to Pasolini's reflection on the intellectual's commitment in this period.

In the same article, Pasolini also expanded on a distinction he had made in the poem and in his letter to Allen Ginsberg, between the Italian and the American student movements, which elucidates his critique of the *sessantottini*:

> I have no critique of the American and German student revolts: on this I agree with Moravia: they are the most beautiful events of the century; because they invent a new revolutionary substance and a new form (in America from scratch: from bourgeois entropy; in Germany in order to rebuild what Hitler had physically eliminated).[16]

He was "completely on the side of American and German students" because "they act and speak in a way incomprehensible to their fathers." In Italy (and in France) on the other hand, "young and old speak the same language ... Never have two generations understood one another so well. Never have two generations confronted one another with such reciprocal understanding of their ends and means."[17] The existing language of protest, Marxism, limited the possibilities of Italian and French students, while their American and German peers were free to invent an extraordinary new language. His suggestion for the former was to identify their fathers' responsibilities (*colpe*) and the mistakes that their fathers had not yet recognized. If they wanted to tear apart the bourgeois system, they needed to be aware of their position within a totality that anticipated and co-opted even students' rebellion. Only this awareness could produce a kind of action and discourse that were truly scandalous.

Subsequent responses to the *Sessantotto* focused on two broader issues that the student protest had brought into play: the first was the need to redefine his intellectual identity, once the identification with youth was challenged by young people's actions; the second was the redefinition of a form of *impegno* that could involve artists and intellectuals, in view of the call to action that was issued by the young. The protest of 1968 forced Pasolini to acknowledge that this generation's experience of youth was radically different from his own, a quarter century earlier. There was very little cultural continuity between these children and their "fathers," because the historical conditions that defined the generation of the *sessantottini* were radically new, and stronger than any common experiences of youth as a life cycle, which Pasolini had assumed and celebrated. His identification with adolescence corresponded to a glorification of change and hybridity, but also to an existence at the margins of the social order. When young people began to take action, he saw them becoming incorporated into a patriarchal order on which they lacked perspective. Their actions, and the cultural change that accompanied them, also compelled intellectuals and artists to rethink their social role, a particularly problematic task for someone like Pasolini who had shaped his poetics on an unorthodox Communism and the idea of rejuvenating the legacy of a great literary tradition. Many articles and poems written in 1968 and 1969 reflect at length on these problems, while the two films realized in those years, *Teorema* and *Porcile*, provide his poetic contribution to the *Sessantotto*.

Wanting to Be Orphans, Refusing to Be a Father: *Il Caos*

"At the end of the Sixties, orphanhood becomes a slogan" states historian Luisa Passerini, quoting a graffiti on a university wall that summarized a feeling shared by many young people in that period: "I want to be an orphan."[18] The need to establish their autonomy induced the *sessantottini* to reject paternal authority in many forms. Pasolini's verse libel,

"The PCI to the Young!" which referred to them as *"figli di papà"* who would soon fill their fathers' position of power, could hardly have hit a more sensitive spot. Although the debate that it stirred confirmed the success of the provocation, Pasolini's further reflection on the student movement articulated a more complex father-children relationship. While those "ugly verses" had provokingly emphasized the bond between bourgeois children and their fathers, further considerations induced the author to acknowledge the existence of an unbridgeable gap between the two generations. Separating fathers and children was not merely age difference, but a cultural divide.

He explored that relationship, which included him as a reluctant father, in a series of short articles published in the popular magazine *Il Tempo Illustrato*. Similarly to the *Dialoghi* he had maintained in the PCI newspaper *Vie Nuove* in the early 1960s, Pasolini's collaboration with the weekly *Il Caos* in the 1968–70 period gave him the opportunity to comment on current events, which naturally included student protests. Whereas the Communist weekly had invited him in order to attract younger readers, *Il Tempo Illustrato* wanted to take advantage of his maverick reputation and his critical appraisal of the student movement, a clear indication of the change in Pasolini's reputation.[19] Immediately, in an attempt to justify a collaboration that might surprise his readers, Pasolini began a reflection on his role as a public intellectual, which spanned over several weeks: it regarded issues of authority, age, and contemporary youth. Because of the coincidence of several factors – 1968, his intense activity of these years, his recurrent identification with youth throughout his career – redefining his intellectual position meant also renegotiating his relationship with youth: "A young person who awakes (to culture) today cannot but see me as part of this sort of paternal AUTHORITY that overhelms him. Well, I don't want to allow that.")[20] Pasolini used *Il Caos* as an arena in which he could challenge the authority that he felt already accompanied his celebrity.

Identification with youth had been for Pasolini a way to express his aversion to authority in the form of ossified conventions, normalizing discourses of development, and stifling moral codes. At the end of the 1960s that identification clashed both with his age (46 in 1968) and the fame he enjoyed as a public intellectual. Like many Italian writers before and after him, Pasolini could count on his opinions having resonance beyond literary circles. In addition to that, his work in cinema, collaboration with widely circulating newspapers, and frequent press reports of his appearances in court granted Pasolini a higher degree of name and face recognition than most poets in his time. As he had done in the pages of *Vie Nuove* in 1964, even in *Tempo* he professed discomfort with that celebrity, and with the authority it conferred on his statements. Earlier, he had purportedly agreed to play the game of celebrity because, he claimed, "those who, through the cultural industry or through the help of a current of thought, or a party organization, or chance, become 'myths,' 'authorities,' acquire new duties towards themselves and towards others."[21] Now, while he admitted "I inescapably belong to an undifferentiated AUTHORITY," he reopened the discussion considering his changed relationship with young people and with the Communist Party.[22]

The renegotiation of his paternal authority began with a reasserting of his marginal position with respect to the Communist Party, one of the "great fathers" questioned by the student movement. As a "*compagno di strada*," a fellow traveller rather than an intellectual fully committed to party politics, he could take advantage of the space for self-expression in a commercial magazine, like *Il Tempo Illustrato*, through a relationship that would be "personally friendly" but "ideologically cynical." Through his self-identification as a fellow traveller, ironically introduced by the crow in *Uccellacci e uccellini*, Pasolini reoccupied an ambiguous position that he had professed since the publication of *Le ceneri di Gramsci*. However, the famous Trotsky phrase "fellow traveller" also introduced the role assigned to intellectuals by the student movement, according to Rossana Rossanda's essay *L'anno degli studenti*, which Pasolini reviewed in the same issue. Rossanda's definition of intellectuals as "fellow travellers," that is, external witnesses to the struggle of the students and young workers, forced Pasolini to reconsider his critical role as an intellectual and his potential identification with young protesters. As an external witness to the student movement, an intellectual must establish another form of presence in order to fulfil his critical role: "He must somehow try to be present, at least pragmatically and existentially, even if theoretically his presence cannot be proved!"[23] A substantial part of Pasolini's activity that year constitutes an attempt to establish alternative forms of presence in consideration of the conditions created by the student movement.

His disidentification with authority became more explicit as a refusal to play a fatherly role to the younger generation, which he expressed in an article titled "La volontà di non essere padre" (The Will Not to

Be a Father). His age and the activism of contemporary young people forced a father role upon him that he did not accept:

> When I observe, with love or loathing, with complicity or anger, etc., the members of the Student Movement, one feeling is constant and certain: the will to not consider myself as their father. There are many reasons for this. There is, certainly, in me, a general will not to be a father (that is, not to assimilate myself to my father and to fathers in general), etc. And maybe there is also the rivalry of a father (who is a father despite himself) against his children: (a father) who therefore tries to deny his fatherly position in order to deny his children their rights as children.[24]

Having founded his critical discourse on an anti-authoritarianism, which he identified with the absolute confrontation of youth, he could not accept a fatherly role without questioning his entire poetics, particularly at a time when paternal authorities were under attack. However, he explained his "will not to be a father" also with "objective reasons," namely the fundamental difference between the students' generation and his own. Father-children relationships are based on cultural continuity, and the transformation of Italy in post-war years created a radically different generation of children:

> 1) the human and cultural precociousness of the members of the latest generation (who will certainly read these naïve lines of mine with "adult" irony): because of that, they don't look at all like children (or, in any case, there is also in them a veiled, mysterious will not to be children); 2) the fact that the new generation was born and grew up in a different era, with interests and lifestyles so different: and which, even through the pure and simple fact of living, they experience in a way that is not accessible to us if not from the outside, and as a "prediction."[25]

Pasolini was forced to acknowledge the existence of a historical difference between the young people of the late sixties and his generation. The discontinuity between his experience of youth and theirs only allowed him at best to "predict" what their interests might be, but not to really understand them. Father-children continuity, traditionally based on "different degrees of experience of the same world," was unattainable because 1960s children grew up in a "post-humanistic" world, radically different from the world of their fathers.

Young *sessantottini* had grown up in a time of economic growth and prosperity, which extended to larger segments of the population lifestyles previously limited to the bourgeoisie. This experience incorporated them in a patriarchal order on which they lacked, in Pasolini's view, an external perspective. As he saw young people become integrated in a system he condemned, Pasolini's attention turned to a subcohort of that generation that still occupied a marginal position: young women. Highlighting the masculine gender implicit in general terms such as *"figli"* and *"studenti,"* which he used as gender-neutral too, he articulated his willingness to fulfil his paternal responsibilities towards female students:

> Instead, when I see female students – bold, proud, factious, moving companions – usually so petite, pale, weak – or comically childlike – so scantily dressed as to seem part victim and part slut – with their petit bourgeoisie imprinted on their pretty skin, and in their eyes which stare full of uncertainty and, together, of so much idealism and consciousness, I am deeply moved. To one of these female students, tender and defiant, I really feel like a father.[26]

Unlike their male counterparts, young women seemed to maintain those liminal features that connoted cultural authenticity in Pasolini's world view. Because their relationship to paternal authority was not based on the expectation that they replace their fathers, as was the case with bourgeois sons, they represented a true alternative to the incorporation of young men in a self-perpetuating bourgeois system. Young women, female students, even when perceived as daughters, maintained an otherness with respect to existing power structures that could truly subvert them. They could embody an absolute confrontation that did not run the risk of falling back into existing forms through which neo-capitalist power reproduces itself. As Colleen Ryan-Scheutz argues, daughters are the last bulwark of authenticity among young people, allowing Pasolini "to extend his assault on the father, on neo-capitalist culture, and on patriarchy at large."[27] Young women complicate the generational conflict and reintroduce alterity into youth.

Generational Conflicts: Rebellious Children and Fascist Fathers

A further elaboration of the historical difference between the two generations is found in the poem "La Maturità di Dutschke" (Dutschke's

Maturity), which was commissioned by *Tempo* after the attempted assassination of the leader of the German student movement in April 1968.[28] Even though chronologically Rudy Dutschke should be his son, Pasolini relates to him in brotherly terms, as if the German student leader were a young version of him. "Per tutto il periodo in cui tu non eri nato, / io ho ragionato. Non so nel ventre di quale madre tu stavi. / Non l'ho fecondata io, quella donna, questo è certo. / Eppure, se considero il lungo periodo di tempo, / che per me passò dopo la nascita e per te prima, / non c'è dubbio: ti sono padre. / Perché allora, ti guardo con l'occhio del figlio?" (Long before you were born, / I reasoned. I don't know in whose mother's womb you dwelt. / It was not I who impregnated that woman, this is certain. / Yet, if I consider the passage of time / after my birth and before yours, / there can be no doubt: I am your father. / Why, then, do I look at you through a son's eyes?)[29] Pasolini and Dutschke belong to different historical cohorts, but they are connected in the poet's mind by a perceived common struggle against a specific political generation: Nazi-Fascism as a sort of *Über*-father. Pasolini recollects his own coming-of-age as a rebellion against his Fascist "fathers": "Non ho mai usato una sola parola / usata dai miei padri (eccetto che per augurargli l'Inferno). / La loro criminalità e il loro odio per la ragione / sono dei puri e semplici pesi nella mia vita" (I never used a single word / used by my fathers [except for wishing that they go to Hell]. / Their criminality and their hatred for reason / are pure and simple burdens on my life).[30] Similarly, in Germany, generational rebellion in 1968 was complicated by an uncomfortable overlap between family and national issues – parents' unresolved relationship with the defeated Nazi regime – while in Italy the Resistance had at least partially exorcised that burden.[31]

The perceived parallelism between his interlocutor's situation and his own – "la borghesia dalle cui viscere misteriosamente sei nato, / l'ho vista coi miei occhi" (the bourgeoisie from whose viscera you were mysteriously born / I saw it with my own eyes) – allows the poet to address Dutschke on equal terms and offer him brotherly advice: "Non lasciarti ingannare dalla loro buona volontà, / dalla loro tormentata sensibilità, dalla loro comica timidezza! Sono tutti terrorizzati, padre mio, capo." (Don't let their good will fool you, or their tormented sensibility, or their comic shyness! They are all terrified, father, boss.) Because of that continuity, the young Sozialistischer Deutscher Studentenbund leader is equipped to carry on the rebellion initiated by the poet, whose choice to address him as "father" indicates a definitive abdication of power. The poet has passed on the results of his struggle with the Fascist fathers to those younger than him, like Dutschke, who have acquired, consequently "a paternal authority" (un' autorità ... paterna). Because of that authority they are confident: "E i tuoi giovani coetanei / vanno per la strada maestra, non per i sentieri." (And your young peers/ choose the highway, not the trails.)[32]

The imaginary encounter with the leader of the German student movement brought to the surface an earlier generational conflict, which had been formative for Pasolini and absent from the *sessantottini*'s experience. Originated as a reflection on the 1968 revolt, the poetic address to Dutschke occasioned a recollection of the poet's own youth, and a refashioning of his coming-of-age as a rebellion against the Fascist regime, which Pasolini further developed in interviews. In two long interviews, with Jean Duflot and Oswald Stack, he recognized a connection between the difficult relationship he had with his father and the latter's acceptance of Fascism.[33] He reconstructed his cultural coming-of-age – the discovery of Rimbaud, French Symbolist poets, Italian Hermeticism – as an early form of anti-Fascism. Political and cultural anti-Fascism were thus linked to Oedipal conflict and situated at the origin of his poetics, in a retrospective shaping of authorial self that became particularly important at this time, when age and fame challenged his anti-authoritarianism. The generational gap between those who defined their identity in relation to Fascism and those who did so in relation to the economic miracle appeared unbridgeable, and the fundamental difference lay in the function exercised by humanistic culture.

Besides allowing the mature poet to showcase his own rebellious youth, the frequent references to his coming-of-age under Fascism introduced a decisive point in Pasolini's critique of the '68 generation, which would inform his 1970s essays: the importance of humanistic culture for his emancipation from Fascism. He returned to the topic of an alleged cultural decline among the young in the poem "La poesia della tradizione" (The Poetry of Tradition), which resumes the direct appeal to young people found in "The PCI to the Young!" and broadens it to a generational issue: "Oh unfortunate generation! / What will happen tomorrow, if that ruling class – / when they were fledglings / they didn't get to know the poetry of the tradition." The memory of *Eredi*, his youthful project based on the idea of entering and altering an existing genealogy of poets, informs, by contrast, his critique of the *sessantottini*, a generation growing up among people who scorned tradition and "took literally their mock-ribald irony / erecting juvenile barriers against the ruling class of the past." Because contemporary youth came of age in a world that "wanted to discredit history –its (own); / it wanted to wipe the slate clean of the past – its (own)," the student protest responds, in his view, to an inherent dynamic of neo-capitalism, which "ask(s) its new children to help it / contradict itself, in order to continue." Pasolini's critique is based on the idea that in breaking ties with the humanistic tradition, the students reject a powerful instrument with which they could carry out their critical duty as young intellectuals. In what appears as a democratic gesture, the rejection of a tradition that sets bourgeois students apart from young workers, they eschew the chance to exercise a powerful act of confrontation in favour of a more pragmatic revolution: "poor Calvinist generation as at the bourgeoisie's origins / adolescently pragmatic, childishly active / you sought salvation in organization / (which can't produce anything but more organization)." In so doing they perpetrate "treasons leading to blackmail / and thus unhappiness."[34]

Action has taken precedence over contemplation, pragmatic goals over visionary ideals: *organizzar* (to organize) prevails over *trasumanar* (to transfigure) even in another poem, "Trasumanar e organizzar," which gives the collection its title: "you've spent the days of your youth / speaking the jargon of bureaucratic democracy / never departing from the repetition of formulas, / for organizing can be signified not through words / but through formulas, yes." While in Dante's verse words are insufficient to express the divine experience, transcending human limits, in Pasolini's version they are unnecessary to express action, or the practical goal of the revolution. So while young people reject conformity nominally, with their actions they in fact conform: "…distancing themselves from culture, young protesters automatically opt for action and utilitarianism, and resign themselves to the situation in which the system strives to integrate them."[35] By rejecting traditional humanistic culture in the name of modernization, the *sessantottini*'s disobedience simply obeys the practical requirements of consumer power.

Young people's actions in 1968 imposed a redefinition of *impegno* on Pasolini's part. In particular, the imbalance he observed between the pragmatic and visionary components of the *Sessantotto* induced him to further reflect on the relationship between action and poetry as forms of protest. His ambivalent participation in the occupation of the Venice Film Festival organized by the Association of Cinema Authors (ANAC) indicated some discomfort with the possibility of partaking in direct action. Initially opposed to boycotting the festival altogether, he accepted the invitation to participate with *Teorema*. He would "continue to cynically exploit the system" in order to express his views through the film.[36] A week later, however, he reached an agreement with ANAC concerning the form of the protest and decided to take part in the occupation. At that point he wrote an open letter to the director of the festival, Luigi Chiarini, clarifying his current support for the protest, but also praising him for his dedication to the festival. He invoked "the advent of children (*figli*) on the scene" as the phenomenon that forced intellectuals of his generation to review their positions: on one hand the awareness of being a "father" and of the duties that such position imposed; on the other a renewed hope in the possibility to uproot the "bourgeois malady" that had crystallized inside him.[37] The sit-ins in Venice were violently interrupted by the police. *Teorema* was still screened for the critics, but Pasolini encouraged them to leave the theatre as an expression of dissent. The majority of critics, however, stayed and Pasolini later granted a press conference. Although he had pre-emptively justified his behaviour by stating that he was not afraid of "any contradiction, any backtracking, any ridicule," his inconsistent behaviour, playing protest one day and fulfilling his obligations to the producer the next, attracted criticism.[38]

The concern with the excessively pragmatic goals he noticed in the students' actions, and the desire to find a critical space for writers and artists operating within cultural institutions, inspired a conversation between Pasolini and his friend, the writer Alberto Moravia, in the pages of *Tempo Illustrato*. Occasioned by a dispute that arose within the jury of a literary prize, on the possibility of expressing dissent through an award, the dialogue between the two writers focuses on the relationship between literature and action. Moravia distinguishes between two forms of protest – confrontation (*contestazione*) and revolution (*rivoluzione*) – by saying that the former "sta a metà strada tra la critica e la rivoluzione" (stands halfway between critique and revolution). *Contestazione* is more radical than critique, he says, inasmuch as "it questions the validity of institutions, but it also maintains a 'demonstrative' quality that true revolutions don't possess."[39] He then situates literature, and art in general, in the realm of confrontation, ascribing its effect to its ambiguity and symbolic value. Literature and art are thus forms of action. Pasolini's pointed questions clearly indicate his personal interest in the definition provided by Moravia, which resonates with his own dynamic view of poetic discourse, and with his critique of the limited "reasonable and practical" goals of the Italian student movement. A creative approach that goes beyond practical goals allows for the engagement of artists regardless of their direct involvement in political activity. When Moravia observes that in Italy *contestazione* prevails over *rivoluzione*, Pasolini reflects that "consequently, it would be our duty to abandon creative ambiguity and switch to revolutionary clarity. But couldn't one achieve the same goal by stressing ambiguity in an abnormal and scandalous way?"[40] Clearly, Pasolini favours "creative ambiguity" over "revolutionary clarity," that is, poetic, rather than political, action.

Moravia's definition of literature as *contestazione*, an ideal confrontation of the establishment that did not exclude ambiguity, appealed to Pasolini because it described the function he attributed to both youth and poetry. Just as the polysemic and expressive language of poetry undermined by its very presence the conformity of neo-capitalism, the inherent ambiguity and permanent transformation of youth challenged stifling conventions and established patterns. Blurring the distinction between being and doing, youth, in Pasolini's interpretation, had a transformative effect on society even without engaging in political action. By challenging fixed categories, youth was intrinsically rebellious. Young people's presence had the effect of *contestazione*, a power capable of disrupting the rational bourgeois system, equivalent, or even superior, to any organized actions. Conversely, by embracing "revolutionary clarity" young people lost some of the transformative power that depended on their exclusion from the social system. Both youth and poetry, as forms of *contestazione*, were being challenged, in Pasolini's view, by the social transformation of Italy: young people had embraced action and occupied a different place in society; poetry had lost its expressiveness due to the linguistic homogenization of the country. Consequently, his preoccupation as a poet who identified with youth was to find ways to express difference through youth and poetry under the new conditions. Cinema as "the written language of action" would respond to this double necessity.

Challenged by the students' actions and his own celebrity, Pasolini's disidentification with authority required him to renegotiate his paternal role and redefine the critical function of poetry. Such redefinition led him to claim the value of poetry as action; though he sought support in the identification with marginal groups that came to replace young people as signifiers of difference. "There is no difference between what an intellectual 'does' and what an intellectual 'does for somebody,'" he stated in response to an article signed by representatives of the Italian student movement at the Festival of New Cinema in Pesaro, published in the New Left journal *Ombre Rosse*. Commenting on black activist Stokely Carmichael's statement that "we are not interested in what intellectuals can do, but in what they can do for us," which was chosen as an epigraph for the article, Pasolini responded that poetic discourse was a form of action. "Doing," in that sentence, must be interpreted in the Greek sense of *poetare (poiein)*, the act of poetic creation, and its effect depends also on the existential condition of the intellectual. Poetry, when issued from a place of difference, *does*. Intellectuals, he claims, are not authorities; rather, they occupy a marginal position: "The intellectual is a reject, in the sense that society relegates him outside of itself, puts him on record, discriminates him, attaches a sign to him, so as to either damn him or integrate him." In a rhetorical move that is frequent in later essays, Pasolini identifies with minorities, foregrounding his own sense of difference: intellectuals share the discrimination of which black people are victims in the United States; they "experience in actuality the same condition of alterity as the black man."[41] Because poets speak from a marginalized condition, poetry maintains its performative function, even in a world that expects action.

As an alternative to the rational actions and verbal excess of the student movement (and of his own poetry), Pasolini reclaimed the space of *contestazione* for youth through cinema as poetry. Although most of his films represented young people or showed their effect on contemporary society, *Teorema* and *Porcile*, the films of *Sessantotto*, reflect specifically on the position of adolescents in the universal bourgeois condition created by capitalism. Unlike the students' actions, which ultimately strengthen the bourgeois system, the absolute confrontation taking place on the screen produces a scandal that destroys the bourgeois family. *Teorema* and *Porcile* attack the bourgeoisie in a radical way, but they do so without subscribing to what Pasolini called "Fascism of the Left," or neo-Zhdanovism. They are not directly political films, but poetic reflections that invite the viewer to assume an active role in the construction of meaning. As such they employ in visual terms a similar poetic strategy as the one attempted in the poems of *Trasumanar e organizzar*. But while the "new Italian" language proved inadequate to the expressive task, cinema expressed the poetry of youth. On screen young people can simply "be" a transformative presence, without doing much. Indeed, the "written language of action" shows the ambiguous coincidence of being and doing that characterizes youth in two particularly static films.

The Cinematic Poetry of Youth: *Teorema*

The paradox that combining the intrinsic dynamism of youth with cinema could produce a distinctly static film is evident in *Teorema*, a poetic confrontation of the bourgeois world inspired by the ambiguous presence of youth.[42] Shot in the spring of 1968, while the student protest was at its apex in Italy, and presented at a protest-ridden Venice Film Festival in September of the same year, *Teorema* is Pasolini's true poetic contribution to the cultural and political debate of the *Sessantotto*. Initially conceived and partially written as a verse tragedy, the project developed simultaneously into a novel and a film.[43] Together with *Porcile*, made the following year, *Teorema* was the first of Pasolini's films to focus primarily on the bourgeois world that most of his previous works criticized indirectly. Its theoretical premise, the universality of the bourgeois condition that he saw as invalidating the ideological approach of the *sessantottini*, imposed the new focus and the choice of a form that challenged the rationality of Marxism and liberalism. *Teorema* is thus a visual poem, and requires a non-narrative fruition. As a matter of fact, Pasolini acknowledged to have found inspiration for the film in the poetic and existential revolt initiated by the Beat Generation:

> You need to go back to the general context of the years around 1965. These are the times of the *beat generation*. Ginsberg, Ferlinghetti, Kerouac in the United States, and some movements of poetic protest, launch a poetic movement that enhances despair. It is at that time that the revolt against materialism (*il dominio della società del benessere*) culminates, in poetry and the arts. Everyone knows that this revolt would then lead to the explosion of the student protest, in American universities and, later, in May, in France.[44]

While he acknowledged the fundamental role of the Beats and other poetic movements in generating the core of ideas that were developed and expressed in the student protest, Pasolini highlighted in particular the existential aspect of their poetics, their critique of materialism and their expression of a "despair" that did not translate into concrete actions: "I do not offer any solution. In order to do so, I should have found some myself. No, they are open films ... They don't offer results or solutions. Like the above-mentioned poetic movement, they are 'poems in the form of a howl of despair.'"[45]

The prologue, shot in a documentary style, introduces the main function of the movie: asking questions, raising doubts. A handheld camera moves around a group of workers, in front of a factory in northern Italy. The owner of the factory has just donated it to the workers, and the interview reveals the author's ironic attitude towards the acquisition of power which, as shown in his explicit comments on the *Sessantotto*, he saw as the misguided objective of the protest. The camera moves among the workers, showing only their backs, while the interviewer questions them on their future, now that the owner has donated the factory to them. The confused movement of the camera, which never faces the interviewees, and only shows us the face of the interviewer, renders the bewilderment of the workers, and their lack of a definite position on the issue. When the interviewer suggests that the workers' situation will not really change, that "the protagonist of the story remains the bourgeois," and that "the bourgeoisie is changing its own condition," thus depriving the working class of a revolutionary possibility, they can only agree. When he invites them to enumerate the problems that the bourgeoisie will face once its incorporation of all of humanity is complete, the workers are puzzled and cannot answer. "If the bourgeoisie succeeds in identifying all of humanity with itself, it will no longer have a class struggle to win, neither with the army, nor with the nation, nor with the institutional church…" repeats the interviewer. "Can you answer these questions? Can you answer these questions?" The question, repeated twice, is left hanging as the film title appears on the screen.

After the prosaic prologue, a sudden shift to a different visual style – the low-angle shot of a cloudy volcano peak, accompanied by the jazz motif that will punctuate the entire movie – opens the film as poem.[46] The setting moves to an elegant mansion and the pace slows down. The members of a wealthy Milanese family are introduced one by one. A mysterious young man (Terence Stamp) comes to visit, seduces each member of the household, including the maid, then leaves, as abruptly as he had arrived. Both his arrival and departure are announced by a dancing mailman named Angelino (Ninetto Davoli). The experience throws all family members in despair, and their lives unravel: Emilia, the maid (Laura Betti), goes back to her village, fasts for a long time, performs miracles, and finally chooses to be buried alive in a construction site. Pietro, the artistically inclined adolescent son (Andrés José Cruz Soublette), tries to evoke the lost lover through painting, but his experiments with avant-garde techniques result in increasing frustration, anger, and self-destruction. Odetta, the teenage daughter (Anne Wiazemsky) unable to react to the young man's departure, falls into catatonia, and is eventually carried away in an ambulance. The mother, Lucia (Silvana Mangano), compulsively tries to reproduce the guest's seduction with other young men whom she picks up on the street. She finally seeks refuge in a deserted country church. Unlike his wife, Paolo, the father (Massimo Girotti), does not try to substitute anyone for the mysterious visitor, even when the opportunity presents itself. Instead, he renounces his possessions and, after disrobing in the crowded Milan train station, walks off into a desert, where his howl of despair seems to continue past the end of the film. The father's renunciation ties the movie ending to the initial interview, thus recasting the questions asked in the prologue.

The attack on bourgeois conventions, and particularly on the family as its central institution, resonates with the *sessantottini*'s rejection of paternal authority, even as its peculiar form illustrates the author's disagreement with the practical goals of their protest. The protagonist family is a perfect representative of the bourgeoisie, almost cliché in its conformity to class standards: the father is an industry magnate, the son a popular high school student with many friends and a girlfriend; the daughter an introverted girl with an almost pathological admiration for her father; the mother a beautiful woman who spends her days following the conventions of her class. Their universality and the cinematic style, which works against psychological realism, turn the narration into a parable. The opening sequence, silent and shot with a purple/sepia filter, removes their life from the immediacy of the present. The denaturalization produced by this style culminates in a scene at the dinner table: rather than being the meeting point for the ideal family, the silent table becomes the stage for the destruction of the conventions on which the family stands. The static shot, central perspective, unbalanced disposition of the characters around the table, and the lack of dialogue denaturalize the scene.[47] In sharp contrast to this somber and motionless scene, the dancing and smiling mailman, Angelino, delivers a telegram announcing the Guest's arrival. The message marks the cut to a more naturalistic sequence, which only enhances the unnaturalness of the previous one: the camera now pans over a crowded living room, registering the background noise and snippets of conversation between various family members and their party guests. This context provides the backdrop against which the mysterious young man appears and exercises his power.

The plot ostensibly sets up a generational clash, where the youthful energy of the Guest disrupts the stale practices of bourgeois living exemplified by his hosts. The transformation he causes, however, goes far beyond the alternation of forces that Pasolini saw as the misguided objective of the Italian protest, and questions the prosaic confrontation of the *sessantottini* through a poetic revolution.[48] Youth does not take over the existing system, but instead challenges its premises and forces it to confront itself. *Teorema* sets out to prove the following: the bourgeoisie is so alienated from authentic life that if it came into contact with the sacred, the encounter would destroy not only the family as an institution, but the subject as he/she is defined by that institution. This destruction proves *per absurdum* that the materialistic values and social conventions characterizing middle-class life constitute the identity of its subjects, regardless of gender or age. The entire family lives in this alienated condition, and all members are uniquely and equally transformed by their encounter with the sacred. Consequently, instead of a conventional narrative, in which events are organized according to an internal cause-effect sequence, the film has an abstract structure, which corresponds to the mathematical statement of the title and takes its premises to extremes. The introduction of each character, the arrival in the home and the five "seductions" are presented sequentially but are to be considered as simultaneous.

The sacred assumes the shape of a handsome young man, whose body becomes the vehicle for its revelation to each of the family members. The young man embodies a form of authenticity that is lost in the bourgeois world, and that Pasolini typically associated with primitive, impure, marginal forms of life.[49] Odetta and her friend's comments in English, as they look at him across a crowded room, immediately acknowledge his foreign handsomeness: *"Who is that boy?"* asks Odetta's friend. *"A boy,"* she replies. In the novel *Teorema* the Guest is described as exceptionally handsome and foreign-looking:

> Straordinario prima di tutto per bellezza: una bellezza così eccezionale, da riuscire quasi di scandaloso contrasto con tutti gli altri presenti. Anche osservandolo bene, infatti, lo si direbbe uno straniero, non solo per la sua alta statura e il colore azzurro dei suoi occhi, ma perché è così completamente privo di mediocrità, di riconoscibilità e di volgarità da non poterlo nemmeno pensare come un ragazzo appartenente a una famiglia piccolo borghese italiana. Non si potrebbe neanche dire, d'altra parte, che egli abbia la sensualità innocente e la grazia di un ragazzo del popolo ... Egli

è insomma socialmente misterioso, benché leghi perfettamente con tutti gli altri che stanno intorno a lui, in quel salone magicamente illuminato dal sole.

Extraordinary first of all for his beauty: a beauty so exceptional that it creates an almost scandalous contrast with all the other people present. Even on a closer look, in fact, one would think him a foreigner, not only because of his height and his blue eyes, but because he completely lacks the mediocrity, recognizability, and vulgarity that one would normally associate with a petit bourgeois Italian family. On the other hand, neither could one say that he has the innocent sensuality and grace of a lower class boy ... All in all, he is socially mysterious, although he fits in perfectly with all the people sitting around him, in that magically sunlit living room.[50]

Simultaneously familiar and utterly foreign, the handsome young visitor exercises an irresistible attraction on his hosts. He is the object of their desires, gives himself to them, yet challenges the bourgeois sense of ownership and control. His alterity is not class coded, even though his arrival was announced by the proletarian Angelino, who embodies the "innocent sensuality and grace" of the lower classes. The ambiguous identity of the visitor, both at home in the bourgeois world and foreign to it, allows him to access and shatter the existential alienation of the family. He speaks a radically different language and introduces alterity into a condition that has become so universal that it does not recognize anything outside of itself.[51]

As signalled by the book of Rimbaud's poems that the young man reads, the poetry of youth destroys existing categories and introduces a new perspective. Its vehicle is the body, the young male body at the centre of the screen. Since the prosaic, communicative language of the middle class is a tangible sign, for Pasolini, of the loss implicit in a bourgeois transformation of Italian society, speech is replaced by bodily presence. It is crucial that the instrument of authentic expression and radical transformation is poetry. In order to subvert the logical, rational system through which the bourgeoisie perpetuates itself, and to go beyond the rational and pragmatic limits of Marxist discourse, youth expresses its difference through its poetic presence. It is equally significant that youth, as the social group embodying difference, is not class-specific. If young sub-proletarians embodied that alterity in the society of the 1950s, after the economic miracle extended bourgeois values and lifestyle to a wide segment of the population, youth maintains that connotation here even without the class specificity, and remains the only force of resistance. The poetry of youth, expressed in the language that is most foreign to the bourgeois condition, makes each member of the family aware of his or her inauthenticity.

The mysterious young man is a truly revolutionary presence inasmuch as he "scandalizes everybody" without age, gender, or class distinction.[52] In a world in which social and sexual identities are strictly defined, his indefinite identity echoes the shifting representations of youth in modern culture. He offers himself to each family member and is to each what he or she needs him to be. His behaviour exposes the constructedness of their identities and, in so doing, questions the very basis of the bourgeois world. Since words are vehicles for empty conventions in that world, they are no longer sufficient to establish authentic contacts. The body becomes therefore the instrument for a new experience, which reveals each individual to him or herself. The experience provides each of them with a poetic lens through which their previous condition appears unacceptable. By giving each character a different perspective on their life, the poetic look challenges their conventional roles, such as they are presented at the beginning of the film, and disrupts the certainties on which their bourgeois world stands. The scandal it produces makes that world fall apart. Alienation from the sacred in a bourgeois lifestyle that is becoming universal is the existential problem that should concern young people. Young people alone, in fact, could reintroduce that poetic world view that is missing from the "practical and rational" world of the bourgeois fathers, and represents the only resistance to bourgeois alienation.

Thematically, the clash of the prosaic with the poetic is rather disastrous. As the Guest's departure is imminent, one-on-one encounters become occasions for each of the family members to share their self-awareness: the son has become aware of his difference, the mother of the emptiness of her life, the daughter of her pathology; the father has lost his identity, which was built on "the idea of order, of the future, and above all of possession," in his own definition. Only Emilia, the servant, does not verbalize her realization, but simply acts upon it: she returns to her rural village and re-enters her community as a saintly figure. She becomes a new "source of the scandal" in her own world, as the old woman observing her confirms: *"Uh Signur, che scandalo!"* Emilia has apparently *"trasumanato"*: she is transfigured and, consequently, treated like a saint by her rural community. The dynamic effect of poetry, conveyed by the young Guest, has translated into a form of action that is not "pragmatic and reasonable."

The corollaries of the theorem offer a range of outcomes, all of which reveal the characters' incompatibility with the bourgeois world as it was presented at the beginning. Odetta's inability to come to terms with her world is reproduced through the camera work: a 360-degree pan shot of her in the living room conveys her disoriented state. Such confusion is enhanced by the following shots: the extended shots of her gaze, only completed with delayed counter-shots of the closed gate, the empty street, and the deserted lawn, heighten her sense of loss and confusion. Her attempts to evoke the Guest's presence fail: the ritual dance in the front yard, reminiscent of the mailman's, has no effect. Her attempt at reconstructing the garden setting where her "epiphany" had taken place is just as disappointing: she measures the space around her, with her feet first, then with a measuring tape, but the counter-shots insistently reveal an empty spot where the Guest had been. As she had anticipated in her parting speech to the Guest, she is thrown back into her childish pathology (or her pathological childhood) and, unable to live with the consciousness of it, she refuses to continue living. The tight fist, shown in a close-up shot, becomes the symbol of her desperate attempt at coming to grips with reality, an attempt that has no solutions.

Odetta's descent into a catatonic state is counterposed with Emilia's transcendence. The difference between the two worlds is highlighted by the contrasting responses of their communities to the women's self-isolation: while Odetta's family confronts her state by medicalizing it, the peasants welcome Emilia as a saint and allow her transcendence to become visible in the form of miracles. This positive response is used as a counterpoint to the destiny of all of the bourgeois family members and then foregrounded in the conclusion of Emilia's corollary. Her self-awareness does not translate into a rejection of the world around her, but rather into a choice to put transcendence at the service of her community. Like the young Guest, Emilia chooses an ambiguous position: she sits between the *trasumanar* and the *organizzar* and brings the sacred into the daily life of her people. This choice turns her into the only positive example provided by the corollaries. The unfolding of her destiny is cross-cut with those of her previous employers and the juxtaposition highlights both the authentic outcome of her contact with the sacred and the limitations of their experiences. By rediscovering the religious experience of her peasant origins, Emilia is the only person who is able to turn the scandalous experience offered to her by the Guest into a model for her own behaviour.[53]

Pietro tries to express his new consciousness through art, but fails miserably and becomes a caricature of the avant-garde artist. His aesthetics express a compulsion to innovate: "Bisogna cercare di inventare nuove tecniche ... che siano irriconoscibili, che non assomiglino a nessuna operazione precedente, per evitare la puerilità, il ridicolo." (New techniques must be invented ... unrecognizable ones, not resembling any previous operation, to avoid childishness, ridiculousness.) His first timid attempts at portrait painting give way to abstract art realized on glass panes, which can be superimposed so as to mask possible mistakes:

> A brushstroke on a glass pane corrects without muddying a previous brushstroke on another glass pane. But everyone must believe that it is not the remedy of an incapable, of an impotent artist! Not at all. Rather, they must believe that it is the result of a firm, undaunted decision, a high and pressing gesture.

The realization of his own weakness only leads to more rebellious experiments, like painting with his eyes shut and urinating on the canvas, which are viewed by Pasolini as analogous to the literary experiments of the avant-garde: merely rebellious gestures that have no social impact beyond the artistic realm.[54]

Lucia tries to remedy the loss of the mysterious Guest by substituting other attractive young men for him. The sense of entrapment that she feels when she leaves these men, signalled by a long shot of her anxious look followed by a counter-shot of a long fence first, then of a quick sequence of statues of saints cut together, pushes her to go back to a confessional form of religion. The cut from Lucia's close-up, as she looks up to what should be the altar, to the empty bench on which Emilia had been sitting in the previous sequences, highlights both Emilia's authentic "sanctity" and the inauthenticity of a type of religion that fails to provide Lucia with alternative values to those of her class. Unlike Lucia, Paolo does not try to substitute anyone for the mysterious visitor even when the opportunity offers itself to him in the train station: his epiphany is so overpowering that he has to renounce his possessions, on which his identity is based. "What would happen to me if... if I decided to get rid of everything, and donated my factory to the workers?" he wonders. As he disrobes in the middle of the Milan train station, the camera zooms out to position his ritual action at the centre of a larger frame and then cuts to a close-up of his naked legs making their way among the crowd and walking off into the desert. The heaviness of his stride alludes to the absence of the young visitor who, like Gerasim in Tolstoy's story *The Death of Ivan Ilych* referred to earlier in the film, was able to give the aching legs some relief. The absence of Paolo's naked body from the screen, and his feet on the dark earth of the desert, are juxtaposed with Emilia's body being buried; a minimal graphic match between the two frames, dominated for the most part by the brown earth of the desert image that has constelled the film at irregular intervals, points to an imminent resolution.

As a matter of fact, the desert motif functions both as a continuity and a disruption device. Presented from the beginning, with the opening credits, the image of the slopes of a smoky volcano is then inserted as a non-diegetic shot at irregular intervals throughout the film: after the sexual intercourse between the Guest and Emilia; when Pietro, the son, first uncovers the Guest's body; when the father is awakened in the middle of the night and sees his son and the Guest in the same bed; when the Guest reads Tolstoy to Paolo and, later, when they drive out into the countryside together. However, the encounters between the Guest and the mother, and the daughter, are not punctuated by the desert shot, which only occurs in reference to them after the Guest's departure. We are encouraged to interpret the desert shot as the sign of an epiphany, and we follow it as a clue to a possible resolution. The final sequence, which blurs the distinction between diegetic and non-diegetic, challenges even our symbolic interpretation.

Emilia's decision to be buried alive represents a possible resolution of the film's thematic and formal elements, and reveals its relationship to Pasolini's poetry. Emilia chooses to be buried near a construction site that marks the advance of capitalism and its gradual destruction of the rural world to which she belongs. Her natural aide in this self-sacrifice is the old woman who has been the first witness to her scandalous presence, and who first acknowledged Emilia's sanctity in the previous sequences.[55] Emilia's tears are visually associated with the excavator sitting next to her burial ground, and the frame composition recalls one of Pasolini's most famous poems, "The Tears of the Excavator." In the eponymous poem, tears are shed for "what changes even / if to become something better" (ciò che muta, anche / per farsi migliore).[56] In the poem, the howl of the excavator, expanding to become the howl of the whole neighbourhood, of the city, of the world, brings back the poet, and the readers, to the present, after a long and nostalgic recollection of the past, and alludes to a future that "doesn't cease for even an instant / to wound us."[57] Emilia's tears, springing from the earth, refer both to an irretrievable past and to a future that must begin from the wound opened by the Guest's arrival. Her declaration to her aide, the only words she utters in the whole film, substantiate the impression that the tears should be considered as a new beginning: "Don't worry" she reassures the old woman who is burying her, "I didn't come here to die, but to cry ... and mine won't be tears of sorrow. No, they will be a source, which won't be a source of sorrow..." Like the excavator's, Emilia's tears are a rite of transition that involves pain, but does not exclude hope.

However, Emilia's tears are also juxtaposed with Paolo's final howl in the desert. The film's closing sequence is constituted by cross-cut shots of Paolo and Emilia's destinies. The continuity suggested by the characters' physical contact with the earth suggests that they have both acted upon their epiphany. However, while Emilia's function has already been symbolically defined, Paolo's wandering in the desert seems destined to continue indefinitely, just like the howl that concludes the film. The despair that his howl manifests appears thus to be the only certain message offered by the film. While the scene of Emilia's buried body, accompanied by the same musical theme that accompanied the title and opening credits, would provide at least some external closure to the film, the choice to end on Paolo's howl leaves the circle, and the theorem, open.

The "theorem" of the title is based on the hypothesis of the irruption of a poetic look into a bourgeois lifestyle and promises to show the consequences of that revolution in a series of "corollaries." However, the film is far from being a logical demonstration of universal laws. Just like the embodiment of the sacred is not a clear cut, easily identifiable character, *Teorema* is not a linear process that leads from established premises to clear and proven conclusions. The poetic lens offered by the mysterious Guest to his hosts is placed on the camera as well: the look offered by this film is thus just as disruptive to our certainties as it is to the family on the screen. The theorem remains open: rather than proving a point irrefutably, the film raises important questions and leaves them suspended. It creates expectations in the viewers and then proceeds to disregard them. The theorem is never closed and the consequences of the irruption of a different look in conventional bourgeois life are as many as the family members affected by it.

The lack of resolution between the geometric structure and the film's interpretive openness reflects the distance between the false certainties that Pasolini sees manifested in neo-capitalism and the immense doubts that afflict those who can look at reality with a poetic lens. The film provides this lens at both the thematic and the formal level: by the Guest and by the film itself. Through the parable of the mysterious young man of scandalous beauty, the film shows us how the irruption of a poetic body in a bourgeois world can mine its foundations and make life unacceptable to its subjects. Through its form, it turns the viewers into the bourgeois family of the parable and shatters our certainties about the world. The film attracts us with its beauty and intrigues us with its mystery; it frustrates our expectations as viewers; it provides us with a poetic lens, which allows us to obtain both a critical distance and a closer look at our bourgeois, neo-capitalistic world and its taboos. It scandalizes us with the naked body on the screen, but even more with the absent body: the one that has been missing from our relationship with the world. It places us in a position analogous to that of the bourgeois family in the case studied. It refuses to provide definite answers because there are as many answers as there are viewers. For this reason, it invites us to acknowledge our own specificity, to become aware of the constructedness of our "naturalistic" view of reality, and to add our own corollary. In the "difficulty" of the film lies a major part of its critical value. The intellectual involvement required of the viewer, who needs to fill in the many gaps in this suspended theorem, is a model for the kind of critical involvement that the author wishes to encourage with respect to neo-capitalist society.

The attack of youth on the bourgeois world, on its decrepit conventions, and on the family succeeds through the revolutionary power of the young body. Revolutionary change in Italian society does not require an ideological program, Pasolini claims, but an encounter with what has become truly foreign. The encounter with the young Guest is an encounter with the Other, which according to the bourgeois parameters of education, is a fundamental condition of the *Bildung* process. The subjects of formation, those who need to know the Other in order to know themselves, are in this case not only bourgeois young people, but even their parents. Their process of self-discovery requires a poetic lens that provides a different perspective on themselves and their world. In this sense, *Teorema* represents another (sub)version of the classic *Bildungsroman*: the body of youth, divine presence and object of everyone's desire, becomes the instrument of education for an entire family.

The sense that young people could initiate a positive change in a neo-capitalist society where the bourgeois condition has become universal clearly underlies this film, which can thus be considered as Pasolini's contribution to the protest of *Sessantotto*.

Disobeying the Almighty Father: *La sequenza del fiore di carta*

Reluctant father figure to a generation that was culturally different from his own and had severed ties with paternal figures, Pasolini criticized young people mainly for the form of political engagement they had chosen, which deprived them of the qualities he valued most in youth: irrationality, changeability, innocence. In addition, by relinquishing the legacy of their anti-Fascist historical fathers, *sessantottini* were also depriving themselves of the cultural instruments that had served Pasolini and his peers in their own intellectual coming-of-age: the sense of a literary tradition that the *eredi* could enter and alter.

It is easy to see traces of this contradictory relationship even in Pasolini's short film *La sequenza del fiore di carta* (The Sequence of the Paper Flower), shot in the summer of 1968 for an envisaged compilation of contemporary interpretations of parables from the Gospel. Initially called *Vangelo '70*, the collective project was later reconfigured as a series of European responses to the Vietnam War, and eventually titled *Amore e Rabbia* (1969). Besides Pasolini's, it included episodes by Carlo Lizzani, Bernardo Bertolucci, Jean-Luc Godard, and Marco Bellocchio.[58] *La sequenza del fiore di carta* took inspiration from the Bible episode in which Jesus curses the fig tree for being barren, and the tree withers and dies. In Pasolini's contemporary take, it is God, the supreme Father, who strikes down Riccetto, a young man who doesn't hear his calls and does not produce the expected fruits.

Riccetto (Ninetto Davoli), a carefree young man, dances and strolls leisurely in a busy Via Nazionale in Rome. A 1960s incarnation of the *ragazzi* of the Roman novels, he seems at home in the busy street at midday. His tight-fitting jeans and ankle boots match the modern city: Fiat 500s and 600s swarm by, delivery trucks park near the sidewalk, people of all ages and occupations crowd the scene. Riccetto hops along, starts casual conversations, flirts with a young woman, and smiles. He apparently has no destination and no worries. His innocence is untouched by the grim black-and-white archival footage superimposed on the lively and colourful urban scene: airplane bombings, combat zones, anti-war demonstrations, and several other images from contemporary news. He also does not hear, or does not listen to, the numerous appeals from God: "I want your fruits, your first fruits ... The fruits of your knowledge and will." Riccetto continues his trivial conversations, deaf to the suffering of other innocent people whom we see in the superimposed news images.[59] The paradox of his condition is made explicit in God's demands: "It is true, you are innocent, and those who are innocent do not know, and those who do not know, do not want, but I am your God and I order you to know and want. It is contradictory, I know, maybe it is even insoluble, because if you are innocent you cannot have knowledge and will." The appeals continue in different voices (including Pasolini's), and become more and more pressing, but to no avail. God's punishment follows: after a series of explosions, Riccetto's dead body is shown on the pavement, in a vertical shot suggesting God's point of view. Next to him lies the big red paper flower, which he had been holding during his cheerful dance.

Recalling both the hawthorns and the red flags of *Il sogno di una cosa*, as well as the flowers offered by American students to policemen in peace rallies, the oversized poppy adds to the exemplary function of the parable a specific significance in relation to the discourse of youth. It connotes the simplicity and cheerfulness of Riccetto's youthful life, and its fleetingness. Indirectly, it also evokes the potential intrinsic in his position outside of history, as per Pasolini's view. Riccetto holds the oversize flower like a flag, drawing a significant parallel with the documentary images of protesters carrying banners against the war.[60] The flower falls with him, perhaps as a reminder of the reason for Riccetto's death. The dance sequence celebrates those qualities and Riccetto's vitality. On the other hand, his death is presented as a necessary punishment for his disobedience, as if to say that his deafness to the Father's calling – albeit constitutive of his innocence, which is predicated on ignorance – cannot be tolerated in the contemporary world. The *impegno* required of young people, the *Sequenza* seems to say, causes them to lose what makes them unique. If at the end of *Ragazzi di vita* a new Riccetto could be expected to replace one that was lost, that assumption could no longer be made in 1968. While remaining outside of the social order guaranteed youth's vitality, in entering history youth was losing itself.

6 *Giovani Infelici*: Consumer, Disobedient, Unhappy Youth

Consuming Disobedient Adolescence: *Porcile*

Events and debates of the *Sessantotto*, centred on young people as new social and political agents, compelled Pasolini to redefine his own poetics. They challenged a critical stance based on his identification with youth as a hybrid condition, external to the patriarchal order, and on the cultural authority assigned to left-wing intellectuals by the Communist Party in the immediate post-war years. His response, expressed in different media throughout the late 1960s, focused on renegotiating his relationship with "children" who suddenly appeared foreign to him, and who in turn viewed him as a "father" to reject; and also concentrated on redefining an alternative type of *impegno* that was suitable for the new power structure created by neo-capitalism. Young people's activism foregrounded an epochal transformation of Italian society, which, in Pasolini's view, required a more creative approach than the one chosen by the student movement. Responding also to the homogenization of Italian language, which reduced the expressive possibilities for poetry, Pasolini focused on cinema as a new poetic language. His cinema of poetry offered an original contribution to the critique of bourgeois conventions, and assigned a role to youth that partially redeemed their actions in the streets. As the debate grew tenser after 1968, Pasolini's cinema and essays reflected on young people as increasingly caught in the role of disobedient children, and on the responsibilities of their historical fathers for their unhappiness.

Teorema and *Porcile* offer complementary examples of how cinema can be used to reflect on the specificity of consumer modernity, and at the same time offer the space for imagination that Pasolini saw missing in the 1968 protest. The poetic look that, in *Teorema*, irrupts in a traditional bourgeois family, subverting its conventions and questioning its values, is directed, in *Porcile*, at the devastating effect of neo-capitalism on that same class. The bourgeois condition, taken as timeless and universal in *Teorema*, is here observed through a historical perspective that highlights the different functioning of power in neo-capitalistic societies. Consequently, while *Teorema* introduced youth as a foreign presence that shattered a traditional family, *Porcile* comments in particular on the role of "disobedient children" in consumer society. Explicit references to organized student protests and a biting irony on the revolutionary aspirations of young bourgeois convey the author's beliefs regarding the inutility of their demonstrations, which he had explained profusely in articles and poetry throughout 1968.[1] As an alternative to a form of protest that, in Pasolini's view, values "action and utilitarianism" just like the system it purports to oppose, *Porcile* proposes a discourse based on ambiguity, reflection, and polysemy.[2] Through a poetic use of images the film shows the violence implicit in the new power structure and the horror masked by the semblance of civilization. As a form of resistance to a power system that co-opts its disobedient children and is strengthened by their opposition, Pasolini proposes a film that encourages viewers to reflect on that inevitable incorporation. *Porcile* deploys a poetic gaze that de-familiarizes neo-capitalism and engages the viewer in the construction of sense. Performing the ambiguous function of *contestazione*, *Porcile* raises problems rather than providing solutions: it "suspends the meaning" in the Barthesian sense.

Shot in the spring of 1969, *Porcile* is the result of the alternate montage of two completely different storylines: one episode, which gives the film its title, is set in a neoclassical villa in Godesborg, Germany, in 1967, and stylizes the prosaic reality of bourgeois life: Julian Klotz, a bourgeois young man, rejects both positions envisaged for him by his class – obedient or disobedient child, faithful heir to his father's wealth or active participant in his generation's protest against their fathers – and finds solace only in the "infinite repetition of the same thing": sexual intercourse with pigs. The revelation of this unspeakable habit forces his father into a merger of his empire with Mr. Herdhitze's, an ex-Nazi who has undergone plastic surgery. The German episode is a highly staged drama, set in the ornate rooms of an elegant villa. Both visually and verbally it is very static: symmetry and geometry dominate the shot composition, repetition and redundancy dominate the dialogue. The characters are typically standing still or moving slowly within the limits of the imposing architecture, either facing one another or walking side by side towards the camera. The narrative is governed less by internal causation laws than by a *deus ex machina* intent on proving that the bourgeoisie eats its children.

Cross-cut with the Godesborg episode is a story set on the desert slopes of a volcano in a historically unspecified time. Wandering in the desert is a young man, played by Pierre Clémenti, who is driven by hunger to eat butterflies and snakes. He fights with a soldier left behind by his troop, kills him, and eats him. A second cannibal, played by Franco Citti, soon joins him and their killings continue until one of the victims of their attacks manages to escape and denounce them to the authorities of a town nearby. Captured with a trick, they are sentenced to death by ground crucifixion in the same desert where they used to roam. Even stylistically this episode differs widely from the German one. Shot on the brown earth of Mount Etna, which often occupies most of the frame, the desert episode is virtually free of audible dialogue, with the exception of the final statement uttered by the protagonist before being executed. Its visual discourse exceeds the limits of the simple narrative structure: expressionistic acting, sudden camera movements, and frequent lens changes suggest an expressive reading.[3]

Consistent with the culture of 1968 from which the film originates, the cluster of ideas at its core regards young people and their relationship with their fathers. In a bourgeois world that expects either obedience or disobedience, young people can either be heirs or protesters. Julian's girlfriend, Ida, is a protester, but could become an heir, if only he were to accept her love. The mere contemplation of this possibility already indicates Pasolini's conviction of the futility of the students' demonstrations. Julian is neither, and only that ambiguous position guarantees his independence, albeit temporarily. His rebellion is highlighted by the actions of the Clémenti character: the cannibal, breaking all taboos of human society, functions as a signifier of total, authentic revolt.[4] The simple narrative depicts the novelty of neo-capitalist power in its incorporation of even authentic forms of dissent. In the neo-capitalist world, Julian can no longer hold his ambiguous position: his secret alternative to the rational bourgeois order is discovered and tolerated. The violence and finality of his co-optation are rendered explicit through the actions of the other young man, Clémenti: the cannibal is arrested and sentenced to death.

The analogies between the two young male protagonists and their rebellious actions support illustrative interpretations of the montage.

Maurizio Viano, reading *Porcile* in psychoanalytical terms as the apotheosis of Pasolini's realist mode, interprets Pierre Clémenti's character as a "visual dramatization of Julian's unconscious. Slaying the father, cannibalism, and pleasure sum up 'the other scene' as the exclusive locus of Freudian discourse."[5] Marco Antonio Bazzocchi sees the two tales as allusions to Pasolini's personal story, to the "irreducible difference of the homosexual and the intellectual." Consequently, Julian and the cannibal are "two faces of the same personality, two complementary strategies" employing the "opposing weapons with which Pasolini himself experimented: aggression and despair, absolute revolt and mild silence."[6] It is undeniable that Julian and the Pierre Clémenti character are intended as parallel figures, young rebels disobeying their fathers' world, and that cannibalism is a forceful image meant to make the cultural anthropophagy of the modern world explicit. However, I would like to suggest that the film goes beyond illustrating the impossibility of absolute rebellion in contemporary society. The juxtaposition of the desert tale with the modern does shed light on the dynamics of neo-capitalism, but the multiplication of perspectives that the interaction produces has a function that is perhaps more important. The proliferation of meanings adds density to a phenomenon that is too easily accepted and reminds the viewer of the complexity of the world that neo-capitalism simplifies.

The pigsty of the title refers, at the most literal level, to the place where Julian's true independence from the bourgeois world is played out: the pigs are the object of his desire and the agents of his disappearance in the end. The pigsty is the locus of the young man's ambiguity, of his refusal of the "either/or commitment" that both his girlfriend and his parents expect.[7] However, as a critique of neo-capitalism realized in 1968, a film titled *Porcile* obviously plays on the epithet "pigs" used by the young protesters in the sixties to refer to the bourgeois. One cannot forget the pigsty of the opening credits when, after a long silent sequence, the first line uttered in the film, by Ida, is "We are two bourgeois, Julian, and here we are analysing ourselves, in accordance with our privilege." A few minutes later, when Julian's parents, in bed, explicitly refer to themselves as "pigs" and wonder about Julian's future as a "pig," the metaphor has become so explicit that it is a parody of itself: "When is Julian going to start fattening like a pig? Or calling me 'pig'?" asks the father. Julian, on the other hand, refuses to eat and to live either "fattening like a pig" or rebelling against the "pigs." His absolute desire for real pigs prevents him from taking a stand in a "pigs"' world. The desire prevents him from either marrying Ida and becoming a "pig" like his parents, or joining Ida in the student protest against the "pigs" in Berlin. The metaphor is pushed to a grotesque extreme by the exchange of comments on pigs and Jews between Mr. Klotz and Mr. Herdhitze in the course of the conversation that will lead to the revelation of Julian's secret. Finally, once Julian's metaphorical incorporation by neo-capitalist power is complete, the pigsty becomes the locus of his literal consumption.

Anticipating some of Pasolini's reflections that became well-known through his articles of the 1970s, the movie addresses in visual terms the transition from old to new capitalism: a transformation that replaced the *Palazzo*, Pasolini's metaphor for the old power structure, based on violence and repression, with the "penitentiary of consumerism," which controls its subjects through hedonism and tolerance. The old separation between power holders and subjects is delegitimized in a system in which "leaving the Palace you fall back into a new inside."[8] This new kind of power destroys traditional cultures and replaces them with "a fictitious form of progress and tolerance": the sense of freedom and modernity it engenders is an effective instrument of cultural homogenization, and an equally effective neutralizer of conventional types of social critique.[9] Customary forms of resistance are a component of the new power network and allow it to regenerate: "Rhetorical disobedience, ... created and manipulated by power as a contradiction to itself and above all as a guarantee of modernity," is an integral part of consumer society.[10] Not only does the new power produce satisfied consumers, it also tolerates its disobedient children, incorporating them in order to renew itself. "Apparently ... they fight against this neo-capitalism, but actually they unknowingly obey its sacrilegious needs."[11] Incapable of any real opposition, young people who inhabit this "penitentiary" can only relate to neo-capitalism as consumers and/ or consumed.

Besides exposing this paradoxical position occupied by young people in a modern consumer society, *Porcile* employs visual poetry to reinstate some of the complexity lost as a result of modernization. As was shown in previous chapters, Pasolini deplored an increased attention to the denotative function of language in contemporary Italy.[12] The regularity that facilitated communication came at the expense of the expressive force of regional diversity: it sacrificed "the metaphorical nature of language in favor of its metonymic nature," producing texts "without shadows, without ambiguity, without drama."[13] Besides exposing the effects of economic and social change, a non-normative critique of neo-capitalism must then recreate some of the ambiguity that prevents cultural products from becoming instant commodities.[14] Poetry is the vehicle for highlighting that complexity, the medium for recuperating the expressiveness that, as previously shown, has a performative function. As an alternative to a verbal language impoverished by homogenization, poetic discourse, offered in visual form in *Porcile*, exposes the true nature of consumer modernity and resists consumption by suspending the sense and encouraging the viewer to actively participate in its creation.

"*Sens suspendu*," the expression that Pasolini explicitly appreciates in his essay "The End of the Avant-Garde," characterizes for Roland Barthes a type of art that endeavours "not to generate meanings, but to not fill them exactly." The French theorist, in the interview from which Pasolini quotes, discusses contemporary cinema as a metonymic art, and underlines the possibilities it offers of finding meaning outside the signified: "The relationship between signifier and signified (that is, the sign) at first seems to be the foundation itself of every 'semiological' reflection, but later one comes to have a much vaster vision of the 'meaning'…."[15] Pasolini, who is trying to create "inconsumable films," movies that can resist commodification, finds it to be "a stupendous epigraph for what could be a new description of the commitment."[16] As Ward has shown, it is particularly "the switch in emphasis he finds in Barthes' work from the denotative to the connotative function of language" that attracts Pasolini.[17] The interest in connotation resonates with his search for a more expressive form, in film, to counter the "communicative" transformation of the Italian language. A new form of commitment in a neo-capitalist age needs to maintain a critical approach while resisting the tendency to simplification and normativity.

Rather than finding reassurance and fulfilment of desire, the viewer of *Porcile* is disoriented, invested with the task of making sense of the apparently dissonant images on the screen, and left with the impression that the puzzle does not have a univocal solution. Positioned within the apparently controlled universe of modern capitalism, we are nevertheless discouraged from identifying with any of its heroes or victims. The ambiguity of our position is sustained by a variety of strategies including elliptical narration, anti-naturalistic performance, and an alternate montage that opens up several interpretive possibilities. The goal is to defamiliarize consumer modernity and allow us to establish a critical relationship. However, even as he suspends meaning for a substantial part of the movie, allowing the contiguity of the two episodes to multiply the possibilities of interpretation and reflection, for Pasolini "meaning may be suspended, but not infinitely deferred."[18] As events in both narratives unfold towards their tragic conclusions, a particular point of view is introduced, which brings a new tone to the film and proposes an approach that is not strictly intellectual: the poetic gaze of the young Maracchione (Ninetto Davoli).[19] Functioning as the only direct link between the two narratives, and the eyewitness to the scandal of consumption, Maracchione models a different way of looking at both stories, which questions easy solutions and encourages doubt.

Consumer modernity is represented in the film through the visual metaphor of the modern pigsty. Presented with the opening credits, the pigsty is thus a metaphorical establishing shot for the film as a whole: we are in the pigsty, though we might not be aware of it. Visually opposed to the new power, the Klotzes' palace, shot frontally and positioned at the centre of the frame, serves as contrast to the pigsty, shot from the inside and filling the frame. We are always *inside* the penitentiary/pigsty, whereas we could either be *inside* or *outside* the palace. Despite the stately external appearance, the old power is deteriorating, a weakening also connoted by Mr. Klotz's physical disability. Its demise is precipitated by the pigsty: the literal one, housing Julian's pigs, and the possible blackmailing to which his secret subjects his family, and the metaphoric one, that is, Mr. Herdhitze's "healthy" neo-capitalistic empire. In the old power system, the pigsty represented for Julian a real alternative to the Palace. The either/or rational order of the traditional bourgeoisie, presented in the memorial stone at the film opening, established a binary code for its children. In the father's words:

> If he had been obedient, I would have taken him under my wings and together we would have flown over the glorious smokestacks of our Cologne, furnace of buttons and cannons. If, instead, he had been disobedient, I would have crushed him.

As young bourgeois, Julian and Ida are determined by their class: as heirs to their parents' wealth or young protesters, their actions are part of a ritualized event that allows bourgeois power to renew itself.[20] Julian's difference lies in his ambiguous position, which stalled the functioning of his father's power: in the repetition of the same act in the pigsty, he found a space of resistance to the linear progression of bourgeois capitalism. As the son who was neither obedient nor disobedient, he was inconsumable. He did not follow his father in his pride for the "glorious smokestacks" that embodied his economic power, or marry Ida, the girl of whom his parents approved, but he did not even join her and the other young people in their protest against their fathers. His secret desire arrested the linear progression and perpetuation of power. Once that desire becomes acknowledged and accepted by Mr. Herdhitze's new capitalism, the pigsty ceases to be a locus of resistance. That tolerance negates Julian's only possibility of rebellion: leaving the Palace he can no longer find a real "outside."

Julian's relationship with his parents' world is reflected in the form of the film. In the first part of the episode, his ambiguous position is visualized through his immobility. While his parents move in a space organized around a central perspective, and come to the foreground by passing through a sequence of doors that recede in the distance, Julian stands motionless in a bi-dimensional world. He is first introduced in a shallow-focus shot, with his back to the camera, facing a genealogical tree on a wall. In the following scenes, also in shallow focus, he and Ida are always positioned symmetrically around a central line against an elaborate backdrop of frescoes and ornate furniture, which fill the scene. Julian shares each frame with both Ida and the signs of his family's wealth, and yet he embraces neither. The first exception to this style marks the crisis of Julian's static and ambiguous position: alternate tracking shots show Julian and Ida walking along opposite sides of the fountain in front of his house. Although both were contained in one frame before, now they belong to separate frames, and the symbol of the Klotzes' empire recedes in the distance. The retreating camera precedes Ida and Julian as they move away from the house and towards a final confrontation. This takes place in the foreground of a very long shot, framed on a central perspective with the Klotzes' palace in the vanishing point. Julian is no longer in the Palace, and yet he is not going to the pigsty. The symmetric recomposition of the frame seals their relationship, and the negated kiss marks Julian's transition to the last, desperate, locus of resistance: catatonia.

Visually associated through montage to Clémenti's first act of cannibalism, Julian's fall into catatonia is his ultimate act of rebellion. His position between life and death – "an embalmed saint: neither dead nor alive" – makes him a scandalous presence in an environment where positions are so clearly defined. Everything and its opposite can be said of him, as the dialogue between his mother and Ida demonstrates, and nothing that either of them says holds truer than anything else.

Julian is a "Chaplin" but also "a mannerist St. Sebastian." Shot from the feet, he is presented as a martyr, or a Christ-like figure: "the fatalist martyr, an ambiguous saint."[21] The cross-cut of the two episodes comments on his ambiguous status. Although he is immediately associated with the Pierre Clémenti character, both liminal figures that assume a different identity in their own world, Julian is also visually matched with Clémenti's victims. The body of Clémenti's first prey, right before undergoing consumption, is juxtaposed with the first shot of Julian in bed. Later, the naked bodies of the two young people brought to the desert as bait, to capture Clémenti and his gang, are again associated with Julian's motionless body. At this stage, Julian is thus both consumer and consumed. However, his status changes following the compromise between his father and Herdhitze, the exchange of "a story of pigs for a story of Jews."

A second memorial stone, parallel to the one introducing Julian's ambiguous position with respect to his world, presents the new power that will incorporate him. Julian's father reads it, accompanying himself with his harp. The alternative between obedience and disobedience to fathers was significant in the old power system embodied by "smokestacks smokestacks smokestacks" visually modifying the land. That was Klotz's old capitalism. On the contrary, "nobody can see [Herdhitze's] factories: are they transparent? Levitating?" His wealth is apparently "coming up from nowhere." His empire does not stand in an obvious relationship of continuity with the past, nor does it exist in an antagonistic relationship with difference. Herdhitze has a new name, a new profession, and a new face; he is *"nuovo di zecca"* (brand new), as Klotz remarks. The irony of this comment is the key criticism expressed by the alternate montage: Herdhitze is *not* new. He is an ex-Nazi, who used to conduct experiments on the bodies of Jews. The plastic surgery he underwent, in Italy, is a metaphor for the transition from "old, clerico-Fascist power" to new consumerist power.[22] The visible, repressive power of the past is given a facelift, reshaped and renamed; the result is a "new" economic power, which is equally cruel, but in a less visible way. The new capitalism, embodied by Herdhitze, incorporates Julian's difference and thus voids his ambiguous position. The act of incorporation, of consumption, is marked by Clémenti's capture in the desert story. Julian's sudden recovery from catatonia and his appearance on the screen as a healthy eater mark the completion of that act of consumption. The compromise has redefined what his unnamed desire guaranteed to him: the possibility of living *in limine*, of remaining ambiguous, of wandering the non-linear space of the desert. The merger of the two economic empires determines his incorporation in a different system of consumption: the new consumer power knows and tolerates his desire, transforming it into a commodity.

The alternate structure of the film exposes the violence implicit in the new power. The physical violence represented in the desert story illustrates the violence implicit in consumer modernity.[23] The extreme actions performed by the Clémenti character in the desert tale visualize the violence that Herdhitze's world subtly masks: the disciplinary power of the penitentiary. In a way, the physical consumption of which Clémenti is an agent foregrounds the metaphorical consumption of which Julian is a subject. Rather than a direct representation of Julian's unconscious, as Viano claims, the desert episode offers a visualization of neo-capitalistic power's unconscious, so to speak: it is the representation of a social phenomenon, not a psychological one. As young people, Julian and the Pierre Clémenti character are the protagonists of the penitentiary of consumerism, and thus the subjects of a homogenizing power that consumes them, while apparently responding to their desires. The desert scene makes the mechanism visible and shows what the apparent transparency of neo-capitalism obscures: the violence implicit in consumer power and our complicity. At the same time, the metahistorical episode suggests the type of total disobedience that is only hinted at in Julian's secret desire for pigs: the breaking of all taboos summarized in the only words uttered by Clémenti: "I killed my father, I ate human flesh, and I quiver with joy." "A symbol of revolt taken to its ultimate consequences, ... it is a form of extremism, an extremism pushed to the limit of scandal, of rebellion, of horror."[24] In the irrationality of this existential rebellion is a suggestion of what the author sees missing in contemporary protest.

Visibility plays a key role in determining power relations and a peculiarity of the new disciplinary power is a reversal of the relationship between subject and object of vision.[25] The juxtaposition of the physical violence of the desert to the psychological violence of the modern world, and the play on the literal and metaphorical meaning of consumption in *Porcile*, encourage the viewers to question assumptions about modernity. On the other hand, in opposing the pigsty to the Palace, the film posits our presence *within* the penitentiary of consumerism, and therefore our involvement in its operation. Assuming that such condition is inescapable, the film tries to make us look at it with different eyes: to see neo-capitalism for what it is – a disciplinary system;

to be aware of our participation, but also to defamiliarize it enough that its horror scandalizes us, stupefies us, and engages us in a more profound way. However, that awareness needs to be separated from the rational process, which sustains neo-capitalism, hence the need to engage visual strategies that open gaps of signification in the text and "suspend the meaning."

Perhaps because Barthes introduces Brecht's work as a preliminary example of suspended sense, the estrangement effect produced in the German playwright's theatre could be called upon to describe the strategy at work in *Porcile*. This premise becomes obvious when Mr. Klotz states that "the times of Brecht and Grosz are not over," underlining the film's purpose to demonstrate quite the opposite.[26] *Porcile* does use an estrangement effect to make us reflect on the "pigsty" in which we live. The elliptical montage, both between the two episodes and within each, enhances the sense of a collage of separate images. More specifically, many stylistic choices in the German episode interfere with narrative realism and identification: from the fragmentation of the story in autonomous tableaux with sudden interruptions, to the stylized use of the camera, to the choice of *mise-en-scène*, whose symbolic function often prevails over rules of narrative coherence. The acting in the German episode is purposefully anti-naturalistic.[27] The viewer must never forget that on the screen are actors playing bourgeois: moving and speaking unnaturally slowly, the actors seem to assess the effect produced by their words. They take an established position before they initiate dialogue – usually in a symmetrical order with respect to the centre of the frame. They recite their lines, often rhyming with one another, as if reading. No emotion touches their voices even when they discuss the most disturbing subjects. The frequent addition of expressions such as "Trallallà" at the end of a statement reinforces the sense of detachment of the characters from their utterances. The stiffly delivered lines lack any psychological realism and, together with the rest of the *mise-en-scène*, create a staged effect that distances the viewers from the situation and prevents identification.

However, emotional estrangement only partially explains the film's critical strategy. If *Porcile* is an example of the Brechtian/Barthesian "suspended sense" film, its debunking of the mechanisms of power relies as strongly on poetic discourse as on the distancing effect produced by the structural and stylistic choices enumerated so far. The film requires an active engagement on the viewer's part: not only to understand the difficult dialogue in the German episode (a story not governed by internal narrative laws), or to follow the often puzzling actions in the desert episode (a poem whose richness does not lie in its narrative structure), but to make sense of the interplay of the two. Analogy and parallelisms only partially explain the interweaving, and the acts of interpretation required involve the viewer in the production of sense. However, the film is not constrained by the alternation of the stories, precisely because the analogies are never perfect. Every allusion is only one of many points of contact between the desert and the pigsty, but never summarizes the entire relationship. A little like the metric structure of a poem, exceeded by the poetic movement of the verses, the alternate structure is a framework counterpointed by visual poetry, a structure that both limits and encourages an expressive reading of the poetic discourse. The viewers are invited to fill the gaps and participate in the creation of meaning. However, if identification is discouraged and both *mise-en-scène* and montage enhance ambiguity, ultimately the critical distance encouraged by the film is aimed at eliciting a certain kind of empathy rather than detachment. In an attempt to separate awareness of one's position within the neo-capitalist network from the rationality that sustains that network, distance is pursued as a way to see things with different eyes, to strip them of the common causality. While the play of signification between the two episodes partially uncovers the dark side of consumer modernity, the multiplication of perspectives is aimed primarily at adding ambiguity to the narrative and leaving us stupefied, not reassured; with the sense of knowing less, not more. The look that the film elicits from the viewer is thus an "ingenuous" gaze that can see the horror of consumption in the rational reality of neo-capitalism: the poetic gaze of Ninetto/Maracchione.

Recurring signifier of the hybridity of youth in Pasolini's poetry and film since his appearance in *Uccellacci e uccellini*, Ninetto appears once again as the liminal character, a messenger between disparate worlds. His playful dance, accompanied by the sound of a flute, introduces a change of pace in the gloomy desert tale, necessary to guide the viewer through the complex cluster of events that follow. Just like in *Teorema*, where the mailman, Angelino, announces the arrival of the mysterious guest and later his imminent departure, Ninetto's appearance in *Porcile* marks an important moment of transition. Mr. Herdhitze is entering the Klotzes' villa and news of the cannibals' attacks in the desert is reaching authorities. Both events point to the end of Julian's ambiguous existence outside the patriarchal order: his metaphorical consumption by Mr. Herdhitze's tolerant neo-capitalism is clearly linked to Pierre

Clémenti's loss of freedom. The pigsty has definitely ceased to be the locus of Julian's resistance: co-opted by the tolerant power championed by Mr. Herdhitze, it has become everyone's space. Its mystery has been revealed, its disruptive power controlled. However, the feeling of reassurance for a re-established order is not the film's desired effect. Nor is the simple recognition of the new power's poorly hidden ties to its horrific past. Beyond a mere exposition of the act of consumption, the open-ended structure of the film invites a different approach to the news of the inescapability of the new power. That approach is suggested by Ninetto's otherwise unjustifiable presence in the desert and his crossing over to the Godesborg villa. As Viano has noted, Ninetto and Maracchione are, "spectators to the events."[28] However, their functionality to the film is not, I suggest, in their being "outside the difficult rational discourse which is the dominant mode of the film," but in their showing a different way of looking from within (ibid., 234). Taking the viewers inside the film perhaps for the first time, Maracchione's gaze guides us beyond the reflective stage. His stupefied, scandalized look on the sacrifice of consumption is a suggestion of the position that the film elicits from us.

The insertion of a specific character sharing a particular point of view partially closes the open play of signification that the film's form otherwise encourages. As the witness of consumption both in the desert and in Godesborg, Ninetto/Maracchione provides the only direct link between the two storylines. Positioned inside the world of the film, and yet distant spectator, he casts the unhardened look on events that the film suggests we adopt: a look that is capable of being scandalized. In the desert episode, whose signifying system is based on physical action and visuality, he is introduced as the dancing clapper inside a big church bell. The poetic look, in this episode, is expressed directly through the camera eye. The time dilation, the rapid alternation of long shots and close-ups at a high angle, the final revelation of the mode of the execution places us, as viewers, in Ninetto/Maracchione's perspective. His innocent look is foregrounded when he witnesses the trial involving Pierre Clémenti and his gang, and it comes to coincide with ours at the moment of their execution: the camera is behind his head, and we see the long preparation for the execution as a point-of-view shot. The long shot of the bodies being devoured by dogs is the image that Maracchione transports into the other tale: the distance that informs his testimony.

In the Klotzes' villa, in a system based primarily on the word, Maracchione gives voice to the innocent look of Gustava, the little girl who witnessed Julian's consumption.[29] However, he was also a direct witness to the other consumption and he brings that experience to his account. The pain and incredulity in his voice as he discloses the news of Julian's death to Herdhitze is inspired by that experience: the slow and painful consumption of Clémenti's body by the dogs in the desert, so distant and yet so close, parallels the fierce and perfect consumption of Julian's body by the pigs in the pigsty, so incredible and yet so real. The enormity of the message motivates the request that his interlocutor be the "toughest member of the new society." Klotz leaves the room and we are left with Herdhitze to hear it. However, while he can listen impassively to the report, focusing on the practical details, we cannot avoid seeing again, in our mind, the scene of Clémenti in the desert. To Herdhitze, Julian is now just like the "Jewish Bolsheviks" of his past: bodies he used to collect for his scientific experiments, that conveniently disappeared when the war ended, leaving no evidence. If no traces are left of him, "not even a button," the act of consumption is perfectly accomplished. But we cannot quite believe that the order and transparence of the system is re-established.

Because we have shared Maracchione's distant gaze upon the horror of Clémenti's death, the horror of Julian's death in the pigsty is closer, even if only evoked by a second-hand account. At the end of his testimony we are left, like the young messenger, with a disconcerting invitation to silence. Whether we choose to respect it and become accomplices in the new power, or to denounce it, is the decision left to us. If we want to be consumers of the products of new capitalism and accomplices in its false tolerance, we can raise a glass of beer with Klotz and Herdhitze and merge in their business. We will then accept the disappearance of humanistic culture and the opportune masking of violence that consumer power implies. We will take advantage of the Italian expertise in facelifts and forget our past. Accepting this complicity means accepting to be consumed, like Julian, by "the pigs." However, if we accept Ninetto/Maracchione's poetic look on consumption, and see its violence – not only the pigs, but the dogs in the desert as well – we will not be able to keep our mouths shut, like Herdhitze intimates that we do. As viewers of *Porcile*, we are made aware of our position within the Palace and the pigsty of neo-capitalism, and of the unavoidable consequences of that incorporation. The violence of this system, rather than simply removed to a distant past, is made all too evident to us through the cannibalistic analogy. In the present day, violence is not offered with gruesome detail, but is instead evoked only through

Ninetto/Maracchione's words and his distant gaze upon the young cannibal's execution. His stupefied look on the horror of consumption defamiliarizes it, removes from the acceptance of what is too close, allowing us to see it as if from a distance. The gaze he shares with us is the poetic look that Pasolini saw missing from the *Sessantotto*: a gaze that re-establishes opacity to the world and makes us aware of its complexity.

In both *Teorema* and *Porcile*, Ninetto signals the irruption of a peculiar form of youth in worlds that no longer recognize it: young people are the bearers of a poetic look which, in Pasolini's view, questions the bourgeois system more effectively than their actions in the streets or the words of their slogans. This form of youth belongs primarily to the imagination, but the hybrid young man-character Ninetto embodies this idea well when contemporary young people move in a different direction. Or rather, because the form of youth he embodies is mainly nourished by the imagination, and stands just outside the modern world, it does not fall prey to consumption, or consumerism. This seems the only way in which youth can maintain its privileged status in Pasolini's poetics. Ninetto guaranteed a steady presence of this hybrid form in Pasolini's cinema and poetry, until he too, grew up. In 1971, Ninetto fell in love with a girl, and two years later he got married. Pasolini wrote to his friend, the writer Paolo Volponi: "Ninetto è finito. Dopo quasi nove anni Ninetto non c'è più. Ho perso il senso della vita." (Ninetto is finished. After almost nine years, Ninetto is no longer there. I lost the meaning of life.)[30] The sense of irreparable loss accompanying Ninetto's maturation added to Pasolini's conviction that an entire generation was beyond his reach.

Beyond the *Sessantottini:* Neo-capitalism as the New Fascism

The generational conflict that characterized the student revolt of 1968 acquired a different configuration in the 1970s. The young people who in 1968 had imagined themselves and been perceived as members of a single cohort soon complicated that unified generational discourse. Increasingly politicized, they split into myriad revolutionary groups, and challenged the control of the unions and historical left-wing parties in the factories. Numerous strikes and occupations, promoted and coordinated by these activists throughout 1969, grew into a generalized struggle involving the large factories in Milan and Turin, as well as the smaller manufacturing works in the provinces. Demands included better work conditions and salary equity between different categories of workers, but the solidarity between factory workers and university students nourished revolutionary hopes in the Italian New Left.[31] On the other hand, in the perceived need for discipline and organization, some of these groups reproduced the hierarchical and male-centred models of the historical parties that they were questioning. Many young women who had participated both in the student rallies and in the workers' strikes, began to point out the patterns of oppression and self-oppression present in the "liberation movement."[32] The feminist movement, which would attain national resonance in the mid-1970s, gained its strength here.

The success of a season of intense struggle, the "hot autumn" of 1969, was, however, a combined effort of new groups and old unions that had learned to channel the energy of youth into their strategies and regained control of the factories. The experience favoured the further radicalization of some members of the New Left, who modelled their struggle on South American guerrillas and supported the use of violence to counter the violence of the state. The latter became undeniable after the bombing of a bank in Milan's Piazza Fontana, in December 1969. The "strategy of tension," a plan through which the state misrepresented right-wing terroristic acts as the work of left-wing organizations, in order to justify the imposition of repressive measures against public protest, further radicalized some revolutionary groups, who chose violence and clandestinity. Ideologically committed and willing to forgo the path to maturity established by society and join underground "families" of like-minded peers, these young men and women were carrying the mission of political renewal of the country to its extreme.[33] The massacre of Piazza Fontana functioned as a watershed of the era: it declared the end of the *Sessantotto* as a period of popular and largely peaceful protest and the beginning of Italy's darkest period since the war, the *anni di piombo*. The diaspora of the *sessantottini* produced a variety of groups, "collectives," and "avant-gardes," ranging from environmentalists and pacifists to terrorists, from Maoists and Leninists to feminists and gay activists, whose social impact would become visible over the next decade.

While young people identified with a growing variety of constituencies, and the category of youth became less and less definitive, Pasolini's social analysis in the 1970s focused on their conformity. While young people's actions and political choices differentiated them, he declared that they had become indistinguishable from one another. The superficial markers of 1960s youth – long hair, blue jeans – were so widespread as to no longer carry the political meaning they did when they transgressed a norm. They had become a fashion, which not only did not free the subjects wearing them, if they had ever done so, but instead confined them. Pasolini described the effects of consumer capitalism on young people in numerous essays and newspaper articles, published between 1973 and 1975. By undertaking action young people had allowed themselves to be co-opted by a power they did not understand, and consequently had become its victims.

In general, Pasolini's analysis of the transformation of Italy in the 1970s focused on its transition from a traditional, rural, or paleo-capitalist culture to a modern, urban, consumer culture, which had entered the late capitalist phase almost without realizing it. His observations, not inherently original, gained strength from a passionate rhetorical style, which underscored the emergency of the situation and the physical evidence of his theoretical points. Published mainly in the authoritative and conservative newspaper *Corriere della Sera*, Pasolini's articles on the bourgeois homogenization of Italian society acquired the weight of personal indictments against a system that challenged everyone's independence. He defended his own freedom of thought, previously justified through a self-exclusion from the centres of cultural hegemony, through a relentless, repeated, and outrageous provocation of power holders. The changes he perceived were so radical that he defined them collectively, with a formula that would be permanently associated with him, as an "anthropological revolution":

> The "middle class" has radically – I would say anthropologically – changed: its positive values are no longer reactionary and clerical values, but the values ... of hedonistic consumer ideology and of the resultant modernist American-style tolerance. It was the same Power – through the "development" of superfluous goods, the imposition of desires for consumption, fashion, information (particularly, in an imposing manner, television) – that created these values, cynically throwing out traditional values and the Church itself, which was their symbol.[34]

The cultural homologation undergone by different strata of society, through the introduction of consumer lifestyles and materialistic values, produced a form of "Development" (*Sviluppo*), "a pragmatic and economic fact," which did not correspond to real "Progress" (*Progresso*), "an ideal (social and political) notion." The apparent "social promotion and liberation" granted by the availability of consumer goods ensnared the lower classes in this Development and dissociated them from the idea of Progress.³⁵ Pasolini focused on this distinction in several articles, which outlined a model of emancipation imposed from above, but masked as acquired freedom and prosperity, and experienced as such by young people in particular.

Often quoted for their prophetic outlook on Italian society and their status within Pasolini's parable as a dissenting intellectual, these articles also contain what I consider to be Pasolini's last word on youth, that is, his last original contribution to a discourse on adolescence that had shaped his oeuvre for thirty years.³⁶ The protest of 1968 was quickly receding into the past and young people featured in these essays as victims, rather than agents, of a transformation whose violent outcome threatened to annihilate even the eternally redeeming power of youth. In their inauthentic coming-of-age as consumers they were confined to a youthful ghetto, which proved to be much more effective in cutting ties between fathers and children than any previous form of generational conflict. Casting young people as victims of the epochal changes of the sixties was instrumental to an invitation to a self-critique, which Pasolini extended to the intellectuals of his own generation. Recognizing the responsibility of the "fathers," who allowed this radical transformation to happen, was equivalent to admitting the failure of a generation of left-wing intellectuals: those who had identified *impegno* with the cultural formation of the lower classes in a hegemonic project in the 1950s, and who had been unable to understand and adapt to the social and cultural changes in the 1960s. Despite their efforts to establish continuities between the *Sessantotto* and the Resistance, the "fathers" were ultimately to blame, in Pasolini's view, for a-critically accepting, perhaps even encouraging, the "Development" of Italy into a bourgeois country. Pasolini belonged to this cohort, even if his "heretical" relationship with Communism may have lessened his feelings of guilt. As shown in chapter 2, in the 1950s, while both conservative institutions and left-wing parties promoted a national coming-of-age in the name of integration, productivity, and prosperity, Pasolini drew attention to the limits of a blueprint of individual and national development that obscured difference. The results of that model of development were now noticeable on the bodies of young people, patently conforming to an international model of youth, which he viewed as inauthentic.

Pasolini interpreted the changing significance of long hair for men as the visible sign of the neo-capitalist transformation of the country in the famous article "The Discourse of Hair," which opens the collection

Scritti corsari.[37] The choice of subject shows not only the centrality of young people in his socio-cultural analysis, but also how once again youth had become a symbol in the discourse of a mature writer. The "*capelloni*," long-haired youths, were a "new human category," whom he had first encountered while travelling in Prague in 1965. Their newness consisted of the non-verbal language that expressed their protest against consumer society: "the discourse of hair," a "silent and exclusively physical message," fully replaced words in young people's relationship with the world. Their silence corresponded to a form of protest by presence: they had "nothing to add orally and rationally to what [their] hair [said] physically and ontologically." In 1966–7, the "discourse of long hair" could potentially set up an absolute critique to consumer society by creating "new religious values within the bourgeois entropy." The physical and irrational nature of that protest, the "language of physical presence," overcame his instinctive aversion to the hairstyle:[38]

> I understood and felt an immediate aversion to those two. Later I had to take back my aversion, and defend the long-haired boys from attacks by police and Fascists: I was naturally on the side of the Living Theatre, of the Beats, etc., and the principle that made me stand on their side was a rigorously democratic one.[39]

He instinctively disliked those youths, but then rationally convinced himself to stand on their side. Pasolini's contradictory reaction to this encounter summarizes his complex relationship with youth in this period. As long as their protest against consumerism was non-verbal, exercised merely through physical presence, young people created "an antibody to such civilization" and earned his approval. By 1968, the *capelloni* were integrated in the student movement and long hair "fluttered in the wind with the red flags on the barricades": their language increasingly expressed "left-wing 'ideas.'" But the excess verbiage characterizing the period, in Pasolini's view, didn't spare the long-haired apostles: the presence of long hair was no longer sufficient and was "demoted to a distinctive function." Hair was "reabsorbed in the verbal fury" and ceased to express unambiguously left-wing ideas (ibid., 274). No longer uniquely associated with a specific political stance, long hair became simply a marker of youth. It became "a perfect mask" for both a left-wing and a right-wing subculture, thus even allowing infiltrations by *agents provocateurs*. Fast-forward to 1972, in Persia. In the central streets of Isfahan, walking among the "ancient boys," "dignified and humble sons, with their beautiful necks, their beautiful clean faces under proud innocent forelocks," Pasolini noticed two "monsters": not strictly *capelloni*, but boys whose hair was "cut European-style: long in the back, short in the front, stringy from the (forced) straightening, artificially stuck around the face, with two ugly wisps over their ears." (ibid., 276). The hairstyle communicated to the viewer the boys' "privileged international modernity," their sense of belonging to an elite of "bankers, students, sons of *nouveau* [sic] *riches* who work in the oil companies," in short, bourgeois. In recognizing this signal, Pasolini concluded that the subculture that produced the *capelloni* had been appropriated and absorbed by the dominant subculture, which transformed what was once a revolutionary style into a bourgeois fashion reserved for youth. The dominant subculture was none other than youth subculture, which transcended ideological and national divides.

Pasolini's "discourse against long hair" condemned a revolutionary gesture that created a "youth ghetto," de facto isolating young people from older generations. The style that successfully distinguished young people as a social group produced, in Pasolini's view, undesired results: setting young men apart from their fathers, long hair became "an insurmountable barrier" that prevented youth from entering into a "dialectical relationship" with their elders. The radical protest expressed by the non-verbal language of long hair lost its poignancy in establishing a transversal group. The co-optation by televisions and popular culture transformed a radical gesture into a fashion, a normative choice for young people rather than a revolutionary one. Letting one's hair grow long became a forced act, akin to putting on a mask ("the repugnant masks that young people put on their faces"): the gesture highlighted their bourgeois belonging and voided the significance of youth as the essentially anti-bourgeois force he believed it to be. Once signifiers of difference, young people had come to embody conformity.

Even blue jeans, the staple of rebellious youth style, offered the pretext for an analysis of Italy's secularization. Commenting on the success of Oliviero Toscani's advertising campaign for Jesus Jeans, Pasolini discussed the ads as a sign of the transformation of Italy into a secular, consumerist country. The slogans "Chi mi ama mi segua" (He who loves me follows me), and "Non avrai altro jeans all'infuori di me" (Thou shalt have no jeans besides me), attached to a close-up picture of a young, jeans-clad behind, created outrage in the Vatican. Its reaction, which could be justified in a paleo-capitalist world, was devoid of meaning in the current situation: "The Church made a pact with the devil, i.e., with the bourgeois State" and accepted its consumerism, "a new spirit which would initially compete with religion ... and would end up taking its place in providing people with a total and exclusive view of life."[40] In the cynicism of the ad that used one of the commandments as a slogan, Pasolini identified an indicator of the secularism of the new ruling class: "The new industrialists and the new technicians are completely secular, but of a secularism that no longer competes with religion." In the new value system created by the "bourgeois entropy," these slogans were "the nemesis – albeit unconscious – which punishes the Church for its pact with the devil" (ibid., 283).

More broadly, the focus on youth and generational discourse underlies Pasolini's definition of neo-capitalism as a "new Fascism." The comparison with the centralized, brutal power of the Fascist regime confers an ominous aspect to neo-capitalism, an apparently democratic, tolerant, yet normalizing power. The specter of violence and repression, allegedly exorcised long before in the democratic identity of post-war Italy, resurfaces in a new type of conformity enforced through non-coercive means: "No Fascist centralism succeeded in doing what the centralism of consumer culture did."[41] While the central model imposed by Fascism, "reactionary and monumental," had been only superficially accepted, leaving the various local cultures substantially untouched, the model imposed by the new power supplanted the specificity of local cultures with a "mass hedonism" diffused through modern media. The effectiveness of new Fascism consisted in its lack of coercion and constraint; on the contrary, it created desires and models to which individuals willingly conformed. Although the new Fascism employed consumerism instead of violence, as Pasolini's analysis highlighted, it also focused its attention on youth just like the Fascist regime did. The new power created models for young people to emulate "Young Man and Young Woman": "They are two People who value life only through Consumer Goods" (ibid., 290). These models proposed by television erased class and cultural differences that had characterized youth before the economic miracle: young sub-proletarians, once proud of their "illiterate popular model," were now ashamed of it and aspired to a petit bourgeois condition that they used to despise. Petit bourgeois youths, for their part, tried unsuccessfully to reproduce the models of youth seen on television, and became "strangely coarse and unhappy" (ibid., 292). The homogenization (*omologazione*) of young people from different social classes, determined by a shared disdain for culture, produced a condition that Pasolini defined as "unhappiness."

The new Fascism voided the distinction between social classes, between centre and periphery, between the Left and the Right. "Development" produced standardized young people: "culturally, psychologically, somatically ... nothing distinguishes" young neo-Fascists from young Communists. In a way, neo-capitalism produced the "new man" that was the model for Fascist youth policies. Despite their capillary nature, Pasolini argued, the latter had only partially succeeded because humanistic culture allowed young people of the 1930s and '40s to see beyond the ideals imposed by Fascism, and maintain an ambivalent relationship. The young citizens produced by neo-capitalism, on the contrary, reflected the complete homologation to a model not imposed from above but shaped through the creation of desires:

> Deciding to let one's hair grow to shoulders' length, or cutting one's hair and growing a moustache ...; deciding to wear a bandanna on one's head or to pull a cap down on one's eyes; deciding whether to dream of a Ferrari or a Porsche; carefully following TV programs; knowing the titles of a few best-sellers; wearing aggressively fashionable pants and t-shirts; having obsessive relationships with young women kept ornamentally at one's side, but at the same time, pretending that they are "free" etc.: all these are cultural acts. Now, all young Italians perform these same acts, have the same physical language, are interchangeable.[42]

The economic boom of the sixties and the rapid urbanization, together with the reform of the school system and the diffusion of television, effected a democratization of habits that all previous attempts at unification had failed to achieve: young people were the natural target for a cultural model based on the notions of newness and modernity. Development was thus both the means and the product of the new Power. Because young people under Fascism had maintained a strong link to the culture of their fathers, to which they could return once they took off their *Balilla* uniforms, the control that the regime exercised on them could remain superficial. In the domain of neo-capitalism, on the contrary, consumer culture "profoundly transformed young people, touched them deeply, gave them new sentiments, new ways of thinking, of living, new cultural models." Therefore, in successfully transforming young people, Pasolini concluded, "consumer culture fully realized the intent of Fascism."[43]

Sharing Responsibilities: Fathers and Children

In this apocalyptic scenario, the focus on the children (*i figli*) as victims of the new power allowed Pasolini to reflect on the responsibilities of the fathers. In a bold rhetorical move, he commented on the terrorist attacks in Brescia (1974) and Milan (1969) alongside the results of a national referendum which, despite fears to the contrary, confirmed the legalization of divorce. The cultural transformation that led a majority of Italians – presumably left-wing – to uphold divorce, he claimed, also changed the nature of the young right-wing extremists who put bombs in those public places. The latter were no more Fascists than the young supporters of divorce were Communists, in the traditional sense of these words. Neo-capitalism voided traditional oppositions of their ideological meaning, because it created an alternative culture, which replaced all pre-existing categories.[44] Responsibility for this radical change rested with the fathers, and Pasolini included himself in the category of "progressive, anti-Fascist, left-wing men," who did not prevent the "genocide." In the course of a famous dispute with Italo Calvino, who accused him of looking back nostalgically to a lost world, Pasolini explicitly assigned to the fathers responsibility for the wrongdoing of the children. Nothing predestined a young man to be a Fascist, he claimed, recuperating the timeless notion of the innate goodness of youth:

> They are not the fatal and destined representatives of Evil. ... It is an atrocious form of despair and neurosis which pushes a young man to such a choice; and maybe a single slightly different experience in his life, a single simple encounter, would have been enough for his destiny to be different.[45]

The acceptance of responsibilities, as a father, for the wrongdoing of children, concluded Pasolini's lifetime reflection on youth. While school and university reforms, the passing of the Statute of the Workers, legislation on divorce, and the debate on abortion were among the most prominent outcomes of the debates stirred by the *Sessantotto*, Pasolini saw them as manifestations of a disciplinary power.[46] The functioning and effects of this new Power, introduced in *Scritti corsari*, were further explored in later articles, published in the newspapers *Corriere della Sera* and *Il Mondo*, and later collected in *Lettere luterane*. The discourse of youth reached a bitter conclusion in these articles, which focused on the catastrophic effects of the new Fascism on young Italians. The normalizing effects of the new power, argued Pasolini, were particularly visible on the young: "Young people who were born and grew up in this time of false progressiveness and false tolerance are paying for this falsity (the cynicism of the new power that destroyed everything) in the most atrocious way" (ibid.). Creating a false sense of sexual liberation, the new power produced a heteronormative society based on the "consumer couple," whose sexual behaviour was imposed, while homosexuality was tolerated at best by progressive elites to "gratify their conscience."[47] Young men were "traumatized by the obligation imposed by [sexual] permissiveness," while young women conformed to the myth of the new woman, expected to be "there, ready, immediately, always available."[48] The normalizing new power confined young Italians to a condition of forcible "freedom," which was particularly insidious because it was less noticeable than open repression.

The catastrophic effects of the "anthropological mutation" could be observed not only in young people's social and sexual behaviour, but also on their bodies: "The children who surround us, especially the youngest, the adolescents, are almost all monsters. Their physical aspect is almost terrifying, and when not terrifying, it is annoyingly unhappy. Horrible manes, caricatural hairdos, pale complexion, dull eyes."[49] Their physical appearance, which clearly contravened the aesthetic ideal of adolescent bodies celebrated in Pasolini's earlier work, were actually, in his interpretation, the external symptom of a profound discomfort: "Their eyes avoid your gaze, their thoughts are perpetually elsewhere, they have both too much respect or too much contempt, too much patience or too much impatience" (544). Their alien look, which Pasolini described through specific physical features, disclosed their belonging to a radically new peer culture, foreign to any form of youth that he, as a father, could identify with. Pasolini saw young people, young men particularly, as trapped in their youthful clothing and hairstyle, not liberated by it. The sartorial choices that identified them publicly as modern youths transformed the redemptive function ascribed to them by bourgeois society into an obligation: while their look indicated rebellion (or, because their rebellion became part of a youthful look) "their revolt [was] codified." Their "unhappiness," a condition that uniquely characterized this generation in Pasolini's account of it, was a product of their new condition within the social order. Youth was "happy" when not burdened by the historical and moral codes of contemporary society. By entering history as social subjects, young people lost that "happiness" (innocence) that qualified them as a moral alternative to a corrupt society. Now, distinguished only by that superficial dress style, they were integrated in the system that they were allegedly challenging. A paradox emerges from this assessment: modern society had imagined into being a form of youth that was simultaneously rebellious and integrated. The generation resulting from this operation was comprised, in Pasolini's view, of children who were both obedient and disobedient, or rather obedient by being disobedient. Youth had become once again, as it had been during Fascism, a cultural label that could be used to deflect attention from other conflicts, or to project the specter of renewal onto a substantially conservative society.

Pasolini's assessment of the position of young people in the society of the early 1970s as broadly analogous to the ambiguous cult of youth during Fascism accounted for the generational discourse he introduced. Despite having earlier rejected a fatherly role, he now accepted it and invited his own generation to take responsibility for the present situation. His condemnation of the children, his "suspension of love for them," implied an assumption of responsibility for what the children had become. All "fathers," regardless of their political affiliation, were to blame for having trusted young people, the *sessantottini*, with the renewal of society. Both Fascists and anti-Fascists, both right-wing and left-wing fathers, had believed in the younger generation's project to change the course of Italy as a democratic nation. In spite of their own experience with Fascism, they had not recognized the implications of transforming a cultural construction of youth into political action. The obvious differences between a top-down program aimed at mobilizing youth to support a totalitarian regime and a spontaneous initiative drawing together a historical cohort around the idea of radical institutional transformation lost relevance in the context of Pasolini's depiction of neo-capitalism as the new Fascism. The new power manipulated young people in ways that were comparable to the means employed by the Fascist regime: celebrating on one hand their "disobedience," while on the other institutionalizing it so that, to all intents and purposes, it became a "new [form of] obedience."[50]

Totally deprived of agency by a lack of perspective, young people born in the ambit of this "new Fascism" could no more see it for what it was than could the young people born during the Fascist regime.[51] However, while young Italians born during Fascism, like Pasolini, could rely on humanistic culture to develop an anti-Fascist conscience, contemporary youths had rejected that value. For this reason, the responsibility for the current situation had to be shared. The fault of the fathers was to entrust the renewal of society to young people, thereby signing off on the transformation of Italy into a neo-capitalistic country. The children's was to have failed to recognize the value of literature and art in their revolutionary discourse. The fathers had let young people's desires dictate what Pasolini called a unification of two histories, the bourgeoisie's and the lower classes', under the aegis of consumer society. Young proletarians and sub-proletarians had repudiated their geographically and class-specific culture, which guaranteed intergenerational continuity, in the name of an international and democratic peer culture. They sustained globalizing Development instead of exercising the resistance they had embodied in a paleo-capitalist society. The fathers did not recognize in time that even the youth of the lower classes (*il popolo*) were coming of age as consumers. The children must then be punished for their fathers' mistakes.

Gennariello: A Concise Study Guide to Pasolini

Whether the pedagogical treatise *Gennariello* constituted that punishment or an example for his generation is a matter of debate. Organized as a series of lessons published in the weekly *Il Mondo*, the treatise is addressed to an imaginary pupil, Gennariello, a 15-year-old Neapolitan bourgeois boy. Combining the physical features of the sub-proletarian *ragazzi* – slim, with shiny black eyes, hair cut short on the neck and long on the forehead, a good soccer player – with the bourgeois propensity for education, Gennariello is a miraculous creature. His geographical origin – Naples, "the last plebeian metropolis" whose participation in a history "not strictly Italian" renders it "virtually classless" – guarantees that even a bourgeois boy is full of "vitality." Averting possible criticism regarding ulterior motives in his specific physical requirements, Pasolini adds that the only prerequisite is the pupil's "likability" (*simpatia*), which he could equally find in "a Concettina," a southern young woman. However, the descriptions of Gennariello's peers in several chapters make it clear that he is a special youth. His absence from the dialogue is also made explicit: "Naturally, if read by others, this pedagogical text of mine is a lie, because you are not there: your talk, your voice, your smile."[52] It is clear that the pupil has to be imagined into being so that the teacher can illustrate his ideas on education, on contemporary Italy, on youth. None of these ideas are new to Pasolini's readers, but the new format condenses and streamlines analyses that were previously scattered among various articles and interviews.

The project outlined includes preliminary lessons on "the pedagogical value of objects," on peer education, on "diseducational" institutions such as school and mass media. Only after these introductory lessons are completed will the teacher take up "the most important subjects": sex, behaviour, religion, politics, art. The illustration of the plan and of the principles informing each selection constitutes the only explicitly pedagogical part of the treatise, which is otherwise a digest of Pasolini's critical positions in the seventies. The outspoken criticism characterizing the "pirate writings," combined with a self-imposed simplification consistent with the didactic goal, make of *Gennariello* a sort of "CliffsNotes" version of Pasolini's view of society. As if in a short study guide, the author provides the key points of his critical perspective: social milieu determines a child from his birth and any other form of education can only add layers to the socio-economic substratum; his own humanistic culture affects his aesthetic approach to the world but he does not think that poverty is the worst evil; the economic emancipation of the lower classes brought about by the economic miracle had side effects that degraded them; young people have conformed to a state of imposed disobedience that renders them ugly and unhappy; materialism and hedonism have replaced Catholicism as the dominant faith. The likeable but presumably impatient Gennariello, addressed directly at least once in each chapter, can thus receive a quick illustration of many lessons that, if we believe their content, he cannot actually take in.

At the basis of this project is what Enzo Golino called a "pedagogy of scandal," through which Gennariello must learn to deconsecrate everything. In the conditions created by the new Power, falsely secular and anti-authoritarian, this means also learning not to be afraid of "sacredness and sentiments."[53] The model for these acts of deconsecration is the author himself, whose homosexuality confines him to the condition of "tolerated":

> As long as the person who is "different" lives his "difference" in silence, confined to the mental ghetto assigned to him, everything is fine; and everyone feels gratified by the tolerance they grant to him. But as soon as he says a word on his experience of "difference," or simply, dares utter words "coloured" by his experience of "difference," a lynching is unleashed, like in the darkest clerico-fascist times.[54]

After presenting the young to adults as archetypes of difference for decades, he now offers himself as a model for the type of transgression he encourages in the pupil. Young people have become conformist, and they must be taught to reject conformity. The straightforward didactic approach, which the teacher considers indispensable, does not offer more chances of success. Quite the contrary: the casting of young people as pupils comes with an explicit admission that communication is impossible. The generational gap is undeniable: the teacher and the imagined pupil speak completely different languages. They were shaped by the "qualitatively different" physical and cultural environments in which each grew up: "The physical reality of the periphery educated me to certainty, to a profound, certain and irreplaceable love. It educated you to uncertainty, to a lack of love determined by a false certainty, cruel and merciless" (ibid., 579). Where the teacher experienced continuity, the pupil experiences the conformity of innovation. Little can the words of the teacher do against the "language of things," which taught Gennariello to distrust teachers: "My role as a pedagogue is irreparably questioned. One cannot teach if he doesn't at the same time learn" (ibid., 575). The possibility of learning seems however as hopeless as that of teaching.

The real lessons come to Gennariello from his peers: "They are carriers, unknowing and therefore much more aggressive, of absolutely new values, which only you and they experience. We – your fathers – are excluded from them. What is more, those values are untranslatable into our language."[55] Once again, Pasolini discusses youth in the familiar format: he makes parallels between his own youth and Gennariello's, comparing peer pressure during Fascism and neo-capitalism; he attempts a generational portrait of contemporary youth, divided into obedient and disobedient children; he remarks bitterly – more so than usual – on their unhappiness, caused by their feeling "undesired" in a world in which the birth of a child is no longer seen as a blessing.[56] Obedient young people include, in the seventies, those faithful to the conformity of rebellion, and their teachings are no less difficult to oppose than those of young Fascists in the thirties. Gennariello should therefore learn to distance himself from all forms of obedience, which produce unhappiness. Very few young people could be defined truly disobedient: "the very few surviving extremists, maladjusted people, deviants, and – these truly rare – '"the learned."' They could represent a positive model, but they never make it into the treatise, which is interrupted soon thereafter.

Gennariello, necessary interlocutor, does not have the opportunity to speak. From imagined audience to featured character, he makes explicit a dynamic underlying all of Pasolini's oeuvre: his frustrated desire to establish a channel of communication with youth, which translated into the creation of young characters. In creating a pupil to his own specifications, the teacher admits to his limitations: no real adolescent exists who could live up to this literary ideal, but one could still be imagined into being. *Gennariello* thus thematizes Pasolini's wish to speak to and for youth, which often resulted in discussions about youth. Gennariello's presence in the text, however, also reflects the relationship between author and reader. As readers we are implicitly cast as pupils, sharing with Gennariello the lessons of the *"mirabile maestro."* This education, however, is complicated by Gennariello's specific characterization and subsequent silence. His textual presence, a pupil who does not question his teacher, asks that we listen in silence too. It is the opposite of what Ninetto/Maracchione had asked us to do in the conclusion of *Porcile*. Pedagogy separated from poetics betrays the view of youth that shaped Pasolini's oeuvre. It is no coincidence that the treatise is unfinished.

In choosing youth as a referent and a subject of identification, Pasolini had embraced in a unique way the generational call to *impegno* issued to anti-Fascist intellectuals in post-war Italy. Through youth discourse he contributed to a Gramscian project of cultural emancipation, whose premises he shared, while questioning some of its ideological limitations. Through literary notions of adolescence as an irrational force he challenged a progressive discourse that he perceived as too rigid. His analyses of the transformation of youthful lifestyles from the 1940s to the 1970s traced Italy's coming-of-age not as linear progress, but as a composite phenomenon whose costs at times outweighed its benefits. The poetry of youth, expressed in verbal or visual form, became an instrument of resistance in an increasingly pragmatic world that seemed to have no place for poets. Aesthetics and ethics were inseparable components of his dialogue with youth, be that real or imagined. Thus, when the form of commitment that had defined his generation "fell out of style," as he put it, the position of difference from which he continued to speak, and which he had repeatedly assigned to youth, proved to be his most enduring legacy.

Epilogue
Coming of Age as Sadists: *Salò* and the Repudiation of Youth

Much has been written about *Salò*, Pasolini's last completed film, which was released only a few weeks after he was brutally murdered in November 1975.[1] The display of violence in the movie and his violent death, at the hands of Pino Pelosi, a young male prostitute with whom Pasolini had spent the last few hours of his life, wrote a gruesome ending to his saga of youth. This *ragazzo di vita* was similar to many he had known, worked with, written about, or solicited for sex in the twenty-five years he had lived in Rome. Perhaps fittingly, he was the first to speak publicly about Pasolini after his death: to the police, the court, and the press. *Salò* added to these pronouncements the disturbing images of young men and women being annihilated, victims of the perverted desires of aging men.[2] The murder, Pelosi's statements, and the movie together projected an image of adolescence that redefined much of what Pasolini's oeuvre had celebrated, namely his belief in the irrepressible and unknowable qualities of youth, beyond all adult attempts to control, mould, and understand.

The unfinished treatise *Gennariello* summed up the signs of a social transformation, which troubled the author: the disappearance of authentic youth due to consumerism and incipient globalization. The extent of that transformation had become clear on the occasion of the first television broadcast of his film *Accattone*. Although at the time of shooting, in 1961, the film portrayed an existing social group, in 1975 the young sub-proletarian characters appeared anachronistic. Pasolini claimed that, were he to reshoot his first movie again in 1975, he wouldn't find "a single young man who [was], in his 'body,' even vaguely similar to the young men who [had] portrayed themselves in *Accattone*."[3] The young *borgatari* featured in that movie and in his

Roman novels were likeable (*simpatici*) because they were proud of their social standing. A decade later, they had become "sad, neurotic, uncertain, full of a petit bourgeois anxiety" (ibid., 678). Most importantly, they were ashamed of their working-class status and tried to emulate bourgeois youths. Observing that even sub-proletarian *ragazzi*, the epitome of youthful authenticity, wished to participate in the globalized form of youth created by consumer culture, had Pasolini admitting to an underlying desire for conformity in youth that was not historically specific.

He acknowledged his change of mind via a retroactive explanation in "Abiura dalla *Trilogia della vita*" (Repudiation of the *Trilogy of Life*), an essay through which he explicitly bid farewell to youth as a symbol of resistance:

> The youths and boys of the Roman sub-proletariat – the ones I have projected in the old and resistant Naples, and later in the poor countries of the Third World – if now they are human garbage it means that potentially they were such also then; they were, therefore, imbeciles compelled to be adorable, squalid criminals compelled to be likeable rascals, vile good-for-nothings compelled to be saintly innocents, etc. The collapse of the present implies the collapse of the past.

In the previous three years, he had attempted to recover the innocence of youth by celebrating an ideally free pre-capitalistic sexuality in the *Trilogy of Life*: *Il Decameron* (1971; *The Decameron*), *I racconti di Canterbury* (1972; *The Canterbury Tales*), and *Il fiore delle mille e una notte* (1974; *Arabian Nights*). Creative adaptations of canonical narratives in the Western and Middle-Eastern traditions, the three movies responded to what Pasolini saw as the "unreality" of present conformity by portraying the supposed "reality" of a pre-modern world in which sexuality functioned as a form of resistance to repression. Free of the social conditioning imposed by modernity, the young bodies on the screen allegedly expressed an authentic sexuality, which could serve as an antidote to the forced sexual liberation of the 1970s. When such attempts produced instead a barrage of criticism, and more importantly, inspired B- and X-rated mock-sequels with such titles as *Decameron proibitissimo: Boccaccio mio statte zitto* (1972; *Sexy Sinners*) or *Decameron n.3: Le più belle donne del Boccaccio* (1972; *Decameron's Jolly Kittens*), he had to admit that his films had been "manipulated by the power structure."[4] However, his recantation, regardless of the degree of irony one sees in it, reaffirmed his critical view of contemporary youth.⁵ Since his critics had failed to understand the ideological implications of his visual and narrative choices in the *Trilogia*, he would have to represent the transformation in more explicit terms.⁶ The consequent "commitment to a greater legibility (*Salò?*)," which concluded the *abiura*, set up expectations for an unambiguous critique of contemporary adolescents in his next film.

Salò, o le 120 giornate di Sodoma (1975; *Salò, or the 120 Days of Sodom*) offered such a critique by visualizing the analogy between neo-capitalism and Fascism, which he had drawn in his "pirate writings." His view of contemporary adolescents as the products of a new Fascism, which accomplished the mission of historical Fascism, was rendered as a cult of youth gone awry, transformed into fetishism of youthful bodies. The film moves the action of Marquis de Sade's eighteenth-century novel to 1944, in the Italian Social Republic (RSI), the puppet state created by Nazi Germany after the fall of Mussolini. Although not the actual geographical location of the movie, the Salò of the title, a town on Lake Garda where the "republic" had its official seat, becomes an allegory for modern power.⁷ The film portrays the escalating violence perpetrated by four aging libertines on sixteen captive adolescents, culminating in outright torture and murder.⁸ After a brief prologue (called the "Anti-Inferno") depicting the arrests of the young people, the entire movie is a series of extremely stylized *tableaux*, corresponding to successive stages of their descent into *gironi* of a Dantean hell: the Circle of Manias, the Circle of Shit, and the Circle of Blood. While the prologue is shot outdoors in a naturalistic style reminiscent of Resistance films, once the boys and girls are captured they never leave the elegant art deco villa where they are held, which stands as another incarnation of the inescapable *Palazzo* of modern power.

The nexus youth-pleasure-power, central to Pasolini's analysis of the functioning of neo-capitalism, is here perverted into a fantasy control of youthful bodies by aging authorities.

The libertines – a judge, a monsignor, a banker, and a nobleman – embody state institutions, while the victims are bourgeois or petit bourgeois adolescents largely indistinguishable from one another. Three middle-aged prostitutes tell erotic stories intended to inspire the libertines, while a fourth plays the piano. Guards, servants, and *fouteurs*, well-endowed young men, complete the cast. Sexual acts and practices of subjugation are performed according to an elaborate narrative and dramatic *mise-en-scène*, based on the ideas of repetition and excess, which the dignitaries present as the basis of their ethos. The result is the "inconsumable" film that Pasolini had attempted to create since choosing cinema as an antidote to cultural consumerism.

The "last-word" status of *Salò* in Pasolini's filmography has been assessed in many convincing analyses.[9] Its lucid, if disturbing, study of contemporary power dynamics via allegorical displacement caused general outrage: graphic images upset the audience, while the analogy between literary sadism and historical Fascism angered intellectuals.[10] Thus, the film achieves its intended goal of non-commodifiable artistic expression. It also brings Pasolini's contribution to the discourse on youth to an unequivocal close. First of all, it pushes the critique of contemporary youth as culturally undiscerning, falsely liberated, compulsively heterosexual, and promiscuous to visual and ideological extremes. Reduced to nameless and interchangeable bodies, or worse, anuses, young men and women are deprived of all humanity. They are incarcerated, sodomized, fustigated, subjected to coprophagia, necrophilia, mutilation, and death. In a cruel if somewhat humorous *contrappasso*, they are even punished for their consumption of objectionable cultural products (distasteful to Pasolini, at least) by being forced to eat, literally, excrement.

Sadism functions as a perverse form of education in a vicious boarding school, whose rules are as detailed as they are absurd.[11] The stories, the meticulous descriptions, and the role play are pedagogical strategies aimed at teaching the young about the pleasure of sodomy, incest, necrophilia, sadism, masochism, exhibitionism, and voyeurism.[12] Two books regulate the pedagogical process: one contains the rules, the other the names of pupils who contravene them. The main principle is the transgression of all norms, which makes transgression itself a norm. In the interval between the enunciation of the rule and the punishment, the pupils are periodically lined up for inspection, either naked or dressed in outfits resembling school uniforms, and frequently tested via stage performances.[13] Two young men are even singled out as subjects of a *Bildung* that will lead them to be socialized in the system of the aging libertines.[14] Consistently with Pasolini's assessment of contemporary youth as forcibly disobedient children, the perverse educational experiment succeeds: young people, arbitrarily cast as victims or guards when they were first captured, eventually participate in their own subjugation. They betray one another, and those who survive are willing to become voyeurs, just like the perpetrators. As an allegory of the modern world, hence, *Salò* ratifies the conformity of adolescence.

As a meta-cinematic reflection on voyeurism, however, the film also comments on the manipulation of youth in cultural objects produced by adults. Through various on-screen viewers/voyeurs, *Salò* equates the filmmaker and the audience to the libertines who exploit innocent young bodies.[15] Yet the very principles that arouse the libertines – excess and repetition – exclude the viewers from pleasure. Such exclusion favours an intellectual engagement, which allows the images to have a performative effect, analogous to that exercised by the poetic gaze in *Teorema* and *Porcile*.[16] Thus, at the formal level, *Salò* could be viewed as a third episode in a "Trilogy of Modern Youth." In *Teorema*, the irruption of a youthful poetic look questioned the identity of a stultified bourgeois family; in *Porcile* the empathetic gaze of Ninetto/Maracchione elicited a new perspective on the invisible violence of neo-capitalism, and created a form of resistance to (youth) consumption. *Salò* implicates the viewers in the fetishism of youth on screen while condemning young people for their lack of resistance. Redressing the fallacy of innocence that underlies the *Trilogy of Life*, *Salò* resists the commodification of youth by portraying young people as complicit in their own co-optation.[17]

In order to set up such resistance, *Salò* arrests the play of signification that had allowed youth to be a defining concept for Pasolini's own poetics and ethics. While *Teorema* and *Porcile* relied on polysemy and ambiguity to showcase the revolutionary power of youth and its resistance to consumption, the exactitude of *Salò* leaves no doubt as to the powerlessness of adolescents, or worse, their complicity in their own submission. Although many of his poetic and cinematic reflections focused on a tension between being and doing, which was embodied in youth, that tension is absent from *Salò*. The film stages a perverted pedagogy, which results in a completed coming of age. Early on, as one of the young victims is being brutally sodomized, the others watch and sing "Sul ponte di Perati," the Friulian song containing the famous verse "la meglio zoventù va soto tera" (the best of youth goes underground). Making use of that verse once again, now restored to its original context, Pasolini closes the play of signification on youth inaugurated by *Poesie a Casarsa*. No longer displaced or idealized, youth ceases to stand for something other than young bodies. The best of youth in those early poems was part of a natural landscape that cannot even be imagined in the dark claustrophobic rooms of the house of horrors. A close-up of the young victims singing along with the libertines and the guards, confirms that the best of youth will now go, definitively, "*soto tera*."

Notes

Introduction

1 Pasolini, "Roma 1950: Diario," in *Tutte le poesie* vol.1, ed. Walter Siti (Milan: Mondadori, 2003), 699. Hereafter *Poesie 1* in parenthetical references in the text and endnotes. *The Selected Poetry of Pier Paolo Pasolini: A Bilingual Edition*, ed. and trans. Stephen Sartarelli (Chicago: University of Chicago Press, 2014), 139.
2 *La meglio gioventù*, written by Stefano Rulli and Sandro Petraglia and directed by Marco Tullio Giordana, tells the story of a middle-class Roman family from the early 1960s to the 1990s. The protagonists, brothers Nicola and Matteo, choose opposite sides of the barricades in the student protest: the former as an activist, the latter as a policeman. Pasolini's comments on the student rallies are not mentioned in the film, but they clearly shape Matteo's argument with his brother's girlfriend, Giulia, who criticizes the police's use of violence to repress a student demonstration in Turin, where part of the miniseries takes place. Matteo highlights a different perspective, exemplified by his colleague and friend Luigi, a southern young man for whom the service represented a chance of upward mobility, who was injured in the clashes.
3 The poem "The PCI to the Young!" was published in the magazine *l'Espresso* in the spring of 1968, as a commentary on clashes between students and policemen at the Faculty of Architecture in Rome. The poem and the controversy it stirred are discussed in chapter 5.
4 Patricia Meyer Spacks, *The Adolescent Idea: Myths of Youth and the Adult Imagination* (New York: Basic Books, 1981), 291.
5 It was Natale De Zotti, the principal of the middle school in Valvasone, Friuli, where Pasolini worked in 1948, who defined him as a "wonderful teacher."

The poet Andrea Zanzotto, who grew up in a nearby town, reports the principal's appreciation for Pasolini's innovative pedagogy, based on the "active methods" of Carleton Washburne and of Dewey's "honest work," which were revolutionary for a provincial school in 1940s Italy. See Zanzotto, "Pedagogia" in *Aure e disincanti nel Novecento letterario*, 145.

6 Stephen Burt, *The Forms of Youth: Twentieth-Century Poetry and Adolescence* (New York: Columbia University Press, 2007), 5.
7 Existing scholarship addresses specific configurations of youth in Pasolini's work. Young people are the primary subjects of education in Enzo Golino's study of Pasolini's oeuvre as a "polyphonic *Bildunsgroman*," *Pasolini: Il sogno di una cosa: Pedagogia, eros, letteratura dal mito del popolo alla società di massa* (Bologna: Il Mulino, 1985). Marco Antonio Bazzocchi focuses on young people's bodies as an absolute force that can disrupt the bourgeois world in *Teorema*. See the essay "La letteratura, i giovani e la rappresentazione della sessualità" in *Il secolo dei giovani: Le nuove generazioni e la storia del Novecento*, ed. Paolo Sorcinelli and Angelo Varni (Rome: Donzelli, 2004), 187–211; and the chapter "*Teorema*: mito e tragedia borghese" in his book *I burattini filosofi: Pasolini dalla letteratura al cinema* (Milan: Bruno Mondadori, 2007), 107–27. Colleen Ryan-Scheutz's analysis of daughters in Pasolini's film considers them as signifiers of authenticity who could either revive the traits of maiden mothers in poetry and early films or represent an alternative to the disappointing "sons" in the late 1960s. See *Sex, the Self, and the Sacred: Women in the Cinema of Pier Paolo Pasolini* (Toronto, Buffalo, and London: University of Toronto Press, 2007), 102–34.
8 For Pasolini's biographies see Nico Naldini, *Pasolini, una vita* (Turin: Einaudi, 1989); Enzo Siciliano, *Vita di Pasolini* (Milan: Rizzoli, 1978); Barth David Schwartz, *Pasolini Requiem* (New York: Pantheon Books, 1992).
9 In the extensive bibliography existing on Pasolini, Robert S.C. Gordon's *Pasolini: Forms of Subjectivity* (Oxford: Clarendon Press, 1996) is indispensable. This study is indebted to Gordon's detailed analysis of Pasolini's construction of subjectivity through formal experimentation, and to the notion of "active and subjective signifying practices," which help understand the oscillations between a strong authorial presence and the fluidity of its manifestations.
10 In the fall of 1949, rumours started circulating about Pasolini's homosexuality in the small towns of Friuli where he had relocated during the war. He was an active member of the local Communist Party and a beloved elementary, then middle school, teacher. After he had met with fifteen- and sixteen-year-old boys at a county fair in the town of Ramuscello, and allegedly masturbated in nearby fields, Pasolini was charged with

"corruption of minors and obscene acts in a public place," and convicted of the latter. The charges would be dropped two years later, at appeal, but in 1949 the scandal – the loss of employment, the expulsion from the party – ruined his life in Friuli and induced him to move to Rome. See Naldini, *Pasolini, una vita*; Siciliano, *Vita di Pasolini*; Schwartz, *Pasolini Requiem* for biographical accounts of the Ramuscello events. For a juridical account see Laura Betti, ed., *Pasolini: cronaca giudiziaria, persecuzione, morte* (Milan: Garzanti, 1977).

11 Zygmunt Baranski reassesses Pasolini's claims of the early influence of Gramsci on his ideology against his writings in the chapter "Pasolini: Culture, Croce, Gramsci," in *Culture and Conflict in Postwar Italy*, ed. Zygmunt Baranski and Robert Lumley, 139–59.

12 Michel Foucault, "Les matins gris de la tolerance," *Le Monde*, March 23, 1977, trans. Danielle Kormos as "Grey Mornings of Tolerance," *Stanford Italian Review*, 2:2, Fall 1982: 73.

13 For a reading of Pasolini's oeuvre through a pedagogical lens see Golino, *Pasolini: Il sogno di una cosa*, and Zanzotto's essay "Pedagogia," in *Aure e disincanti nel Novecento letterario* (Milan: Arnoldo Mondadori, 1994), 141–52.

14 Patrizia Dogliani, *Storia dei giovani* (Milan: Bruno Mondadori, 2003). This concise book offers an introduction to the main issues relating to the youth question in Italy, in an international (mostly European) framework. It also provides an extended bibliography on the subject. The "long century of youth," which Dogliani introduces in response to historian Eric J. Hobsbawm's definition of a "short twentieth century," starts with the nation-building movements of the early nineteenth century, which recruited young militants in order to rejuvenate stale politics. On this subject see also Sergio Luzzatto, "Giovani ribelli e rivoluzionari," in G. Levi and J.C. Schmitt, *Storia dei giovani*, vol. 2: *L'età contemporanea* (Rome: Laterza, 1994).

15 Already in the debates leading to the French Revolution notions of "regeneration" shifted from the religious to the political realm, appealing to young people's vital energies, courage, and impulse to eradicate the corruption of the ancient world. Edmund Burke, in "Philosophical Enquiry into the Origin of our Ideas on the Sublime and the Beautiful" (1757) recorded a change in aesthetic taste juxtaposing the sublime – pursued through passion, eccess, terror, infinity – with the beautiful – expression of measure, rationality, serenity, control. Youthful rebelliousness and passion found expression in the *Sturm und Drang* movement: in the re-established myth of Prometheus (Goethe, 1773) and in the existential angst of the young Werther (*Die Leiden des jungen Werther*, 1778). For an overview of pre-Romantic and Romantic debates on youth in Italy see Andrea

Battistini, "I miti letterari della giovinezza alle soglie del romanticismo," in *Il mondo giovanile in Italia tra Otto e Novecento*, ed. Angelo Varni (Bologna: Il Mulino, 1998), 11–39.

16 Later in life, Pasolini often referred to those readings as stimulating his early "cultural anti-Fascism." See for instance, Pasolini, *Il sogno del centauro*, ed. Jean Duflot (Rome: Editori Riuniti, 1983), and *Pasolini on Pasolini: Interview with Oswald Stack* (London: Thames and Hudson, 1969). For an in-depth exploration of Pasolini's intellectual development, see Fabio Vighi, *Le ragioni dell'altro: La formazione intellettuale di Pasolini tra saggistica, letteratura e cinema* (Ravenna: Longo, 2001).

17 Naomi Greene follows Pasolini's recollections about the importance of Rimbaud for his formative years and speculates convincingly that he must have been "entranced, certainly, by Rimbaud's adolescent genius," but also "drawn to Rimbaud's youthful passion and rebellion, his scandalous and doomed love affair with the married poet Paul Verlaine, and finally, his romantic flight from Europe in to the dark heart of Africa." Greene, *Pier Paolo Pasolini: Cinema as Heresy* (Princeton, NJ: Princeton University Press, 1990), 6.

18 The importance for young Pasolini of an ethical component to poetics is evident, for instance, in his early interest in the poetry of Eugenio Montale, Giuseppe Ungaretti, and Giovanni Pascoli. When describing his intention to write a thesis on Pascoli in a letter to Carlo Calcaterra, who would be his supervisor, he refers to the *Fanciullino* (*The Child*), Pascoli's essay on poetics, as an example of "conciliation of the autonomy of art ... with a human morality which does not exclude a utilitarian end, or, somehow, [an end] almost foreign to poetry." See Pasolini to Carlo Calcaterra, March 1944, in *Antologia della Lirica Pascoliana*, ed. Marco Bazzocchi (Turin: Einaudi, 1993), 219.

19 Pier Paolo Pasolini, "Le ceneri di Gramsci," *Le ceneri di Gramsci: Poemetti (1957)*, in *Poesie 1*, 815–26, "Gramsci's Ashes," trans. Stephen Sartarelli, in *The Selected Poetry of Pier Paolo Pasolini*, 169–85. Parenthetical references indicate section and line.

20 "The aura of the foreignness of the cemetery, and hence the sense of Gramsci's continuing exile, is created by images of England and Englishness" scattered throughout the poem. Gordon, *Forms of Subjectivity*, 151.

21 While it is undeniable that this Gramsci "*giovinetto*," as literary critic Alberto Asor Rosa defined the poet's interlocutor, does not correspond to historical accounts of the political theorist, this characterization creates an alter ego for the poet and situates youth in the margins. Asor Rosa's famous definition of Gramsci as a "Silvia Marxistizzata" (Marxified Silvia)

in "Ceneri" highlighted, through a comparison with Giacomo Leopardi's poem, Pasolini's characterization of the political theorist as "an adolescent betrayed by the audacity of his own tension, confined in loneliness, in death as he had been in life, by men's offence, by the cruelty of history." Like the prematurely dead Silvia of Leopardi's eponymous poem, Gramsci embodies the loss of hope, or in this case the death of a political ideal. Alberto Asor Rosa, *Scrittori e popolo* (Turin: Einaudi, 1988), 323–4.

22 I agree with Alessia Ricciardi, and Carla Benedetti, in stressing the importance of Pasolini's interest in a "poetic of potentiality." As Ricciardi argues, and Benedetti before her, "his attachment to the notion of a work that has to be kept in a state of potentiality is an important key in understanding Pasolini's last endeavours in particular." Alessia Ricciardi, "Pasolini for the Future," *CIS* 2:1 (2011). See also Carla Benedetti, *Pasolini contro Calvino* (Turin: Bollati Boringhieri, 1998).

23 Fabio Vighi traced Pasolini's adoption of irrationality as a cognitive tool and the search for a new poetic language in his formative years, to the influence of decadentism. See Fabio Vighi, *Le ragioni dell'altro*, 48–9.

24 See Michael Mitterauer, *A History of Youth* (Oxford, UK, and Cambridge, MA: Blackwell, 1993), 1–34.

25 Kristin Ross, "Rimbaud and the Resistance to Work," in *Rimbaud: Modern Critical Views*, ed. Harold Bloom (New York: Chelsea House, 1988) quoted in Stephen Burt, *The Forms of Youth*, 14.

26 I follow the distinction outlined by Mark Roseman in the introduction to *Generations in Conflict: Youth Revolt and Generation Formation in Germany 1770-1968* (Cambridge: Cambridge University Press, 1995). Dogliani also discusses the "fluidity" of generations, produced by a process of self-identification whereby shared experiences jettison the purely biological characteristics of a generation. See Dogliani, *Storia dei Giovani*, 8–9.

27 Many well-known poems of the nineteenth and early twentieth century feature "fanciulli." Readers of Italian literature will be familiar with Ugo Foscolo's sonnet "A Zacinto" ("Né più mai toccherò le sacre sponde / ove il mio corpo fanciulletto giacque"; or with Giacomo Leopardi's *canto* "Il sabato del villaggio": "I fanciulli gridando / sulla piazzuola in frotta / e qua e là saltando, fanno un lieto romore." Children and adolescents, both "fanciulli" and "giovanetti" frequently appear in Umberto Saba's *Canzoniere*: "Il fanciullo," "Il fanciullo appassionato," "Fanciulli al bagno," "Il giovanetto." Playful children even populate Eugenio Montale's *Ossi di Seppia*, where human presence is otherwise scarce: "I fanciulli con gli archetti / spaventano gli scriccioli nei buchi" and "La farandola dei fanciulli sul greto / era la vita che scoppia dall'arsura."

Chapter One

1 See Tracy Koon, *Believe, Obey, Fight: Political Socialization of Youth in Fascist Italy, 1922–1943* (Chapel Hill and London: University of North Carolina Press, 1985), 29.
2 The youth question, or *problema dei giovani*, occupied the Fascist press very early in the history of the regime, particularly in the journal *Critica Fascista*. Tracy Koon argues that it was "one of the most frequently debated issues in the Fascist press" and that it persisted throughout the duration of the regime." The problem of the young is the central problem of fascism," said Minister of National Education Giuseppe Bottai (Bottai, "Funzione della gioventù," *Critica Fascista*, March 1, 1933. Quoted in Koon, 220). For an overview of the debate and Mussolini's response, see Koon 218–23.
3 The complex figure of Giuseppe Bottai, minister of national education from 1936 to 1943, was described both as "the most Fascist of all the Fascists" and an opportunistic politician who did not believe in the conformity enforced by the regime. He came to Fascism through *arditismo* and Futurism, and believed in the revolutionary ideal initially propounded by Fascism, but he became one of the key enforcers of the regime policies. His plan to "make way for youth" was based on his belief in Fascism as continuing revolution, and in the need for a new ruling elite that would save Italy from decay. His views found sympathizers among young people but clashed with Mussolini's vision of the young as docile followers of orthodoxy. See Koon 143–8.
4 Pasolini wrote excitedly about preparing for the *pre-Littoriali* to his friends and he was disappointed when the competitions were suspended due to the war. See his letters to Franco Farolfi in Pier Paolo Pasolini, *Le Lettere 1945–1954*, ed. Nico Naldini (Turin: Einaudi, 1986) 22, 33 (hereafter *Lettere 1*). Trans. by Stuart Hood as *The Letters of Pier Paolo Pasolini* (London: Quartet Books, 1992) 112, 119 (hereafter *Letters*). For a description of the *Littoriali*, see Koon 202–7.
5 See his letter to Franco Farolfi in winter 1941: "I often go to play basketball – I am hopeless but I have a lot of fun. Sport is truly my most pure, continual, spontaneous consolation. Now I have a desperate desire to go skiing – I dream of the Dolomites as a lofty world, above the clouds, sunny, loud with shouts and laughter. Do you remember how on the top of the peaks the wind raises clouds of fine snow when everything is clear? The little wooden bedrooms, the village children, and all the other magnificent things? And think too that we are reaching our twentieth year without a [celebratory] ball. It's sad – not to say disgusting – but we are virile and warlike." Pasolini to Franco Farolfi, Bologna, Winter 1941, in *Lettere 1*, 28–9 (*Letters*, 116).

6 In the context of his study on the "work of subjectivity" in Pasolini's oeuvre, Robert Gordon has pointed out the "articulated attempt to find a role and voice for the self into the context of debates over youth and the role of the intellectuals." Gordon, *Forms of Subjectivity*, 32.
7 Ruth Ben-Ghiat, *Fascist Modernities: Italy 1922-1945* (Berkeley: University of California Press, 2001), 13. For a discussion of Fascism in generational terms see also Dogliani, *Storia dei Giovani*, 103–6.
8 See Ben-Ghiat, *Fascist Modernities*, 100–1.
9 Ben-Ghiat convincingly argues that "culture served this generation of intellectuals as a compensatory sphere within the Fascist state" (ibid. 13).
10 While many critics have focused on the instrumental role these youth journals played in providing an arena for a development of a "left-wing Fascism," which would later evolve into anti-Fascism, Ben-Ghiat provides a more nuanced articulation of the complex relationship between youth groups and the regime. Her study focuses particularly on the appeal of the patronage system and other policies put in place to create a new Fascist elite and the exposure, on the part of the latter, of the gap between revolutionary rhetoric and normalizing practice. See Ben-Ghiat, 93–122.
11 "Giovinezza" was the title of the official song of the Fascist National Party (PNF), of the Italian army, and of the regime. Composed by Giuseppe Blanc and Nino Oxilia in 1909, it was originally a university song and then the official song of the *arditi*, the elite shock troops of WWI. The mystique of action and heroism accompanying the *arditi*, and the black shirts and fezzes they wore in combat, carried over when many of them joined the first Fascist *squadristi*. The song also transitioned from the *arditi* to the PNF, with new lyrics commissioned by Mussolini, which connect the springtime of life with the rejuvenation of Italy.
12 On the eternal youth of the Duce see Laura Malvano, "The Myth of Youth in Images: Italian Fascism" in *A History of Young People in the West*, 250–1.
13 Barbara Spackman, *Fascist Virilities*, 41 (quoting Marina Addis Saba, *La corporazione delle donne: Ricerche e studi sui modelli femminili nel ventennio fascista*, Rome: Vallecchi, 1988). Spackman provides several convincing examples of how the divided interpellation of women in Fascism generated responses that exploited the ambivalence implicit in the rhetoric of virility, on which the interpellation often stood, to denaturalize the notion of woman thus constructed. On the contradictory representation of women see also Victoria De Grazia, *How Fascism Ruled Women* (Berkeley and Los Angeles, CA: University of California Press, 1992).
14 *Architrave*, the GUF journal published in Bologna between 1940 and 1943 as a "monthly review of politics, literature and art," was a representative

of that "left-wing Fascism" aiming to revive the original revolutionary spirit corrupted by the regime's hierarchical fossilization. It was directed by Roberto Mazzetti and had, among its collaborators, Renzo Renzi, Giovanni Testori, and Alfonso Gatto. (*Architrave: mensile di politica, letteratura e arte*. Gruppo universitario fascista Bologna, <<http://db.archiviostorico.unibo.it/it-it/edicola-degli-studenti/elenco-delle-annate.aspx?idC=61687&idRivista=11993&LN=it-IT>> [Archivio Storico Università degli Studi di Bologna. Accessed on March 1, 2014]. Pasolini contributed several articles in 1942, mostly of literary criticism. See Pier Paolo Pasolini, *Saggi sulla letteratura e sull'arte*, ed. Walter Siti and Silvia De Laude (Milan: Arnoldo Mondadori, 1999, hereafter *SLA*) and *Saggi sulla politica e la società*, ed. Walter Siti and Silvia De Laude (Milan: Arnoldo Mondadori, 1999, hereafter *SPS*). Shortly after the publication of "Cultura italiana e cultura europea a Weimar, in September 1942, *Architrave* was shut down by censorship. It reopened in December with a new editorial board, which was meant to restore the journal to conformity. See Patrick McCarthy, "Pasolini e *Il setaccio* alla ricerca di parole politiche" in *Pasolini e Bologna*, Davide Ferrari and Gianni Scalia, eds. (Bologna: Pendragon, 1998). *Il setaccio* (The Sieve) was published in Bologna between November 1942 and March 1943. Pasolini was part of the editorial board and contributed to all six issues with literary and art criticism, drawings, poems, and reviews. Frequent disagreement opposed him to Giovanni Falzone, the editor-in-chief, regarding conformity to political guidelines and the limits of the journal's scope set by its relationship with the GIL as a youth organization. See, for example, Pasolini's letters to Fabio Luca Cavazza in February 1943 (*Lettere 1*, 154–8; *Letters* 193–5). The co-editor, Italo Cinti, a "Futurist painter with anti-Fascist views" in Luciano Serra's words, broke with the Falzone's line and transformed *Il setaccio* into a culturally vital journal, animated, thanks to Pasolini, by the contributions of Mario Ricci, Fabio Mauri, Luigi Vecchi, Giovanna Bemporad, and Fabio Luca Cavazza. On these and other Fascist youth journals see Marina Addis Saba, *Gioventù italiana del Littorio: La stampa dei giovani nella guerra fascista* (Milan: Feltrinelli, 1973).
15 Roberto Mazzetti, "Atto di nascita," *Architrave* 1 (1940).
16 Mazzetti, "Atto di nascita," *Architrave* 1 (1940).
17 Agostino Bignardi, a schoolmate of Pasolini at Liceo Galvani, would later become the leader of the Italian Liberal Party (PLI) and a member of the Chamber of Deputies in the Italian Parliament.
18 Bignardi, "Noi, i giovani," *Architrave* 4 (1941).
19 "La guerra attuale è la rivoluzione che cammina in Europa, distruggendola nelle sue strutture anguste e irrazionali, rinnovandola dal profondo e

portandola verso una impensata unità di vita continentale." (The present war is the revolution which is advancing through Europe, destroying its narrow and irrational structures, profoundly renewing it and leading it towards an as yet unconceived unity of life on the continent.) *Architrave* 4 (1941).

20 "Note sui giovani," *Architrave* 5 (1941). My translation of these early texts respects the convoluted style of the original in so far as comprehension is deemed possible. Often an ambiguous word choice challenges the translator's task, and the English version must be the product of a hermeneutical operation. For instance, I have tried to unpack the phrase "[i valori] delle storiche maturità" because of the crucial significance of generational discourse to the general argument of the chapter and of the book. However, the combined choice of the words "historical" and "maturity," untranslatable in the plural form of the original, strongly suggests the idea of generations following one another in a continuum, attaining maturity by standing on the shoulders of their fathers.

21 Pasolini participated in one of the so-called "cultural bridges" ("Ponte Culturale Weimar-Firenze"), international meetings of young representatives from Fascist countries organized between 1940 and 1943. Young intellectuals met to discuss assigned topics and to compete for literary and artistic prizes. See Koon, *Believe, Obey, Fight*, 151. The article was subsequently republished in *Il setaccio* in January 1943.

22 "Cultura italiana e cultura europea a Weimar," in *SPS*, 5–6.

23 Carlo Manzoni, "Teatro: Repertorio," *Il setaccio* I (1942): 11–12.

24 Riccardo Castellani was, with Cesare Bortotto, one of Pasolini's friends from Casarsa who contributed to *Il setaccio* upon Pasolini's request, according to Nico Naldini. Pasolini would found with them in 1944–5 the "Academiuta di lenga furlana," an association for the promotion of Friulian culture, through poetry readings, concerts, and publication of the journal *Stroligùt di cà da l'aga*. Bortotto and Castellani also taught science and mathematics, respectively, in the little school that Pasolini and his friends opened in the village of Versuta, near Casarsa, for children who couldn't reach their schools due to the bombings. See Naldini, *Vita di Pasolini*, 47–8, 63, and Gordon, *Forms of Subjectivity*, 33–4, Barth David Schwartz, *Pasolini Requiem*, 148.

25 Riccardo Castellani, "Sui concetti di 'fede' e 'giovinezza'," *Il setaccio* 3 (1942).

26 Pasolini had high expectations of his participation in this journal. He expressed his hopes in a letter to Franco Farolfi: "I am overwhelmed by exams – but above all what concerns me is the founding within the ambit of the GIL of the review *Il setaccio* from which my real career will perhaps begin." Pasolini to Franco Farolfi, Bologna, October 1942, in *Lettere 1*, 144 (*Letters*, 187).

27 Pier Paolo Pasolini, "I giovani, l'attesa," in *SPS*, 11.
28 Gordon, *Forms of Subjectivity*, 24–5.
29 Pasolini to Luciano Serra, but addressed also to Francesco Leonetti and Roberto Roversi, Casarsa, August 1, 1941, in *Lettere 1*, 63 (*Letters*, 138).
30 Nico Naldini quotes the definition, given by Francesco Leonetti, in his introduction to Pasolini's letters. See *Lettere 1*, xxxi.
31 Among the projects conceived in this period is a "critical-poetic" anthology to be called *Sul concetto d'eredismo*. See letter to Luciano Serra, but addressed also to Francesco Leonetti and Roberto Roversi, Casarsa, August 1, 1941, in *Lettere 1*, 63 (*Letters*, 138).
32 Fabio Vighi identifies in the project "un proposito diacronico, se recuperare la tradizione al presente significa già inserire la poesia nel *continuum* della storia." *Le ragioni dell'altro*, 24.
33 Letter to Luciano Serra, but addressed also to Francesco Leonetti and Roberto Roversi, Casarsa, August 1, 1941, in *Lettere 1*, 62 (*Letters*, 138).
34 Pasolini to Franco Farolfi, Bologna, Spring 1941, in *Lettere 1*, 37 (*Letters*, 121).
35 Pasolini to Franco Farolfi, Casarsa, August 1940, in *Lettere 1*, 11 (*Letters*, 105).
36 Pasolini to Franco Farolfi, Casarsa, September 1940, in *Lettere 1*, 13 (*Letters*, 106).
37 Colleen Ryan-Scheutz, *Sex, the Self, and the Sacred*, 19.
38 Paolo Bartoloni defines exile as "life in the company of a presence which has been lost … The usual is always 'there,' before the eye of the exile and yet removed from it, unreachable." Overcoming the opposition between exile as self-enforced isolation and as juridical exclusion for political reasons, Bartoloni's definition focuses on the search, common to both, for a space of potentiality, "the threshold at which authenticity and inauthenticity become indistinguishable and ultimately irrelevant as an ontological paradigm of subjectivity." *On the Cultures of Exile, Translation and Writing* (West Lafayette, IN: Purdue University Press, 2008), 81.
39 On the dialectical nature of exile writing see Sophia McClennen *Dialectics of Exile: Nation, Time, Language, and Space in Hispanic Literatures* (West Lafayette, IN: Purdue University Press, 2004)
40 The exile poem addressed to the maternal land calls to mind Ugo Foscolo's sonnet "A Zacinto," while the lexical choice of "spirito vivente" and "arboree ombre" strongly evokes D'Annunzio's famous poem "La pioggia nel pineto": "E immersi / noi siam nello spirto / silvestre, / d'arborea vita viventi." The symbolic significance of the hawthorn flower in relation to youth in Pasolini is further explored in chapter 3.
41 Pasolini to Luciano Serra, Casarsa, July 1941, in *Lettere 1*, 52 (*Letters*, 131).

42 Ibid. The first version of the poem, included in this letter, contained the words "Perduta Elèusi," but in the subsequent letter Pasolini asks his friends to revise the poem and replace Elèusi with "Syon."
43 Pasolini to Luciano Serra, Casarsa, July 1941, in *Lettere 1*, 53 (my translation).
44 Pasolini to Luciano Serra, Casarsa, August 1941, *Lettere 1*, 85 (*Letters*, 153).
45 Echoing Eugenio Montale's "Falsetto" ("Esterina, i vent'anni ti minacciano, / grigiorosea nube / che a poco a poco in sé ti chiude'), "Severina in the dark air" is the first line of the poem, which is actually untitled. In sending it to his friends for comments, Pasolini asks them explicitly to suggest a title. He also footnotes the poem with a self-commentary that connects this to the three poems addressed here on the topic of "nostalgia for the present time." He does not however receive any helpful suggestions, because in the following letter he solicits further readings from his friends, particularly of the "untitled" poem, "which seems to me one of my greatest achievements." See Pasolini to Luciano Serra, Casarsa, September 1941, in *Lettere 1*, 109–10 (*Letters*, 166–7).
46 Pasolini to Luciano Serra, Casarsa, August 20, 1941, in *Lettere 1*, 107–8 (*Letters*, 166).
47 Dialectical in nature, youth writing is comparable to exile writing as it is described by Sophia McClennen. Borrowing her account of "the most salient dialectical tensions found in exile writing," and replacing "youth" for "exile," we may say that young Pasolini's writing depicts youth as both a physical and mental condition; as a state that both liberates and confines the writer; as both spiritual/abstract and material; as personal/individual and political/collective; as both unique and universal. Youth heightens both regionalism and cosmopolitanism, both nationalism and globalization. Writing is both a way to express youth and to supersede it. Youth writing recuperates the past and re-imagines it. See McClennen, *Dialectics of Exile*, 30.
48 Bartoloni maintains that "in the experience of enforced exile the subject demonstrates that what matters above all else is communion with similar individuals and the sharing of a set of conditions of belonging, including language, without which the subject feels bereft of significance and, ultimately, of life." Although poetic isolation, unlike political exile, is voluntary seclusion rather than traumatic punishment, the writings inspired by these experiences of separation similarly seek an audience of peers. *On the Cultures of Exile, Translation and Writing*, 82.
49 Pasolini to Franco Farolfi, Winter 1941 – II, *Lettere 1*, 29 (*Letters*, 116).
50 Pasolini to Franco Farolfi, Bologna, Winter 1941, in *Lettere 1*, 30 (*Letters*, 117).
51 "Have you ever heard in some philosophy or other of the concept of breaking the chains which tie one to the past by an act of pure will? That is

what I am trying to do. I want to kill a sick and hypersensitive adolescent who tries to pollute my life as a man as well – and he is already moribund – but I shall be cruel to him even if basically I love him because he has been my life up to today's threshold." Pasolini to Franco Farolfi, Bologna, January-February 1941, in *Lettere 1*, 34 (*Letters*, 120).

52 "I am very fed up with this university culture which consists of dust and palimpsests." Pasolini to Franco Farolfi, Bologna, June 1941, in *Lettere 1*, 41 (*Letters*, 124).

53 The song titled "Bandiera Nera (Black Flag)" is included in the section "Songs of 1915–1918 War" in *Canzoniere Italiano*, edited by Pasolini and published in 1955 (Florence: Guanda, 1975). It was known also as "Sul ponte di Bassano" from its first verse, and was rewritten in WWII as "Sul ponte di Perati." See A. Virgilio Savona and Michele L. Straniero, *Canti della grande guerra*, vol. 2 (Milan: Garzanti, 1981).

54 Pasolini, *Tutte le poesie*, vol.1, 10. Hereafter *Poesie* in parenthetical references in the text and endnotes. The Italian version accompanying the dialect is Pasolini's. The English translation, unless otherwise specified, is mine. "Il nini muàrt" is translated by Stephen Sartarelli as "Dead Boy" in *The Selected Poetry of Pier Paolo Pasolini*, 63.

55 Narcissus, as Robert Gordon shows, "is established here as the focus of a network of archetypal elements in Friulian landscape" and "is constantly recast in evolving patterns of associative imagery" in these and later poems. Narcissistic figuration reoccurs, according to Gordon, in *L'usignolo della Chiesa Cattolica* and *La nuova gioventù*. Guido Santato notes that the recurrent combination youth-death in Pasolini's poetry starts here: "Narcissus is reflected in the death that eternalizes him: he is the ideal image of a childhood immortalized by death, which it joins directly, without encountering the anti-aesthetic degradation of maturity (a universe to which he does not belong)." G. Santato, *Pasolini: L'opera* (Vicenza: Neri Pozza, 1980), 40. On the figure of Narcissus in Pasolini's poetry and prose see also Asor Rosa, *Scrittori e Popolo*; Jean-Michel Gardair, *Narciso e il suo doppio* (Rome: Bulzoni, 1996); Giorgio Nisini, *L'unità impossibile* (Rome: Carocci, 2008).

56 "Ab l'alen tir vas me l'aire / Qu'eu sen venir de Proensa: tot quant es de lai m'agensa (With my breath I inhale the air / which I feel blowing towards me from Provence / everything from there so delights me)." See Veronica Mary Fraser, *The Songs of Peire Vidal: Translation & Commentary* (New York: Peter Lang, 2006), 100.

57 For a more detailed discussion of Manzù's *David*, see Maria Sole Cardulli "Giacomo Manzù, l'opera del mese: 19 maggio 2012,"

http://www.museomanzu.beniculturali.it/index.php?it/137/ms-cardulli-19-maggio-2012-giacomo-manz-lopera-del-mese (accessed 12/2/2012).
58 See Introduction, n.10 for a brief summary of the Ramuscello events.
59 This "time of Friuli," according to Guido Santato, is "a-historical, or meta-historical time: an abstract, mythical dimension, never historically determined; otherwise the Orphic time of living nature, of continuous, *ab aeterno* cycles of dawn and dusk, spring and fall, birth and death." Santato, *Pier Paolo Pasolini: L'opera*, 9.
60 The title is taken from a twelfth-century song by troubadour Jaufre Rudel, "Lanquan li jorn son lonc en mai" (When the days are long in May).
61 Most of the poems contained in this section were initially collected in the volume *Dov'è la mia patria*, published by the *Academiuta* in 1949. For a more detailed analysis see Santato, *Pasolini: L'opera*.
62 When published in the collection *Dov'è la mia patria*, the poems "Mi contenti," "I dis robàs," "La giava," "Arba pai cunìns," "Bel coma un ciavàl," "Vegnerà el vero Cristo," and "El cuòr su l'acqua" were each preceded by a caption indicating the speaker's name and his dialect. For example: "A Valvasone Bruno Lenardus canta 'Mi contenti.'" The suppression of the captions in *La meglio gioventù* accentuates the common elements even in the variety of languages.
63 The acknowledged model, recalled in the title, is François Villon's *Le Grand Testament*. See *The Complete Works of François Villon*, trans. Anthony Bonner.
64 Santato, *Pier Paolo Pasolini: L'opera*, 83.
65 On the critical rejection of the concept of generations among anti-Fascists see Luisa Passerini, "Youth as a Metaphor for Social Change," *A History of Young People in the West*, vol. 2, ed. G. Levi and J.C. Schmitt (Cambridge, MA: The Belknap Press of Harvard University Press, 1997), 286.

Chapter Two

1 Quoted in Laura Betti, ed., *Pasolini: cronaca giudiziaria, persecuzione, morte* (Milan: Garzanti), 61.
2 Millicent Marcus, *Italian Film in the Light of Neorealism* (Princeton, NJ: Princeton University Press, 1986), 23.
3 The judicial proceedings and their political and cultural context are described in *Pasolini: cronaca giudiziaria, persecuzione, morte*, ed. Laura Betti.
4 Objections justified on literary grounds attacked primarily Pasolini's use of the Roman dialect in a realist novel. Particularly influential among these was the response of prominent Marxist critic Carlo Salinari. He interpreted the use of dialect as a "linguistic equivocation" (equivoco linguistico),

and as a symptom of an ideological limitation. The use of dialect reveals, according to Salinari, "a typically formalist and decadent literary taste" (un gusto letterario tipicamente formalista e decadente) which revelled in "the filthiest, most abject, sordid, unseemly, and turbid aspects" (gli aspetti più sporchi, abbietti, sordidi, scomposti e torbidi) of the Roman sub-proletariat. According to Salinari, by denying his characters access to work and historical consciousness, Pasolini deprived realism of its positive intent and reduced it to a "simple representation of ugliness and vice." See Carlo Salinari, *Preludio e fine del realismo in Italia* (Naples: Morano, 1965), 55–9. The review was originally published in the literary and political weekly *Il Contemporaneo* as "I cinque dello Strega," September 9, 1955. Quoted in *Pasolini: cronaca giudiziaria, persecuzione, morte*, ed. Laura Betti, 60. On the debate between Salinari and Pasolini regarding his novel see also Joseph Francese, "Pasolini's 'Roman Novels,' the Italian Communist Party, and the Events of 1956," in *Pier Paolo Pasolini: Contemporary Perspectives*, ed. Patrick Rumble and Bart Testa, 22–39 (Toronto: University of Toronto Press, 1994).

5 For a convincing analysis of the original role played by the "narrative voice's refusal to acknowledge our presence as outsiders coming into a new environment and to share with us the kind of welcoming background information we expect a kind host or a conventional narrative voice to supply" see David Ward, *A Poetics of Resistance: Narrative and the Writings of Pier Paolo Pasolini* (Madison, NJ and London: Fairleigh Dickinson University Press: 1995), 64.

6 In the published English translation of the novel, the title phrase "Ragazzi di vita" is rendered simply as "the *ragazzi*," a foreignizing choice, which conveys the otherness of this social group to the intended reader.

7 Fritz Martini, "*Bildungsroman*: Term and Theory," in *Reflection and Action: Essays on the Bildungsroman*, ed. James N. Hardin (Columbia, SC: University of South Carolina Press, 1991), 41.

8 Santato considers Riccetto "a roughly sketched protagonist" because he is the only one of the *ragazzi* who shows, albeit confusedly, "some awareness of his past, and thus who has a past." Santato, *Pier Paolo Pasolini: L'opera*, 205.

9 Pasolini, *Ragazzi di vita* (Milan: Garzanti, 1955), trans. Emile Capouya, *The Ragazzi* (Manchester: Carcanet Press Ltd., 1986), 7. Hereafter, parenthetical in-text references indicate page number of the original and the published translation, separated by a semicolon.

10 My translation. The published translation mixes up war refugees and squatters, whereas their relative importance in the social food chain becomes relevant in my subsequent analysis.

11 Thomas Jeffers, *Apprenticeships: The Bildungsroman from Goethe to Santayana* (New York: Palgrave Macmillan, 2005), 13.
12 See Franco Moretti, *The Way of the World: The Bildungsroman in European Culture*, trans. Albert Sbragia (London and New York: Verso, 2000 [1987]), 4–6.
13 Mobility and interiority constitute, according to Franco Moretti, the crucial characteristics of the youth portrayed in the *Bildungsroman*, and make that genre the "symbolic form of modernity." Ibid., 5.
14 Thomas L. Jeffers claims that "to go through such a novel is an occasion not only for a reader's individual cultivation (his vicarious growing up, or re-growing up) but for a generation of readers' collective cultivation ... When the educated members of a generation read the early printings of *Wilhelm Meister* or Dickens's *David Copperfield*, for instance, their consciousness and conscience were, in the authentic Joycean sense, forged." Thomas Jeffers, *Apprenticeships: The Bildungsroman from Goethe to Santayana*, 4.
15 Pasolini, an avid sportsman, started playing basketball in the GUF (*Gruppi Universitari Fascisti*) team in Bologna in 1940. He mentions it with an ironic tone in a letter to his friend Franco Farolfi as a privilege worth bragging about, even though "I shudder to think of the pitiful figures we will cut." Pasolini to Farolfi, Bologna, Fall 1940, in *Lettere 1*, 19 (*Letters*, 110).
16 Basketball was introduced in Italy at the beginning of the twentieth century. In 1909 Ida Nomi translated into Italian the rules established by James Naismith and introduced the game as appropriate for girls. Its popularity increased during the First World War thanks to the presence of American soldiers in Europe and the involvement of YMCA centres in various cities. The first official basketball game was played in Milan in 1919 between two military teams. It became more popular at the national level in the 1930s, when it was included in the University Games. See Saverio Battente and Tito Menzani, *Storia sociale della pallacanestro in Italia* (Manduria: Lacaita, 2009).
17 See Golino, *Pasolini: Il sogno di una cosa*, 49.
18 My translation. The translation by Emile Capouya, "a walled-in field" misses the adventurous connotation implicit in Pasolini's choice of the word "prateria," instead of the standard "prato." The vast courtyard of the *Ferrobeton* factory is transfigured in Riccetto's mind into the prairie of a Western movie, of which the boy becomes the protagonist. With two pistols stuck in his belt and a submachine gun slung over his shoulder, he hops on a horse's back, ready to ride off.
19 The imagination of Riccetto and his friends is likely shaped by popular Hollywood adventure movies starring Errol Flynn, like *Captain Blood*

(1935) and *The Sea Hawk* (1940). However, adventure movies with a pirate theme were also produced in Italy since the silent era. Numerous adaptations of popular Emilio Salgari novels were produced in the 1920s: *Il Corsaro*, by Augusto Genina; *Il Corsaro Nero, Il figlio del Corsaro Nero, Gli ultimi filibustieri*, and *Iolanda, la figlia del Corsaro Nero*, all written, directed, and starring Vitale Di Stefano. In 1941 Enrico Guazzoni adapted both *I pirati della Malesia* and *La figlia del Corsaro Verde*. See Gian Piero Brunetta, *Cent'anni di cinema italiano*, vol. 1 (Rome: Laterza, 1998).

20 The intersection of these institutions, church and prison, in Italian culture is well exemplified by the Regina Coeli jail in Rome, which occupies the site of a former Salesian convent. Founded in 1643 by Anna Colonna Barberini, the building was repurposed after national unification when many ecclesiastical properties were acquired by the State, and has served as the city's main jail since 1884. The other correctional facility of some relevance for the *ragazzi* is the Istituto Romano San Michele, conversationally referred to as "Porta Portese" in the novel, due to its location near the famous city gate. Like many prisons in Italy, San Michele a Ripa Grande has a composite history, which blurs the distinction between incarceration and rehabilitation, confinement and cure. Founded by the Odescalchi family in the seventeenth century as a multipurpose institution, the Ospizio Apostolico di San Michele was initially the site of an orphanage and a poorhouse. A juvenile correctional facility was added in 1704 and remained in use, through the various changes undergone by the rest of the institution, until 1972. In the course of the eighteenth century, the ever-expanding complex came to include a hospice for old people, a church, and a women's prison. An in-depth analysis of the "cultural and material palimpsest" offered by Italian prisons can be found in Ellen Nerenberg, *Prison Terms: Representing Confinement During and After Italian Fascism* (Toronto: University of Toronto Press, 2001).

21 Ward, *A Poetics of Resistance*, 70.

22 While Riccetto introduces himself using his last name first, as is the practice in official situations in Italy, the translation uses the first name-last name order that is natural in English.

23 For an anthropological overview of initiation rituals, which mark the transition from childhood to adolescence, see the seminal Arnold van Gennep, *The Rites of Passage*, trans. Monika B. Vizedom and Gabrielle L. Caffee (Chicago: University of Chicago Press, 1960). Victor Turner based his study of the liminal period on van Gennep's distinction of three phases in all rites of transition – separation, margin, and aggregation – in *The Forest of Symbols: Aspects of Ndembu Ritual* (Ithaca, NY: Cornell University Press, 1967).

In this transitional period, he claims, the subject is "structurally, if not physically, 'invisible,'" and "ritually polluting," according to the view that "what is unclear and contradictory (from the perspective of social definition) tends to be regarded as (ritually) unclean," a theory advanced by Mary Douglas in another seminal work, *Purity and Danger: An Analysis of Concepts of Pollution and Taboo* (London and Boston: Routledge & Kegan Paul, 1969). The emphasis on the liminal period is particularly relevant for Pasolini's treatment of adolescence in *Ragazzi*: the variable period of time in which the boys are "neither here nor there" or "betwixt and between," as Turner would say, is the focus of the novel, rather than the tension towards an eventual socialization.

24 My translation. The published translation, "since the school building had collapsed," is more explicit than the original.
25 Robert Gordon calls this threshold the "point of entry into consciousness and history." *Forms of Subjectivity*, 127.
26 Enzo Golino reads this ending as ambiguous: "Is this behavior determined by maturity or cowardice? Pasolini leaves the reader hanging between the two solutions ... The novelist's imagination hasn't yet crafted the pedagogical motivation to justify Riccetto's potential heroic act, as he will do for Tommaso Puzzilli." *Pasolini: il sogno di una cosa*, 56–7.
27 Although Santato reads Riccetto's behaviour as "pre-moral, a purely animal conservation instinct which works at an exclusively biological level of existence," in which cynicism has no part, the clear contrast between the swallow rescue in chapter 1 and Genesio's drowning indicates that Riccetto's self-preservation instinct is a product of his coming of age, as is the rationalization attempt. Santato, *Pasolini: L'opera*, 207.
28 See Franco Moretti, *The Way of the World*, 6–10.
29 Ibid., 7.
30 Moretti, *The Way of the World*, 7. Following semiotician Yuri Lotman, Moretti distinguishes between two models of *Bildungsroman*: one organized according to a principle of classification, the other a principle of transformation. While both principles coexist in all narratives, the prevalence of one over the other determines the meaning assigned to individual events. When classification prevails, "narrative transformations have meaning in so far as they lead to a particularly marked ending; ... the meaning of events lies in their *finality*"; when transformation prevails, "what makes a story meaningful is its narrativity, its being an open-ended process."
31 I am considering the archetypal plot posited for the *Bildungsroman* by Jerome Buckley in *Season of Youth*: "A sensitive child grows up in the

provinces, where his lively imagination is frustrated by his neighbors' – and often by his family's – social prejudices and intellectual obtuseness. School and private reading stimulate his hopes for a different life away from home, and so he goes to the metropolis, where his transformative education begins. He has at least two love affairs, one good and one bad, which help him revalue his values. He makes some accommodation, as citizen and worker, with the industrial urban world, and after a time he perhaps revisits his old home to show folks how much he has grown. No single *Bildungsroman* will have all these elements, Buckley says, but none can ignore more than two or three." J.H. Buckley, *Season of Youth: The Bildungsroman from Dickens to Golding* (Cambridge, MA: Harvard University Press, 1974), 18, quoted in Thomas Jeffers, *Apprenticeships*, 52.

32 David Ward has convincingly analysed this dynamic of reader disorientation at both the macro-level and the micro-level, showing how it is more a result of "the narrative voice's deeply embedded position in the fabric of these stories" and its failure to act as "a mediator between text and reader" than of the use of dialect. D. Ward, *A Poetics of Resistance*, 64–5.

33 In a way, the readers' *Bildung* is not unlike the result of the "urban pedagogy" that Rome, "stupendous and miserable city," effected on the poet of "Il pianto della scavatrice" (The Tears of the Excavator). Robert Gordon remarks that this poem emphasizes "the duration and the process of learning and also the pedagogical agency of the city." The outcome of this experience is "a growth beyond isolation towards reality and knowledge, hence towards a plenitude of the subject in harmony with the other" (*Forms of Subjectivity*, 100). While "Pianto" can be considered as a "triumphant *Bildungsroman*," at least inasmuch as the harmony between the subject and history is achieved, the *Bildung* process of which the reader is the subject in *Ragazzi* frustrates that harmony.

34 "Representations of childhood and adolescence have played a major role in Italian cinema" claims Marcia Landy in her seminal essay "A Cinema of Childhood," which offers a useful overview of such representations from the silent era to the early 1990s (in Landy, *Italian Film*, Cambridge, MA: Cambridge University Press, 2000, 234–60). In addition to Landy's essay, a discussion of the role played by children in post-war Italian cinema can be found in Millicent Marcus' essays on Rossellini's *Open City*, De Sica's *Bicycle Thief*, and Taviani's *Night of the Shooting Stars* included in the volume *Italian Film in the Light of Neorealism*. More recently, the role of the child as focalizer for the film's testimonial impulse was discussed by Millicent Marcus in the paper "Film in the Face of Atrocity: Giorgio Diritti's *L'uomo che verrà* and the

Massacre of Marzabotto" presented at the *Re-visioning Terrorism* conference at Purdue University on September 10, 2011. In cinema of the 1980s and '90s, Àine O'Healy recognized in Francesca Archibugi's films a construction of the "child as witness of adult weakness or ineptitude" that could be connected to a neorealist legacy (O'Healy, "Are the Children Watching Us? The Roman Films of Francesca Archibugi," *Annali d'Italianistica* 17 (1999): 121–36. Nicoletta Marini-Maio analysed how the postmodern construction of childhood as a liminal condition influenced the representation of childhood in two films of Andrea and Antonio Frazzi (Marini-Maio, "The Children Are Still Watching Us: The 'Visual Psycho-mimesis' of *Il cielo cade* and *Certi bambini*," in *Coming of Age On Film: Stories of Transformation in World Cinema*, ed. Anne Hardcastle et al., 40). An argument for the evolution of the child's perspective in contemporary Italian cinema vis-à-vis its absence in society is also found in Paul Sutton's analysis of Michele's role as "physical rescuer," rather than passive witness of traumatic events, in Salvatores' *Io non ho paura*. See Paul Sutton, "The *Bambino Negato* or Missing Child of Contemporary Italian Cinema," *Screen* 46:3 (Autumn 2005): 353–9.

35 Gilles Deleuze defines the role of the child as witness in neorealism as based on his "motor helplessness" in the adult world. The child's exclusion from action makes him a pure seer, who can transform an image into a "purely optical and sound situation" and thus gives objects and settings a new material reality. *Cinema 2: The Time-Image* (London: Continuum, 2005), 3–4.

36 Pier Paolo Pasolini, "New Linguistic Questions," in *Heretical Empiricism*, trans. Ben Lawton and Louise K. Barnett (Washington, DC: New Academia Publishing, 2005), 9. Hereafter *HE* in parenthetical in-text references and endnotes.

37 Connecting the century-old *questione della lingua* to a historical lack of national unity, the 1964 essay acknowledges the situation of *de facto* bi- or trilingualism characterizing Italy one century after its unification: an elite literary language, a bourgeois language of recent creation (*koiné*), a multitude of locally spoken dialects. Pasolini identifies current Italian (*l'italiano medio*), a combination of literary and instrumental language, as the language of the bourgeoisie which, for historical reasons "has not known how to identify itself with the nation but has remained a social class" (*HE*, 4), and a language that does not reflect the fragmented reality of Italy. To use this language as a neutral instrument is to obscure that reality. Given this premise, Pasolini outlines a history of Italian literature in the first half of the twentieth century as a history of the relationship maintained by each author with this *lingua media* and shows how this ordinary language exercises a centrifugal force with respect to literature. Imagining the *lingua*

media as a horizontal line, then, free indirect discourse practised by a bourgeois writer who introduces characters from the working class, peasantry, or the sub-proletariat, takes the shape of "a serpentine line that starting from above, descends – intersecting the middle line – towards the bottom, and then returns once again towards the top – again intersecting the middle line – and then again towards the bottom, etc." (8). The linguistic materials located below the middle line "are elevated into the high or very high zone ... and worked out in an expressive or expressionistic way" (ibid.). While Pasolini introduces the novelist Carlo Emilio Gadda's expressionistic use of a variety of linguistic and sub-linguistic material as the primary example of contemporary plurilingualism, he also brings his own linguistic experiments as examples, describing them as "a kind of experimentalism ... that contained within itself those expressionistic elements of decadence and those sentimental elements of neorealism that [those years] wished to overcome ideologically" (ibid.).

38 Pasolini, *Una vita violenta* (Milan: Garzanti, 1959), trans. William Weaver, *A Violent Life* (Manchester: Carcanet Press Ltd., 1985). Hereafter, parenthetical in-text references indicate page number of the original and the published translation, separated by a semicolon.

39 Santato reads the novel as a result of the influence exercised by the harsh judgment on *Ragazzi di vita* on the part of militant critics such as Carlo Salinari, Antonello Trombatore, and Adriano Seroni. They had particularly noted, he reports, "a lack of political perspective and of 'positive' heroes, the a-moral and pre-ideological layout of the novel, its self-satisfied representation of an abject world without any light of redemption, a taste for filth and bestiality." See Santato, *Pasolini: L'opera*, 210.

40 See Santato, *Pasolini: L'opera*, and Golino, *Sogno di una cosa*.

41 Group narrative characterizes particularly the nightly escapades in the chapters "Notte nella città di Dio" and "Canzoni di vita." Significantly, "Notte" ends with an accident that leaves Tommaso's friend Lello disabled and to all intents and purposes writes him out of the story. He reappears, in the second half of the novel, as a beggar in Via Nazionale, where Tommaso and his girlfriend, Irene, are marvelling at the comforts of middle-class life during an afternoon stroll. Tommaso's scornful disregard of his childhood friend shows how his engagement with an emancipatory approach requires that he sever all ties with the world of the *borgate*: while he disapprovingly notes to himself Lello's resigned and passive demeanour, Irene expresses a more clearly optimistic outlook: "Che ne puoi sapé ... che un giorno pure noi, co' un po' de bona volontà, avemo fortuna e potemo fà la figura nostra!" (Maybe one day, if we work at it, maybe we'll be lucky

and be able to look nice and all). Her hopeful attitude is immediately explained through her allegiance, and her family's, to Communism (*Vita*, 199; 200).

42 The police station, which functions here as an alternative to the school in shaping the young man's identity, is fittingly located in an old Fascist gymnasium. See 27; 34.

43 Founded in 1934 and named after the most famous Italian disciple of Robert Koch, the Istituto Carlo Forlanini was a hospital, sanatorium, and research centre on tuberculosis. It occupied a vast area in the southwest of Rome known as Monteverde. Built according to the most modern technologies of its time, it also included a library, an anatomical museum, classrooms for medical residents, a movie theatre, and an extensive park. Its construction corresponded to the policies on public works and public health introduced by the Fascist regime. According to the memoir of a former nurse, the riots described in the novel actually happened on June 8, 1955, when troops were brought in to replace hospital workers who had gone on strike. Many patients, worried about hygienic precautions not being maintained by replacement staff, sided with the strikers. Police was called in and the violent clashes between agents and protesters ended with several arrests. See Massimo Venanzetti, *Anch'io fui studente al Forlanini: Una giornata con il suo fondatore, tra segreti e curiosità* (Rome: Scienze e Lettere, 2011).

44 On the process of individuation through illness and the role of tuberculosis in the articulation of a modern idea of individuality see Susan Sontag, *Illness as Metaphor* (New York: Farrar, Straus and Giroux, 1977), 30–6.

45 The bill was brought before the Council of Ministers by Minister of Labour Amintore Fanfani in July 1948. While designed primarily for low-skilled workers, the project also offered opportunities for numerous architects and engineers. The call for proposals issued by the State was met with an enthusiastic response among young architects, many of whom relished the professional opportunities that the *INA-Casa* would afford. See Paola Di Biagi, "La 'città pubblica' e l'Ina-Casa" in *La grande ricostruzione: Il piano Ina-Casa e l'Italia degli anni Cinquanta*, ed. Paola Di Biagi (Rome: Donzelli, 2001).

46 See Luigi B. Anguissola, ed., *I 14 anni del Piano INA Casa* (Rome: Staderini Editore, 1963), xxi–xxiii.

47 See John David Rhodes, *Stupendous, Miserable City* (Minneapolis, MN: University of Minnesota Press, 2007), 84–5. Rhodes provides a convincing analysis of the INA-Casa project particularly in relation to its use in Pasolini's cinema. After a thorough analysis of the Tiburtino quarter, and a brief introduction of its use in *Vita*, Rhodes moves on to discussing the Tuscolano II project, which was the setting of *Mamma Roma*. Given the mainly

cinematographic focus of his book, the emphasis is understandable, but the choice of the Tiburtino for *Vita* deserves further attention, particularly in the context of a critique of development.

48 Rhodes, *Stupendous*...,100. Rhodes defines the Tiburtino as the "*ur*-text – the *Rome, Open City* of architectural neorealism," based on its exemplary function in almost every discussion of that style. Ibid., 88.
49 Marcus, *Italian Film in the Light of Neorealism*, 23–6
50 The translation was modified to reflect the original word choice, "harem" for "house," which supports the residents' perception of the quarter as exotic, outlandish.
51 Composed by Domenico Modugno and Riccardo Pazzaglia, the Neapolitan song "Lazzarella" was an instant hit in 1957, also thanks to the romantic comedy it inspired. Directed by Carlo Ludovico Bragaglia, the movie featured Alessandra Panaro, of *Poveri ma belli* fame, and Mario Girotti (later to become famous also as Terence Hill). Lazzarella is a teenage girl from a well-off family who falls in love with a less wealthy boy. Modugno sang the song in the movie, and released it as a B-side of his popular single "Nel blu dipinto di blu," but many Italian singers later covered it.
52 Rhodes, *Stupendous, Miserable City*, 101. Rhodes summarizes Giuseppe De Santis' argument on the importance of the Italian landscape to Italian neorealist film.
53 Susan Sontag, *Illness as Metaphor*, 14, 30.
54 See Sontag: "TB is disintegration, febrilization, dematerialization; it is a disease of liquids – the body turning to phlegm and mucus and sputum and, finally, blood – and of air, of the need for better air." *Illness as Metaphor*, 13.

Chapter Three

1 Pier Paolo Pasolini, *Il sogno di una cosa* (Milan: Garzanti, 1962), trans. Stuart Hood, *A Dream of Something* (London: Quartet Books Ltd., 1988). Hereafter, parenthetical in-text citations indicate page number of the original and of the published translation, separated by a semicolon.
2 See Guido Crainz, *Storia del miracolo italiano: Culture, identità, trasformazioni fra anni cinquanta e sessanta* (Rome: Donzelli Editore, 1996), 72–8.
3 Enrica Capussotti, *Gioventù perduta: Gli anni Cinquanta dei giovani e del cinema in Italia* (Florence: Giunti, 2004), 20–1.
4 For an overview of the coverage on the subject of youth in the years of the economic miracle in the daily *Il Giorno* and the weekly *l'Espresso*, themselves products of the cultural change of this period, see Crainz, *Storia del miracolo*, 70–8.

5 See for instance "È difficile fare all'amore per i giovani di Varsavia," part of a series called *Le nuove generazioni in Europa* (July 4, 1959); "Da Rostock alla città più giovane del mondo: viaggio nella Repubblica Democratica Tedesca" and "Un simposio di studenti parla del 'grande viaggio': In una scuola d'avviamento professionale del Bronx" (October 31, 1959); "I 'teen-agers' preoccupano l'Inghilterra: I ribelli del coffee bar" (April 16, 1960).
6 See, for instance, "Proteggiamo i nostri figli: Amore e vizio" (July 20, 1958); "I paras della banlieue: Chi sono i blousons noirs di Parigi e di Tolone" (August 9, 1959); "Le amicizie eccessive: Sociologi psicologi e magistrati esaminano il caso dei ragazzi squillo romani (May 8, 1960); "La morte stupida non piace ai ventenni: In Francia la gioventù dà segni di insofferenza" (November 6, 1960).
7 See "I giovani del Sud" (July 4, 1959); "Inchiesta sui giovani" (August 1, 1959); "Caso Marzano e 'teddy-boys'" and "Una legge speciale contro la gioventù?" (September 5, 1959); "L'America e i teddy boys" (September 26 1959); "Teddy-boys e coprifuoco" (October 10, 1959); "Pasolini e i teddy-boys" (October 17, 1959). The latter is a response to Pasolini's article published in the previous issue and announced on the magazine cover with the title "La colpa non è dei teddy-boys" (October 10, 1959. Now in *SPS*, 92).
8 Tony Dallara, Betty Curtis, Fred Buscaglione, Adriano Celentano, Vera Nepi, and Mina are interviewed in *Vie Nuove* (July 11, 1959). *L'Espresso* focuses on Mina: "Mazzini urla ma non si spoglia: Mina ragazza di buona famiglia canta per i juke-boxes" (*l'Espresso*, October 18, 1959). *I ragazzi del juke-box* is the first of a new series of *musicarelli* movies, directed by Lucio Fulci, which showcase 1960s' pop music instead of the traditional melodic songs of the 1950s. The success of *I ragazzi del juke-box* was repeated the following year with *Urlatori alla sbarra*, featuring Mina, Adriano Celentano, Joe Sentieri, and Chet Baker. This second movie is also advertised widely in magazines. On *musicarelli* and post-war Italian youth music, see Franco Minganti, "Jukebox Boys: Postwar Italian Music and the Culture of Covering" in *Transactions, Transgressions, Transformations: American Culture in Western Europe and Japan*, ed. Heide Fehrenbach and Uta G. Poiger (New York: Berghahn Books, 2000), 148–65.
9 *L'Espresso* n. 47, October 22, 1959. *Vie Nuove* XIV: 36, September 12, 1959.
10 *Totò, Fabrizi e i giovani d'oggi* (Mario Mattioli, 1960), an otherwise conventional comedy of hindered romance, reflects the popularity of inquiries on the youth condition through a direct quotation of the RAI documentary *Giovani d'oggi*. Unable to get their fathers' approval to marry, the young film protagonists use their participation in the TV inquiry to shock them. Carlo and Gabriella play the part of unhappy, angry youth in an episode

of the documentary dedicated to the influence of the family on contemporary adolescents' behaviour. Following a description of young people as "angry, violent, discontent," the couple appears on screen: Carlo who usually wears a traditional suit, appears on TV wearing jeans and a leather jacket, Gabriella in a plaid skirt and black turtleneck sweater. They criticize their fathers, and Gabriella frowningly announces a (probably untrue) pregnancy. The nationwide scandal will paradoxically convince the fathers to come to an agreement and let them marry.

11 The years between 1959 and 1962 witnessed the production of numerous television inquiries (*inchieste*), which broadcast to the entire nation and reflected upon the changes that Italy was undergoing. With series like: *Viaggio nel Sud* (Virgilio Sabel, 1958, 10 episodes), *La donna che lavora* (Ugo Zatterin and Giovanni Salvi, 1959, 8 episodes), *Noi come siamo. Dialoghi con gli italiani* (Virgilio Sabel, 1960, 7 episodes), *L'agricoltura in Italia* (Fabiano Fabiani, Giuseppe Lisi, and Emanuele Milano, 1960, 6 episodes), *Noi e l'automobile* (Luciano Emmer, 1962, 5 episodes) and the already mentioned *Giovani d'oggi* (Carlo Alberto Chiesa, 1960, 8 episodes), RAI undertook the task of making the material and cultural transformations of Italy visible to Italians. See Aldo Grasso, *Storia della televisione italiana* (Milan: Garzanti, 1992).

12 Blaming the decreased interest in religious practice among young people on the popularity of pinball machines and fussball tables in coffee shops and recreational centres, the officers of *Azione Cattolica* conducted a strenuous fight to have those games confiscated from commercial establishments. With games remaining exclusively in church community centres or PCI branches, the church would only have to compete with the Communists for young people's attention. See Mario Agatoni, "Il flipper in parrocchia" (*l'Espresso*, July 27, 1958). On the popularity and risks of these pastimes see, for instance, "Le macchine a gettone: Al ministero le chiamano giocattoli" (November 3, 1957); "3000 Teddy boys a Milano: Birra a gogo" (June 21, 1959); "I paras della *banlieue*: Chi sono i *blousons noirs* di Parigi e di Tolone" (August 9, 1959); "Perché odiano: I centomila minorenni che terrorizzano la V repubblica" (August 16, 1959); "Casco d'oro di papà: gli ossigenati dei Parioli" (December 20, 1959).

13 Simonetta Piccone-Stella links the phenomenon of *teppismo* (hooliganism) among young people in the 1958–62 period to the economic miracle, and notices a double tendency towards the creation of a generational group: on one hand, "*benessere* was a unifying and homogenizing force" and its effects were evident on adolescents of all classes; on the other, adults outraged at antisocial behaviour tended to "lump ... together individual from different classes, simply calling them all 'youths.'" Simonetta Piccone-Stella, "'Rebels

without a Cause': Male Youth in Italy around 1960," *History Workshop* 38 (1994): 161–2.
14 The ambiguity of rock and roll is particularly charged with negative connotations in *reportages* of this period: "il rock and roll come sfida ai rispettabili valori degli adulti, e il rock and roll come veicolo del rispettabile mito dell'America e del mondo libero." See Alessandro Portelli, "L'orsacchiotto e la tigre di carta: Il rock and roll arriva in Italia," *Quaderni Storici* 58 (1985): 143, quoted in Crainz, *Storia del miracolo italiano*, 77–8.
15 Pasolini, "La colpa non è dei teddy boys," *Vie Nuove*, October 10, 1959. Now in *SPS*, 92.
16 Pasolini, "Il risveglio dei giovani," *Dialoghi con Pasolini, Vie Nuove*, July 16, 1960. Now in *SPS*, 887–8.
17 Enrica Capussotti notices that a gender imbalance among youth models and social subjects remains well into the 1950s: "Insieme ai lavoratori e ai poveri, le donne erano infatti defilate rispetto al modello adolescenziale." Capussotti, *Gioventù perduta: Gli anni Cinquanta dei giovani e del cinema in Italia*, 16.
18 In a letter to Franco Fortini, Pasolini wrote: "I have here an old novel, among my first, written in 1949, which was titled *The Best of Youth*. Now I have used that title for my Friulian poetry; so, in the desperate search for a new title, I was struck by a quote of yours [in that evening on the *Menabò* and industry] A DREAM OF SOMETHING." Pasolini to Franco Fortini, Rome, January 26, 1962, in *Lettere 1955-1975* (hereafter *Lettere 2*), 499.
19 According to historian Paul Ginsborg, the law, introduced by Prime Minister Alcide De Gasperi in 1946 in response to increasing demonstrations on the part of sharecroppers throughout Italy, suggested that landowners contribute part of their revenue to repair war damages to farms and hire unemployed farmhands. Unions took on the task of persuading reluctant landowners to implement the law, and numerous protest rallies were organized with that goal. See Paul Ginsborg, *Storia d'Italia dal dopoguerra a oggi* (Turin: Einaudi, 1989), 144–5.
20 Santato called it "the epic of lost youth and, ... the elegy of missed youth." *Pier Paolo Pasolini: L'opera*, 100. The same definition provides the title to Carla Graziano's critical appraisal of the novel: "Il sogno di una cosa: Un'epica della giovinezza vissuta, un'elegia della giovinezza mancata," *Quaderni del '900* 1 (2001): 47–57.
21 Pasolini, "[Risvolto di *Il sogno di una cosa*]" in *SLA*, 2391.
22 See *Romanzi e Racconti*, vol. 2, 1933–1939 (hereafter *RR2*). Zygmunt G. Baranski illustrates the "tormented elaboration" of *Il sogno di una cosa* in the context of an important argument for the continuity between the Friulian and Roman period in Pasolini's oeuvre. The genesis of the novel

was revealed to have been "even more complicated than has hitherto been imagined" by the publication of the novel *Romans*. See "Pasolini, Friuli, Rome (1950–51)" in *Pasolini Old and New*, ed. Z. Baranski, n. 22, 270–1.

23 P.P. Pasolini, "Un mio sogno": interview granted to *Paese Sera*, April 6, 1962. Quoted in Carla Graziano, "Un'epica della giovinezza vissuta…," 47.

24 Vera Dika, *Recycled Culture in Contemporary Art and Film: The Uses of Nostalgia* (Cambridge, UK and New York: Cambridge University Press, 2003), 10.

25 Svetlana Boym, *The Future of Nostalgia* (New York: Basic Books, 2001), xvi.

26 Giorgio Nisini – following Gordon, Asor Rosa, Borghello, and Tricomi – ascribes this choice to Pasolini's "autobiographical impulse," motivated by a narcissistic desire to clarify once and for all the stages of his literary and political apprenticeship, thus leaving no room for critical speculation. Nisini states that *Sogno* "must be considered a 1962 novel," although the product of a "Proustian, existentialist" type of research. Nisini, *L'unità impossibile: Dinamiche testuali nella narrativa di Pier Paolo Pasolini* (Rome: Carocci, 2008), 153, 155. My translation.

27 For a discussion of the use of free indirect discourse in the Roman novels see Santato, *Pier Paolo Pasolini: L'opera*, 199–204; Renato Barilli, "Ancora sul naturalismo di Pasolini," *La barriera del naturalismo* (Milan: Mursia, 1970); Ward, *A Poetics of Resistance*, 61–9.

28 Daniel Fabre, "'Doing Youth in the Village," in *A History of Young People in the West* vol. 2, ed. G. Levi and J.C. Schmitt, trans. Carol Volk, 37 ("Il paese dei giovani," *Storia dei giovani* vol. 2, 51.) Fabre discusses town festivals as the locus where young people assert themselves as an age group in the Languedoc region of France. His study, conducted in the 1960s, describes practices that had been in use since the seventeenth century and that were undergoing changes at mid-twentieth century. Despite the obvious geographic and cultural differences, the practices he describes are strikingly similar to those portrayed in the novel.

29 Interaction with nature, a prominent characteristic of pastoral definitions of youth, plays an important role in the introduction of the characters. Equal attention is devoted to the landscape and the adolescents populating it, both of which are fresh, dynamic, and colourful, as if the latter somehow were part of the former. According to Fabre, a consistent part of the process of youth affirmation during holidays is expressed through interaction with nature: in the decoration of the dancing floor with branches of different trees, in the picnics near the streams on Easter Monday, and in other outdoor activities, socialization and self-affirmation of adolescents as a social group in rural communities involves physical immersion in nature (see Fabre, "Doing Youth," *A History of Young People*, 2:54–61).

30 Even in Pasolini's early poetry, the image of white hedges is central to the feeling that he called "nostalgia for the present time." See my discussion in chapter 1.
31 Provençal troubadour poetry, which he had studied at the University of Bologna, was among the influences on Pasolini's choice of Friulian dialect for his early poems. At the university he wrote his thesis on Giovanni Pascoli's poetry, a choice he justified by stating that he felt connected to Pascoli by a "brotherly bond." See Marco A. Bazzocchi and Ezio Raimondi, "Una tesi di laurea e una città" in Pier Paolo Pasolini, *Antologia della lirica pascoliana*, ed. M. Bazzocchi (Turin: Einaudi, 1993).
32 The almond blossom also features, albeit less prominently, in the opening sequence and evokes similar literary symbolism. See Frederick A. De Armas, "The Flowering Almond Tree: Examples of Tragic Foreshadowing in Golden Age Drama," *Revista de estudios hispánicos*, 14:2 (1980): 117.
33 The hawthorn appears as a sign of spring also in Jaufre Rudel's song "Lanquan li jorn son lonc en mai" from which Pasolini draws the famous expression "amor de loinh" to describe his love for Friuli. See chapter 1. Further references to the hawthorn (either as *biancospino* or *prunalbo*) in Pascoli's poems can be found in "Sera festiva," where the flower connotes the joyful anticipation of the holiday and the mourning for a dead child; in "Cavallino," where it appears, as it does in the previous poem, in combination with boxwood ("bosso ricciuto"). In "La rosa delle siepi" the hawthorn is the "brother" of the flower on which the poem focuses, its hedges like herds of boys receiving their snack from the older sister, the bramble rose.
34 See Ward, *A Poetics of Resistance*, 48.
35 References to the Resistance in Pasolini's essays, particularly in the 1960s, describe it as "the great days of Hope of the forties," where the commonality of goals overcame ideological differences. He recognizes a similar "mystical" approach to social and political struggle in the American New Left. See "Civil War," *HE*, 143.
36 The detailed nature of this passage, which includes lines of the songs in dialect, can be ascribed to Pasolini's reworking of the manuscript of *Sogno* in the late 1950s, at the same time that he was preparing the anthology of Italian popular poetry *Il Canzoniere italiano*. Nini's song, "E io canto, canto, canto ... ma non so il perchè" corresponds to the *villotta* n. 204, in the section "Malinconia" of the *Canzoniere italiano*, where it is reported in its original Friulian dialect. See Pier Paolo Pasolini, *Canzoniere italiano: Antologia della poesia popolare* (Florence: Guanda, 1975), 52–3.
37 Rock and roll became popular in Italy in the mid-1950s, occupying the contested space that had been created after the war by boogie-woogie

and bebop. In discursive terms, it was often presented as a dangerous epidemic that was spreading to Italy from the United States, England, and Northern Europe. The most frequently underscored aspects of the new rhythm were its "negro" origins and its sexually explicit quality. See Capussotti, *Gioventù perduta*, 217–18.

38 The half-legendary story of Giovanni Battista Perasso, nicknamed Balilla, inspired patriotic poems and songs written during the *Risorgimento*. Among these is the Italian national anthem, *Il canto degli Italiani*, by Goffredo Mameli, which contains a reference to the heroic child: "I bimbi d'Italia / Si chiaman Balilla" (Italy's children / Are all named Balilla). The Opera Nazionale Balilla (ONB), founded in 1926, was the organization for the indoctrination of youth during Fascism. *Balilla* were boys between the age of eight and fourteen, after which they became *Avanguardisti*. *Il Balilla*, published under the aegis of the ONB, was the popular paper for boys in the same period. On the ONB see Koon, *Believe, Obey, Fight*, 94–6; Dogliani, *Storia dei giovani*, 106–21. On the use of the image of Balilla in advertising see Laura Malvano, "The Myth of Youth in Images: Italian Fascism," *A History of Young People in the West*, 232–56.

39 The speakers representing the two older generations at the convention in Reggio Emilia included Carlo Ludovico Ragghianti, one of the founders of the Partito D'Azione and leader of the Tuscan Resistance; the journalist and art critic Antonello Trombadori, an anti-Fascist organizer since his days as a university student in Rome in the early 1940s, and Pasolini himself. While Ragghianti's background in pre-Fascist parliamentary democracy guaranteed, according to Pasolini, "objective, almost 'natural' elements" to his anti-Fascist apprenticeship, the effort put forth by Pasolini and Trombadori to resist the "monstrous condition" of Fascism that surrounded their youth seems "almost miraculous" in retrospect (*Vie Nuove*, July 30, 1960).

40 This letter, titled "Ancora sui giovani," appeared as part of the regular section *Dialoghi con Pasolini* in *Vie Nuove* on July 30, 1960, but is not included in *SPS*. In the magazine it is unusually accompanied by a black-and-white photograph of young men in striped T-shirts crowding a public place. The same picture, in colour, appears on the magazine cover on October 29, with the title "I ragazzi della Nuova Resistenza" (The youth of the New Resistance), to announce a special section featuring texts by Pasolini and Carlo Levi.

41 An important contribution to the discourse on the "New Resistance" and the role of youth therein is found in the articles that Carlo Levi published in the weekly *ABC* in 1960–1, now in Carlo Levi, *Il bambino del 7 luglio*, ed.

Sandro Gerbi (Naples: Avagliano, 1997). Texts by both Levi and Pasolini feature in a prominent reportage that earns the cover of *Vie Nuove* in October 1960: Levi's article, "La Nuova Resistenza," focuses on Rome as capital of Fascism first, locus of inception of the Resistance in 1943, and now avant-garde of the New Resistance after the July rally. Pasolini's poem, "La croce uncinata," is also inspired by Rome. It is prefaced by a justification of its "painful and pessimistic ... political indignation." At the time of the poem's composition, in April 1960, Pasolini explains, the hope for change expressed in the summer protests seemed unthinkable. The shame of a Fascist revival ("una vergogna, triste come la notte / che regna su Roma, regna sul mondo"; a shame, sad as the night / which reigns on Rome, reigns on the world) felt upon the appointment of the Tambroni government, was relieved by the awareness that his indignation was shared by a majority of Italians, "among whom, especially, the young." (*Vie Nuove*, October 29, 1960). For an analysis of the "New Resistance" in the writings of Carlo Levi see Philip Cooke "Carlo Levi and the Tambroni Affair," *The Voices of Carlo Levi*, ed. J. Farrell (Oxford: Peter Lang, 2007).

42 See Capussotti, *Gioventù perduta*, 17.
43 According to Capussotti the success of the *maggiorate* is to be viewed as the effect of the construction of a positive image of national popular culture, which provided a double antidote: for the Church, against Communist ideas spread by neorealism, and for the Communists, against the influence of bourgeois and American models. See *Gioventù perduta*, 153–61.
44 Capussotti, *Gioventù Perduta*, 157
45 Giovanna Grignaffini, "Verità e poesia: Ancora di Silvana Mangano e del cinema italiano," *Cinema e Cinema*, 30:42 (January–March 1982).
46 Colleen Ryan-Scheutz has shown how Casarsa and the world of his maternal family help define Pasolini's "concepts of beauty, goodness and authenticity" and the friendship with women like Giovanna Bemporad, Pina Kalc, and Silvana Mauri influenced his life and thought. *Sex, the Self, and the Sacred*, 20.
47 See Piera De Tassis, "Corpi recuperati per il proprio sguardo: Cinema e immaginario negli anni '50," *Memoria*, 6 (1982). Capussotti also maintains that "group and individual photography worked, if we accept Lacan's theories on identity formation, as 'mirror stage' for young women in the Fifties." Capussotti, *Gioventù perduta*, 151–2.
48 Michael Mitterauer, *A History of Youth*, 120–1.
49 Capussotti, *Gioventù Perduta*, 152.
50 For a discussion of *Riso Amaro* and the interaction between realism and popular romance see Marcus, "De Santis's Bitter Rice: A Neorealist Hybrid," *Italian Film in the Light of Neorealism*, 76–95.

51 See Moretti, *The Way of the World*, 7.
52 This gesture, which together with other "Manzonian echoes," led David Ward to compare Pasolini's novel to *The Betrothed* and thus to perceive it as outdated, marks instead the distance of *Il sogno di una cosa* from that world (*A Poetics of Resistance*, 47). Unlike Lucia's vow, Cecilia's decision to take the veil seems more motivated by her psychological inability to enter into a generational struggle than dictated by unflinching faith.
53 In this respect, although the novel remains "on the threshold of history," as Carla Graziano claims, the narrator's ambiguous position towards the past does not preclude knowledge. Instead it opens up a space for reflection. See Graziano, "Un'epica della giovinezza vissuta...," 52–3.
54 See Gianfranco Contini, "Dialetto e poesia in Italia," *L'Approdo*, April-June 1954. Quoted in Santato, *Pier Paolo Pasolini: L'opera*.
55 Pam Cook, *Screening the Past: Memory and Nostalgia in Cinema* (London and New York: Routledge, 2005), 4.

Chapter Four

1 Linguist Tullio De Mauro estimated that only 2.5 per cent of citizens spoke Italian at the moment of national unification in 1861. Although the Tuscan dialect of Dante, Petrarch, and Boccaccio had been adopted as a literary language over three centuries before, the majority of Italians continued to speak regional dialects in their daily lives until the twentieth century. For a concise overview of the linguistic question, see Brian Richardson, "Questions of Language," *The Cambridge Companion to Modern Italian Culture*, ed. Zygmunt Baranski and Rebecca West, (Cambridge, UK and New York: Cambridge University Press, 2001), 63–79.
2 See Philip Cooke, *The Legacy of the Italian Resistance*. Gian Piero Brunetta also notices how production of movies about Fascism and the Resistance resumed, after a ten-year hiatus, with Roberto Rossellini's *Generale Della Rovere* (1959). Among these new films, *Il carro armato dell'8 settembre* (Gianni Puccini, 1960) and *La lunga notte del '43* (Florestano Vancini, 1960), had screenplays co-written by Pasolini. Brunetta, *Cent'anni di cinema italiano*, 187–90.
3 See Luca Gorgolini, "I consumi," *Il secolo dei giovani*, ed. Sorcinelli and Varni, 224–7.
4 See Paul Ginsborg, *Storia d'Italia dal dopoguerra a oggi*, 400–19. On the deregionalization of youth culture see also Mitterauer, *A History of Youth*, 235–40.

5 Luisa Passerini, *Autobiography of a Generation*, 27.
6 David Ward, "Intellectuals, culture and power in modern Italy" in *The Cambridge Companion to Modern Italian Culture*, ed. Baranski and West, 90.
7 A partisan and leader of the Partito d'Azione, and president of the National Liberation Committee (CLN), Ferruccio Parri was appointed prime minister of the compromise government, which was formed at the end of the war. For a detailed description of the process through which Parri was chosen and his symbolic significance in post-war years, see Philip Cooke, *The Legacy of the Italian Resistance*. The epithet "Resistance prime minister" and the report of the statement made by Parri at the university of Rome are also in Cooke, 110.
8 David Forgacs argues that "the Resistance came to be seen from the Left no longer as a consensual anti-Fascist alliance which had laid the basis of the post-war state, but as a 'failed revolution,' a movement whose radical aspirations to political and social regeneration had been defeated by the restoration of capitalism and liberal democracy, with which the PCI had fatally colluded and which had been firmly entrenched in the late 1940s by the economic and political support of the US government." David Forgacs, "Fascism and Anti-Fascism Reviewed," in *European Memories of the Second World War*, ed. Helmut Peitsch, Charles Burdett, and Claire Gorrara (New York: Berghahn Books, 1999), 187.
9 According to Cooke, the slogan "La Resistenza è stata rossa, non tricolore (Resistance was red, not tricolor)" was still popular on banners in 1970s demonstrations. See Cooke, *Legacy*, 124. Feminist historiography in the 1970s sought to recuperate the "other half" of Resistance narrative, obscured in the "tricolore Resistance" to show the important contribution of women to the anti-Fascist struggle and the continuity between those efforts and the feminist movement of the 1970s. For an overview of these works see Forgacs, "Fascism and Anti-Fascism Reviewed," 191–3.
10 Quoted in Nico Naldini, "Cronologia," Pier Paolo Pasolini, *Per il cinema*, ed. Walter Siti and Franco Zabagli (Milan: Arnoldo Mondadori, 2001), xcix.
11 Pasolini, "New Linguistic Questions," in *HE*, 19.
12 Pasolini, "The End of the Avant-Garde," in *HE*, 133.
13 Pasolini, "The Written Language of Reality," in *HE*, 205.
14 Ibid.
15 Maurizio Viano, *A Certain Realism: Making Use of Pasolini's Film Theory and Practice*. (Berkeley, Los Angeles, and London: University of California Press, 1993), 3.
16 He wrote the first screenplay in collaboration with Giorgio Bassani for a film realized by Mario Soldati: *La donna del fiume*. Then he collaborated

with various filmmakers, among whom were Mauro Bolognini, Francesco Rosi, Federico Fellini. With Fellini he co-wrote some scenes for *Le notti di Cabiria* and *La dolce vita*. Bolognini was instrumental in helping Pasolini find a producer for *Accattone*, Alfredo Bini, when Fellini turned the film down.

17 See Brunetta, *Cent'anni di cinema italiano*, 217. Pasolini himself confirmed this transition from painting to cinema on several occasions. See Pasolini, *Il sogno del centauro*, ed. Jean Duflot, and *Pasolini on Pasolini: Interview with Oswald Stack*.
18 Pasolini's filmography counts twenty-two films. His essays on cinema, including the previously mentioned "Cinema of Poetry" and "The Written Language of Reality," were published in 1966 in various reviews and then collected in the volume *Heretical Empiricism*. Preliminary versions were presented at the *1st Mostra Internazionale del Nuovo Cinema di Pesaro*, a new film festival dedicated to young filmmakers, in 1965.
19 Michel Foucault, " Grey Mornings of Tolerance," 73.
20 Pasolini, "Cento paia di buoi: Scaletta preparatoria," in *Le regole di un'illusione. I film, il cinema*, ed. Laura Betti and Michele Gulinucci (Rome: Associazione Fondo Pier Paolo Pasolini, 1991), 83.
21 Michel Foucault, *The History of Sexuality, Volume 1: An Introduction*, 6.
22 Foucault noticed, in commenting on the misleading subtitle to the French edition of the movie, *Enquête sur la sexualité* (Inquiry into Sexuality), that Pasolini delivers "street conversations about love," rather than a scientific investigation. The tension between the inquiry and the "meetings" is inherent in the movie rather than a product of its translation. See "Grey Mornings of Tolerance," 72.
23 Ibid., 73.
24 Michel Foucault, "Grey Mornings of Tolerance," 72.
25 Pasolini, "The end of the avant-garde," in *HE*, 125.
26 See Pasolini, *Le regole di un'illusione*, 128.
27 Like Bernardo Bertolucci's *Prima della rivoluzione* (1964), Paolo and Vittorio Taviani's *I sovversivi* (1965), Marco Bellocchio's *I pugni in tasca* (1966), and several other films realized in the mid-1960s, *Uccellacci* translates into images a crisis of identity that accompanies this period of transition to post-ideological commitment. Lino Miccichè defines them as sharing "the double motif of the disappointed (or unfounded) past hope and the necessity (or impossibility) of refounding the future." *Il cinema italiano degli anni Sessanta* (Venice: Marsilio Editori, 1975), 165.
28 On *Uccellacci e uccellini* as a film of crisis see Maurizio Viano, *A Certain Realism*, 147–9.

29 As film historian Gian Piero Brunetta observed, "reality coexists with the symbolic dimension, allegory and fable." Brunetta, *Il cinema italiano contemporaneo*, 201.
30 For an exhaustive analysis of *Il sorpasso* as an Italian road movie, see Angelo Restivo, *The Cinema of Economic Miracles: Visuality and Modernization in the Italian Art Film* (Durham, NC and London : Duke University Press, 2002), 56-60.
31 The review *Officina*, published bimonthly between 1955 and 1958 in Bologna (two issues of a second series were published in 1959 in Milan), reunited the *Eredi* group from the 1940s: Pasolini, Roberto Roversi, Francesco Leonetti were the editors, but regular collaborators included also Franco Fortini, Gianni Scalia, and Angelo Romanò. Consistently with the legacy of *Eredi*, *Officina* combined a critical assessment of the literary canon (essays on Giovanni Pascoli, Giacomo Leopardi, and Alessandro Manzoni opened the first three issues) with an anthology of contemporary poetry and prose. Pasolini made explicit *Officina*'s connection to his youth project in the essay "La posizione" (April 6, 1956). The variety of the contributors' individual positions found common ground in a commitment to literature above all extra-literary issues – political activity, critical militancy – which were dear to some editors. See Giancarlo Ferretti's introductory essay to the volume *Officina: Cultura, letteratura e politica negli anni cinquanta* (Turin: Einaudi, 1975).
32 On Totò's hybridity see Brunetta, *Cent'anni di cinema italiano*, vol.1, 208–9.
33 Pasolini, "Avvertenza," *Alì dagli occhi azzurri*, in *RR2*, 889.
34 Marco Antonio Bazzocchi, "I riccioli di Ninetto," in *Fratello Selvaggio: Pier Paolo Pasolini tra gioventù e nuova gioventù*, ed. Gian Maria Annovi (Massa: Transeuropa, 2013), 24. See also Marco Antonio Bazzocchi, *Pier Paolo Pasolini* (Milan: Bruno Mondadori, 1998), 133–6.
35 The adjective "crepuscular," which evokes the extenuating light at the end of the day, was adopted by literary critic Giuseppe Antonio Borgese in 1910 to refer to a group of young Italian poets whose melancholic tone and unassuming style implied a surrender of the traditional role of poetry. Pasolini's choice of words here suggests the perception of New York as the nexus of youth, political activism, and poetry.
36 The photographs were taken by Italian photographer Duilio Pallottelli.
37 The Student Nonviolent Coordinating Committee (SNCC) was an organization of the American civil rights movement founded in 1960 by students who had been organizing sit-ins against segregation in the South. They organized "Freedom Rides" in which "blacks and whites traveled together on buses going through the South, to try to break the segregation pattern in

interstate travel." In 1963, their activity included organizing black people to register to vote. In the late sixties, led by Stokely Carmichael, their protest focused on Black Power and the Vietnam War. See Howard Zinn, *A People's History of the United States: 1492- Present* (New York: Harper Perennial, 1995), 444, 447, 451, 475.

38 Pasolini rectified some of the statements that Fallaci had too freely "translated" into "common speech." Overall, though, he confirmed his positive impression. See "Civil War," in *HE*, 142–9.

39 Pasolini, "Civil War," in *HE*, 143.

40 Ibid.

41 Ibid., 147.

42 In the previously quoted interview with Fallaci he summarized his limited appreciation for American literature as follows: "I never liked American literature ... I don't like Hemingway, nor Steinbeck, very little Faulkner: from Melville I go straight to Allen Ginsberg." "Un marxista a New York," in *SPS*, 1600.

43 A detailed discussion of Pasolini's relationship with the Italian student movement can be found in chapter 5.

44 Beside Michael Schumacher's and Barry Miles' complete biographies of Allen Ginsberg, a detailed account of Ginsberg's public appearances and of his reception can be found in Jane Kramer's book *Allen Ginsberg in America* (New York: Random House, 1969).

45 Fernanda Pivano offers numerous anecdotes of Ginsberg's visits to Italy in her book *Amici scrittori*. During his visit in 1967, she narrates, "he requested to see one of Pasolini's films. During the intermission, a young man approached him and asked 'Are you Mr. Ginsberg?' Ginsberg replied: 'One of them.' leaving him stunned. But he was equally stunned when, the next day, after visiting the Uffizi and Orsammichele [in Florence], he saw on a wall in Piazza del Duomo, a spray-written sign saying: 'Ginsberg you are a god.' Fernanda Pivano, *Amici scrittori* (Milan: Mondadori, 1996), 215.

46 Pasolini to Allen Ginsberg, Milan, October 18, 1967, in *Lettere 2*, 631. Only the first two pages of the original text in Italian are available; the whole letter is available only in the English translation made by Allen Ginsberg and Annette Galvano for publication in the "Lumen/Avenue A" review. Where a comparison is possible, the translation appears often inaccurate, when not completely distorting the meaning of the original. I therefore rely on the Italian text, where possible, providing my own translation. Here, the English translation erroneously said "flowers only to be found in forests."

47 Pasolini to Allen Ginsberg, Milan, October 18, 1967, in *Lettere 2*, 631

250 Notes to pages 140–50

48 In his suggestions to the organizing committee of a demonstration march in support of peace in Vietnam, to be held in Berkeley in November 1965, Ginsberg wrote: "Masses of flowers – a visual spectacle – especially concentrated in the front lines. Can be used to set up barricades, to present to Hell's Angels, police, politicians, and press and spectators whenever needed or at parade's end." Allen Ginsberg, *Deliberate Prose: Selected Essays 1952–1995*, ed. Bill Morgan (New York: Harper Collins, 2000), 10.
49 Pasolini to Allen Ginsberg, Milan, October 18, 1967, in *Lettere 2*, 631
50 Pasolini to Allen Ginsberg, Milan, October 18, 1967, in *Lettere 2*, 632.
51 Ibid., 632–3. Italian original missing.
52 Pasolini, "The Written Language of Reality," in *HE*, 198.
53 Ibid., 205.
54 Pasolini, "Quips on Cinema," in *HE*, 227.
55 Pasolini, "The Cinema of Poetry," in *HE*, 172.
56 Carla Benedetti refers to a "performative" relationship with reality as opposed to a "constative" one. See Carla Benedetti, *Pasolini contro Calvino. Per una letteratura impura* (Turin: Bollati Boringhieri, 1998), 131.
57 Dante Alighieri, *Commedia: Paradiso*, ed. Emilio Pasquini and Antonio Quaglio (Milan: Garzanti, 1986), I :70–1.
58 Enzo Golino, *Il sogno di una cosa*, 142.
59 Pasolini, "La nascita di un nuovo tipo di buffone" (The Birth of a New Type of Buffoon), in *Trasumanar e organizzar* (Milan: Garzanti, 1971).
60 Pasolini, "The Screenplay as a 'Structure that Wants to Be Another Structure,'" in *HE*, 189.
61 Kristin Ross, "Rimbaud and the Resistance to Work," in *Rimbaud: Modern Critical Views*, ed. Harold Bloom. Quoted in Stephen Burt, *The Forms of Youth*, 14.
62 Kristin Ross, *The Emergence of Social Space*, quoted in Burt, 14.
63 Burt, *The Forms of Youth*, 3.

Chapter Five

1 The journal *Quaderni Rossi* (Red Notebooks) was founded by a group of young dissident intellectuals who had abandoned the PCI after Khrushchev's revelations regarding Stalin's crimes at the 1956 convention of the PCUS, the Communist Party of the Soviet Union.
2 The Istituto Universitario di Scienze Sociali was founded in 1962 in Trento by initiative of the progressive wing of the Christian Democratic Party, with the purpose of educating "social architects" who could understand and

steer the neo-capitalist transformation of Italy. Breaking with an intellectual tradition that had shown little interest in social sciences, the school of sociology in Trento attracted a geographically and socially composite student body, since it also admitted students with technical high school degrees (previously only admitted to the faculties of agriculture and economics). The first student occupations started in Trento in 1966. See Nanni Balestrini and Primo Moroni, *L'orda d'oro: 1968–1977* (Milan: Feltrinelli, 1988); Rossana Rossanda, *L'anno degli studenti* (Rome: De Donato, 1968).

3 Although I rely primarily on the definitive version of the poem, published in *Empirismo Eretico*, and on Ben Lawton and Louise Barnett's translation of *Heretical Empiricism*, I quote here the first published version, in *l'Espresso*, June 16, 1968, which included the line "I hate you, like I hate your daddies," because it was quoted in every article referring to the poem in 1968. That line was expunged from subsequent publications.

4 Pasolini, "The P.C.I. to the Young!," in *HE*, 150.
5 Ibid., 151.
6 Ibid., 153.
7 Ibid., 151.
8 Lorenza Mazzetti, "Il PCI ai giovani," *Il lato oscuro*, *Vie Nuove*, June 20, 1968.
9 Pasolini, "The P.C.I. to the Young!," in *HE*, 153.
10 Ibid., 156.
11 Ibid., 157.
12 Pasolini, "Perché siamo tutti borghesi" (Why We Are All Bourgeois), in *SLA1*, 1651.
13 Ibid., 1652.
14 Ibid., 1655.
15 Ibid., 1655–6.
16 Ibid., 1657.
17 Ibid.
18 Luisa Passerini, *Autobiography of a Generation: Italy, 1968*, trans. Lisa Erdberg (Hanover, NH: Wesleyan University Press, 1996), 29.
19 For a discussion of Pasolini's relationship with *Il Tempo Illustrato* and his development in this venue of the "forceful maverick role which will be further crystallized in SC [*Scritti Corsari*] and LL (*Lettere Luterane*]" see Robert Gordon, *Forms of Subjectivity*, 61–7.
20 Pasolini, *Il Caos*, in *SPS*, 1094.
21 Pasolini, "Chi può scandalizzarsi" (Who Can Be Scandalized), *Dialoghi con Pasolini*, in *SPS*, 1025.

22 See "Dopo un anno" (After One Year), "Chi può scandalizzarsi," and "I problemi sul tappeto" (Problems on the Table), *Dialoghi con Pasolini*, in *SPS*, 1025–7.
23 Pasolini, *Il Caos*, in *SPS*, 1098.
24 Ibid., 1137.
25 Ibid.
26 Ibid., 1137–8.
27 Ryan-Scheutz, *Sex, the Self and the Sacred*, 134.
28 Born in East Germany but educated in West Berlin, Dutschke joined the Berlin SDS (Sozialistischer Deutscher Studentenbund) in the mid-1960s. A student of Marxism from an early age, he was also influenced by the writings of the Frankfurt School. He became a leader of the student movement, advocating an international organization of dissent in solidarity with the Viet Cong and with South American *guerrilleros*. When a radical right-wing worker, spurred by the repressive campaign led by the conservative press of the Springer group against "Dutschke the Red," shot and nearly killed him, he became the symbol of anti-authoritarianism throughout Europe.
29 Pasolini, "Dutschke," *Trasumanar e organizzar*, 23.
30 Ibid.
31 On the distinctive features of the 1968 movement in Germany, see Mark Roseman, "Introduction," *Generations in Conflict*, 1–46.
32 The reference in the last line is to the famous poem "Be the Best of Whatever You Are," which Martin Luther King quoted in several of his speeches: "If you can't be a highway, then just be a trail, / if you can't be the sun, be a star." One section of the poetry collection *Trasumanar e organizzar* is titled "Per i sentieri."
33 See Pasolini, *Il sogno del centauro*, ed. Jean Duflot, 21–2, 26–7, and *Pasolini on Pasolini: Interview with Oswald Stack*, 11–13, 17–18.
34 "La poesia della tradizione," in *Trasumanar e organizzar*, 122. Trans. Norman MacAfee and Luciano Martinengo, "The Poetry of Tradition" in *Pier Paolo Pasolini: Poems* (New York: Random House, 1982), 214–18.
35 Pasolini, *Il sogno del centauro*, 68.
36 Pasolini, "Perché vado a Venezia" (Why I Am Going to Venice), *Il Giorno*, August 15, 1968 in *SPS*, 164.
37 Pasolini, "Ho cambiato idea per farla cambiare" (I Changed My Mind to Make Others Change Theirs), *Il Giorno*, August 22, 1968 in *SPS*, 164.
38 Ibid., 172.
39 Pasolini, *Il Caos*, in *SPS*, 1126.
40 Ibid.
41 Ibid., 1157.

42 Among the many existing analyses of *Teorema*, particularly relevant for this discussion are the ones in Marcus, *Italian Cinema in the Light of Neorealism*; Greene, *Pier Paolo Pasolini: Cinema as Heresy*, Ryan-Scheutz, *Sex, the Self, and the Sacred*, Viano, *A Certain Realism*.

43 Pasolini described the realization of the two works as painting with the right hand on a golden backdrop (the literary text), while with the left hand painting frescoes on a huge wall (the film.) Neither form is meant to be predominant; they overlap and should be considered complementary. See Naldini, *Pasolini: Una vita*, 317.

44 Pasolini, *Il sogno del centauro*, 79.

45 Pasolini, *Il sogno del centauro*, 79.

46 The piece is "Tears for Dolphy" by American saxophonist Ted Curson. In the published credits it appears erroneously as "Ted Cursen [sic]: "Per la morte di un sax alto." See Betti and Gulinucci, eds., *Le regole di un'illusione. I film, il cinema* (Rome: Associazione Fondo Pier Paolo Pasolini, 1991). 191. "Tears for Dolphy" was most recently used in Vincent Gallo's film *Brown Bunny*.

47 Millicent Marcus interprets the two dinner table scenes, one before the Guest's arrival and one before his departure, as evidence that he is the theorem, the law establishing balance where it was lacking. See *Italian Cinema in the Light of Neorealism*, 250.

48 Poet Andrea Zanzotto described the film as "la testimonianza di quel salto di qualità nell'esistenza che è l'irruzione dello sguardo poetico" (the testimony of that qualitative leap in our existence that is the irruption of the poetic look). "Su *Teorema*," in *Aure e disincanti nel Novecento Letterario* (Milan: Arnoldo Mondadori, 1994), 162.

49 "Più sacro dov'è più animale / il mondo" (The world is more sacred where it is more beastly). Pasolini, "L'Umile Italia," *Le ceneri di Gramsci*, in *Poesie 1*, 804.

50 Pasolini, *Teorema*, in *RR2*, 905–6.

51 In his 1968 interview with English journalist Oswald Stack, Pasolini described adapting his original idea to suit Terence Stamp. The resulting character is, according to Pasolini, "a generically ultra-terrestrial and metaphysical apparition: he could be the Devil, or a mixture of God and the Devil. The important thing is that he is something authentic and unstoppable." *Pasolini on Pasolini: Interviews with Oswald Stack*, 157.

52 He scandalizes everybody like the Pazzariello in Elsa Morante's book, which Pasolini reviews in a poem: "È facile scandalizzare i Borghesi. / Meno facile è scandalizzare "Tutti." / Il Pazzariello, lui, scandalizza "Tutti." "Il mondo salvato dai ragazzini (Continuazione e fine)," *Trasumanar e organizzar*, 39.

53 For an analysis of Emilia's saintliness and her transition from service to one to service to many, see Ryan-Scheutz, *Sex, the Self, and the Sacred*, 150–7.
54 See Pasolini, "The End of the Avant-Garde," in *HE*, 121–41.
55 Specifying that Susanna Pasolini, the author's mother, plays this woman adds another layer of interpretation to her function, particularly in the case of a filmmaker, like Pasolini, who always chose his actors for what they were in real life. Susanna Pasolini had made her cinematic debut as Mary in *The Gospel According to St. Matthew*, a part that her role in this film seems to quote, both visually and symbolically.
56 Pasolini, "Il pianto della scavatrice," in *Poesie 1*, 849. Trans. Norman MacAfee and Luciano Martinengo as "The Tears of the Excavator" in *Pier Paolo Pasolini: Poems*, 25–53.
57 Ibid.
58 The planned film included, beside the directors who eventually contributed to *Amore e Rabbia*, also Valerio Zurlini. His parable adaptation developed into a feature film, *Seduto alla Sua Destra* (1968; *Black Jesus*) based on the life of Congolese independence leader Patrice Lumumba.
59 On the ideas of innocence and knowledge in the film see also Sam Rohdie, *The Passion of Pier Paolo Pasolini*, 41.
60 Analogously, Riccetto's dead body on the pavement evokes that of Che Guevara, seen only a few minutes before in the superimposed clips.

Chapter Six

1 See Ryan-Scheutz, *Sex, the Self, and the Sacred*, 121–4.
2 See Pasolini's comments on this choice in Duflot, *Il sogno del centauro*, 68–9.
3 One cannot help but acknowledge a certain similarity between the styles of these two episodes and the two types of theatre that Pasolini criticizes in his "Manifesto per un nuovo teatro," also written in 1968: *Teatro della Chiacchiera* (a traditional, bourgeois theatre based on the perfect reconstruction of bourgeois settings and situations) and *Teatro del Gesto o dell'Urlo* (anti-bourgeois, avant-garde theatre based on physical presence and on the desecration of the word). Pasolini responds to these two types of theatre by proposing the *Teatro di Parola*, aimed at an intellectual audience (just like the film being discussed here) and looks to establish a critical relationship with the audience, rather than at "ritually confirming" shared views. "Manifesto per un nuovo teatro," *Il sogno del centauro*, 133–5. Trans. David Ward, in *A Poetics of Resistance*, 179–91.

4 Pasolini defined the young cannibal as "not ... a savage immersed in the natural state," but "an outlaw intellectual." Cannibalism, as a system of signs, has the same function as sex did in *Teorema*: "extremism pushed to the limit of scandal, of rebellion, of horror." The choice of Pierre Clémenti, a young star of the French *Nouvelle Vague*, supports this interpretation of the cannibal as a young rebellious intellectual. Pasolini, *Il sogno del centauro*, 88–9.
5 Viano, *A Certain Realism*, 234.
6 Bazzocchi, *Burattini Filosofi*, 76.
7 Viano, *A Certain Realism*, 224. Focusing on the parents-children relationship, Ryan-Scheutz summarizes Julian and Ida's position as follows: "Viewed in opposing terms as they relate to parental figures, Julian epitomizes the great danger of political indecision, while Ida epitomizes the negative fate of the co-opted younger generation." Ryan-Scheutz, *Sex, the Self, and the Sacred*, 115.
8 Pasolini, "Fuori dal Palazzo," *Lettere luterane* (hereafter *LL*), in *SPS*, 621.
9 Ibid.
10 Pasolini, "Soggetto per un film su una guardia di PS," *LL*, in *SPS*, 625.
11 Pasolini, *Il sogno del centauro*, 68.
12 See in particular the sections "A New Poetry of Youth" and "The Written Language of Action" in chapter 4.
13 Pasolini, "The End of the Avant-Garde," in *HE*, 128.
14 For a discussion of the use of allegory in *Porcile*, *Teorema*, and *Salò* as an antidote to commodification see Mark Rappaport "The Autobiography of Pier Paolo Pasolini," *Film Quarterly*, 56:1 (Autumn, 2002): 2–8.
15 Roland Barthes, quoted in "The End of the Avant-Garde," in *HE*, 136.
16 Ibid. Pasolini defined his activity in the late 1960s as attempts to resist the mechanisms of the cultural industry by making "difficult, indigestible films." Betti and Gulinucci, eds., *Le regole di un'illusione*, 190
17 Ward, *A Poetics of Resistance*, 139.
18 Ibid.
19 David Ward's comment on deferred fulfilment was written with regard to Pasolini's concept of the screenplay: "Suspended sense is the result of deferring fulfillment of meaning from the moment the screenplay is read to the moment the film based on the screenplay is seen. Meaning may be suspended, but not infinitely deferred" (*A Poetics of Resistance*, 140). However it is applicable to this film and generally to Pasolini's interest in "suspended sense."
20 As Ryan-Scheutz suggests, Ida's enthusiasm for the student protest in Berlin reflects the position criticized by Pasolini in his poetic commentary to the Valle Giulia events of 1968: "She proves so completely convinced, co-opted, and caught up in the student agenda that she does not grasp the

way in which Julian sees what is truly different." Ryan-Scheutz, *Sex, the Self, and the Sacred*, 117.
21 Pasolini, *Centauro*, 51. This shot is also used by Pasolini to represent Ettore on the contention bed in the final sequence of *Mamma Roma*. (See Marco Antonio Bazzocchi, *I burattini filosofi*, 154–5). Ettore is another outsider who resists integration. He lives in a perennial dream-like state, variously interpreted as a lack of historical consciousness, which assimilates him to the classic characters of Pasolini's Roman novels, or as a disaffection with the particular reality in which he is forced to live.
22 Maurizio Viano views "the ironic reference to Herdhitze's facelift done in Italy" as a reference to Italian *trasformismo*. *A Certain Realism*, 227.
23 Richard Neupert's accurate analysis of the narrative strategies resulting from interrelations between the two stories in *Porcile* includes "parallelism, displacement, and allegorical illustration." Allegorical illustration is obviously at work in the representation of violence in the two stories. Richard Neupert, "A Cannibal's Text: Alternation and Embedding in Pasolini's Pigsty" *Film Criticism*, 12:3 (Spring 1988): 46.
24 Pasolini, *Il sogno del centauro*, 89.
25 In Foucault's account, traditional power systems were based on "the spectacle of the scaffold," a visual reminder of power for those excluded from it, who were identified as subjects in their act of watching the exercise of sovereign power. The new power is based on a surveillance system subjecting individuals to the gaze of an invisible eye: "a single gaze [that] see[s] everything constantly." Michel Foucault, *Discipline and Punish: The Birth of the Prison* (New York: Random House, 1977), 173. This system, exemplified by Bentham's *Panopticon*, induces "in the inmate a state of conscious and permanent visibility that assures the automatic functioning of power" (ibid., 201). The *Panopticon*, writes Foucault, "is a machine for dissociating the see/being seen dyad: in the peripheric ring, one is totally seen, without ever seeing; in the central tower, one sees everything without ever being seen" (ibid., 202). The result of this dynamic is the subjection of individuals without the use of force. As a reflection on the effects of neo-capitalism, *Porcile* assumes the functioning of this mechanism and the complicity of the viewers in their own subjection. What we are watching is thus not a "spectacle of the scaffold," but rather a section of *Panopticon*.
26 The statement is used multiple times by Pasolini to refer to the crisis of ideology of the late 1960s. It makes its first appearance in *Uccellacci e uccellini*, where the crow says that "the times of Brecht and Rossellini are over." It also concludes the first article of the *Manifesto for a New Theatre*, where Pasolini promises that "in the entirety of this manifesto, Brecht will never

be named": "One thing is certain: the days of Brecht are gone forever." Pasolini, *Il sogno del centauro*, 132.
27 Pasolini uses precisely the word *straniamento* (estrangement) to describe the type of performance he expected from actors in *Teorema* and *Porcile* and specifies: "In *Porcile* the detachment of the character from him or herself is taken much further [than in *Teorema*]." *Le regole di un'illusione*, 208–9.
28 Viano, *A Certain Realism*, 233.
29 In another parallel to *Teorema*, Gustava recalls the children who are Emilia's only company when she returns to her village and carries out her role as "witness to the scandal." Besides Ninetto, they are the other obvious bearers of the kind of look Pasolini elicits from the viewers: an ingenuous, pre-rational perception of the bourgeois world.
30 Pasolini to Paolo Volponi, Rome, August 1971, in *Lettere 2*, 707.
31 See Paul Ginsborg, *Storia d'Italia dal dopoguerra a oggi*, 423–33.
32 See Passerini, *Autobiography of a Generation*, 98–9.
33 Subsequent acts of public violence that formed part of the "strategy of tension" took place in Brescia's Piazza della Loggia (1974), on the Italicus Express train travelling on the Florence–Bologna line (1974), and at the Bologna railway station (1980). State institutions were found to have been involved with far-right groups in organizing these attacks, which were thus defined "stragi di Stato" (State massacres).
34 Pasolini, "Studio sulla rivoluzione antropologica in Italia," *Scritti corsari*, in *SPS*, 308.
35 See Pasolini, "Sviluppo e Progresso," *Scritti corsari*, in *SPS*, 455–8.
36 Golino interprets them as the extreme point of a "mass pedagogy," when every occasion offers a pretext for a lecture. *Pasolini: Sogno di una cosa*, 187–204. See also Enzo Golino, *Tra lucciole e Palazzo. Il mito Pasolini dentro la realtà* (Palermo: Sellerio, 1995); Gordon, *Forms of Subjectivity*; Rinaldi, *L'irriconoscibile Pasolini* (Rovito [CS]: Marra Editore, 1990).
37 The article was first published in the *Corriere della Sera* in January 1973, with the title "Against Long Hair."
38 Marco Bazzocchi explained the aesthetic and erotic value of short hair in Pasolini's symbolic system by comparing the nape of the neck to the convex part on the inside of the knees of boys, which Pasolini indicated as the object of his earliest sexual desire. Young men with hair cut short on the nape of the neck, and longer in front, in the style of the 1950s, are ontologically different from the hippies of the late 1960s, whose hair covers the neck. See Bazzocchi, *Pier Paolo Pasolini*, 189, and "I riccioli di Ninetto" in *Fratello Selvaggio*, ed. Gian Maria Annovi, 21.

39 Pasolini, "Il 'discorso' dei capelli," *Scritti corsari*, in *SPS*, 271.
40 Pasolini, "Analisi linguistica di uno slogan," *Scritti corsari*, in *SPS*, 280–1.
41 Pasolini, "Acculturazione e acculturazione," *Scritti corsari*, in *SPS*, 291.
42 Pasolini, "Il vero fascismo e quindi il vero antifascismo," *Scritti corsari*, in *SPS*, 316.
43 Pasolini, "Fascista," *Scritti corsari*, in *SPS*, 519.
44 See Pasolini, "Studio sulla rivoluzione antropologica in Italia," *Scritti corsari*, in *SPS*, 307–12.
45 Pasolini, "Limitatezza della storia e immensità del mondo contadino," *Scritti corsari*, in *SPS*, 324.
46 Pasolini, "Fuori dal Palazzo," *Lettere luterane*, in *SPS*, 622.
47 See Pasolini, "Il coito, l'aborto, la falsa tolleranza del potere, il conformismo dei progressisti," *Scritti corsari*, in *SPS*, 372–9.
48 Pasolini, "Soggetto per un film su una guardia di PS," *Lettere luterane*, in *SPS*, 629.
49 Pasolini, "I giovani infelici," *Lettere luterane*, in *SPS*, 543.
50 See Pasolini, "Pannella e il dissenso," *Lettere luterane*, in *SPS*, 604–10.
51 In several interviews Pasolini referred to his early relationship with Fascism as natural. To Jean Duflot he said that he "ingenuously accepted [Fascist society], hardly imagining that a different one could exist." (*Il sogno del centauro*, 26). He answered Oswald Stack's question on whether he felt the weight of Fascism, stating "No, because I was born in a Fascist age and a Fascist world and I didn't notice Fascism, just as a fish does not notice he is in the water." *Pasolini on Pasolini*, 17.
52 Pasolini, "Gennariello: Paragrafo primo: Come ti immagino," *Lettere luterane*, in *SPS*, 553.
53 See Enzo Golino, *Pasolini: Il sogno di una cosa*, 195.
54 Pasolini, "Gennariello: Paragrafo terzo: Ancora sul tuo pedagogo," *Lettere luterane*, in *SPS*, 559.
55 Pasolini, "Progetto dell'opera," *Lettere luterane*, in *SPS*, 564.
56 This remark recalls Pasolini's polemical stance against abortion, which he had taken a few months before in an article titled "Il coito, l'aborto, la falsa tolleranza del potere, il conformismo dei progressisti" (Coitus, Abortion, the False Tolerance of Power, the Conformity of Progressives), *Scritti corsari*, in *SPS*, 372–9. He defined legalized abortion as another way to "make [heterosexual] coitus even easier," removing the last obstacle to it, thus sanctioning the heterosexual couple as the norm imposed by consumer power. The article, which appeared with the title "Sono contro l'aborto" (I Am Against Abortion) (*Corriere della Sera*, January 19, 1975), generated a heated debate in the major newspapers. Many intellectuals criticized

Pasolini for substantially supporting the position advocated by the Church and conservative parties (similarly to his critique of the Valle Giulia students). Among the many feminists who objected to his position, Dacia Maraini ("Una femminista contro Pasolini," *La Stampa*, January 25, 1975) aptly drew attention to the fact that in that article he never posited the question from the point of view of women. For an overview of the debate see "Note e notizie sui testi," in *SPS*, 1769–71.

Epilogue

1 See Gordon, Viano, Rohdie, Greene, *Cinema as Heresy* and, more specifically, "*Salò*: The Refusal to Consume"; Rumble and Testa, eds., *Pier Paolo Pasolini: Contemporary Perspectives*; Serafino Murri, *Pier Paolo Pasolini: Salò o Le 120 Giornate di Sodoma* (Turin: Lindau, 2001); Gary Indiana, *Salò or the 120 Days of Sodom* (London: British Film Institute, 2000); Erminia Passannanti, *Il corpo & il potere: Salo' o le 120 Giornate di Sodoma di Pier Paolo Pasolini* (Leicester, UK: Troubador, 2004); Armando Maggi, *The Resurrection of the Body: Pier Paolo Pasolini from Saint Paul to Sade* (Chicago and London: The University of Chicago Press, 2009).
2 See Naomi Greene on concomitant readings of Pasolini's murder and *Salò*. Greene, *Cinema as Heresy*, 218–23.
3 Pasolini, "Il mio *Accattone* in Tv dopo il genocidio," LL, in *SPS*, 677.
4 Pier Paolo Pasolini, "Abiura dalla Trilogia della Vita," in *SPS*, 599. "Repudiation of the Trilogy of Life," trans. Ben Lawton, *HE*, xvii.
5 Even Patrick Rumble's persuasive analysis of the repudiation as an ironic text maintains that the *abiura* contains "an even more intense and focused ideological critique" of Italian youth and the progressive discourse of sexual liberation. Rumble reads the text as both "an abjuration of how his films had been instrumentalized by the forces of false tolerance, and a recantation of an irrational or even utopian nostalgia for a lost innocence," but also a rhetorical defence akin to those of Boccaccio and Chaucer. Rumble, *Allegories of Contamination*, 98, 84.
6 Pasolini had discussed this misinterpretation also in another essay, claiming that critics didn't understand that "ideology was there … it was right there, in the giant dick on the screen, above their heads that didn't want to understand." Pier Paolo Pasolini, "Tetis," in *SPS*, 262.
7 Pasolini provocatively stated that this was his "first film about the modern world." Quoted in Greene, *Cinema as Heresy*, 205.
8 Patrick Rumble provides an interpretation of *Salò* as a Dantean allegory in "*Dopo Tanto Veder*: Pasolini's Dante after the Disappearance of the

Fireflies," Amilcare Iannucci, ed. *Dante, Cinema, and Television* (Toronto, Buffalo, and London: Toronto University Press, 2004).

9 See Viano, Greene, Indiana, Murri.
10 See Greene for a useful analysis of reactions by contemporary Sade scholars, such as Klossowsky, Barthes, De Beauvoir, Sollers, and Blanchot, whose commentaries *Salò* directly calls into question through direct citations by the libertines, and a suggested bibliography in its opening credits. Greene, *Cinema as Heresy*, 200–8.
11 Erminia Passannanti discusses the link between sadism and education in *Salò* and describes the villa as a "reversed barracks or school." Erminia Passannanti, *Il corpo & il potere*, 16, 43.
12 Gary Indiana observes: "While the victims are utterly expendable, the outrages perpetrated on them are pedagogical. They will 'learn' abjection from their captors, who initiate them into the process of their own annihilation." Indiana, 56–7.
13 Gary Indiana also notes the analogy with inspections of children in private schools and the film's rendering of Sade's Salon "as a sort of homicidal boarding school." See Indiana, 37, 56.
14 See Roberto Chiesi's analysis of the process of socialization that turns two of the young victims, Rino and Umberto, into willing collaborators of the libertines. Their successful apprenticeship makes the young men as pleased by violence as the older men. Roberto Chiesi, "Una nuova gioventù di spettatori e conniventi," *Fratello selvaggio*, ed. Gian Maria Annovi, 133–5.
15 Naomi Greene claims that "in this ferocious meta-cinema, Pasolini indicts himself on several counts: as a user of adolescent bodies in both life and film, he, like the libertines, manipulates bodies, tells stories, arranges numbers. He too is a master of spectacle, an organizer of rites, an expert, as *Salò* demonstrates, at turning violence into theatre." Naomi Greene, "*Salò*: The Refusal to Consume" in *Pier Paolo Pasolini: Contemporary Perspectives*, ed. Patrick Rumble and Bart Testa, 239.
16 See Gordon, 261.
17 Viano also maintains that "*Salò* corrects the errors of *La Trilogia della vita*, where Pasolini thought he could celebrate a joy that was not his ... Although still relying on the self-serving fallacy that reduced reality to sex, Pasolini left behind, at last, the dream of an innocent enclave outside history." *A Certain Realism*, 296.

Bibliography

Published Works by Pier Paolo Pasolini

Antologia della lirica pascoliana: Introduzione e commenti. Edited by Marco Antonio Bazzocchi. Turin: Einaudi, 1993.
Canzoniere italiano: Antologia della poesia popolare. Edited by Pier Paolo Pasolini. Florence: Guanda, 1975.
Le ceneri di Gramsci: poemetti. Milan: Garzanti, 1957.
Per il cinema, 2 vols. Edited by Walter Siti and Franco Zabagli. Milan: Arnoldo Mondadori, 2001.
Heretical Empiricism. Translated by Ben Lawton and Louise K. Barnett. Washington, DC: New Academia Publishing, 2005 (First English Edition by Indiana University Press, 1988).
Le lettere: 1945–1954. Edited by Nico Naldini. Turin: Einaudi, 1986. Translated by Stuart Hood as *The Letters of Pier Paolo Pasolini*. London: Quartet Books, 1992.
Le lettere: 1955–1975. Edited by Nico Naldini. Turin: Einaudi, 1986.
Tutte le poesie, 2 vols. Edited by Walter Siti. Milan: Arnoldo Mondadori, 2003.
Pier Paolo Pasolini: Poems. Translated by Norman MacAfee and Luciano Martinengo. New York: Random House, 1982.
Ragazzi di vita. Milan: Garzanti, 1955. Translated by Emile Capouya, *The Ragazzi*. Manchester: Carcanet Press Ltd., 1986.
Romanzi e racconti, 2 vols. Edited by Walter Siti and Silvia De Laude. Milan: Arnoldo Mondadori, 1998.
Saggi sulla letteratura e sull'arte. 2 vols. Edited by Walter Siti and Silvia De Laude. Milan: Arnoldo Mondadori, 1999.
Saggi sulla politica e sulla società. Edited by Walter Siti and Silvia De Laude. Milan: Arnoldo Mondadori, 1999.

The Selected Poetry of Pier Paolo Pasolini: A Bilingual Edition. Edited and translated by Stephen Sartarelli. Chicago and London: The University of Chicago Press, 2014.
Il sogno di una cosa. Milan: Garzanti, 1962. Translated by Stuart Hood, *A Dream of Something*. London: Quartet Books Ltd., 1988.
Teatro. Edited by Walter Siti and Silvia De Laude. Milan: Arnoldo Mondadori, 2001.
Trasumanar e organizzar. Milan: Garzanti, 1971.
Una vita violenta. Milan: Garzanti, 1959. Translated by William Weaver, *A Violent Life*. Manchester: Carcanet Press Ltd., 1985.

Secondary Works

Addis Saba, Marina. *La corporazione delle donne: Ricerche e studi sui modelli femminili nel ventennio fascista*. Rome: Vallecchi, 1988.
Addis Saba, Marina. *Gioventù italiana del Littorio: La stampa dei giovani nella guerra fascista*. Milan: Feltrinelli, 1973.
Alighieri, Dante. *Commedia: Paradiso*, edited by Emilio Pasquini and Antonio Quaglio. Milan: Garzanti, 1986.
Allen, Beverly, ed. *Pier Paolo Pasolini: The Poetics of Heresy*. Saratoga, CA: ANMA Libri, 1982.
Angelini, Franca. *Pasolini e lo spettacolo*. Rome: Bulzoni, 2000.
Anguissola, Luigi B., ed. *I 14 anni del Piano INA Casa*. Rome: Staderini Editore, 1963.
Annovi, Gian Maria, ed. *Fratello selvaggio: Pier Paolo Pasolini tra gioventù e nuova gioventù*. Massa: Transeuropa, 2013.
Antonello, Pierpaolo and Florian Mussgnug, eds. *Postmodern Impegno: Ethics and Commitment in Contemporary Italian Culture*. Oxford and New York: Peter Lang, 2009.
Ariès, Philippe. *Centuries of Childhood*. Trans. Robert Baldick. New York: Knopf, 1962.
Asor Rosa, Alberto. *Scrittori e popolo: Il populismo nella letteratura italiana contemporanea*. Turin: Einaudi, 1988 (1st ed. Rome: Samonà e Savelli, 1969).
Balestrini, Nanni and Primo Moroni. *L'orda d'oro: 1968–1977*. Milan: Feltrinelli, 1988.
Baranski, Zygmunt G., ed. *Pasolini Old and New: Surveys and Studies*. Dublin: Four Court Press, 1999.
Baranski, Zygmunt G. "Pier Paolo Pasolini: Culture, Croce, Gramsci" in *Culture and Conflict in Postwar Italy*, edited by Zygmunt G. Baranski and Robert Lumley. New York: St. Martin's Press, 1990.

Barilli, Renato. "Ancora sul naturalismo di Pasolini." In *La barriera del naturalismo*, Milan: Mursia, 1970.
Bartoloni, Paolo. *On the Cultures of Exile, Translation and Writing*. West Lafayette, IN: Purdue University Press, 2008.
Battente, Saverio and Tito Menzani. *Storia sociale della pallacanestro in Italia*. Manduria: Lacaita, 2009.
Battistini, Andrea. "I miti letterari della giovinezza alle soglie del romanticismo." In *Il mondo giovanile in Italia tra Otto e Novecento*, edited by Angelo Varni. Bologna: Il Mulino, 1998.
Bazzocchi, Marco Antonio. "I riccioli di Ninetto." In *Fratello selvaggio: Pier Paolo Pasolini tra gioventù e nuova gioventù*, edited by Gian Maria Annovi. Massa: Transeuropa, 2013.
Bazzocchi, Marco Antonio. *I burattini filosofi: Pasolini dalla letteratura al cinema*. Milan: Bruno Mondadori, 2007.
Bazzocchi, Marco Antonio. "La letteratura, i giovani e la rappresentazione della sessualità." In *Il secolo dei giovani: Le nuove generazioni e la storia del Novecento*, edited by Paolo Sorcinelli and Angelo Varni. Rome: Donzelli, 2004.
Bazzocchi, Marco Antonio. *Pier Paolo Pasolini*. Milan: Bruno Mondadori, 1998.
Bazzocchi, Marco Antonio and Ezio Raimondi. "Una tesi di laurea e una città." In Pier Paolo Pasolini, *Antologia della lirica pascoliana*, edited by Marco Antonio Bazzocchi. Turin: Einaudi, 1993.
Bellocchio, Piergiorgio. "Disperatamente italiano." In *Saggi sulla politica e sulla società*, edited by Walter Siti and Silvia De Laude. Milan: Arnoldo Mondadori, 1999.
Ben-Ghiat, Ruth, *Fascist Modernities: Italy 1922–1945*. Berkeley, University of California Press, 2001.
Benedetti, Carla. *Pasolini contro Calvino. Per una letteratura impura*. Turin: Bollati Boringhieri, 1998.
Betti, Laura and Michele Gulinucci, eds. *Le regole di un'illusione. I film, il cinema*. Rome: Associazione Fondo Pier Paolo Pasolini, 1991.
Betti, Laura, ed. *Pasolini: cronaca giudiziaria, persecuzione, morte*. Milan: Garzanti, 1977.
Boym, Svetlana. *The Future of Nostalgia*. New York: Basic Books, 2001.
Brunetta, Gian Piero. *Il cinema italiano contemporaneo: Da "La dolce vita" a "Centochiodi."* Rome: Laterza, 2007.
Brunetta, Gian Piero. *Cent'anni di cinema italiano*. 2 vols. Rome: Laterza 1998.
Brunetta, Gian Piero. *Forma e parola nel cinema: Il film muto, Pasolini, Antonioni*. Padua: Liviana Editrice, 1970.
Buckley, Jerome Hamilton. *Season of Youth: The Bildungsroman from Dickens to Golding*. Cambridge, MA: Harvard University Press, 1974.

Burt, Stephen. *The Forms of Youth: Twentieth-Century Poetry and Adolescence.* New York: Columbia University Press, 2007.

Capussotti, Enrica. *Gioventù perduta: Gli anni Cinquanta dei giovani e del cinema in Italia.* Florence: Giunti, 2004.

Cook, Pam. *Screening the Past: Memory and Nostalgia in Cinema.* London and New York: Routledge, 2005.

Cooke, Philip. *The Legacy of the Italian Resistance.* New York: Palgrave Macmillan, 2011.

Cooke, Philip. "Carlo Levi and the Tambroni Affair" in *The Voices of Carlo Levi*, edited by Joseph Farrell. Oxford: Peter Lang, 2007.

Contini, Gianfrano. "Dialetto e poesia in Italia." *L'Approdo* 3 (1954): 10–13.

Crainz, Guido. *Storia del miracolo italiano: Culture, identità, trasformazioni fra anni cinquanta e sessanta.* Rome: Donzelli Editore, 1996.

De Armas, Frederick A. "The Flowering Almond Tree: Examples of Tragic Foreshadowing in Golden Age Drama," *Revista de estudios hispánicos* 14:2 (1980).

De Grazia, Victoria. *How Fascism Ruled Women: Italy 1922–1945.* Berkeley and Los Angeles: University of California Press, 1992.

De Tassis, Piera. "Corpi recuperati per il proprio sguardo: Cinema e immaginario negli anni'50." *Memoria* 6 (1982).

Deleuze, Gilles. *Cinema 2: The Time Image.* London: Continuum, 2005.

Di Biagi, Paola. *La grande ricostruzione: Il piano Ina-Casa e l'Italia degli anni cinquanta.* Rome: Donzelli, 2001.

Dika, Vera. *Recycled Culture in Contemporary Art and Film: The Uses of Nostalgia.* Cambridge, UK and New York: Cambridge University Press, 2003.

Dogliani, Patrizia. *Storia dei giovani.* Milan: Bruno Mondadori, 2003.

Douglas, Mary. *Purity and Danger: An Analysis of Concepts of Pollution and Taboo.* London and Boston: Routledge & Kegan Paul, 1969.

Duflot, Jean, ed. *Il sogno del centauro.* Rome: Editori Riuniti, 1983.

Fabre, Daniel. "'Doing Youth' in the Village." In *A History of Young People in the West*, vol. 2, edited by G. Levi and J.C. Schmitt, translated by Carol Volk. Cambridge, MA: The Belknap Press of Harvard University Press, 1997.

Ferrari, Davide and Gianni Scalia, eds. *Pasolini e Bologna.* Bologna: Pendragon, 1998.

Ferrero, Adelio. *Il cinema di Pier Paolo Pasolini.* Venice: Marsilio, 1977.

Ferretti, Gian Carlo. Preface to *I dialoghi*, by Pier Paolo Pasolini. Edited by Giovanni Falaschi. Rome: Editori Riuniti, 1992.

Ferretti, Gian Carlo. *Pasolini: L'universo orrendo.* Rome: Editori Riuniti, 1976.

Ferretti, Gian Carlo. *Officina: Cultura, letteratura e politica negli anni cinquanta.* Turin: Einaudi, 1975.

Ferretti, Gian Carlo. *Letteratura e ideologia: Bassani, Cassola, Pasolini*. Rome: Editori Riuniti, 1964.
Forgacs, David. "Fascism and Anti-Fascism Reviewed." In *European Memories of the Second World War*, edited by Helmut Peitsch, Charles Burdett, and Claire Gorrara. New York: Berghahn Books, 1999.
Fortini, Franco. *Attraverso Pasolini*. Turin: Einaudi, 1993.
Foucault, Michel. *The History of Sexuality: Vol. I.:An Introduction*. New York: Vintage Books, 1990.
Foucault, Michel. "Les matins gris de la tolerance." *Le Monde*, March 23, 1977. Translated by Danielle Kormos as "Grey Mornings of Tolerance," *Stanford Italian Review* 2:2 (Fall 1982).
Foucault, Michel. *Discipline and Punish: The Birth of the Prison*. New York: Random House, 1977.
Francese, Joseph. *Cultura e politica negli anni Cinquanta: Salinari, Pasolini, Calvino*. Rome: Lithos 2000.
Fraser, Veronica M. *The Songs of Peire Vidal: Translation & Commentary*. New York: Peter Lang, 2006.
Gardair, Jean-Michel. *Narciso e il suo doppio: Saggio su La nuova gioventù di Pasolini*. Rome: Bulzoni 1996.
Gillis, John. *Youth and History*. New York: Harcourt, Brace, Jovanovich, 1974.
Ginsberg, Allen. *Deliberate Prose: Selected Essays 1952–1995*. Edited by Bill Morgan. New York: Harper Collins, 2000.
Ginsborg, Paul. *Storia d'Italia dal dopoguerra a oggi*. Turin: Einaudi, 1989.
Golino, Enzo. *Tra lucciole e Palazzo. Il mito Pasolini dentro la realtà*. Palermo: Sellerio, 1995.
Golino, Enzo. *Pasolini: Il sogno di una cosa*. Bologna: Il Mulino, 1985.
Gordon, Robert S.C. *Pasolini: Forms of Subjectivity*. Oxford: Clarendon Press, 1996.
Grasso, Aldo. *Storia della televisione italiana*. Milan: Garzanti, 1992.
Graziano, Carla. "Il sogno di una cosa: Un'epica della giovinezza vissuta, un'elegia della giovinezza mancata." *Quaderni del '900*. 1 (2001): 47–57.
Greene, Naomi. "*Salò*: The Refusal to Consume." In *Pier Paolo Pasolini: Contemporary Perspectives*, edited by Patrick Rumble and Bart Testa. Toronto, Buffalo, and London: University of Toronto Press, 1994.
Greene, Naomi. *Pier Paolo Pasolini: Cinema as Heresy*. Princeton, NJ: Princeton University Press, 1990.
Grignaffini, Giovanna. "Verità e poesia: Ancora di Silvana Mangano e del cinema italiano," *Cinema e Cinema* 30 (January–March 1982).
Hobsbawm, Eric J. *The Age of Extremes: A History of the World, 1914–1991*. New York: Pantheon Books, 1994.

Indiana, Gary. *Salò or The 120 Days of Sodom*. London: British Film Institute, 2000.
Jeffers, Thomas. *Apprenticeships: The Bildungsroman from Goethe to Santayana*. New York: Palgrave Macmillan, 2005.
Koon, Tracy. *Believe, Obey, Fight: Political Socialization of Youth in Fascist Italy, 1922–1943*. Chapel Hill and London: University of North Carolina Press, 1985.
Kramer, Jane. *Allen Ginsberg in America*. New York: Random House, 1969.
Landy, Marcia. "A Cinema of Childhood." In *Italian Film*. Cambridge: Cambridge University Press, 2000. 234–60.
Levi, Carlo. *Il bambino del 7 luglio: dal neofascismo ai fatti di Reggio Emilia (1952–61)*. Edited by Sandro Gerbi. Naples: Avagliano, 1997.
Levi, Carlo. "La Nuova Resistenza." *Vie Nuove* 43 (1960).
Levi, Giovanni and Jean-Claude Schmitt. *Storia dei Giovani* (vol. 2). Rome: Laterza, 1994. Translated by Camille Naish as *A History of Young People in the West*, edited by Giovanni Levi and Jean-Claude Schmitt. Cambridge, MA: The Belknap Press of Harvard University Press, 1997.
Maggi, Armando. *The Resurrection of the Body: Pier Paolo Pasolini from Saint Paul to Sade*. Chicago and London: The University of Chicago Press, 2009.
Malvano, Laura. "The Myth of Youth in Images: Italian Fascism." In *A History of Young People in the West*, edited by Giovanni Levi and Jean-Claude Schmitt. Cambridge, MA: The Belknap Press of Harvard University Press, 1997.
Mantegazza, Raffaele. *Con pura passione. L'eros pedagogico di Pier Paolo Pasolini*. Palermo: Sudnordsud (Edizioni della Battaglia), 1997.
Marcus, Millicent. *Italian Film in the Light of Neorealism*. Princeton, NJ: Princeton University Press, 1986.
Marini-Maio, Nicoletta. "The Children Are Still Watching Us: The 'Visual Psycho-mimesis' of *Il cielo cade* and *Certi bambini*." In *Coming of Age On Film: Stories of Transformation in World Cinema*, edited by Anne Hardcastle, Roberta Morosini, and Kendall Tarte. Newcastle Upon Tyne: Cambridge Scholars Publishing, 2009.
Martini, Fritz. "*Bildungsroman*: Term and Theory." In *Reflection and Action: Essays on the Bildungsroman*, edited by James N. Hardin. Columbia: University of South Carolina Press.
Mazzetti, Lorenza. "Il PCI ai giovani," *Il lato oscuro*, *Vie Nuove*, June 20, 1968.
McClennen, Sophia. *Dialectics of Exile: Nation, Time, Language, and Space in Hispanic Literatures*. West Lafayette, IN: Purdue University Press, 2004.
Meyer Spacks, Patricia. *The Adolescent Idea: Myths of Youth and the Adult Imagination*. New York: Basic Books, 1981.
Miccichè, Lino. *Il cinema italiano degli Anni '60*. Venice: Marsilio Editori, 1975.

Minganti, Franco. "Jukebox Boys: Postwar Italian Music and the Culture of Covering." In *Transactions, Transgressions, Transformations: American Culture in Western Europe and Japan*, edited by Heide Fehrenbach and Uta G. Poiger, 148–65. New York: Berghahn Books, 2000.

Mitterauer, Michael. *A History of Youth*. Translated by Graeme Dunphy. Oxford, UK and Cambridge, MA: Blackwell, 1993.

Moretti, Franco. *Il romanzo di formazione*. Turin: Einaudi, 1999 (1986). Translated by Albert Sbragia as *The Way of the World: The Bildungsroman in European Culture*. London and New York: Verso, 2000 (1987).

Murri, Serafino. *Pier Paolo Pasolini: Salò o le 120 giornate di Sodoma*. Turin: Lindau, 2001.

Naldini, Nico. *Pasolini, una vita*. Turin: Einaudi, 1989.

Naldini, Nico. *Nei campi del Friuli: La giovinezza di Pasolini*. Milan: Vanni Scheiwiller, 1984.

Nerenberg, Ellen. *Prison Terms: Representing Confinement During and After Italian Fascism*. Toronto: University of Toronto Press, 2001.

Neubauer, John. *The Fin-de-Siècle Culture of Adolescence*. New Haven, CT and London: Yale University Press, 1992.

Neupert, Richard. "A Cannibal's Text: Alternation and Embedding in Pasolini's Pigsty." *Film Criticism* 12:3 (Spring 1988): 46–57.

Nisini, Giorgio. *L'unità impossibile: Dinamiche testuali nella narrativa di Pier Paolo Pasolini*. Rome: Carocci, 2008.

O'Healy, Àine. "Are the Children Watching Us? The Roman Films of Francesca Archibugi." *Annali d'Italianistica* 17 (1999): 121–36.

Parussa, Sergio. *L'eros onnipotente: erotismo, letteratura e impegno nell'opera di Pier Paolo Pasolini e Jean Genet*. Turin: Tirrenia Stampatori, 2003.

Passannanti, Erminia. *Il corpo & il potere: Salo' o le 120 giornate di Sodoma di Pier Paolo Pasolini*. Leicester, UK: Troubador, 2004.

Passerini, Luisa. *Autobiography of a Generation: Italy, 1968*. Translated by Lisa Erdberg. Hanover, NH: Wesleyan University Press, 1996. (*Autoritratto di gruppo*. Florence: Giunti, 1988).

Piccone-Stella, Simonetta. "'Rebels without a Cause': Male Youth in Italy around 1960." *History Workshop* 38 (1994): 157–78.

Pivano, Fernanda. *Amici scrittori*. Milan: Mondadori, 1996.

Portelli, Alessandro. "L'orsacchiotto e la tigre di carta. Il rock and roll arriva in Italia." *Quaderni Storici* 58 (1985): 135–47.

Rappaport, Mark. "The Autobiography of Pier Paolo Pasolini." *Film Quarterly* 56:1 (Autumn 2002): 2–8.

Restivo, Angelo. *The Cinema of Economic Miracles: Visuality and Modernization in the Italian Art Film*. Durham, NC and London: Duke University Press, 2002.

Rhodes, John David. *Stupendous, Miserable City: Pasolini's Rome*. Minneapolis: University of Minnesota Press, 2007.
Ricciardi, Alessia. "Pasolini for the Future." *California Italian Studies* 2:1 (2011).
Richardson, Brian. "Questions of Language." In *The Cambridge Companion to Modern Italian Culture*, edited by Zygmunt Baranski and Rebecca West. Cambridge, UK and New York: Cambridge University Press, 2001.
Rinaldi, Rinaldo. *L'irriconoscibile Pasolini*. Rovito (CS): Marra Editore, 1990.
Rinaldi, Rinaldo. *Pier Paolo Pasolini*. Milan: Mursia, 1982.
Rohdie, Sam. *The Passion of Pier Paolo Pasolini*. Bloomington: Indiana University Press; London: British Film Institute, 1995.
Roseman, Mark, ed. *Generations in Conflict: Youth Revolt and Generation Formation in Germany 1770–1968*. Cambridge: Cambridge University Press, 1995.
Ross, Kristin. "Rimbaud and the Resistance to Work." In *Rimbaud: Modern Critical Views*, edited by Harold Bloom. New York: Chelsea House, 1988.
Rossanda, Rossana. *L'anno degli studenti*. Rome: De Donato, 1968.
Rumble, Patrick. "*Dopo Tanto Veder*: Pasolini's Dante after the Disappearance of the Fireflies." In *Dante, Cinema, and Television*, edited by Amilcare Iannucci. Toronto, Buffalo, and London: University of Toronto Press, 2004.
Rumble, Patrick. *Allegories of Contamination: Pier Paolo Pasolini's Trilogy of Life*. Toronto, Buffalo, and London: University of Toronto Press, 1996.
Rumble, Patrick and Bart Testa, ed. *Pier Paolo Pasolini: Contemporary Perspectives*. Toronto, Buffalo, and London: University of Toronto Press, 1994.
Ryan-Scheutz, Colleen. *Sex, the Self, and the Sacred: Women in the Cinema of Pier Paolo Pasolini*. Toronto, Buffalo, and London: University of Toronto Press, 2007.
Salinari, Carlo. *Preludio e fine del realismo in Italia*. Naples: Morano, 1965.
Santato, Guido. *Pier Paolo Pasolini: L'opera*. Vicenza: Neri Pozza, 1980.
Savona, Antonio Virgilio and Michele L. Straniero. *Canti della grande guerra*, vol. 2, Milan: Garzanti, 1981.
Scalia, Gianni. *La mania della verità: Dialogo con Pier Paolo Pasolini*. Bologna, Cappelli Editore, 1978.
Schwartz, Barth David. *Pasolini Requiem*. New York: Pantheon Books, 1992.
Siciliano, Enzo. *Vita di Pasolini*. Milan: Rizzoli, 1978.
Sontag, Susan. *Illness as Metaphor*. New York: Farrar, Straus and Giroux, 1977.
Sorcinelli, Paolo and Angelo Varni, eds. *Il secolo dei giovani: Le nuove generazioni e la storia del Novecento*. Rome: Donzelli, 2004.
Spackman, Barbara. *Fascist Virilities: Rhetoric, Ideology, and Social Fantasy in Italy*. Minneapolis and London: University of Minnesota Press, 1996.
Stack, Oswald, ed. *Pasolini on Pasolini: Interviews with Oswald Stack*. London: Thames and Hudson, 1969.

Sutton, Paul. "The *Bambino Negato* or Missing Child of Contemporary Italian Cinema." *Screen* 46:3 (Autumn 2005): 353–9.
Turner, Victor. *The Forest of Symbols: Aspects of Ndembu Ritual*. Ithaca, NY: Cornell University Press, 1967.
Van Gennep, Arnold. *The Rites of Passage*. Translated by Monika B. Vizedom and Gabrielle L. Caffee. Chicago: University of Chicago Press, 1960
Varni, Angelo, ed. *Il mondo giovanile in Italia tra Otto e Novecento*. Bologna: Il Mulino, 1998.
Venanzetti, Massimo. *Anch'io fui studente al Forlanini: una giornata con il suo fondatore, tra segreti e curiosità*. Rome: Scienze e Lettere, 2011.
Viano, Maurizio. *A Certain Realism: Making use of Pasolini's Film Theory and Practice*. Berkeley, Los Angeles, and London: University of California Press, 1993.
Vighi, Fabio. *Le ragioni dell'altro: La formazione intellettuale di Pasolini tra saggistica, letteratura e cinema*. Ravenna: Longo, 2001.
Villon, François. *The Complete Works of François Villon*, Translated by Anthony Bonner. New York: Museum Press, 1961.
Ward, David. "Intellectuals, culture and power in modern Italy." In *The Cambridge Companion to Modern Italian Culture*, edited by Zygmunt Baranski and Rebecca West. Cambridge, UK and New York: Cambridge University Press, 2001.
Ward, David. *A Poetics of Resistance: Narrative and the Writings of Pier Paolo Pasolini*. Madison, NJ and London: Fairleigh Dickinson University Press, 1995.
Zanzotto, Andrea. "Pedagogia." In *Aure e disincanti nel Novecento letterario*. Milan: Arnoldo Mondadori, 1994.
Zanzotto, Andrea. "Pasolini poeta." In *Aure e disincanti nel Novecento letterario*. Milan: Arnoldo Mondadori, 1994.
Zanzotto, Andrea. "Su *Teorema*." In *Aure e disincanti nel Novecento letterario*. Milan: Arnoldo Mondadori, 1994.
Zinn, Howard. *A People's History of the United States: 1492–Present*. New York: Harper Perennial, 1995.

Periodicals Consulted

Architrave: mensile di politica, letteratura e arte. Gruppo universitario fascista Bologna, 1940–43. <<http://db.archiviostorico.unibo.it/it-it/edicola-degli-studenti/elenco-delle-annate.aspx?idC=61687&idRivista=11993&LN=it-IT>>
L'Espresso: Settimanale di politica, cultura ed economia. 1959–63.
Il setaccio: Rivista mensile della G.I.L Bolognese. November 1942–March 1943.
Vie Nuove: Settimanale di sinistra. 1959–63.

Index

action 8, 12, 14, 19, 21, 30, 34, 85, 97, 115, 120, 143–7, 158, 165-8, 175, 177, 183, 194, 198, 206, 213, 222, 229, 234, 255
adolescence (*see also* youth): as anti-authoritarianism 7, 10; as audience 35, 89, 122, 210; as conformity 120, 147–8, 210–11, 214; as continuous transformation 9, 11, 13, 26, 35, 60, 83; as a correlative of the poet 5, 7, 10; as danger 85–7, 90–2; as (self)-exclusion from power 4, 7, 12, 51, 60–1, 154, 158; as exile 30, 32–3, 35–6; as indeterminacy 3, 7, 11, 36, 91, 147–8, 232; as a literary construction 3, 5, 12, 47, 154, 210; as a modern myth 5, 7, 12, 47; as non-conformity 4; as potentiality 4, 7, 26, 91, 211; as rebellion 100, 138, 158, 163–4, 184–5, 189, 191, 205, 209, 219, 255; as rejuvenation 7, 12, 104, 222; renewal 12, 17, 51, 89, 96, 103, 136, 197, 206–7; as resistance, 5, 66, 70, 83–5, 137–8, 147, 156, 174, 183, 186, 188–9, 194, 207, 210–12, 215; as a social subject 5, 10, 12, 47, 120, 158; as trans-historical 90–2, 96, 104, 114, 231; as uncertainty 7, 36, 162, 209; in Italian cinema 233
anni di piombo (Years of Lead) 10, 197
anti-Fascism (*see also* anti-Fascist Resistance) 18, 118, 164, 219, 222, 246
Architrave 20–4, 222–4
authenticity 9, 84, 135, 162, 172, 212, 217, 225, 244

Barthes, Roland 187, 192, 255, 260
"Battle of Valle Giulia" 150
Bazzocchi, Marco Antonio 134, 185, 217, 219, 242, 248, 255–7
Beat Generation 169, 200
Ben-Ghiat, Ruth 222
Berlinguer, Giovanni 49–51, 71, 79
bicycles 29, 91, 96
Bignardi, Agostino 21, 223
Bildung 13, 49, 69–70, 82, 111, 120, 179, 214, 233
Bildungsroman 8, 50–2, 66, 69, 179, 229–30, 232–3
Bologna 5, 10, 18, 20–1, 28, 30, 35, 37, 122, 124–5, 128, 217, 219, 221–7, 230, 242, 248, 257
Bolognini, Mauro 86, 90, 247

borgate 10, 51, 55, 60–1, 64, 66, 69–70, 72–6, 83, 123, 137, 235
Bottai, Giuseppe 17, 19, 221
bourgeoisie 90, 139, 155, 162–3, 165, 168, 170–3, 184, 188, 207, 234
Brecht, Bertholt 134, 192, 256–7
Burt, Stephen 5, 217, 220, 250

Cambria, Adele 123
Carmichael, Stokely 168, 249
Casarsa della Delizia 29–32, 34–9, 41, 43–4, 115, 224
Castellani, Riccardo 24, 224
Cederna, Camilla 123
Cézanne, Paul 28
Chiarini, Luigi 166
coming of age 9, 14, 50, 65, 123, 207, 211, 215, 232, 234
coming-of-age novel (see also *Bildungsroman*) 72
Communism 6, 18–19, 82, 158, 199, 236
compagno di strada 133, 160
consumerism 11, 116–17, 136, 138, 186, 191, 196, 200, 202, 211, 214
Corriere della Sera 198, 204, 257–8

D'Annunzio, Gabriele 31, 225
daughters 4, 11, 65, 125, 162, 217
Davoli. *See* Ninetto
De Sade, Marquis 213
De Sica 69, 233
death 6, 8, 33–4, 38, 43–4, 46, 66–7, 79, 82–3, 112–13, 118, 122, 177, 181, 184, 189, 195, 211, 214, 220, 227–8
Democrazia Cristiana (Christian Democrats) 71, 117–18, 250
development 5, 8–9, 13, 49–52, 54, 58, 67, 70–1, 73–5, 79–80, 83, 116, 119–20, 122, 155–6, 159, 198–9, 203, 207, 219, 222, 237, 251

dialect 6, 9, 120, 234, 242, 245; Friulian dialect 3, 16, 36–7, 44–5, 48, 93, 115, 227–8, 242; Roman dialect 13, 69–70, 72, 228, 93, 228–9, 233
Dogliani, Patrizia 7, 218, 220, 222
Duflot, Jean 164, 219, 247, 252, 258
Dutschke, Rudy 162–4, 252

economic miracle 10, 13, 85, 116, 119, 129, 149, 164, 173, 202, 208, 237, 239
education 7, 16–17, 52, 61–6, 83, 96, 103, 116–17, 121, 125–6, 135, 149, 179, 207–8, 210, 214, 217, 221, 233, 260
emancipation 6, 13, 50–1, 66, 71, 83, 90, 104, 117, 119, 125–6, 155, 164, 199, 208, 210
Eredi 26–7, 36, 47, 103–4, 127, 133, 164, 180, 248
exile 8, 26, 30, 32–3, 35–6, 80, 219, 225–6

Fallaci, Oriana 123, 136, 249
Falzone, Giovanni 24, 223
Farolfi, Franco 18, 26, 28–9, 35, 221, 224, 225–7, 230
Fascism 4–5, 10, 12, 15, 17–21, 24–6, 47, 85, 102, 107, 118, 141–2, 163–4, 196, 202–3, 205–6, 209, 213–14, 221–3, 243–4
fatherlessness 57, 60
fathers 8, 14, 19, 21, 58, 67, 91, 113, 117, 119, 140–2, 149, 151–3, 156–64, 174, 180, 182–5, 189–90, 199, 201, 203–4, 206–7, 209, 224, 238–9
figli di papà 72, 78, 151–3, 159
flower children 6, 147, 152
flowers 41, 42, 96, 112, 139–41, 152, 154, 181, 242, 249–50
Foscolo, Ugo 31, 220, 225
Foucault, Michel 6, 123–5, 127, 129, 218, 247, 256

Friuli 3, 6, 10, 13, 30, 35–9, 41, 43–5, 48, 92, 94, 98, 107, 114, 127, 154, 216–8, 228, 241–2

Galve, Roberto 153
gaze 13, 31, 42, 84, 98–9, 104, 106, 109, 175, 183, 188, 193–6, 205, 215, 256
generational discourse 3, 4, 9, 11–5, 17–19, 21–3, 25–6, 27, 47, 92, 96, 101–3, 113, 115–8, 119–20, 133, 137, 151, 153–4, 156, 158–62, 164–6, 196, 199, 201–2, 206, 210, 224
Ginsberg, Allen 138–40, 142, 149, 152, 157, 169, 249–50
Giordana, Marco Tullio 3, 216
Gioventù Universitaria Fascista (GUF) 17–18, 20–1, 222, 230
Godard, Jean-Luc 180
Golino, Enzo 10, 61, 145, 208, 217, 217–18, 230, 232, 235, 250, 257, 258
Gordon, Robert S.C. 6, 217, 219, 222, 224–5, 227, 232–3, 241, 251, 257, 259–60
Gramsci, Antonio 6–8, 160, 218–20, 253

hair 59, 105, 108–10, 112, 132, 197, 199–201, 203, 207, 257
homosexuality 6, 125, 205, 208, 217
Hughes, Langston 44–5
ideology 10, 20, 90, 121, 152, 198, 218, 256, 259

Il Mondo 6, 67, 204, 207, 219, 253, 263
Il setaccio 20, 24–5, 223–4
Il Tempo Illustrato, 159–60, 251
immaturity (*see also* unripeness) 4, 9, 66
impegno 93, 130, 133, 145, 158, 165, 181–2, 199, 210
INA-Casa 74, 77–80, 236

individuation 67, 73, 80, 82–3, 236
innocence 7, 11, 13, 19, 47, 70, 92, 94, 96, 109, 114, 132, 135, 180–1, 206, 212, 215, 254, 259
irrationality 6, 142, 147; and youth 9, 66, 82, 135, 149, 180, 191, 200, 210, 220, 223, 259; and cinema 144, 147; Italian language 9–10, 121, 144, 182, 187

l'Espresso 86–7, 102, 150–1, 153, 216, 237–9, 251
Leonetti, Francesco 18, 26, 133, 225, 248
Leopardi, Giacomo 220, 248
Levi, Carlo 218, 228, 241, 243–4
liminality 8, 11, 26, 61, 66, 71, 79, 134, 148, 162, 190, 193, 231–2, 234
Littoriali della Cultura e dell'Arte 18, 20, 28, 221
Longhi, Roberto 18, 122

Macciocchi, Maria Antonietta 89
Mafai, Miriam 88–9, 103
Manzù, Giacomo 39, 41, 227
marginality 7, 8, 12–13, 49–51, 56, 58, 120–1, 135, 154, 160, 162, 167–8, 172
Marxism 9, 84, 129–30, 141–2, 154–7, 169, 252
masculinity 19, 28, 106–7, 128
Masters, Edgar Lee 23, 45
maturity 9, 24, 34, 67–8, 104, 147–8, 163, 197, 224, 227, 232
Mazzetti, Lorenza 153, 223, 251
Milan 10, 18, 87, 125–6, 138, 149, 171, 176, 196–7, 204, 230, 239, 246, 248
Montale, Eugenio 27, 219–20, 226
Moravia, Alberto 123, 128, 150, 157, 166–7

Movimento Sociale Italiano (MSI) 71, 102
Musatti, Cesare 123
Mussolini, Benito 16–18, 20, 213, 221–2

Narcissus 38, 40–2, 227
neo-capitalism 6, 9, 122, 155–7, 165, 167, 179, 182–3, 185–7, 191–3, 195–6, 202–4, 206, 209, 213, 215, 256
Neoavanguardia 143
neorealism 74–5, 84, 135, 228, 233–5, 237, 244, 253
"new Fascism" 5, 196, 202–3, 205–6, 213
New York 136–9, 154, 248–9
Ninetto (Davoli) 115, 122, 130–5, 170, 180, 188, 193–6, 210, 215, 248, 257
nostalgia 3, 5, 13, 26, 29–30, 32–6, 38, 43–4, 47, 67, 92–4, 97, 99–100, 107, 113–14, 226, 241–2, 245, 259
Nuovi Argomenti 150, 155

Officina 65, 133, 248
Ombre Rosse 168
Opera Nazionale Balilla (ONB) 17, 243
orphans 14, 149, 158

Paese Sera 137, 241
Palazzo 149, 186, 213, 255, 257–8
Partito Comunista Italiano, PCI (Italian Communist Party) 6, 13, 50–1, 71, 89–90, 117–19, 129–30, 142, 149–51, 154–7, 159, 164, 216, 229, 239, 246, 250–1
Pascoli, Giovanni 31, 96, 219, 242, 248
Pasolini, Pier Paolo: "Abiura dalla *Trilogia della Vita*" 212–13, 259; *Accattone* 122–3, 211, 247, 259; *Alì dagli occhi azzurri* 134, 248; *Il Caos* 158–9, 251–2; *Le ceneri di Gramsci*
(The Ashes of Gramsci) 7–8, 160, 219, 253; *Comizi d'amore* (Love Meetings) 11, 14, 115, 123–4, 126–7, 129; *Il Decameron* (The Decameron) 212; *I dialoghi* 264; *Empirismo Eretico* (Heretical Empiricism) 143, 234, 247, 251, 261; *Il fiore delle mille e una notte* (Arabian Nights) 212; *Gennariello* 14, 207–11, 258; *Lettere luterane* (Lutheran Letters) 204, 251, 255, 258; *Mamma Roma* 122–3, 236, 256; *La meglio gioventù* (The Best of Youth) 16, 36, 39–40, 48, 92, 114, 216, 228; *Poesie a Casarsa* 13, 36–8, 45, 215; *Porcile* (Pigsty) 14, 122, 135, 158, 168–9, 182–3, 185–7, 191–3, 195–6, 210, 215, 255–7; *I racconti di Canterbury* (The Canterbury Tales) 212; *Ragazzi di vita* (The Ragazzi) 8, 15, 45, 50–1, 60, 68–9, 71, 74, 83, 112, 120, 181, 229, 235, 261; *La Ricotta* 134; *Salò, o le 120 giornate di Sodoma* (Salò, or the 120 Days of Sodom) 14, 211, 213–5; *Scritti corsari* (Pirate Writings) 14, 200, 204, 208, 213, 251, 255–7; *La sequenza del fiore di carta* 122, 180; *Il sogno di una cosa* (A Dream of Something) 10–11, 13, 84–5, 91–3, 104, 132, 154, 181, 217–8, 230, 232, 237, 240, 245, 250, 258, 262, 265; *Teorema* (Theorem) 11, 14, 122, 135, 158, 166, 168–9, 172, 178–9, 182–3, 193, 196, 215, 217, 253, 255, 257, 269; *Trasumanar e organizzar* (To Transfigure and Organize) 145–8, 165, 168, 250, 252–3, 262; *Trilogia della Vita* (The Trilogy of Life) 123, 212, 215, 259, 260; *Uccellacci e uccellini* (The Hawks and the Sparrows) 14, 115, 122,

274 Index

130–1, 134–5, 160, 193, 247, 256; *Il Vangelo Secondo Matteo* (The Gospel According to St. Matthew) 123, 134, 254; *Una vita violenta* (A Violent Life) 8, 50, 71–2, 83–4, 90, 132, 235, 262
Passerini, Luisa 158, 228, 246, 251, 257
past 9, 13, 22–3, 26–7, 29–30, 32, 34, 36, 38, 44, 84, 92–4, 103, 113–14, 117, 178, 190, 195, 212, 226, 229, 245
pedagogy 6–7, 10, 123–6, 129, 130, 135, 149, 207–9, 210, 214–15, 217, 218, 232, 233, 257
Pelosi, Pino 211
Pied Piper of Hamelin 35
Pivano, Fernanda 139, 249
poetry: as the expression of youth 8, 9, 11–13, 15, 23, 34, 36, 44, 120, 139, 143, 147–8, 164, 167, 173, 210, 255; in Pasolini's youth 6–8, 11, 13, 15, 26–8, 30, 32, 47, 49; cinema as poetry 10, 14, 115, 121–2, 135, 143–4, 168, 174–5, 186–7, 193, 247; as a critical tool 139–40, 143, 145–7, 167, 168, 210, 217
power 7, 12, 14, 16, 19–20, 101, 122, 124, 129–30, 135, 139, 141–2, 147, 151, 153–4, 159, 162, 164–5, 167, 170–1, 179, 182–4, 186, 188–92, 194–5, 198–9, 202–6, 208, 212–15, 246, 249, 256, 258
prison 63–4, 72–4, 76, 79–80, 231, 256
progress 13, 21, 28, 51, 114, 146, 155, 186, 198–9, 210, 257
proletariat 8, 50, 52, 64, 69, 71, 137, 207, 212, 235
Proust, Marcel 31, 96, 241
Provence 38, 227

Quaderni Piacentini 117, 156
Quaderni Rossi 117, 149, 156, 250

Renzi, Renzo, 18, 223
(anti-Fascist) Resistance 8, 89, 98, 102–4, 113, 116, 118, 133, 137–8, 141, 147, 163, 199, 213, 242–6
revolution, 7, 18–9, 21, 88, 97, 113, 118, 135, 137, 150, 154–5, 165–6, 172, 178, 198, 218, 221, 224, 246
Rimbaud, Arthur 7, 11–12, 142, 148, 164, 173, 219–20, 250
Risi, Dino 131
Rome 4–5, 10, 18–19, 43–4, 49–51, 54–5, 61–2, 69, 75, 80, 86, 102, 118, 122, 128, 132, 150, 180, 211, 216–19, 222, 227, 231, 233, 236–7, 240–1, 243–4, 246–7, 251, 253, 257
Rossanda, Rossana, 160, 251
Rossellini, Roberto, 69, 134, 233, 245, 256
Roversi, Roberto, 18, 26, 225, 248
Ryan-Scheutz, Colleen, 11, 30, 162, 217, 225, 244, 252–6

sagra (county fair), 94–5, 97–9, 105, 112
school: during Fascism 7, 17, 28–9; as temporary housing 53–5; as a locus of apprenticeship 17, 72–3, 149–50, 203–4, 208, 214, 216–17, 224, 232–3, 236, 260
Serra, Luciano, 18, 26–7, 223, 225–6
Sessantotto (1968) 9, 11–12, 13–14, 115–16, 147, 149–50, 153–4, 155–6, 158–9, 163–5, 168–70, 180–5, 196–7, 199–200, 204, 216, 220, 251–5
singing 30, 42, 46, 76, 78, 86, 97, 99–101, 112, 215
sons 4, 11, 162, 201, 217
Sontag, Susan 80, 236–7
Spackman, Barbara 20, 222
Stack, Oswald 164, 219, 247, 252–3, 258
student movement 4, 135, 154, 200;

American student movement 143, 149, 157; German student movement, 163–4, 252; Italian student movement 139, 143, 149, 151, 153–4, 156–7, 159–61, 167–8, 182, 249
sub-proletarian, sub-proletariat 8, 50–1, 69–72, 75, 83, 134, 137, 173, 202, 207, 211–12, 235
"Sul ponte di Perati" (song) 215, 227

Tambroni, Fernando 102, 244
Teddy boys 6, 10, 13, 84, 86–7, 90, 238–40
teleology 52, 69
Totò 86, 130–4, 238, 248
tuberculosis 80, 236

Ungaretti, Giuseppe 25, 27, 34, 219
University of Bologna 5, 10, 18, 22, 26, 30, 36, 122, 124, 128
unripeness 26, 147

Viano, Maurizio 121, 185, 191, 194, 246–7, 253, 255–7, 259–60
Vidal, Peire 38, 227
Vie Nuove 13, 85–91, 102–3, 132, 139, 153–4, 159–60, 238, 240, 243–4, 251, 266, 269
virility 107, 222
vitality 7, 9, 11, 19, 51, 55, 83, 181, 207
Volponi, Paolo 196, 257

Ward, David 64, 98, 112, 187, 229, 231, 233, 241–2, 245–6, 254–5

youth (*see also* adolescence): and the Catholic Church 61–2, 64, 109, 117, 239; and change: generational change 12, 22–3, 25, 125–6, 158–9, 198; and historical/social change 7, 19, 44, 50–2, 57, 60, 69, 71, 73, 75, 79, 82–3, 85, 87, 89, 91–2, 105, 107, 116–17, 120, 125–6, 129, 135, 142, 144, 146, 149, 179–80, 187, 199, 206, 228, 237, 244; and personal change 27, 57, 65–7, 79, 82-3, 158–9; and clothing 53, 57, 59, 60, 65, 72, 86–7, 95, 96, 102, 104, 105, 108, 137, 197, 201, 203, 222, 243; and the economic miracle 10, 13, 85, 116, 119, 129, 149, 164, 173, 202, 208, 237, 239; and Fascism 4–5, 10, 12, 15, 17–21, 24–6, 47, 102, 118 163–4, 196, 202–3, 205–6, 209, 213–14, 221–3, 243–4; and the Italian Communist Party (PCI) 13, 50–1, 71, 89–90, 117–19, 149–51, 154–7, 159, 164, 216, 239; and nature 9, 37, 112, 241, 96, 139–40, 181; and social mobility 9, 51, 60, 116; and sports: basketball, 18, 62, 221, 230; skiing 18, 221; soccer 18, 53, 56, 62, 72, 78, 89, 207; and tradition 4, 7, 9, 18, 23, 26–7, 36, 80, 96, 99–100, 104, 113, 138, 148, 158, 164–5, 180, 251–2

www.ingramcontent.com/pod-product-compliance
Lightning Source LLC
Chambersburg PA
CBHW030308080526
44584CB00012B/491